Acknowledgements

An author's work can only be unique in the expression of ideas, which rarely, if ever, claim just one originator. Ideas are the result of countless interactions with people who influence the path one takes.

I wish to express sincere gratitude for the wonderful people who have helped and inspired me to create this book, *Missed Fortune*.

To my wife and sweetheart, Sharee, thank you for having great faith in my abilities. Thanks for the countless hours of help in pursuit of all our endeavors.

To my six children and my extended family, thank you for your understanding and encouragement while I focused on the completion of this work. May we build a million more memories together.

I offer special thanks and deep appreciation to Lee Brower, who so graciously took time to help co-author chapter 23, which contains the most powerful message in this work. You have inspiring insights and an incredible heart!

I wish to express gratitude to my wonderful and dedicated staff: Patrese Burke, my administrative assistant, for her diligent service; Emron Andrew and Aaron Andrew, for hours of late-night and early-morning editing and proofreading; Adrea Reynolds, Scott Reynolds, and Vickie Jorgenson for help with editing. Thanks also to Larry Kiser for his help.

I express heartfelt appreciation to Heather Beers for her incredible work of editing—a wonderful talent! Thanks also to Clarence Tang and Stephanie Harrell for their professional editing and great attitudes. Also, I appreciate Clyda Rae Blackburn for her valuable input.

I am grateful to Toni Mertin at tmdesigns for the layout and design of this book. You have always come through beautifully! Thanks to Kristin Varner for your unique and professional art work and illustrations. You have extraordinary talent!

I am especially grateful for the many teachers and mentors in my life—thank you Dan Sullivan, Lee Brower, Adrienne Duffy, and Leo Weidner, my coaches. Thanks to all my fellow entrepreneurs in the Strategic Coach program for their encouragement. Special thanks to John Unice, Craig Collins, Jerry Davis, Todd Ballenger, Jack Tilton, Paul Barton, Marv Neumann, and the late David Merrill, for the sharing of ideas and the brainstorming during our careers that have contributed to this work.

MISSED FORTUNE

Dispel the Money Myth-Conceptions—
Isn't It Time *You* Became Wealthy?

DOUGLAS R. ANDREW

Published 2002-2003

by Paramount Publications

Salt Lake City, Utah U.S.A.

ISBN: 0-9740087-1-0

NOTICE TO READER

The materials in this book represent the opinions of the author and may not be applicable to all situations. Due to the frequency of changing laws and regulations, some aspects of this work may be out of date, even upon first publication. Accordingly, the author and publisher assume no responsibility for actions taken by readers based upon the advice offered in this book. You should use caution in applying the material contained in this book to your specific situation and should seek competent advice from a qualified professional. Please provide your comments directly to the author.

To my family and posterity
Who will be the Successor Trustees of
Our Family Empowered Bank
Where all of our
Human, Intellectual and Financial Assets
Are deposited for the
Enrichment of each Family Member's
Health, Happiness and Well-being
Into Perpetuity

May the principles and insights
Contained in this book
Bring you
Clarity, Balance, Focus and Confidence
To help you accomplish
Your Greatest Dreams

Table of Contents

SECTION II
Freeing Yourself From Traditional Money Traps and Tax Traps

SECTION III
Understanding Which Investment Vehicles Are
Best to Use for Safe Accumulation of Wealth

SECTION IV
Using Dynamic Strategies to Enhance, Preserve, and Perpetuate Wealth

Preface

In nearly thirty years as a practicing financial planner, I've never met a person who couldn't find a use for an extra $1 million, especially if he had not yet accumulated his first million!

Millions of people want prosperity, many even take steps to achieve it, but few actualize the goal. Why? Missteps—flawed strategies—something this books calls "money myth-conceptions."

Many people dream of becoming instantly rich by winning a lottery, sweepstakes, or large prize in a game show. In that setting, most "winners" hit it big through total luck, perhaps combined with a small degree of knowledge and skill. The sad reality is that most people will never be lucky enough to win big at any game of chance, because winning such games almost always requires a series of highly random events to fall into a proper, unlikely order. Even for those few who do win, studies show the vast majority—even those who have $100,000 or more dumped in their laps—have absolutely nothing to show for it twenty-four months later! It has vanished—spent or lost in speculative ventures.

Unfortunately, self-made millionaires are also perceived by many as being "lucky." I have observed that what most people refer to as "luck" occurs when opportunities are encountered by people prepared and actively pursuing goals. I prefer to think of LUCK as an acronym representing:

Laboring

Under

Correct

Knowledge

Missed Fortune empowers the reader with the knowledge to attain a greater degree of financial independence.

But I'll warn you, this book is not for financial jellyfish.

You will find concepts here that rattle conventional thought, and that will spur you to action. This book is for the individual who wants to hear new strategies—and who wants do DO SOMETHING with those strategies.

This is no storybook, either. While you will learn through interesting examples, case studies and illustrations, there are plenty of technical details—simply explained—that will educate everyone from the novice to the expert. If you would rather learn general concepts, skim the numbers and charts. If you want to study the evidence, it's provided for you.

SHUNNING IGNORANCE

The worst form of ignorance is when we judge or reject something we know little or nothing about. Many people, including professional CPAs, attorneys, and financial advisors, are often guilty of prejudging little-known concepts like those contained in this book (**fig. 0.1**). I have discovered when they take time to learn about principles herein, they usually do a 180-degree turn-around and become a proponent of concepts they now understand better.

There are other financial traps besides ignorance, such as a false sense of job security. "Corporate downsizing" has become the watchword of management teams whose only concern is the bottom line. Loyalty between employee and employer is becoming a thing of the past. Positions held for years by individuals are suddenly lost in the name of increased profitability. Global competition in wages and resources impacts many American families.

In 1995, I attended a convention where Dan Sullivan, the "Strategic Coach" identified three overriding trends ushering in the twenty-first century. He stated:

1. *"The consumers, not the manufacturers, now call the shots."*
   The introduction of microtechnology into society is dramatically altering political, economic, and social relations, so those who consume now dictate the future to those who manufacture products, services, and knowledge.

Money Myth-Conceptions

2. *"Knowledge is more valuable than capital, equipment,
   and property."*
   The spread of new methods throughout society through
   expanded communications networks continually decreases
   the value of capital, equipment, and property that are tied
   up in old ways of doing things.

3. *"Human creativity is now overwhelming human conformity."*
   No existing organization can survive unless it adapts to the
   creative activities of consumers. Structures of conformity—
   political, economic, or social—which attempt to suppress
   creativity are doomed to decline into disintegration.

Accidents, illness, disability, economic changes, and unemployment, are among uncertainties a family faces. Benjamin Franklin once observed, "The only sure things in life are death and taxes!" To that observation you might well add Murphy's Law, which promises, "If anything can go wrong, it will!"

Bleak though the future may seem, there is a way to avoid most of these pitfalls—education. This book will educate you. It will reveal twenty-three common misconceptions related to money and the accumulation of wealth. I call them "money myth-conceptions." Along with these misconceptions, this book also reveals twenty-three wealth-enhancement strategies, based on true reality concepts that self-made millionaires have used for decades to build wealth!

So, whoever wants to be a millionaire, read on! You will not be disappointed with the wealth of information that follows. I assure that you will gain further insight into financial opportunities you didn't even know existed.

For most of you who choose to continue reading this book, I need to issue a warning: You may never view your house, mortgage, retirement plans, savings, investments, and insurance the same way. The additional knowledge and insight you will gain by reading this book will either force you to implement the strategies and concepts you learn or will leave you forever wondering how much more your financial net worth could have been had you done so.

The great motivational speaker and author, Zig Zigler, has said:

> You train fleas by putting them in a jar with the top on it. Fleas jump, so they will jump up and hit the top over and over and over again. As you watch them jump and hit the top, you will notice something interesting. The fleas continue to jump, but they are no longer jumping high enough to hit the top. Then, and it's a matter of record, you can take the top off and though the fleas continue to jump, they won't jump out of the jar. I repeat, they won't jump out because they can't. The reason is simple. They have conditioned themselves to jump just so high. Once they have conditioned themselves to jump just so high, that's all they can do.

Don't stay trapped in that jar. Too many people make the mistake of asking people trapped in the same jar, "How do we get out of here?" I assure you their opinions will likely never help you get out, because the instructions are found on the outside. In other words, if you want to be a millionaire, don't rely on the advice of those who aren't!

I am going to teach you what most millionaires do—what banks, credit unions, and insurance companies do. You have the power and ability to use some of the identical strategies these financial institutions use to literally become a millionaire!

A NOTE TO THE READER

In order to avoid the perception of gender bias I have used the feminine gender in odd chapters and the masculine gender in even chapters, excepting specific examples where gender makes a difference for illustrative purposes.

Introduction

When my wife, Sharee, and I married, I was in my junior year of college. I had recently returned from serving a two-year missionary assignment for my church in the wonderful country of Korea. Sharee and I met and dated in high school, corresponded by letter while I labored in Korea, and continued our relationship upon my return. After marriage, we were excited to begin life together as newlywed husband and wife.

After witnessing poverty in Korea first-hand, I had a strong desire to provide for our family and to become financially independent.

Sharee became pregnant three months after we married. During the first trimester of her pregnancy, she became deathly sick due to complications with her liver and pancreas. Requiring several episodes of hospitalization, she seriously threatened miscarriage several times. Miraculously, our first daughter Mailee was born in perfect physical condition, and the doctor, who had delivered thousands of babies (including my wife), wept at the miracle.

Blessed though we were with the birth of Mailee, our share of the hospital and doctor bills not covered by insurance was $30,000, which equates to well over $100,000 today.

At the time, I had been doing undergraduate studies in preparation for law school, hoping to become an estate-planning attorney. I had obtained licenses in investment securities and insurance to put myself through school; however, in my senior year of college, I found myself frustrated. The many incidents that hospitalized my wife took my focus away, and I kept putting school on hold—dropping then resuming classes the following semester.

Amid this frustration I talked to the dean of my college. He discovered I was earning an average of $6,000 a month part time while in school, which was nearly double his university salary. Additionally, after interviewing several estate-planning attorneys, I found many of them, if they had to do it over again, would have chosen to become financial planners. They would have preferred to provide clients the investment wisdom and vehicles to achieve financial independence, rather than offer legal instruments to protect wealth.

With the help of school counselors, I realized my true desires and abilities lay in, investment planning, and my career focus changed. I can honestly say from that point on, I have looked forward to Monday mornings my entire career because they dawn new weeks with exciting challenges as I help others achieve financial independence.

My first financial goal was not just to earn my first million dollars by age thirty but to actually have a million dollar net-worth. I remember seeing an illustration in a college money-management textbook with the heading, "Two Ways to Stack up a Million." The first example demonstrated a thirty-year-old person taking a lump sum of $10,000 and setting it aside at 15 percent interest compounded annually which grew to $1,331,755 over thirty-five years.

A second example showed the same thirty-year-old setting aside $1,000 per year for thirty-five years (a total of $35,000) at 15 percent interest, also compounded annually, which grew to $1,013,345.

I was confident I could discipline myself to do this. However, I quickly learned about several critical factors that would affect the desired result:

1. How was the effect of paying taxes on the growth of my money going to affect the outcome?
2. Where could I invest my money to be confident of averaging 15 percent interest?
3. How would inflation affect the purchasing power of my million dollars?
4. Was I too impatient to wait thirty-five years for my million dollars?

I began to learn how to alleviate and legally avoid unnecessary tax, and how to achieve tremendous wealth with rates of return far less than 15 percent—even as low as 6 percent! I learned how to have inflation work for me instead of against me. Most important, I learned how to accomplish all this in a relatively short period of time, with minimal risk.

During my journey toward financial independence, I have observed some common misconceptions prevalent in our society and economy today. In the following chapters, I address twenty-three of them head on, each in turn. In these chapters, I also explain the reality of true principles that can make the difference of hundreds of dollars a month, turning into thousands per year, which can turn into millions over a lifetime!

Each chapter of this book contains a wealth enhancement strategy. Collectively, these strategies can make the difference of millions of dollars in a person's net worth. They have benefited me; it's time they benefit you!

Successfully Managing Equity

to Increase Liquidity, Safety,

Rate of Return, and

Tax Deductions

CHAPTER 1

The $25,000 Mistake

Avoid the trap that ensnares millions of Americans!

COMMON MYTH-CONCEPTION

The best way to pay off a home early is to pay extra principal on your mortgage.

REALITY

No method of applying extra principal payments to your mortgage is the wisest or most cost-effective way of paying off your house.

A bout 4 percent of American households have a financial net worth in excess of $1 million. Eighty percent of them did not inherit it. If you live in a free-enterprise system, have the ability to earn some money, and are willing to put some of that money to work, you can literally become a millionaire with discipline. It will not happen overnight, but it can and it will happen gradually if you adhere to the principles contained in this book. Yes, you can be a millionaire—even a multi-millionaire—and your greatest catapult is probably sitting right under your own roof! Two-thirds of American households have equity in their home. In the first section, comprising chapters 1 to 11, I reveal several equity management strategies that can dramatically enhance your net worth. Because, your home is probably your greatest financial asset, the key to enhancing net worth is managing the equity in your home to increase liquidity, extend safety, improve rate of return, and maximize tax deductions. Learn how to avoid the $25,000 mistake millions of Americans make.

If you believe the following to be TRUE:
- Your home equity is a prudent investment;
- Extra principal payments on your mortgage save you money;
- Mortgage interest should be eliminated as soon as possible;
- Substantial equity in your home enhances your net worth;
- Home equity has a rate of return.

When would be the best time to discover the *real* TRUTH?

Now's the time to educate and empower yourself with the knowledge you need to attain financial independence.

Most homeowners cling to the misconception that the best method of accelerating the payoff of their homes is simply to make extra principal payments on their mortgages. Some homeowners are lured into thinking that bi-weekly payment plans are the answer. Others rely on fifteen-year rather than thirty-year mortgage amortizations. In actuality, none of these methods proves to be the wisest method of accomplishing a "free and clear" home.

You can accumulate sufficient cash in a conservative, tax-deferred mortgage acceleration plan to pay off your home just as soon or sooner—sometimes in less than half the time—than with the traditionally accepted methods previously described. Additionally, you will have the following advantages:

1. Maintain flexibility, liquidity, and safety of principal by allowing home equity to grow in a separate side fund where it is accessible in case of emergency, temporary disability, or unemployment.

2. Maximize the only real tax-deductible interest allowed non-business owners by keeping the loan balance as high as possible until you have the cash accumulated to pay off your home in a lump sum. In a typical tax bracket you can actually pay off a $150,000, thirty-year mortgage in $13^1/2$ years using the same cash outlay required by a fifteen-year mortgage. This is possible partly due to the use of $12,000 to $20,000 (depending on your tax bracket) of Uncle Sam's money instead of your own money.

3. Maintain control and portability of your home equity to allow an increase in its rate of return. Most homeowners relocate an average of every seven years. Your home may likely sell much easier and for a higher price with a high mortgage balance than with a low mortgage balance (see chapter 11). Regardless of real estate market conditions, your equity should always be kept highly liquid.

Consider this personal beatitude: "Blessed are the flexible for they shall not get bent out of shape."

Truly, in this turbulent day and age, there is nothing more constant than change. It is imperative that we as American taxpayers stay flexible when new situations arise, either from tax legislation, inflation, or other external influences over which we have no control.

I once heard someone say, "If pro and con are opposites, I wonder if progress is the opposite of Congress." After being in the financial planning arena for about thirty years, I have found many changes have taken place with regard to the way Congress treats various financial instruments. However, a couple of things have held constant through those years. Firstly, home equity, most people's greatest asset, is commonly misunderstood and mismanaged. Secondly, most Americans are conditioned to spend rather than save.

Americans tend to focus more on consuming than on conserving. Today, the average American family saves between 2 and 3 percent of its income, while in Asia the average family saves 17 to 18 percent of its income. In India, families save 21 percent of their income. It has always amazed me that while many of us devote significant time and energy getting an education so we can earn a living, few of us take enough time to learn what to do with our money after earning it! Most Americans spend more time each year planning their summer vacations than they do planning their finances.

Most homeowners approach the goal of outright home ownership—part of the American dream—in a traditional fashion. They feel that saving mortgage interest and paying off the loan early is accomplished best by applying extra principal to the mortgage, usually with one of four methods:

1. Biweekly or "Canadian amortization"
2. Doubling the principal
3. Target-year
4. Mortgage-term reduction

BIWEEKLY METHOD

The craze of the last decade has been the biweekly or "Canadian amortization" method. Many people are lured into making biweekly mortgage payments through an intermediary or escrow agent in order to magically pay off their mortgages eight to ten years early by making an extra mortgage payment each year.

Biweekly plans work basically as follows: Many Americans are paid on a biweekly basis—one paycheck every two weeks—for a total of twenty-six paychecks per year. If they were to make one-half their mortgage payment out of each paycheck, they would consistently make one half-mortgage payment every two weeks. This would result in twenty-six half-mortgage payments, or a total of thirteen full-mortgage payments, in each calendar year. Through this method, a homeowner, without missing the money, can make an extra mortgage payment against her amortization each year, which generally shaves eight to ten years off her mortgage.

To help people discipline themselves, agencies establish escrows and charge an average of $500 for this procedure. Its main selling feature is the budgeting convenience, as mortgage payments then coincide with the biweekly paycheck, but these agencies also promote the interest-expense savings and the mortgage-term reductions. (Note: disciplined individuals can avoid set-up and management fees by applying this method independently. These individuals then earn their own interest on "the float"—which is the opportunity to earn interest by pooling money while waiting for it to accumulate to an amount deemed worthy of applying to the principal of the mortgage. The biweekly method may seem to suffice, but keep reading, there is a better way.)

DOUBLING THE PRINCIPAL METHOD

Another popular method is the "double principal" method, wherein a person uses an amortization schedule to calculate the amount of principal being paid, then pays double that principal amount with each payment.

For example, a $150,000 mortgage on a thirty-year mortgage amortization at 8 percent interest has a principal and interest payment of $1,100.65 (**fig. 1.1**). The first year, the average monthly amount applied to the principal is just slightly over $100. Using this method, you would send the mortgage company an extra $100 each month. At the outset, doubling the principal may be a very manageable payment, but as years pass, the principal portion of the monthly payment gradually increases and could become too steep. According to the theory, over the years the principal portion of the monthly payment increases, a person's income should also increase, enabling an extra principal payment.

While this method may help a person pay off the mortgage considerably earlier—even reducing a typical thirty-year mortgage term by as much as seventeen years—lifting a calf every day after it is born doesn't ensure that when the calf becomes a full grown cow, you can still lift it. Keep reading, there is a more feasible way.

| Fig. 1.1 | 30-YEAR MORTGAGE ANALYSIS |

Principal $150,000 Rate 8.00%
Balance $150,000 Type Amortized
Payment $1,100.65 Years 30

END OF YEAR	[1] LOAN BALANCE	[2] PRINCIPAL PAYMENT	[3] INTEREST PAYMENT	[4] TOTAL PAYMENT	[5] TAX SAVINGS	[6] NET PAYMENT AFTER TAX
1	$148,747	$1,253	$11,955	$13,208	$4,065	$9,143
2	147,390	1,357	11,851	13,208	4,029	9,179
3	145,920	1,470	11,738	13,208	3,991	9,217
4	144,328	1,592	11,616	13,208	3,949	9,258
5	142,605	1,724	11,484	13,208	3,905	9,303
6	140,738	1,867	11,341	13,208	3,856	9,352
7	138,716	2,022	11,186	13,208	3,803	9,405
8	136,526	2,190	11,018	13,208	3,746	9,462
9	134,155	2,371	10,836	13,208	3,684	9,523
10	131,587	2,568	10,640	13,208	3,617	9,590
11	128,805	2,781	10,426	13,208	3,545	9,663
12	125,793	3,012	10,196	13,208	3,466	9,741
13	122,531	3,262	9,946	13,208	3,381	9,826
14	118,998	3,533	9,675	13,208	3,289	9,918
15	115,171	3,826	9,382	13,208	3,190	10,018
15 YR TOTAL		**$34,828**	**$163,290**	**$198,120**	**$55,516**	**$142,598**
16	111,028	4,144	9,064	13,208	3,082	10,126
17	106,540	4,488	8,720	13,208	2,965	10,243
18	101,680	4,860	8,348	13,208	2,838	10,370
19	96,416	5,264	7,944	13,208	2,701	10,507
20	90,715	5,701	7,507	13,208	2,552	10,655
21	84,542	6,174	7,034	13,208	2,392	10,816
22	77,856	6,686	6,522	13,208	2,217	10,990
23	70,614	7,241	5,967	13,208	2,029	11,179
24	62,772	7,842	5,366	13,208	1,824	11,383
25	54,280	8,493	4,715	13,208	1,603	11,605
26	45,082	9,198	4,010	13,208	1,363	11,844
27	35,120	9,961	3,247	13,208	1,104	12,104
28	24,332	10,788	2,420	13,208	823	12,385
29	12,649	11,683	1,524	13,208	518	12,690
30	0	12,649	555	13,204	189	13,015
30 YR TOTAL		**$150,000**	**$246,230**	**$396,230**	**$83,718**	**$312,512**

Notes:
a. Tax Savings [5] assumes a state and federal marginal tax bracket of 34.00% multiplied by the interest payment [3].
b. Mortgage interest is generally tax deductible, however, certain limitations are applicable. Please review with your tax advisor.
c. Net Payment After Tax [6] equals Total Payment [4] less Tax Savings [5].

TARGET-YEAR METHOD

A homeowner using the target-year method determines the year to pay off the mortgage. Let's say you want to pay off the mortgage in the twenty-second year. You then calculate how much extra you need to pay toward the principal each month to have it paid for by that target year.

This is very easy to do if you possess a financial calculator or financial software. Simply enter three of four variables—present value of the mortgage, interest rate, and target number of years—and solve for the fourth variable—the required monthly payment to meet the target.

If you are not in possession of such software, you can contact your lender or other financial professional and ask them to calculate the extra you must pay each month to reach your goal. Another approach is to determine how much extra you can afford to pay each month. Based on that payment, your lender or financial professional can solve for the number of years it would take to pay off your mortgage. While the target-year method will enable you to pay off your mortgage in a particular timeframe, read on for a more cost efficient way.

MORTGAGE-TERM REDUCTION METHOD

During the 1990s, because of the low-interest financial climate, many people wanted to refinance their homes to obtain lower interest rates. Upon refinancing, many discovered a new mortgage based on a fifteen-year amortization and a lower interest rate often required a monthly payment close to previous payments on their higher interest thirty-year mortgage. Many decided to "bite the bullet" and take out a fifteen-year mortgage.

The shorter-term mortgage method is supported by many professionals. I have attended college finance classes in which professors taught it was smarter to use a fifteen-year mortgage amortization rather than a thirty-year mortgage amortization. But there is still a wiser way.

BURSTING THE BUBBLE

What is neither understood nor taught is that all four traditional approaches contain major disadvantages most homeowners don't consider. These disadvantages, which we will discuss in greater detail in the next few chapters, include:

1. Losing control of your home equity
2. Increasing the after-tax cost of owning your home
3. Increasing your risk of foreclosure and, therefore, the risk of losing your equity
4. Dramatically reducing the return on your equity dollars
5. Decreasing your ability to sell your home quickly at the best price if needed
6. Unnecessarily extending the time required to become debt-free, thereby increasing your costs

The dream for most Americans is to have full home ownership. We are taught from the time we are young either to avoid or to get out of debt as soon as possible. This is wise advice. Please understand this book is not meant to advocate that people go further into debt. I, too, advise people to get out of debt as soon as possible. However, I advise they do so using the wisest method to maximize flexibility—a method that is not embodied in any of the four traditional methods outlined.

BREAKING THE TRUTH

Let me offer a different definition of what being in debt or out of debt really means to the financially independent person. I consider a home "paid for," even though it may be mortgaged to the hilt, if I have sufficient liquid assets in a safe environment that could wash out the liability of my mortgage. I sleep better at night with my home fully mortgaged, when the equity is removed from my property and repositioned in a safer, more liquid environment. Contrary to popular belief, any conceivable financial setback can likely be best resolved if your home equity is separated from your property rather than trapped in it!

For years I have shown clients who were considering traditional "extra-principal payment" methods how to pay off their homes more quickly and shrewdly, making use of their money—and Uncle Sam's. If homeowners would deposit those extra principal payments in a separate, liquid, and safe side fund instead of giving them to their mortgage companies, they would accumulate enough money to pay off the mortgage in as short a time frame—or even shorter—as with any extra principal payment method. Additionally, with the establishment of a side fund, the homeowner then enjoys advantages which are tremendously greater than giving the money to the mortgage banker.

Every time you pay an extra principal payment to the mortgage banker, you are in essence saying, "Here, Mr. Banker, is some extra money. Don't pay me any interest on that money! If I want it back, I will borrow it back on your terms and prove there's a valid reason why I should have it!" How ridiculous! Yet, every time we pay extra principal payments, this is exactly what we are doing.

Let's suppose I instead deposit the extra-principal amount into a side account. In all likelihood, I will still be able to pay off my home as early, but even if I can't—say, it takes me six months longer—it would still be better for me to use a side fund instead of paying extra principal on my mortgage. Why? Because the liquidity, safety, rate of return, and tax benefits I achieve from having my money available in that side account far outweigh any hypothetical disadvantages. Truth is, I can have all of these benefits and actually pay off my mortgage in a shorter time-frame by using a conservative side fund!

Let me illustrate. If I were to take out a new $150,000, fifteen-year mortgage as shown in **figure 1.2**, you can see my mortgage payment would be $1,433.48. I would pay this monthly payment for fifteen years—equivalent to fifteen annual payments of $17,202 (Column 4). This mortgage payment would be my gross outlay. However, because of the tax benefit I receive by deducting the interest on my mortgage payment on Schedule A of my tax return, I am really not shelling out that much from my pocket. Uncle Sam is in essence paying part of my annual mortgage

15-YEAR MORTGAGE ANALYSIS

Fig. 1.2

Principal $150,000   Rate 8.00%
Balance $150,000   Type Amortized
Payment $1,433.48   Years 15

END OF YEAR	[1] LOAN BALANCE	[2] PRINCIPAL PAYMENT	[3] INTEREST PAYMENT	[4] TOTAL PAYMENT	[5] TAX SAVINGS	[6] NET PAYMENT AFTER TAX
1	$144,603	$5,397	$11,805	$17,202	$4,014	$13,188
2	138,758	5,845	11,357	17,202	3,861	13,340
3	132,429	6,330	10,872	17,202	3,696	13,505
4	125,573	6,855	10,347	17,202	3,518	13,684
5	118,149	7,424	9,778	17,202	3,324	13,877
6	110,109	8,040	9,161	17,202	3,115	14,087
7	101,401	8,708	8,494	17,202	2,888	14,314
8	91,971	9,430	7,771	17,202	2,642	14,560
9	81,757	10,213	6,989	17,202	2,376	14,826
10	70,697	11,061	6,141	17,202	2,088	15,114
11	58,718	11,979	5,223	17,202	1,776	15,426
12	45,744	12,973	4,229	17,202	1,438	15,764
13	31,694	14,050	3,152	17,202	1,072	16,130
14	16,478	15,216	1,986	17,202	675	16,527
15	0	16,478	723	17,201	246	16,955
TOTAL		$150,000	$108,026	$258,026	$36,729	$221,297

Notes:
a. Tax Savings [5] assumes a state and federal marginal tax bracket of 34.00% multiplied by the interest payment [3].
b. Mortgage interest is generally tax deductible, however, certain limitations are applicable. Please review with your tax advisor.
c. Net Payment After Tax [6] equals Total Payment [4] less Tax Savings [5].

payment with money I would have paid in taxes. Column 3 of **figure 1.2** shows that an interest expense of $11,805 the first year, deducted on Schedule A of my tax return as mortgage interest expense, saves me $4,014 in taxes. This results in a net after-tax mortgage payment of $13,188, as shown in column 6.

A WORD OF WARNING

A word of warning and advice—don't let the occasional side trip or detailed numerical explanations distract or discourage you from the message of this book! My goal is to educate and empower you with knowledge rather than entertain. This book will provide numbers for those who want to study specific examples. On the other hand, if your purpose in reading this book is to familiarize yourself with financial concepts, please don't get caught up on trying to comprehend exact numbers, charts or graphs. Simply round the numbers in your head and try to grasp general concepts. In this book, I have tried to take the complex and make it as simple as possible, yet still provide specific evidence to those readers who want proof the concepts I outline are sound.

OF TAX DEDUCTIONS AND TAX BRACKETS

To truly grasp the wealth enhancement strategies proposed in this book, it is essential to understand the basics of tax laws and tax brackets— something over 90 percent of American taxpayers don't understand.

For fifteen years, from the 1986 Tax Reform Act until the 2001 tax year, the bottom two federal tax brackets have held constant at rates of 15 percent and 28 percent. This is true even though the income thresholds for both brackets have increased slightly by a little over 3 percent each year. For the first time since the Tax Reform Act of 1986, Congress reduced the tax rates under the Economic Growth and Tax Relief Reconciliation Act of 2001. The 2001 Act provided for a retroactive implementation of a 10 percent rate bracket to January 1, 2001, which will benefit all taxpayers with a tax liability. The taxable income at which the 10 percent bracket ends ($6,000 for single taxpayers, $12,000 for married taxpayers filing jointly, $10,000 for heads of household) will be adjusted for the years 2007 to 2010 to $7,000 (single), $10,000 (married filing jointly), and $14,000 (heads of household).

The 2001 Act phases in the reduced rates over six years, beginning July 1, 2001. Basically, the two lowest brackets stay constant at 10 percent and 15 percent. The former 28 percent bracket, which had previously been the second bracket, is now the third bracket, and was reduced by 1 percent to 27 percent for tax years 2001 to 2003. It will again be reduced by 1 percent to 26 percent for the tax years 2004 to 2005, and again by 1 percent to 25 percent for the tax years 2006 to

Fig. 1.3	REDUCED TAX RATES TIMELINE			
	2000	**2001* - 2003**	**2004 - 2005**	**2006 - 2010**
1st Bracket	10%	10%	10%	10%
2nd Bracket	15%	15%	15%	15%
3rd Bracket	28%	27%	26%	25%
4th Bracket	31%	30%	29%	28%
5th Bracket	36%	35%	34%	33%
6th Bracket	39.6%	38.6%	37.6%	35%

*27%, 30%, 35%, 38.6% rates became effective July 1, 2001

2010. Likewise, the 31 percent, 36 percent, and 39.6 percent brackets will be reduced by 1 percent in each of the same time frames (**fig.1.3**).

Please keep in mind that even though the 2001 Act has already been passed by Congress, at the time of this book publication, certain members of Congress were proposing legislation to change the tax brackets back to the pre-2001 rates as part of an effort to finance the war on terrorism and other increases in federal spending. Because the principles taught in this book remain the same regardless of changes that determine the precise tax bracket, all figures and examples will be calculated using the 2002 to 2003 tax rates and income tax thresholds under the 2001 Act.

BETWEEN THE BRACKETS

For the sake of simplicity, in the following examples let's make two assumptions regarding tax brackets. Depending on your individual circumstances, you can interpolate these illustrations for your income tax bracket. Regardless of differences in the resulting outcome, the principles remain the same.

The first assumption is that of a typical married couple with a combined gross income in excess of $46,700, but under $112,850. This would put the couple beyond the second tax threshold before deductions and exemptions. In the 2002 tax year, this would be a 27 percent federal tax bracket, or in other words, this couple would pay 27 cents of federal tax for every dollar of income over $46,700. Some taxpayers have the misconception that when you cross the threshold from a 15 percent to 27 percent tax bracket, you pay 27 percent retroactive on all of your income. Not true! You only pay the higher rate on the dollars that exceed each threshold (**fig. 1.4**). Each year these thresholds are adjusted, usually resulting in an increase of about 3.3 percent per threshold.

Fig. 1.4	2002 FEDERAL INCOME TAX THRESHOLDS Taxable Income Endpoints				
FILING STATUS	**10%**	**15%**	**27%**	**30%**	**35.5%***
Single	$6,000	$27,950	$67,700	$141,250	$307,050
Married Filing Jointly	$12,000	$46,700	$112,850	$171,950	$307,050
Married Filing Separately	$6,000	$23,350	$56,425	$85,975	$153,525
Head of Household	$10,000	$37,450	$96,700	$156,600	$307,050
Qualifying Widow(er)	$12,000	$46,700	$112,850	$171,950	$307,050

*Income in excess of these amounts is taxed at 38.6%

The second assumption is that this married couple is filing a joint tax return and lives in a state with a flat-rate state income tax of 7 percent. (Each state has its own income tax rate, which may be higher or lower than 7 percent. Some states do not collect revenue through an income tax.) Thus, the combined federal and state tax rate would equal 22 percent for taxable income in excess of $12,000 and 34 percent for income in excess of the next higher bracket. These figures do not include FICA (Social Security taxes) or Medicare. Those additional taxes are added on top of federal and state income tax in the amount of 7.65 percent, matched by the employer for another 7.65 percent.

Fortunately, federal and state income taxes are only calculated on "taxable" income. Taxable income is calculated as gross personal income (or net business income) less personal deductions and exemptions. These deductions and exemptions are subtracted from the top, not the bottom, of a taxpayer's income—in other words, from the last, not the first, dollars you earn each year.

Hence, if this married couple, filing jointly, has a $60,000 combined gross income and has $10,000 in personal deductions and exemptions, their taxable income—the amount eligible for taxation by the federal and state governments—would be $50,000. If they had not been able to claim $10,000 in deductions, they would have paid a combined $3,400 in federal and state taxes on the last $10,000 they had earned. Therefore, their legitimate $10,000 in deductions saved them $3,400 in federal and state taxes! That's money they would have owed Uncle Sam had they not used those deductions! If the tax withheld from their paychecks during the year exceeded the amount they owed in taxes, this money would be refunded to them after they filed their joint tax return. Otherwise, if they owed taxes after completing their tax return, they would simply pay $3,400 less in taxes.

In most circumstances, under current tax law a taxpayer can deduct mortgage interest expense on both primary and secondary residences. A secondary residence could be a vacation home, cabin, condo, motor home, RV, boat, etc. as long as it meets certain qualifications. There are also restrictions and limits for deductible interest, as we will discuss later. But, by and large, most homeowners or homebuyers can deduct at least some, if not all, of their interest expenses (see chapters 6 and 12).

MARGINAL AND EFFECTIVE TAX BRACKETS

The tax bracket that your last dollars earned put you in, is classified as your "marginal" tax bracket. Your marginal tax bracket is different from your "effective" tax bracket. Your effective tax bracket is the tax percentage rate you pay as compared to your total income. For example, if your combined incomes were $100,000, you might be in a marginal federal tax bracket of 27 percent and a 7 percent state tax bracket— a combined bracket of 34 percent. But, if you have deductions and exemptions of $30,000, perhaps comprised of mortgage interest, IRA contributions, charitable contributions, and dependents in the home who qualify as exemptions, your taxable income may be $70,000. You might pay income tax of only 17 percent on the first $12,000 (which equals $2,040), 22 percent from $12,000 to $46,700 (which equals $7,634), and 34 percent on the remaining $23,300 (which equals $7,922) for a total of $17,596. This is only 17.6 percent of your $100,000 gross income. This is your effective tax bracket, different from your marginal bracket, which is still 34 percent. Again, keep in mind this simple example does not include FICA or Medicare.

With this in mind, ask yourself this question, "When analyzing the actual benefit of a tax deduction, should I calculate it using the effective tax bracket or the marginal tax bracket?"

Consider the deductible mortgage interest of $10,000 in my original example, deducted off the last dollars I earn. I actually save 34 percent of $10,000, or $3,400, of otherwise payable income taxes I wouldn't have saved without the deduction. Consequently, if I want to calculate the true tax savings I achieved by virtue of a deduction, I should always use the marginal tax rate times the amount of the deduction. This is always true when calculating the value of a new deduction unless other deductions and exemptions have already taken my gross income below the threshold. In that case, I may want to use the next lower tax rate to calculate a new deduction's value. With this in mind, let's go back to **figure 1.1**.

During the first year of a thirty-year mortgage I can deduct $11,955 (column 3) of interest expense. In a 34 percent tax bracket I actually save $4,065 (34 percent of $11,955) in taxes if this deduction took my taxable income from, say, $60,000 down to $48,045. As a result, my net after-tax mortgage payments for the year total $9,143 (column 6), even though I made twelve payments of $1,100.65, totaling $13,208 (column 4). This is because after filing my tax return on April 15, I got back $4,065 that year as a credit. In essence, Uncle Sam paid part of my house payment.

If you don't want to wait until April 15 every year for Uncle Sam's contribution towards your house payment, you can change the exemptions on your withholding or pay less estimated quarterly tax payments and realize that money each month (see chapter 12).

If I were to take out a brand new thirty-year mortgage rather than a fifteen-year mortgage, my payment, in fact, would be less. However, we shouldn't just take the differential between the thirty-year mortgage and the fifteen-year mortgage payments, and tuck that in our side fund. We need also to calculate and set aside the difference in tax savings achieved during the first fifteen years of a thirty-year mortgage.

As illustrated in **figure 1.1** and **figure 1.2**, over the life of a $150,000, thirty-year mortgage, a homeowner consistently pays more mortgage interest each year with a thirty-year mortgage than with a fifteen-year mortgage (see circled totals). Most people view this as a negative. That's why they are motivated to take out a fifteen-year mortgage—in order to pay as little interest as possible. However, by taking out a thirty-year amortized mortgage, the potential for tax deductions is greater. Therefore, the net after-tax monthly mortgage payment is substantially less for a thirty-year mortgage than for a fifteen-year mortgage.

If we take the annual difference between the net after-tax payment on a fifteen-year mortgage and a thirty-year mortgage each year (**fig. 1.5**)

Fig. 1.5	PAY OFF A 30-YEAR MORTGAGE IN 15 YEARS USING $18,787* OF UNCLE SAM'S MONEY**				
	PRINCIPAL $150,000			RATE 8.00%	
	[1]	[2]	[3]	[4]	[5]
END OF YEAR	30-YEAR MORTGAGE LOAN BALANCE	15-YEAR MORTGAGE NET PAYMENT AFTER TAX	30-YEAR MORTGAGE NET PAYMENT AFTER TAX	DIFFERENCE BETWEEN NET PAYMENT AFTER TAX	DIFFERENCE EARNING 8% COMPOUNDING
1	$148,747	$13,188	$9,143	$4,045	$4,195
2	147,390	13,340	9,179	4,161	8,856
3	145,920	13,505	9,217	4,288	14,032
4	144,328	13,684	9,258	4,426	19,775
5	142,605	13,877	9,303	4,574	26,144
6	140,738	14,087	9,352	4,735	33,204
7	138,716	14,314	9,405	4,909	41,026
8	136,526	14,560	9,462	5,098	49,687
9	134,155	14,826	9,523	5,303	59,272
10	131,587	15,114	9,590	5,524	69,875
11	128,805	15,426	9,663	5,763	81,600
12	125,793	15,764	9,741	6,023	94,559
13	122,531	16,130	9,826	6,304	108,877
14	118,998	16,527	9,918	6,609	124,690
15	$115,171	16,955	10,018	6,937	$142,147
				$78,699	

$26,976

EXCESS CASH BEYOND MORTGAGE BALANCE

* $18,787 is the difference in additional tax savings using a 30-year mortgage versus a 15-year mortgage for the first 15 years.

** The numbers in this figure were taken from figures 1.1 and 1.2

and deposit that money in a tax deferred, interest-bearing side fund (let's assume 8 percent interest), you will notice that by year fifteen, the conservative side fund (column 5) will have accumulated $26,976 more than is needed to pay off the mortgage (column 1)! This is why I call it the $25,000 mistake millions of Americans make. It's an even bigger mistake if the mortgage is greater than $150,000.

You might say, "But wait a minute, I have to pay 34 percent in taxes on the interest or growth I'm earning on my side fund!" The total in fifteen years from saving the difference between the net payment after tax in column 4 equals a basis in my side fund of $78,699. Even in a tax-deferred investment, the gain we achieve of $63,448 to arrive at a balance of $142,147 (column 5) in fifteen years could be subject to tax. If so, assuming a 34 percent tax rate, we would incur a tax liability of $21,572 (34 percent of our $63,448 gain), meaning we would have only realized $5,404 ($26,976 – $21,572 = $5,404) more than is needed to pay off the mortgage balance of $115,171. (This is true unless we use an investment wherein we can access our gain tax free rather than just tax deferred. This book will teach you how you can accomplish this.)

As I began this chapter, I noted many homeowners today are trying to hasten the goal of accomplishing a free and clear home by making extra principal payments in one fashion or another. What they don't realize is that by setting aside those same dollars in a conservative side fund that is tax advantaged, they can accumulate enough money in that side fund to pay off the mortgage just as quickly, or, as I have shown, even more quickly.

Based on just a $100,000 mortgage, you can actually end up with enough money to pay off your mortgage in the same time-frame as using traditional methods, with up to $20,000 extra to be used at your discretion. If you choose, you can use those extra funds to pay off the mortgage one to two years sooner! That's one advantage of using this method over the traditional methods. What are the other advantages? Keep reading and you'll find out.

WEALTH-ENHANCEMENT STRATEGY NUMBER ONE

- *Establish a liquid side fund to accumulate the funds required to pay off your mortgage, maintain flexibility, achieve substantial tax savings and accumulate excess cash.*

CHAPTER 2

The $150,000 Lesson on Liquidity

Avoid expensive risks. Position yourself to act instead of react.

Home equity is liquid.

When you need it most, you may not have it.
Home equity is usually non-liquid.

If I were your investment consultant and offered a particular investment for your consideration, you would likely ask the following questions:

1. "How **liquid** would my money be?" In other words, you would want to know how easily you could access your money at any given time if you needed it. Liquidity is probably the number one consideration for any prudent investment.

2. "Would my money be **safe**?" Is the investment guaranteed and/or insured? What element of safety is inherent in the investment?

3. "What **rate of return** can I expect?" Most people are usually willing to give up a little safety to get a little return. Even depositing money in a bank requires that we give up some safety to obtain some rate of return. We all want maximum return at minimum risk.

4. "What about the **tax consequences**?" A tax-favored investment will, in the long run, achieve a higher net rate of return by virtue of its tax benefits.

Throughout this book I will explain the application of these important concepts—liquidity, safety, rate of return, and tax benefits—as they relate to wealth enhancement and management.

CRACKING THE NEST EGG

How important is it to have the liquidity necessary to get you through the tough times? How will you cope when unexpected circumstances arise from external forces over which you have no control?

Liquidity is the number one element—the key factor—in determining a wise and prudent investment. Many homeowners believe home equity to be a convenient nest egg from which they can always access cash when needed. However, in a time of dire need, many of them suddenly realize that, no matter how much home equity they have, it is not as liquid as they thought.

Suppose you had been doing what many homeowners do—that is, making extra principal payments on your mortgage every opportunity you had. Over a period of five or six years you would have paid a substantial amount against the principal of your mortgage with those extra payments. What if all of a sudden you found yourself with a physical disability or unemployed? You would go to your mortgage banker and explain, "Hey, Mr. Mortgage Banker, I was faithful all these years; in fact, I even paid you extra money. Will you please let me coast now for a little while since I am way ahead of schedule?"

The mortgage banker would say, "Sorry, you'll have to fill out an application to see if you qualify to borrow that money back."

You might say, "Wait a minute! I've been paying you extra; I am way ahead of schedule! I deserve a break!" Eventually, you would realize it doesn't matter how much extra you have paid on your mortgage balance; your next mortgage payment is due in full in thirty days. In fact, if your mortgage payment becomes delinquent for ninety days, the mortgage banker can foreclose on a trust deed note. If that happens, all your extra efforts to reduce your mortgage quickly—all that extra equity you accumulated in your property—will have been for naught!

I knew a man who owed $100,000 on his home. He got a $90,000 windfall and paid all of it against his mortgage. With only a $10,000 balance remaining, this man became disabled and lost his income. Still, his normal mortgage payment was due the next month. He missed three consecutive payments. He wasn't able to borrow back any of the $90,000 he had just paid because he lacked the ability to repay. His home was foreclosed on!

Physical disability is the number one cause of home foreclosure in America. What's more, the chances of becoming temporarily financially disabled at some point in life are far greater than becoming physically disabled.

Envision taking a $100 bill, putting it in a tin can, and burying it in your backyard. Is that $100 bill liquid? Yes, as long as you can remember where you buried it! What about the hundreds of dollars we tie up

in the bricks, mortar, wood, steel, and concrete of our homes? Are those dollars liquid? No, they are not. The fact is, the money buried in the tin can in your backyard has greater liquidity than the money tied up in your property!

If you were to take a loan application to a bank during a critical time in your life when you were sick, unemployed, or simply had a financial setback, chances are they would say, "Sorry, come back when you have the ability to repay." It doesn't matter how many assets you have, because most banks are not collateral lenders. They love to tie up assets with liens, but their first requirement is that you show your ability to repay. You almost have to prove to the banker you don't need the money before he'll loan it to you!

Most of us are familiar with the golden rule—"Do unto others as you would have them do unto you." There is a different golden rule in finance: "He who has the gold, makes the rules!" For this reason, it is better to have control of your home equity and never access it, than to need it and be unable to obtain it.

ACT—DON'T REACT

Why is liquidity important? Because life is unpredictable. Let's go back to September 1987. If I had been your investment consultant and had advised you to sell all your stocks and convert them into a cash position, I would have been your financial hero! Why? Because the stock market crash of 1987! The people who lacked liquidity during that crucial time period were forced to sell and may have taken a beating. Many scrambled to cover margin accounts due to lack of liquidity. Those who had other resources and liquid funds available were able to ride out the short-term market correction.

One of the purposes of managing equity is to position yourself in a situation where you can *act* upon opportunities rather than be forced to *react* to situations. When fluctuations in the market occur, truly, the smart rich get richer. Unfortunately, in those same circumstances, the poor often get poorer (with respect to knowledge and liquid assets). Those who are able to act—buy on the low market, and sell at the high points—continue to accumulate wealth. Those who have to react and sell when the market goes down end up losing what they had hoped to gain.

During the late 90s, it seemed even "turkey" mutual funds and stocks soared because in a stiff breeze, even a turkey can fly. Then the correction came in September 2000, bringing turkeys and blue chips alike down to earth. I have observed through nearly three decades of financial planning that timing the market doesn't generally work. But investors continue to try. Over the twenty-year period between 1980 and 2000, the average growth of 199 institutional growth funds was approximately 12 percent per year, including all the fluctuations in the market. Yet, personal investor returns only averaged about 2 percent annually during the same time period. This difference reflects the fact that individuals keep getting in and out of the market at the wrong times. The average time investors keep their money in the market is about three years—much too short a time period!

Having liquidity allows you to ride out the tough times. We know the market has never, and will never, go up in an infinitely straight line. We also know it is equally impossible for the market to go down in an infinitely straight line. The market is more like a yo-yo in the hands of a man walking up stairs. There are ups and downs, but in the long term, the market, like the yo-yo, will likely move in an upward direction.

The same is true with real estate appreciation. Real estate markets rise and fall, but over time they generally appreciate. Depending upon where your property is located, that appreciation rate could average 3 percent, 5 percent, or even 7 percent per year.

APPRAISING REAL ESTATE'S VALUE

The reason why property values increase is because the demand for them becomes greater than their supply. Basic economics teaches that whenever the demand for products is greater than their supply, prices go up. On the other hand, if supply exceeds demand, prices fall. This is also true of real estate. At any given time, the demand in certain areas of the country is adversely impacted by various microeconomic conditions, causing real estate prices to drop, leading to depressed markets. At the same time, other areas of the country may be booming, increasing demand, causing their real estate markets to rise.

Let's take a look at Houston, Texas, when the oil prices were down during the early 1980s. Suddenly there was a glut of homes on the market. The homes that had been appraised at $100,000 only a year earlier were forced on the market for $60,000 and $70,000. Sixteen thousand homes were foreclosed on. Homeowners' equity was dramatically affected.

Prior to the recession, the vast majority of those people probably had been making timely mortgage payments. In fact, many of them had probably been making extra principal payments on top of their regular payments. But when they suddenly became unemployed and had to relocate and sell their properties, they lacked liquidity. They tried in desperation to sell their homes, sometimes for much less than their market value had been just a few months earlier. These people did not have bad credit histories; they simply found themselves in a situation where they could not make their mortgage payments.

Many of these people pled with their mortgage companies to let them coast a few months or to let them refinance their homes. Mortgage companies wouldn't let them. Many of them went to their bankers and asked for equity lines of credit based on the equity they had in their homes. The bankers wouldn't help them. Many homeowners had no choice but to turn their homes back to the bank and to lose whatever equity they had built in their properties.

In contrast, the homeowners who had liquid funds available could ride out the market until it recovered, or they could afford to sell their properties at their deflated values. They were able to preserve some or all of the equity they had built.

THE $150,000 LESSON

In 1978, a couple constructed a unique country home, comprising 6400 square feet of living space. Designed like a Swiss chalet, the home was beautifully decorated and was scheduled to be featured in *Better Homes and Gardens*. The couple's home appreciated in value and by 1982 it was appraised for just under $300,000. They had accumulated a significant amount of equity, not because of extra payments made on the property, but because market conditions improved during that four-year period.

This couple thought they had the world by the tail. They had a home valued at $300,000 with first and second mortgages owing only $150,000. They had "made" $150,000 in four short years as a result of property appreciation. They had the misconception that equity in their home had a rate of return when, in fact, it was just a number on a sheet of paper.

Then, a series of unexpected events reduced their income to almost nothing for nine months. They tried desperately to borrow funds to keep mortgage payments current, but without the ability to repay, they couldn't. Three months into the ordeal, they sold a vacation time share and applied $10,000 to bring the mortgage current. After another three months, they sold a rental income duplex, which again brought them out of delinquency.

Realizing there was no way to stay, they put the home on the market to protect their $150,000 of equity. Unfortunately, the real estate market, which previously had been strong, turned soft. After reducing the price of the property several times—from $295,000 to $260,000, $245,000, $225,000, and finally $195,000—they were not able to find a buyer. Sadly, they gave up the home in foreclosure to the mortgage lender.

But the story doesn't end there. The two mortgages on the property were in the amounts of $125,000 and $25,000, respectively. The second mortgage holder outbid the first mortgage holder at the ensuing auction. Much like the original owners, the second mortgage holder felt it was in a good position. The lender knew the home had appraised for $300,000, and that the obligation owing was only $150,000. It thought it could turn around and sell the property to cover the investment.

During the soft market, the home did not sell for another nine months, during which time the lender was forced to pay the first mortgage payment and accrued an additional $30,000 of interest and penalties. By the time the home finally sold—for $30,000 less than the accrued indebtedness on the home—guess who got stuck with the deficiency balance of $30,000 on their credit report? The original owners, of course!

This couple not only had a foreclosure appear for seven years on their credit report, but the report also showed a deficiency balance owing of $30,000 on a home they had lost nearly one year earlier! In a time of financial setback, they lost one of their most valuable financial assets due to the lack of liquidity.

Through this experience, this couple learned some unforgettable lessons. They learned the importance of positioning their assets in financial instruments that maintain liquidity in the event of an emergency. They learned the importance of maintaining flexibility in order to ride out market lows and take advantage of market highs. Most important, *they learned never to allow a significant amount of equity to accumulate in their property without maintaining liquidity.* I know they learned these things, because my wife and I were that couple.

The Most Important Reason to Keep Equity Separated from Property...
LIQUIDITY

SEPARATING EQUITY FROM REAL ESTATE

How do you get cash out of real estate? There are only two ways. You either have to sell the property or separate the equity through a conduit known as a mortgage. Obviously, if the purpose behind this exercise is to own property outright, selling isn't the way to go! Therefore, to get cash out of your home, you must refinance and mortgage your property or obtain an equity line of credit (which is simply another form of refinancing).

You may be asking yourself, "Wait a minute, isn't my goal to get out of debt, not to increase it?" I agree with that goal, and I'll cover how to get out of debt the quickest, smartest way possible later. But for now consider the question of who controls the ability to get cash out of your property? Is it you, the owner? No, it's the bank!

Home equity is not liquid and does not pass the initial test of a prudent and wise investment.

2 WEALTH-ENHANCEMENT STRATEGY NUMBER TWO

- *Position yourself to act instead of to react to market conditions over which you have no control.*
- *Separate as much equity from your property as is feasible, positioning it in financial instruments that will maintain liquidity in the event of emergencies and conservative investment opportunities.*

CHAPTER 3

Separating Home and Equity To Increase Safety

A home mortgaged to the hilt or totally free and clear provides the greatest safety for the homeowner.

REALITY

A home mortgaged to the hilt or totally free and clear provides the greatest safety for the homeowner.

Many people feel comfortable depositing money in federally insured savings accounts or certificate of deposits. These banking accounts, approved by the Federal Deposit Insurance Corporation, are usually attractive to savers for reasons Will Rogers once identified: "I am more concerned about the return of my money rather than the return on my money."

Most people are more concerned with the safety of the principal of their investment than they are with the potential earnings on that investment. And home equity is no different. Most homeowners have the misconception that the equity in their homes is safe, and they are content to leave it there. Is that really the safest place for it?

KEEPING EQUITY SAFE

If I were to purchase a home for $200,000 with a $120,000 down payment, I would incur an $80,000 mortgage. Also, at the time of purchase, I would have a total of $120,000 in equity. Let's say, due to a soft real estate market, the value of the home drops from $200,000 down to $160,000. Did that $40,000 reduction come off the mortgage or off the equity? Most definitely, it came off the equity.

Let's go back to the tin-can illustration in chapter two. If I had a $100 bill buried in my backyard inside a tin can, is the $100 bill safe? Sometimes I jokingly reply, "Yes, as long as my wife doesn't know where I buried it!"

So, are the dollar bills we tie up in our home as safe as the dollar bills we have buried in the backyard? Again, let's go back to Houston. In 1981 and 1982 when oil prices went down, many homeowners tried in desperation to sell their properties. Because the supply of homes was greater than the demand, home values plummeted. Much of the equity people had built for years in their properties was lost when the soft real estate market, forced them to sell and liquidate.

Think if a Houston homeowner, after an earlier appraisal of her home, had removed a large portion of her equity and put it into a safe and liquid side fund accessible for use when market values dropped. Even if the value of her home had gone down, she would have had a sizeable amount of liquid cash on hand.

WHO'S SAFER: YOU OR YOUR LENDER?

Even if the value of the home goes below the mortgage balance, with my equity separated, I am still in a position of control. If the market forces me to sell the property for less than the outstanding loan, then I have cash available to settle all liabilities. I could use that cash to pay off my mortgage balance. Whether I have mortgaged my home to the hilt or own the home free and clear, I still have the same amount of equity, but the liquidity and safety of my equity can be greater if I keep it separate from the property.

My recommendation is that people have their home mortgaged as high as is feasible for their budgets. Some want their homes totally free and clear because it gives them peace of mind. I understand that desire. However, the road to that peace of mind may come at an extremely high price. For equity to be in as safe a position as possible, I contend it must either be repositioned out of a home by mortgaging it to the maximum amount feasible, or left in a home that is totally free and clear. Any place in between is a risky position from a safety and liquidity standpoint.

If a mortgage lender carried a mortgage loan based on a borrower's income, net worth, and the value of her property, conventional guidelines would dictate a loan of 80 percent of the value of the home. If the loan becomes delinquent, the trust deed note or mortgage allows the lending institution to legally foreclose and resell the property. In most markets, homes can be liquidated rapidly for at least 80 percent of the appraised value of the home at the time the loan was taken out. Rarely does the real estate market become so bad that homes will only sell for 60 to 70 percent of their appraised value at the time mortgages were originated. Thus, most conventional first mortgage lenders want a margin of 20 percent as a protection against possible loan default. (If a mortgage lender decides to loan in excess of 80 percent of a home's value, it would protect itself by charging an additional amount known as a mortgage insurance premium [MIP] or private mortgage insurance [PMI].)

Thus, if a borrower had a $200,000 home, and all other considerations were favorable, a mortgage lender would most likely be willing to lend $160,000 keeping a $40,000 cushion. In rising real estate markets, this cushion increases as time passes, and the mortgage lender thus becomes more and more secure.

Consider, for example, a $200,000 home with a $160,000 mortgage. If the value of the home is appreciating at a rate of 5 percent a year, the home will double in value about every fifteen years. Thus, the mortgage institution becomes more secure in its investment because the loan-to-value ratio improves each year. Now let me ask you, "If the mortgage company is continually improving its margin of safety, how does that affect your safety?" In just the opposite way! Your position of safety becomes worse and worse. Each year your mortgage reduces and your home appreciates, your safety is being taken away as far as your investment in your home is concerned. The more equity you accumulate and leave trapped in the home, the less safety your equity investment principal has—meaning, if real estate markets take a sudden turn downward, your equity suffers, and the safety of your investment has been compromised.

SPEEDING YOUR RECOVERY FROM FINANCIAL SETBACKS

Let's say you have a home located right in the middle of a California earthquake zone. If your $200,000 home, without earthquake insurance and with little or no mortgage debt, is destroyed in the earthquake, would you be able to recover from that devastation quickly? Probably not.

On the other hand, if that same home, this time with a $160,000 mortgage and $80,000 cash placed in a liquid, safe, side fund, is destroyed in an earthquake, what then? Yes, you would still owe the mortgage balance, but since the mortgage company likely would have only required fire insurance and not earthquake insurance on your property, you would be in a position of greater control. You would have more leverage as to whether you wanted to negotiate with the mortgage company and release the property to them as is. You would be in a position to negotiate whether you wanted to take some of your liquid side funds to pay off the mortgage on the damaged property. You would have the option to use some of that side money to get into a new home. I assure you, having safety of principal, versus money tied up in your property opens up crucial alternatives for financial recovery.

A gentleman came into my office a few years ago who had been making triple house payments on his $100,000 home. Over a relatively short period of time, he had paid $50,000 of his $80,000 mortgage, leaving him with a balance of $30,000. Then, because of a physical disability and other circumstances beyond his control, he was forced to turn the property back to the mortgage lender, thus losing $70,000 of equity trapped in his home. He lacked both liquidity and protection of the safety of his principal.

The most dangerous position a homeowner can be in is to have a home worth substantially more than the mortgage liens against it. It makes no difference how much the property is worth, nor does it matter if the lien on your property is for $2,000, $20,000, or $200,000. Any type of lien on the property makes it encumbered. This means if the liability is not met, the person or entity to which the liability is due has the right to acquire your property or to be paid before you receive any equity when the property is liquidated.

With that in mind, a $200,000 home with a $20,000 mortgage puts the mortgage company in a position of tremendous safety but puts the owner in a precarious situation with little safety of principal. Whose security are you trying to achieve, the bank's or your own?

As I described in chapter two, my wife and I were lulled into a false sense of security when the home we built for $150,000 appreciated to an appraised value of about $300,000 in four short years. Yet, when our fortunes shifted due to circumstances beyond our control, the investment represented by the equity in our home turned out to be one of the least safe in which we have ever been involved. We lost it all, and owed another $30,000 to boot!

The Second Most Important Reason to Keep Equity Separated from Property...
SAFETY

LOCATION, LOCATION, LOCATION

The three most important factors that determine the fair market value of any real estate property are first, the location of the property; second, the location of the property; third, the location of the property. May I also submit to you the three most important factors for conserving the safety of the principal of any real estate property are first, the location of the equity; second, the location of the equity; third, the location of the equity.

Real estate equity is no safer than any other investment whose value is determined by an external market over which we personally have no control. In fact, due to the hidden "risks of life," real estate equity is not nearly as safe as many other conservative investments and assets. Therefore, home equity does not pass the second test of a prudent and wise investment: safety.

3 WEALTH-ENHANCEMENT STRATEGY NUMBER THREE

*• Separate as much equity from your home as is feasible
 to achieve greater safety of principal.*

CHAPTER 4

Is Your Home Really Safe?

Real properties with high equity and low mortgages get foreclosed on the soonest.

COMMON MYTH-CONCEPTION

Homes with a lot of equity are less subject to foreclosure.

REALITY

Homes with substantial equity are usually the first ones mortgage bankers foreclose on if their mortgages become delinquent.

Unfortunately, many home buyers have the misconception that paying down their mortgages quickly is the best method of reducing the risk of foreclosure on their homes. Although the final mortgage payment certainly reduces the risk of foreclosure, in the interim, all the methods most people use to pay off their mortgages quickly actually increase the risk of foreclosure. Many people who scrape up every bit of extra money they can to apply against their mortgage principals often find themselves with no liquidity. When tough times come, they find themselves scrambling to make their mortgage payments!

THE SOFT MARKET

It is important to understand the value of a home is not contingent upon how much the mortgage is. Rather, the value of a home is contingent upon what the market dictates. In other words, its value is based on whatever buyers are willing to pay for it. Just because you bought a $200,000 home and obtained a $160,000 mortgage does not mean its value will be $200,000 or even $160,000 when you sell it. In soft real estate markets, I have seen homes originally worth $200,000 lose value to $100,000—only 50 percent of the original amount.

Remember the home I bought in 1978? It had an appraised value of $300,000 in 1982, but soon thereafter, it wouldn't sell for even $150,000! With the glut of homes on the market where I lived, most lost some value, but not as dramatically as the 50 percent loss I experienced. Why? My mortgage in 1982 was classified as "jumbo"—in other words, above the average market. In a soft market, the demand for this type of luxury home can be very, very small. Worse, even the few buyers for this type of home know they can obtain one for fifty cents on the dollar, or sometimes even less.

REAL ESTATE AUCTIONS

A mortgage company sells a foreclosed home on auction, usually held at the county courthouse or with the sheriff. The home is awarded to the highest bidder at the time of the auction. After winning, the highest bidder has to pay for the home in full or can be allowed to put down a certain amount immediately—usually around $5,000—then has twenty-four hours to return with the balance. The highest bidder wins regardless of the price. Fairness has nothing to do with the process—it unfolds in simple accordance with the contract agreed upon by both lender and borrower.

In lieu of foreclosure, homeowners may choose to deed over their homes to the mortgage company if the value of the home is close to its anticipated liquidation price on the auction block. In such an arrangement, the homeowner may give up the right to any extra equity that could be realized over and above the mortgage balance and late fees at the time of sale. On the other hand, by deeding over the property, the homeowner is protected from any liability in the event of a low-priced sale.

Many individuals and entities make thousands of dollars by acquiring properties at real estate auctions, then selling them at a profit. As an example, one of my clients obtains weekly lists from the county courthouse of homes scheduled for foreclosure. He studies their loan-to-value ratios and carefully selects those he feels are the best bargains. After touring the properties with selected individuals from his pool of potential home buyers, he attends the weekly auction. He prepares to bid up to a pre-determined amount just below what a client is willing and pre-qualified to buy.

Let's say a home, appraised at $100,000 and carrying a mortgage balance owing less than $60,000, comes up for auction. Because only $60,000 is required to pay off the liability of this home, this man is able to buy it for $.60 on the dollar. Having won the bid on that home, he must immediately pay $5,000 to the court in order to secure his claim. The next day he must pay the balance due—in this case, $55,000—in cash. Depending on the condition of the home, he may then spend an additional $10,000 or so fixing it up over the following weeks. Eventually, he sells the property for, say, $80,000, to his pre-qualified buyer and makes a $10,000 profit.

This man's reputation is so secure, he has a network of mortgage lenders, home foreclosure attorneys, fix-up contractors, and a pool of potential home buyers that keep him busy as a regular bidder. And because he has the means to close a cash purchase of these properties within twenty-four hours, he provides a valuable service and is compensated handsomely.

A great deal of research and skill is required in order not to be occasionally stung buying properties on auction. For example, one day my client, who is an expert at this, witnessed a novice bidder at the auction who thought he had done his homework. He didn't understand why he and the mortgage company were the only ones bidding on a house. After winning the bid, he jumped for joy thinking he had gotten a steal on a home by bidding to pay off the mortgage in the amount of $60,000 on a $100,000 house. After laying down a check for $5,000, he found out there were tax liens amounting to thousands of dollars. He grabbed his $5,000 off the clerk's table and ran out of the courthouse!

FORECLOSURE

It is important to understand every day that goes by, a mortgage banker becomes more secure with the homeowner's loan because usually a home will appreciate over time, even if slowly. Most mortgage bankers realize that geographically limited recessionary periods are somewhat temporary, usually lasting no longer than two to four years.

However, during those recessionary times, homeowners who find themselves in tight straits may plead with their mortgage bankers to let them have some breathing room. They might cite all the extra principal payments they've made on their mortgages as proof of good intent. They might even point to the amount of equity they've built in their properties. Truth is, it doesn't matter. Whether you just barely scraped together last month's required payment or paid an extra $10,000 on top, the next month's mortgage payment is still due (unless your mortgage contract specifically states otherwise).

Principal payments simply reduce the principal balance of the loan. However, regardless of the number and amount of your extra principal payments, the next contractual payment comprised of principal and interest is due in thirty days. If the mortgage becomes delinquent for ninety consecutive days, the mortgage banker has the legal right to fore-close on property secured with a trust deed. If the mortgage is protected by a mortgage contract (rather than by a trust deed note), most state laws protect the homeowner for about six months before a mortgage banker can successfully foreclose and receive full title to the property.

I think the saddest situation is when a homeowner has tried to pay off his home as rapidly as possible, only to find himself in a set of cir-cumstances beyond his worst imaginations. All the equity he was des-perately trying to develop over years of making steep payments on short mortgage terms or extra principal payments on longer mortgage terms is lost—gone in ninety days!

Consider a mortgage banker in Houston when the oil prices plum-meted and over 16,000 homes were foreclosed on. If you were that mort-gage banker, looking at a loan portfolio in which 100 mortgages were seriously delinquent, how would you decide which homes to pursue foreclosure on?

Let's say all 100 of those mortgages had original balances of $200,000 but now have varying balances owing: 10 percent of the mortgages still have nearly $200,000 owing, 10 percent have $180,000 or so owing, 10 percent have $160,000 owing, and 10 percent have $140,000 owing. And so it goes on down the line until you get to the last 10 percent of loans held by the banker—loans held with only $20,000 mortgage balances owing on them.

Having considered your portfolio of delinquent loans, knowing you need to make a quick turnaround, and realizing with the soft market, these 100 homes, are now selling for as little as $100,000, you have to make a decision. The mortgage company you work for doesn't want a large inventory of homes acquired through foreclosure. It's more inter-ested in recovering the money invested in the loans. Thus, you have to consider which ones will sell quickly so you can recover any losses and preserve principal on behalf of investors.

The mortgage company can call any of these loans (declare them immediately due and payable) because they are all in default. Even in a distressed market, a mortgage company will be able to resell those properties because there are always a few anxious investors prepared to pick up properties cheaply, knowing that, prices will rise again as the market bounces back. Maybe the selling price for these homes, originally worth $200,000, will be a mere $80,000, $100,000, or $120,000, but their value will likely rise. Mortgage companies are legally afforded the opportunity to make a profit on foreclosures where possible, which they could return to the foreclosed owners. In reality, however, the mortgage company's only concern is to avoid any losses by covering the mortgage balance due. At the time of liquidation, the homeowner may hope to recover some of the equity in the foreclosed-on home, but the mortgage banker has no motivation to sell the property for any more than necessary to recoup losses.

As the mortgage banker, consider the soft market, the low demand for homes, the falling prices, and the resulting $120,000 average value of the 100 homes in your delinquent portfolio. Which homes would you foreclose on first? The homes with $140,000 and $160,000 mortgages? Or would you foreclose on homes with only $20,000 and $40,000 mortgage balances remaining?

You will likely foreclose first on those people who have the lowest mortgage balances, putting off foreclosures on those with high mortgage balances. In fact, in the latter case, you will most likely work with the homeowners in every possible way to help them keep their homes and payments current.

I have a close acquaintance whose father-in-law is in his early sixties. Due to a series of unfortunate circumstances, this father-in-law and his wife have been unable to make their mortgage payments for over twenty-four months. The mortgage company could have foreclosed on their home mortgage during the first 90 to 180 days of delinquency, but, mainly because of the high loan-to-value ratio of their mortgage, the mortgage lender has bent over backwards trying to assist them. It has extended the time to bring the mortgage current; it has helped to arrange easier payment terms. It has even coached the homeowner, off the record, as to when it is best to file a Chapter 13 bankruptcy and when it is best to convert that to a Chapter 7 bankruptcy in order to buy the most time. The home has a high mortgage balance, and the lender obviously believes by being patient with this couple, it will recover the most money. At this time, those homeowners have lived in their home for over two years without making a mortgage payment!

Homes with substantial equity are the first ones mortgage bankers usually foreclose on because the loan and delinquency can legally be remedied by selling the property quickly to cover their risk and protect their investors—especially in a soft real estate market. A mortgage with a small loan-to-value ratio offers the greatest opportunity for a mortgage banker to protect its interest by using the homeowner's equity to discount the price of the home in the case of delinquency. And remember, even if the home is sold in foreclosure for less than the loan amount, a homeowner may be left with the deficiency on his credit report.

LIQUID EQUITY

A major cause of foreclosure in America is physical disability. The chance of becoming financially disabled is even greater than physical disability, which highlights the importance of having liquid assets. A liquid side fund allows a homeowner the flexibility of using extra dollars for savings and investment opportunities, and the ability to keep the mortgage current if the need arises.

It is extremely difficult to borrow when the ability to repay is lacking. A mortgage banker—or any bank for that matter—is unlikely to loan money even if that individual has substantial collateral. Only lenders who charge high interest rates for the high risk incurred are willing to loan money under those circumstances.

Managing equity in order to maintain liquidity requires a high amount of discipline. Setting aside funds in a liquid position, allowing easy access in case of tough times, requires a homeowner to save the money he might have put toward building equity by making extra principal payments. Then discipline must be exercised not to consume the funds. Those who can maintain this discipline reap the rewards.

Liquidity allows them to "peel off dollars"—dollars that can be used to save, to invest, or to keep mortgages current in case of temporary setbacks. Liquidity also allows a degree of flexibility that not only will keep your credit rating healthy, but will also give your equity far more protection than putting it in the hands of the mortgage banker.

Separate your equity from your home by using a first mortgage, second mortgage, or equity line of credit, and keep it in some type of safe, liquid side fund such as those introduced in Section III.

Every time a mortgage contract is entered into, a homeowner is pledging his home as collateral. A home is usually a person's greatest asset, which is why homeowners often attempt to eliminate their mortgages as soon as possible. But by having the discipline and vision to maintain liquidity in order to have your home work for you, you'll be safer financially and get out of debt more quickly.

4 WEALTH-ENHANCEMENT STRATEGY NUMBER FOUR

- *To reduce the risk of foreclosure during unforeseen setbacks, keep your mortgage balance as high as feasible.*
- *Keep your equity separated into a position of liquidity and safety until you are ready to pay off the mortgage in a lump sum.*

CHAPTER 5

The Return on Equity Is Always Zero

No matter where your property is located, the return on equity is always the same—zero!

COMMON MYTH-CONCEPTION

Home equity has a rate of return.

REALITY

Equity grows as a function of real estate appreciation and mortgage reduction; however, equity has no rate of return.

 One of the greatest misconceptions among homeowners is that equity has a rate of return. In this chapter we will explore the growth of equity as a function of real estate appreciation and mortgage reduction. Even so, equity does not earn a rate of return!

THE VALUE OF REAL ESTATE

Real estate has always been deemed a valuable asset. It has always been a limited commodity. Acquiring property and land has always been associated with wealth.

A gentleman once told me he had bought a lot where he was planning to build a cabin. He had paid $20,000 for the lot several years earlier, but had not yet gotten around to building on the property. It was now worth $40,000. Then he made an interesting comment: "It was one of the best investments I ever made."

When he sensed I wasn't impressed, he asked why. I indicated I could not make a judgment call without getting additional information. I asked him how long he had owned the property. He told me ten years. I asked him if he had paid cash for it. He said, yes. Then I said, "Well, you probably could have done much better elsewhere; you received the equivalent of about 7 percent interest compounded annually on your money. During that same ten-year period, you could have earned at least 11 percent."

He asked how I had figured that out so quickly.

I replied, "The Rule of 72."

THE RULE OF 72

The Rule of 72 is generally used in the financial industry to calculate the number of years it takes to double invested money. You simply take the interest rate, divide it into 72 and the result is the number of years it will take to double your money (**fig. 5.1**). This formula, requiring only simple arithmetic, assumes that no additional principal is added to the investment over the years it is held. Thus, the result of 72 divided by 9

$$72 \div 9 = 8$$

indicates that at a 9 percent interest rate compounded annually, you will double your money every eight years. If you earn 7 percent interest, your money will double every ten years. If you earn 10 percent interest, your money will double every seven years.

Fig. 5.1	THE RULE OF 72

$$\frac{72}{\text{interest rate}} = \text{Years to Double}$$

-or-

$$\frac{72}{\text{years to double}} = \text{Interest Rate}$$

In practical application, the rule could be applied thus: If you started with an investment of $10,000 and earned a 10 percent return, it would be worth $20,000 in seven years, $40,000 in fourteen years, $80,000 in twenty-one years, and so forth. This rule can also be applied to real estate. If your home steadily appreciates at a rate of 5 percent per year, your home will double in value approximately every fifteen years.

As a financial planner I have always found it amusing to project clients' estate value fifteen to thirty years into the future. They are flabbergasted when I tell them their $100,000 home may be worth $400,000 thirty years down the road. I have heard retorts of, "That's highly unlikely. I don't think that will ever happen!" But the rule holds true. Indeed, many of my clients have realized a quadrupling in valuation in only fifteen or twenty years, rather than in the full thirty years that I projected, because the average appreciation rate in their area ended up being far greater than 5 percent.

Rearranging the basic equation for the Rule of 72 also tells us the compound interest you'd have to earn if you wanted to double your investment in a certain number of years. Simply take the number of years in which you'd like to double your money, and divide it into 72 to get the rate of return. So, if you'd like to double your money, in a little over seven years, you can calculate

$$72 \div 7.2 = 10$$

to find you would have to earn about 10 percent interest compounded annually. If you'd like to double your money in ten years, you would have to earn about 7 percent interest.

Using this rule, I was quickly able to determine the gentleman who had purchased a lot for $20,000, which had then doubled in value to $40,000 ten years later, had only experienced a 7 percent annual growth rate on his money. Not that impressive, especially in light of the fact that he had paid cash and tied up an entire $20,000 in his property. This gentleman's story would perhaps have been more impressive had he only paid $2,000 for the property in the form of a down payment, then financed the balance using "other people's money." In that case, the rate of return would have been more complicated to calculate, but would certainly have been better than 7 percent because of the principle of leverage, which we will discuss in chapter 9.

OTHER APPLICATIONS FOR THE RULE OF 72

The principles behind the Rule of 72 can be applied to a broad variety of situations. For example, if you were to retire today and could get by on an income of $3,000 per month, how much would you need thirty years from now to maintain the same standard of living? Assuming a 5 percent inflation rate, and using the Rule of 72, we can calculate that the cost of goods and services will double every fifteen years (5 divided into 72 equals approximately 15). In other words, fifteen years from now, we would need $6,000 per month to buy the same amount of groceries and gas that $3,000 would purchase today. Another fifteen years after that, we would need $12,000 per month to have the same purchasing power. Understanding how to apply the Rule of 72 will help you solve simple financial problems without requiring a financial calculator.

In early 1993, the *Deseret News* and *The Salt Lake Tribune* published an article projecting that Salt Lake City, Utah, would rank seventh out of the nation's top 100 markets for rising real estate values. An average home in Salt Lake City at that time was worth $77,250. Predictions indicated homes would appreciate by 9.6 percent that year and would be worth an average of $84,666 by year's end. They were wrong. The average appreciation rate across Utah's populated Wasatch Front wasn't 9.6 percent, but an amazing 19 percent! By the end of 1993, Salt Lake City was ranked number one in home appreciation values in the nation. Using the Rule of 72, if that appreciation rate were to have continued, homes would have doubled in value within four years.

In 1994 the market pulled back a bit in Salt Lake City, on average appreciating by only 9 percent. Then, in 1995, the market took off again and achieved an average 17 percent appreciation. By 1996, many homes were worth more than double what they were worth just four short years earlier. What would you say the return on equity was in the Salt Lake City area during that four-year period? (Careful, this is a trick question!)

THE RETURN ON EQUITY IS ALWAYS ZERO

The return on equity is always zero! It doesn't matter whether your home is located in Salt Lake City, New Orleans, Honolulu, Houston, or Seattle. Because the mortgage is reducing and the house is appreciating, we have the misconception that equity earns a rate of return. It doesn't! It only grows as a function of the mortgage balance reducing and the home appreciating.

Let's go back to the tin can example. We know the $100 bill in the tin can buried in my backyard is more liquid than the $100 bills tied up in my home (chapter 2). We also know it's safer than the money tied up in my home (chapters 3 and 4). But is that $100 bill earning a rate of return? No, it is not. That much should be obvious. In fact, not only is it not earning a rate of return, but also it is losing value—or purchasing power—because of the increasing cost of living, which we call inflation. What, then, is the difference between rate of return on the $100 bill in the tin can and the dollar bills we tie up in the wood, bricks, mortar, and foundation of our homes? Nothing.

THE PITCHER AND GOBLET

In order to illustrate the concept that equity does not earn a rate of return, I want to use a powerful visual aid. But I need your help. Go to the cupboard and get a pitcher and a goblet, glass, or cup. Fill the goblet with water, then pour the water from the goblet into the pitcher. Imagine the goblet is your home, worth $100,000. It is empty because you have not yet put one dollar into the property.

The pitcher of water represents $100,000 of liquid cash, because for the time being you have that cash sitting in a liquid environment, let's say in the bank. If you or your accountant prepared your financial statement, where would the home be listed on your balance sheet—assets or liabilities? Of course, your home would be listed as a $100,000 asset. How about your $100,000 of liquid cash? It would also be listed as an asset on your financial statement. You would have total assets equaling $200,000. On the next section of the balance sheet, in the liability section, you would also list a $100,000 mortgage, giving you a net worth of $200,000 - $100,000 = $100,000 (assets - liabilities = net worth; **fig. 5.2**).

ASSETS = $200,000

Fig. 5.2	**BALANCE SHEET**
ASSETS	
Home	$100,000
Cash	<u>$100,000</u>
Total Assets	$200,000
LIABILITIES	
Home Mortgage	($100,000)
NET WORTH	
Assets - Liabilities =	<u>**$100,000**</u>

$100,000 Home

$100,000 Cash

Let's examine again the asset section of the balance sheet. It is obviously you have a $100,000 asset (the home) and another $100,000 asset (the liquid cash in the bank) for a grand total of $200,000 in assets. What happens when we take some or all of our cash and pour it into the property (pick up the pitcher of water and pour the liquid water into the goblet)? We just reduced our assets by the amount of cash we poured into the property. If we take all $100,000 of our liquid cash and completely pay off our property, we have just taken two $100,000 assets, together worth $200,000, and combined them into one $100,000 asset, thereby cutting our total assets in half!

If we separate some of the equity or money that is in the house and put it into a liquid position, we have just increased our assets (pour some of the water in the goblet back into the pitcher). If we separate all the equity from a home that was free and clear we have just doubled our assets (pour the rest of the water from the goblet into the pitcher)!

Fig. 5.3

What happens when we pour all of our cash into our property?

$0 Cash

$100,000 Home

We cut our assets in half...
$100,000 IN ASSETS

Let's assume this empty goblet—our house—appreciates at an average 5 percent a year. What will the value of this $100,000 asset be at the end of one year? That's right, $105,000. Isn't that interesting? The house was empty (no equity) and its value still grew to $105,000! Does it make a difference if the house is full of cash—in other words, free and clear of any mortgage (pour the pitcher of water back into the house)? Of course not. If your $100,000 house appreciates at 5 percent a year, at the end of one year, it will be worth $105,000 whether it is mortgaged to the hilt or free and clear!

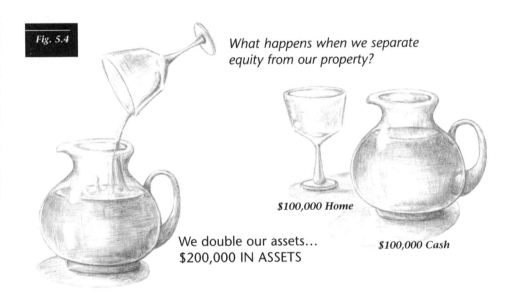

Fig. 5.4

What happens when we separate equity from our property?

$100,000 Home

$100,000 Cash

We double our assets...
$200,000 IN ASSETS

Let's say we have this $100,000 of cash sitting in an investment earning 10 percent (pour the water back into the pitcher). How much money will we have at the end of one year? That's right, $110,000. I was able to earn $10,000 by merely separating my water from my goblet (i.e., separating my cash from my house). What did the house do in the meantime? Its value appreciated by 5 percent while my separated

Fig. 5.5

END OF YEAR ONE

Home Value = $105,000   *Cash Account = $110,000*

*Home Appreciation
Rate = 5%*

Rate of Return on Cash = 10%

Increase in Assets when separated = $15,000.

$100,000 in equity was growing simultaneously at 10 percent. In other words, after having separated the equity, I still earned $5,000 through the appreciation of the home, and I was also able to earn $10,000 on my cash investment for a grand total of $15,000—three times as much as I made without separating my assets. Every time we put extra or excess cash into our properties, we give up the ability to earn a rate of return on that money. Why? Because equity does not earn a rate of return! Let me emphasize again, the return on equity is always the same—ZERO!

Now, you may be sitting there saying, "Well, what about the mortgage? I have to pay interest on the mortgage! There's a cost associated with doing this!" That is true, and I will address that question in depth in the next four chapters, where you will find that your mortgage is your best partner in accomplishing your financial goals. But for now, let me assure you that by removing or separating equity from your property, not only are you able to earn a rate of return, but you will also be able to substantially increase your net worth by doing so!

As I mentioned before, the third test of a wise and prudent investment is that it must earn a rate of return. Home equity passes neither the liquidity test, nor the safety test, nor the rate of return test—three strikes, you're out! And that's just the beginning.

The Third Most Important Reason to Keep Equity Separated from Property...
RATE OF RETURN

5 WEALTH-ENHANCEMENT STRATEGY NUMBER FIVE

- *Separate as much equity from your home as feasible in order to allow idle dollars to earn a rate of return.*

CHAPTER 6

Make Uncle Sam Your Best Partner

Mortgage interest—friend or foe?

There are only four things you can do with money: spend it, lend it, give it away, or own with it. When we deposit money into a savings account, money market account, or certificate of deposit, we are in essence loaning our money to a financial institution. We are putting our money in a "lended" position with institutions most people consider conservative and prudent business entities.

THE IMPORTANCE OF ARBITRAGE

Why are banks so willing to pay you interest to borrow your money? They are willing to do so because they loan that same money to the consuming public at a higher rate of interest. Arbitrage (borrowing at a lower interest rate and putting the money to work to earn a higher rate) allows the bank to generate a return over the cost of obtaining those funds.

Let's use a simple example. Let's say Family A lends $10,000 to the bank, depositing it into a CD earning 6 percent interest. In effect, when they make that deposit, Family A is loaning money to the bank. The bank is willing to pay them a certain amount of interest for that money, which is dictated by the money market and the Federal Reserve. Soon after Family A makes the deposit, Family B goes to the same bank, wanting to borrow $10,000 to purchase, say, an automobile. The bank agrees to loan $10,000 to Family B at 9 percent interest. In the final analysis, who really lent and who really borrowed the $10,000? Family A deposited the money with the bank, thus putting that money into a lended position. After borrowing those funds from Family A, the bank then lent that money to Family B for the purchase of their automobile. Family A and the bank both lent money; on the other hand, both the bank and Family B borrowed money. Did the bank turn a profit? You bet it did!

Banks may borrow money at 6 percent, then loan the money back out at 9 percent and, after management fees and overhead expenses, end up generating between a 1 and 2 percent net profit margin. This arbitrage between what the bank had to pay for that money and what it netted by investing that money allows them to earn a conservative profit.

Many of you have probably heard the old adage: "There are two kinds of people in the world: those who pay interest and those who earn it." This is true to an extent, but more correctly, the adage should say: "There are three kinds of people in the world: those who pay interest, those who earn interest, and those who pay interest in order to earn greater interest"—just like highly profitable banks and credit unions!

FINANCIAL STEWARDSHIP

When interest is charged on indebtedness, I have often heard people cry, "usury!" Sometimes usury has more than one meaning. In the Bible, at times usury implies the lending of money at exorbitant interest rates, but it also means simply charging interest on a loan. The New Testament gives credence to the lending of money with an interest charge for its use. The parable of the talents found in the *Book of Matthew,* chapter 25, verses 14 to 30, and the parable of the pounds found in the *Book of Luke,* chapter 19, verses 12 to 26, offer profound insight to a person's steward-ship. These parables contain deep meaning as they relate to the steward-ship we have, not only to the cultivation of financial assets, but also to human, intellectual, and spiritual capacities (see chapter 23).

As they relate to financial stewardship, these two parables are very insightful. Review for a moment the parable of the talents:

14 For the kingdom of heaven is as a man travelling into a far country, who called his own servants, and delivered unto them his goods.

15 And unto one he gave five talents, to another two, and to another one; to every man according to his several ability; and straightway took his journey.

16 Then he that had received the five talents went and traded with the same, and made them other five talents.

17 And likewise he that had received two, he also gained other two.

18 But he that had received one went and digged in the earth, and hid his lord's money.

19 After a long time the lord of those servants cometh, and reckoneth with them.

20 And so he that had received five talents came and brought other five talents, saying, Lord, thou deliveredst unto me five talents: behold, I have gained beside them five talents more.

21 His lord said unto him, Well done, thou good and faithful servant: thou hast been faithful over a few things, I will make thee ruler over many things: enter thou into the joy of thy lord.

22 He also that had received two talents came and said, Lord, thou deliveredst unto me two talents: behold, I have gained two other talents beside them.

23 His lord said unto him, Well done, good and faithful servant; thou hast been faithful over a few things, I will make thee ruler over many things: enter thou into the joy of thy lord.

24 Then he which had received the one talent came and said, Lord, I knew thee that thou art an hard man, reaping where thou hast not sown, and gathering where thou hast not strawed:

25 And I was afraid, and went and hid thy talent in the earth: lo, there thou hast that is thine.

26 His lord answered and said unto him, Thou wicked and slothful servant, thou knewest that I reap where I sowed not, and gather where I have not strawed:

27 Thou oughtest therefore to have put my money to the exchangers, and then at my coming I should have receive mine own with usury.

28 Take therefore the talent from him, and give it unto him which hath ten talents.

29 For unto every one that hath shall be given, and he shall have abundance: but from him that hath not shall be taken away even that which he hath.

30 And cast ye the unprofitable servant into outer darkness: there shall be weeping and gnashing of teeth.

–Matt. 25:14–30 (King James Version)

As you ponder the meaning of the parable, consider two aspects as they relate to the surface story. First, both the good and faithful servants were rewarded for doubling their talents. The lord of the servants came back after traveling into a far country for a long time. In reference to money earning interest, if that "long time" were fifteen years, based upon the Rule of 72, the servants would have had to earn a rate of about 5 percent interest. If it were ten years, then 7.2 percent interest; if seven years, then 10 percent interest. Second, in verses 26 and 27, some of the harshest words in the Bible are used against the servant who hid his talent and did not multiply it: "Thou wicked and slothful servant." The lord of the servant said he should have at least put the money entrusted to him to the exchangers (banks, credit unions, insurance companies, money management firms, or even stock brokerage firms) so that when he came back, he would have received what he could (even if it only kept up with inflation) with usury (the earning of interest on money in a lended position).

Now review and compare for a moment the parable of the pounds:

12 He said therefore, A certain nobleman went into a far country to receive for himself a kingdom, and to return.

13 And he called his ten servants, and delivered them ten pounds, and said unto them, Occupy till I come.

14 But his citizens hated him, and send a message after him, saying, We will not have this man to reign over us.

15 And it came to pass, that when he was returned, having received the kingdom, then he commanded these servants to be called unto him, to whom he had given the money, that he might know how much every man had gained by trading.

16 Then came the first, saying, Lord thy pound hath gained ten pounds.

17 And he said unto him, Well, thou good servant: because thou hast been faithful in very little, have thou authority over ten cities.

18 And the second came, saying, Lord, thy pound hath gained five pounds.

19 And he said likewise to him, Be thou also over five cities.

20 And another came, Lord, behold, here is thy pound, which I have kept laid up in a napkin:

21 For I feared thee, because thou art an austere man: thou takest up that thou layedst not down, and reapest that thou didst not sow.

22 And he saith unto him, Out of thine own mouth will I judge thee, thou wicked servant. Thou knewest that I was an austere man, taking up that I laid not down, and reaping that I did not sow:

23 Wherefore then gavest not thou my money into the bank, that at my coming I might have required mine own with usury?

24 And he said unto them that stood by, Take from him the pound, and give it to him that hath ten pounds.

25 (And they said unto him, Lord, he hath ten pounds.)

26 For I say unto you, That unto every one which hath shall be given; and from him that hath not, even that he hath shall be taken away from him.

—*Luke 19:12–26 (King James Version)*

Consider again the surface meaning of the story. The nobleman gave his servants a stewardship over money he had given them, and upon his return, he required accountability from each. He rewarded those servants who used the money entrusted them to gain more money with greater stewardship and responsibility. The servant who kept his money laid away in a napkin was rebuked and asked, "Why didn't you even put my money in the bank (in a lended position), so that I might have my money back with some interest?" Subsequently, that which had been entrusted to that servant was taken away. A principle illustrated here is that we either progress or retrogress. We either increase our talents and abilities or else those we have will wither and die.

ATTITUDES ABOUT DEBT

Money in a lended position means there is debt owed by one party or another, or sometimes both. Viewed in this manner, debt and the interest expense that accompanies it can sometimes be your best friend in attaining financial independence, especially if that interest is tax deductible. The common misconception is that the interest on your mortgage is a monstrous expense that needs to be eliminated as soon as possible. The reason for this misconception is clear. As shown in **figure 6.1**, depending on the interest rate of your mortgage, you could pay between 2.5 and 3.5 times the original amount you agreed to pay for your home before it is free and clear. Hence, the first temptation is to eliminate that monster, namely, the interest, by sending extra money to the mortgage banker to be paid on the principal.

Fig. 6.1	LENDERS SELL MONEY	
	30-Year Amortized Mortgage	
AMOUNT BORROWED	INTEREST RATE	AMOUNT REPAID
$100,000	9%	$289,664
$150,000	7%	$359,263
$60,000	8%	$158,493
$250,000	10%	$789,814
$200,000	6%	$431,676

However, by eliminating interest expense through the traditional method of making extra principal payments against your mortgage, you are, in fact, eliminating one of your best partners. This partner is Uncle Sam, who can truly help you accumulate a larger degree of wealth and financial security.

MORTGAGE INTEREST AND TAXES

After the 1986 Tax Reform Act was passed, homeowners rushed out and bundled up everything from vacation expense, credit card debt, and automobile loans in what lenders call "mortgage wrappers." They did this because from 1987 through 1991, the 1986 Tax Reform Act phased out the deductibility of consumer interest expense. After 1991, the only interest the average, non-business owner could deduct was interest incurred on a home mortgage. This is still the case today.

Based on that rule, outlined in the Internal Revenue Code, Section 163, homeowners who itemize deductions on Schedule A of their personal income tax return can deduct any interest paid on debts for which their homes have been used as collateral. This deduction is allowable on one primary and one secondary residence. Properties which qualify as secondary residences under the rules of the Internal Revenue Code include, but are not limited to, cabins, boats (as long as they meet certain requirements, such as having kitchen or bathroom facilities) condominiums, summer homes, and apartments.

Mortgage interest expense incurred on primary and secondary residences on first, second, or even third position mortgages are deductible on your tax return. This is true of up to a $1 million mortgage amount. Any interest paid on mortgage amounts higher than that are not deductible. Also, if a homeowner is borrowing money after the original acquisition indebtedness, the deductibility of that interest is limited to $100,000 over and above the acquisition indebtedness—the amount of original debt still outstanding at the time of refinancing. There is only one exception to this rule: you may increase the deductibility of mortgage interest over and above $100,000 if you use the proceeds to improve your home. In other words, you may borrow up to $100,000 or more of home equity and use the money for anything you want. However, the interest on more than $100,000 is only deductible if you put it back into the home in the form of home improvement expense.

For example, say you bought a $200,000 home. At the time of purchase you paid $100,000 down with money from the sale of a previous home, so, you only took out a $100,000 mortgage. If, after you had paid down your mortgage to $50,000, you decided to refinance or borrow using that home as collateral, your acquisition indebtedness would be $50,000. Thus, you would only be able to deduct the interest on up to $100,000 of new mortgage incurred over and above the $50,000.

For this reason I advise clients to establish the highest amount of acquisition indebtedness possible when they purchase new properties. I want them to create the greatest amount of deductible interest for the equity they want to separate from their property down the road.

If your taxable income last year was $60,000, but you had $10,000 of mortgage interest expense you could deduct on Schedule A of your 1040 tax return, that $10,000 would come right off the top of your $60,000 income, reducing it to $50,000. In the year 2002, a $60,000 taxable income would have required the taxpayer to pay 27 percent in federal tax, plus the appropriate state tax. If we assume a 7 percent state income tax on all income over the $46,700 threshold, that makes 34 percent in combined federal and state taxes. Thus, in taking a $10,000 mortgage interest deduction, you saved 34 percent of that $10,000 in taxes, or

0.34 x $10,000 = $3,400. If you pay mortgage interest and are in a 34 percent marginal federal and state tax bracket (see chapter 1 for an explanation of "effective" and "marginal" tax brackets), by saving you $3,400 in taxes, Uncle Sam is in essence paying over a third of that mortgage interest for you by virtue of the deduction.

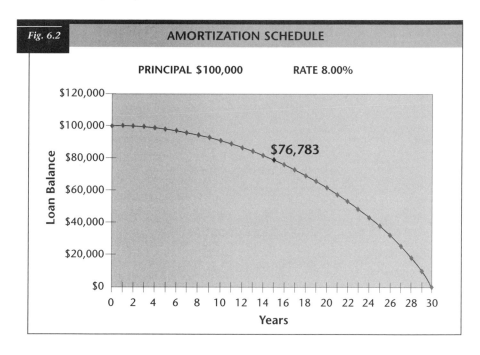

Fig. 6.2 — AMORTIZATION SCHEDULE

PRINCIPAL $100,000   RATE 8.00%

$76,783

If you look at **figure 6.2**, you can see that a long-term mortgage amortization reduces very slowly due to the tremendous amount of interest paid during the early stages. On a thirty-year amortization, you will generally still owe between 75 percent to 80 percent of what you originally owed on the mortgage when you are halfway through the thirty years. Seeing graphs such as these, there is a temptation to do whatever is necessary to eliminate some of that interest expense, like taking out a shorter, fifteen-year mortgage with higher monthly payments.

However, if a person were to take out a brand new, thirty-year, $150,000 mortgage, then discipline himself to set aside money from two areas—the differential between the thirty-year mortgage payment and the fifteen-year mortgage payment, and the tax savings achieved during the first fifteen years of a thirty-year mortgage—into a side fund, that fund will most likely accumulate enough money between year 13 and year 14 to pay off the thirty-year mortgage in full (**fig. 6.3**)!

In fact, another way of looking at it, if the homeowner continued to set aside the differential through the end of year 15, which is when he would have normally paid off the fifteen-year mortgage, he would have accumulated $26,976 over and above the amount needed to pay off the

Fig. 6.3	ACCUMULATING THE NET DIFFERENCE BETWEEN A 30-YEAR 8% MORTGAGE PAYMENT AND A 15-YEAR 8% MORTGAGE PAYMENT IN A SIDE FUND EARNING 8% INTEREST				
END OF YEAR	[1] 30-YEAR MORTGAGE LOAN BALANCE	[2] 15-YEAR MORTGAGE NET PAYMENT AFTER TAX	[3] 30-YEAR MORTGAGE NET PAYMENT AFTER TAX	[4] DIFFERENCE BETWEEN NET PAYMENT AFTER TAX	[5] DIFFERENCE EARNING 8% COMPOUNDING
1	$148,747	$13,188	$9,143	$4,045	$4,195
2	147,390	13,340	9,179	4,161	8,856
3	145,920	13,505	9,217	4,288	14,032
4	144,328	13,684	9,258	4,426	19,775
5	142,605	13,877	9,303	4,574	26,144
6	140,738	14,087	9,352	4,735	33,204
7	138,716	14,314	9,405	4,909	41,026
8	136,526	14,560	9,462	5,098	49,687
9	134,155	14,826	9,523	5,303	59,272
10	131,587	15,114	9,590	5,524	69,875
11	128,805	15,426	9,663	5,763	81,600
12	125,793	15,764	9,741	6,023	94,559
13	**$122,531**	16,130	9,826	6,304	**$108,877**
14	**$118,998**	16,527	9,918	6,609	**$124,690** ◄*
15	115,171	16,955	10,018	6,937	142,147

$26,976

EXCESS CASH BEYOND MORTGAGE BALANCE

Note:
* Notice that you would have enough money in your liquid side fund to pay off the mortgage sometime between the 13th and 14th year.
** Both the 30-year mortgage and the 15-year mortgage are amortized assuming 8 percent interest.

mortgage. Best of all, he would have maintained liquidity and safety of principal in the process. Thank you, Uncle Sam!

MAKING INTEREST WORK FOR YOU

Lenders sell money. That's their business. They provide money to people who need capital. They charge interest, but that doesn't mean you have to make the assumption the interest is your foe. Many major corporate, financial, and even church institutions use debt management to accomplish their goals, even though they may have plenty of assets earmarked to cover their liabilities. For these institutions, debt is a wise and prudent money-management tool. It's easy to see if a bank can borrow money from the Federal Reserve at 4 or 5 percent then turn around and lend that money at 8 percent, they can make a handsome profit, especially on large sums. Why can't you do the same, even if with somewhat smaller sums?

In the next few chapters, I will illustrate how individual homeowners can use the concept of arbitrage to borrow at one interest rate then invest safely to receive a return at a higher interest rate, thereby accumulating wealth. A homeowner's potential to accumulate wealth in this way is enhanced by the fact that mortgage interest is deductible. In other words, when a homeowner uses a mortgage to borrow at, say, 8 percent, it isn't really costing him 8 percent because the interest is deductible (**fig. 6.4**). For now, simply understand that deductible interest, or "preferred interest," as I call it, can become one of your best partners in accumulating wealth. Under current tax law, the only preferred interest available to the average American is mortgage interest.

Many successful businesses and corporations use debt in order to expand and make more money, even sometimes without being able to deduct interest expense. Bonds, debentures, and loans are all financial tools used by some of the nation's largest and most successful enterprises and municipalities. They are willing to pay interest in order to allow themselves opportunities to earn greater interest.

Fig. 6.4	THE COST OF TAX-DEDUCTIBLE INTEREST EXPENSE

Dollar Analysis

- Interest Expense $10,000
- Tax Savings $3,400
- Real Cost of Interest $6,600

Interest Rate	7.00%	8.00%	9.00%
Less Tax Benefit	-2.38%	-2.72%	-3.06%
Effective Interest Rate	4.62%	5.28%	5.94%

Figure 6.4 shows if you are in a 34 percent marginal federal and state tax bracket, the net cost of borrowing money at 8 percent is really only 5.28 percent. The other 2.72 percent is paid by the government in the form of a credit on your income tax return. If you borrow $100,000 and pay 8 percent interest, on the surface you are paying $8,000 in interest. But when you deduct that $8,000 off your gross income on your tax return, Uncle Sam gives you back credit by charging you $2,720 less in taxes. The real cost to you is only $5,280 or 5.28 percent of $100,000. If you want to know the actual cost of funds you've borrowed, remember to calculate the true net cost, based on your income tax bracket, if you are paying preferred interest on those borrowed funds.

Deductible interest is "preferred interest" (**fig. 6.5**). Any other interest expense that you might have—credit card debt, automobile loan expense, etc.—which cannot be deducted, will be deemed "non-preferred interest" expense (unless you have borrowed those funds for business purposes and are now deducting the interest as a business interest expense).

Fig. 6.5	PREFERRED VS. NON-PREFERRED INTEREST EXPENSE		
		A	B
• Income		$50,000	$50,000
• Non-Preferred Interest		-10,000	0
		$40,000	$50,000
• Preferred Interest		0	-10,000
• Available Before Taxes		$40,000	$40,000
• Taxable Income		$50,000	$40,000
• State and Federal Taxes		$17,000 ⟳	$13,600
Difference (TAX SAVINGS) $3,400			

PUTTING YOURSELF IN CONTROL OF YOUR HOME EQUITY

The greatest single debt most people incur is the mortgage on their homes. When they have a new thirty-year mortgage of $150,000 at 8 percent interest, the interest expense for the first year is approximately $11,955. In that same time period, the principal only reduces by $1,253 (**fig. 6.6**). In other words, after the first year or two of payments totaling in the thousands of dollars, homeowners still owe almost the same amount they owed when they started. This discouraging truth may push homeowners to try to eliminate that interest as quickly as possible, when what they really need to do is analyze what can be done to maximize their rate of return and liquidity by making interest their partner.

Americans have a greater incentive to borrow in order to acquire property if the interest is deductible. Consumers borrowing from banks stimulates the economy. The banking system then flourishes profitably. Funds are available and money is not tight, allowing more people to borrow money to acquire property and stimulate the economy even further. Homes are constructed, and as payment, contractors receive the money you've borrowed. They deposit it right back into various financial institutions which are able to lend it out again, and the cycle begins anew. As

Fig. 6.6	30-YEAR MORTGAGE ANALYSIS

Principal $150,000   *Rate* 8.00%
Balance $150,000   *Type* Amortized
Payment $1,100.65   *Years* 30

END OF YEAR	[1] LOAN BALANCE	[2] PRINCIPAL PAYMENT	[3] INTEREST PAYMENT	[4] TOTAL PAYMENT	[5] TAX SAVINGS	[6] NET PAYMENT AFTER TAX
1	$148,747	$1,253	$11,955	$13,208	$4,065	$9,143
2	147,390	1,357	11,851	13,208	4,029	9,179
3	145,920	1,470	11,738	13,208	3,991	9,217
4	144,328	1,592	11,616	13,208	3,949	9,258
5	142,605	1,724	11,484	13,208	3,905	9,303
6	140,738	1,867	11,341	13,208	3,856	9,352
7	138,716	2,022	11,186	13,208	3,803	9,405
8	136,526	2,190	11,018	13,208	3,746	9,462
9	134,155	2,371	10,836	13,208	3,684	9,523
10	131,587	2,568	10,640	13,208	3,617	9,590
11	128,805	2,781	10,426	13,208	3,545	9,663
12	125,793	3,012	10,196	13,208	3,466	9,741
13	122,531	3,262	9,946	13,208	3,381	9,826
14	118,998	3,533	9,675	13,208	3,289	9,918
15	115,171	3,826	9,382	13,208	3,190	10,018
16	111,028	4,144	9,064	13,208	3,082	10,126
17	106,540	4,488	8,720	13,208	2,965	10,243
18	101,680	4,860	8,348	13,208	2,838	10,370
19	96,416	5,264	7,944	13,208	2,701	10,507
20	90,715	5,701	7,507	13,208	2,552	10,655
21	84,542	6,174	7,034	13,208	2,392	10,816
22	77,856	6,686	6,522	13,208	2,217	10,990
23	70,614	7,241	5,967	13,208	2,029	11,179
24	62,772	7,842	5,366	13,208	1,824	11,383
25	54,280	8,493	4,715	13,208	1,603	11,605
26	45,082	9,198	4,010	13,208	1,363	11,844
27	35,120	9,961	3,247	13,208	1,104	12,104
28	24,332	10,788	2,420	13,208	823	12,385
29	12,649	11,683	1,524	13,208	518	12,690
30	0	12,649	555	13,204	189	13,015
TOTAL		$150,000	$246,230	$396,230	$83,718	$312,512

Notes:
a. Tax Savings [5] assumes a state and federal marginal tax bracket of 34.00% multiplied by the interest payment [3].
b. Mortgage interest is generally tax deductible, however, certain limitations are applicable. Please review with your tax advisor.
c. Net Payment After Tax [6] equals Total Payment [4] less Tax Savings [5].

thousands of Americans participate in the buying and selling of real estate, greater economic growth and prosperity results.

One of the main reasons the government allows people to deduct interest expense incurred by home mortgages is to stimulate the economy. Congress understands that economic growth, essential for a thriving free-market economy, is especially important in developing a tax base. This is best achieved by allowing funds that will perpetuate wealth and economic development to be borrowed at attractive, deductible interest rates.

Mortgage lenders funded by investors want to protect their investors from possible losses. Rules are established which allow homeowners and debtors to borrow only up to certain percentages of their home equity unless they can prove they have other assets or the financial wherewithal to responsibly cover that debt. That is why conventional commercial lenders will typically only loan up to 80 percent loan-to-value of a home without charging an additional insurance premium.

In certain situations, homebuyers can get into a home with a nominal down payment or no down payment at all. For instance, the Veterans Administration allows veterans to take out a mortgage without any down payment. However, they may be required to pay some closing costs associated with the mortgage. The Federal Housing Administration also will allow certain qualified homebuyers to purchase a home up to a certain price range with only about a 2.5 percent down payment. But in order to protect the investor who is providing the funds, it charges an extra premium for mortgage insurance in case the mortgage borrower defaults on the mortgage. As soon as the mortgage is paid down to no more than 80 percent of the value of the home, the mortgage insurance premium can be eliminated.

Many banks may loan in excess of 80 percent of the home's value—even up to 100 percent sometimes, although they generally charge higher interest rates to consumers who borrow on the last 20 percent of equity on their home. People may use the borrowed funds for wants and needs such as college funding for children, home improvements, or depreciating assets such as automobiles, boats, RVs, etc. I would never recommend pursuing the latter course. It is never a wise choice to borrow equity from a home for the purpose of acquiring any kind of depreciating asset. One should only borrow home equity to get a safe return on those funds through prudent investing. Remember, the purpose of this book is to teach you how to conserve home equity, not how to consume it.

Fig. 6.7 — **EQUITY CONTROL**

The primary elements for determining a wise
and prudent investment are:

1. **Liquidity**
2. **Safety of Principal**
3. **Rate of Return**
4. **Tax Benefits**

Home Equity Lacks These Primary Elements!

THE FOURTH CRITERION

Remember the three primary criteria for determining a wise and prudent investment (**fig. 6.7**)?

1. Liquidity
2. Safety of principal
3. Rate of return

There is actually a fourth consideration for any investment—taxes. If an investment satisfies the other three criteria, it's already doing well. When the cost of the funds used for the investment is tax deductible, that's even better. And if the investment can offer a tax-favored or even tax-free return, that's like icing on the cake.

It may come as no surprise to you that the people or institutions controlling the money flow also have control on the interest rate at which consumers must borrow funds. Remember the golden rule of finance: "He who has the gold makes the rules!"

Learning how to get into a position of control is absolutely critical. By controlling home equity you can begin to be more in control of the amount of interest you pay, as well as the amount of interest you earn on your own investments. You then learn how to have interest work for you instead of against you. Even though a home can be a wise investment, in the previous chapters, we have dismantled the notion the equity trapped in a home is a wise investment. It does not meet the three criteria for a wise and prudent investment. Furthermore, leaving equity in the property deprives us of the opportunity to take advantage of otherwise payable income tax to increase our wealth. When considering home equity as a sound investment, there can only be one conclusion: It's not!

6 WEALTH-ENHANCEMENT STRATEGY NUMBER SIX

- *Use the difference between preferred and non-preferred interest expense to make interest work for you instead of against you.*

CHAPTER 7

Use Debt for Positive Leverage

"It is often the view from where you sit that makes you fear defeat.
Life is full of many aisles, so why don't you change your seat?"

—ANONYMOUS

Any and all debt is undesirable.

REALITY

Some debt, when managed wisely, can be desirable.

Up to this point, I have assumed you already understand what home equity is. Before proceeding, let me clarify so there are no misunderstandings: equity is the difference between the fair market value of your home and all outstanding loans on the property. If you have a home with a fair market value of $180,000, a first mortgage of $60,000, and $40,000 owing on an equity line of credit, the total loans against the property equal $100,000. The remaining $80,000 represents your equity.

I have often reflected on insight from an anonymous author that has helped me create new opportunities that blossomed into success: "It is only the view from where you sit that makes you fear defeat. Life is full of many aisles, so why don't you change your seat?" Many of us are prone to view life in a traditional way. We tend to reject new ideas simply because they are new and take us out of our established comfort zones. Often we excuse ourselves by saying, "I guess I'm just from the old school."

If you are willing to change your seat by seriously considering a new perspective, you will be amazed at what new opportunities present themselves that can dramatically improve your life! **Figure 7.1** of the caveman, the beaver, and Archimedes shows three perspectives of a stick of wood. The caveman sees it as a means for obtaining warmth and shelter; the beaver sees it as food; Archimedes, on the other hand, views it as a lever for moving the world. It's one object, but all three beings perceive it differently. Thus it is with home equity. Those who learn to change their perception of home equity will be able to use their equity as a lever for moving their financial world into greater wealth and independence.

LENDING AND OWNING

There are basically three sources of income: humankind at work, money at work, and charity. Americans spend hundreds of thousands of dollars attending colleges and universities in the pursuit of knowledge. Most hope to apply that education in a professional endeavor which compensates them monetarily for the unique knowledge and abilities

Fig. 7.1

A lever to move the world...

Ah! Breakfast...

...Ugh. Firewood.

They all see the same thing differently...

they have gained and continue to cultivate. Many are guilty of spending a tremendous amount of time learning how to earn money but don't take enough time learning what to do with that money. As a financial planner, I am constantly amazed at how many people spend far more time planning their summer vacations than they do planning their retirements!

Remember the four things you can do with your money? You can spend it, give it away, lend it, or own with it. The purpose of this book is not to teach wise spending habits. Neither is it to teach wise charitable giving, although I will touch on one dramatic giving strategy in chapter 21. Rather, this book focuses on understanding how to use money in two ways—lending and owning with it to enhance your net worth.

Whenever we put our money in a savings account held by some banking institution, we are putting our money in a lended position. The bank pays us an interest rate for loaning it that money. A bond, another kind of debt instrument, works similarly. We earn interest on it because it represents money we have loaned to a municipality or a corporation that needs those funds. A bond is a primary obligation of the entity that borrowed the funds.

If we put our money in an ownership, or equity, position, we incur greater investment risks, but we also position ourselves to capture appreciation on that equity. This can happen when we purchase stock or when we own real estate.

When banks borrow your money by allowing you to open an account with them, they are putting themselves in your debt. That doesn't mean they're being unwise. To the contrary, because they understand the difference between good debt and bad debt, they thrive. They rely on the proper management of debt to make a profit for themselves and their stockholders.

KEEPING MONEY IN A LENDED POSITION

Prudent investors should strive to have some of their money in an ownership position so as to accumulate wealth and create financial security that can benefit their families and charitable institutions. Even so, it is generally advisable for prudent investors to have some of their money in a lended position even though money in an ownership position seems more desirable. This is because money in a lended position can often pass the liquidity, safety, and rate of return tests, as well as provide tax advantages as good or better than money in ownership positions. I will explain this in more detail in chapter 17.

Often, corporations and non-profit institutions state they are "debt free" or "out of debt." In reality, if you were to look at these large institutions' balance sheets, along with the many assets listed, you would likely see liabilities listed. But businesses or individuals with liabilities on their balance sheets aren't necessarily in debt. When a balance sheet shows an abundance of assets earmarked to wash out any liabilities, the claim to being debt free is justified. It has debt, but is merely using it for management purposes.

CONSUMING VS. CONSERVING EQUITY

When individuals do not learn how to use debt properly, they get into trouble. Because the tax deductibility of consumer debt was phased out by 1991, many Americans were lured into using home equity lines of credit or mortgage debt for consumer debt purposes. They began to consume their equity rather than to conserve their equity. On a summer afternoon you can visit any recreational lake and see home mortgages in the form of boats and jet skis darting across the water. Many consumer items are purchased with home equity lines of credit.

Shortly after the 1986 tax law reform, I saw an amusing advertisement in the lobby of my local bank. The advertisement showed a picture of a home with a car superimposed over it. The caption read, "The IRS thinks this car is a house." The bank was promoting the use of equity lines of credit for consumer purchases, like automobiles. That way, consumers could continue to deduct the interest expense on their cars by using equity from their homes to purchase their cars instead of using only the car as collateral for the loan.

In effect, the bank was "double-collateralizing" auto loans by tying up extremely important assets—homes—and by tying up the cars, which by themselves were sufficient collateral for justifying the loans. The advertised benefit of this tactic, which is still used by many Americans, was that consumers could continue to deduct the interest on their consumer debt. American consumers, on the whole, have a horrible track record of consuming equity rather than conserving it.

On the other hand, some Americans successfully manage equity to help themselves get out of debt. Take, for example, a homeowner who has credit card debt in the amount of $1,000, on which she pays 18 percent

Fig. 7.2	EXCHANGING PREFERRED DEBT FOR NON-PREFERRED DEBT

$1,000 x 18 % 180	Credit Card Debt Interest
$1,000 x 10 % 100	Borrowed Home Equity Interest
$ 80 + 10 % 88	Saved Interest Interest Earned
$ 34 + 10 % $37.40	Taxes Saved (27% + 7%) Interest Earned

So... by moving $1,000 (not spending a dollar) from one pocket to another, we save: $80 + $34 + $11.40 = $125.40
A 12.54% RETURN ON YOUR MONEY!

interest. That 18 percent—$180 per year—is not deductible on her tax return. Thus, her out-of-pocket interest expense on $1,000 of debt is $180. But if she is able to use an equity line of credit to pay off the credit card debt and only pay 10 percent interest, she would only pay $100 of interest. That alone would save her $80 of interest annually. If she itemizes her deductions, she may also qualify to deduct the $100 of interest expense from her tax return. In a 34 percent tax bracket, she would then save $34 on that $100 of interest deduction, and her net cost would only be $66, or 6.6 percent. Furthermore, if she took the $80 of interest savings as well as the $34 of tax savings and put that to work to earn a 10 percent return, she would earn an additional $11.40. In sum, by moving from a non-preferred interest expense position to a preferred interest position, this homeowner could save $80 in interest, $34 in taxes, and make $11.40 in interest, resulting in a grand total of 12.54 percent return on her money (**fig. 7.2**). Disciplined people who use this concept to consolidate debt and reallocate the interest they were paying in a non-preferred status can set themselves on a track to getting out of debt much faster using Uncle Sam as their partner.

There is a danger to this strategy. That danger is the temptation to consolidate debt in order to reduce monthly payments. The tendency is to spend rather than save the difference between the lower, consolidated equity loan payment and the previously unconsolidated consumer debt payments. Thus begins the vicious cycle of debt proliferation and the downward spiral into equity consumption, which ultimately leads to many bankruptcies.

This is perhaps the most important concept I want you to learn from Section I of this book: how to conserve equity. If you can discipline yourself to do so, you will be able to implement the many successful equity-enhancement strategies in this book, which will help you create wealth for your future goals.

Remember, the key to using debt as an instrument that will help you accumulate wealth is to make sure both borrower and lender are in a win-win situation. In teaching educational seminars for over twenty years, I have found most Americans have the same common misconceptions. One of the most amazing misconceptions is that any and all debt is undesirable.

Many of you may be debt free and possibly own homes that are free and clear. To you, especially, I hope to share insights into managing your equity to reposition assets and acquire other properties, better fund your children's college educations, eliminate non-preferred debt, etc. You may not even have realized these opportunities existed. Chapter 14 discusses how many of you who have already paid off your mortgages but are possibly struggling with a lack of cash flow may be able to annuitize the equity in your home to generate a tax-favored income and supplement your retirement—a procedure referred to as "equity conversion."

THE ARITHMETIC OF EQUITY MANAGEMENT

We already discussed how equity does not earn a rate of return; the only way equity grows is when a property's market value increases or when a property's mortgage reduces. A homeowner can only effectively control one of these two factors—the mortgage. We have virtually no control over the conditions affecting a home's market value in any given time period.

In equity management, owning a free and clear home and carrying no debt may appear to be a positive. But, really, it is a negative. When viewed in terms of liquidity, safety, and rate of return, these two factors could very well surprise you with an unpleasant experience.

In arithmetic, we know that multiplying two negative values together makes a positive value. The same goes for equity management.

A mortgage payment can consume as much as 25 to 28 percent of a homeowner's monthly income. (In fact, a mortgage lender will generally not approve a mortgage if the payment exceeds more than 29 percent of a borrower's gross income. Furthermore, a mortgage payment, including tax and insurance escrow plus other installment debt, generally cannot exceed more than 41 percent of the borrower's gross income.) Not only that, but the amount of interest homeowners pay on their mortgages is often enough to double or even triple the eventual cost of their homes. These are clearly perceived as negatives, causing homeowners to anxiously push for the day they can burn their mortgages and own homes that are free and clear.

A second perceived negative in sound financial budgeting is insurance, sometimes referred to as a "necessary evil" for risk management. Insurance is something we are forced to deal with in modern society. If you borrow money from a mortgage company, the mortgage company requires fire insurance in the event of the home being damaged or destroyed by fire. If you own and drive a car, you are required to have adequate liability insurance so you are not financially wiped out compensating a person you might injure. Although not usually required, it would be in your best interests to have adequate health insurance in case of a catastrophic medical illness. If you are married and have a family of two children for whom you hope to provide a future college education, you should have life insurance in case of an untimely death.

Insurance is a form of risk management that is best purchased before the emergency arises and you actually need it. If you found you had a terminal illness, for example, then tried to contact a life insurance agent to buy $1 million of life insurance, what would the life insurance agent likely tell you? She would probably say something like, "Sorry, I can't help you." Just like insurance, it is much better for you to obtain the key to accessing one of your most important assets—equity in the home— before an emergency arises, and it is actually needed.

Like in arithmetic, multiplying the negative of a mortgage and the negative of insurance creates a huge positive—the tremendous enhancement of our net worth.

USING EQUITY FOR POSITIVE LEVERAGE

As you may suspect, I keep my personal home mortgaged to the hilt and separate my equity in order to achieve greater liquidity, safety, and rate of return. In 1990, I purchased a 7,600-square-foot home that had been appraised at $500,000 two years prior. I picked it up in a soft market for $300,000. Ten years later, it had a market valuation of over $1 million—an average annual appreciation rate of 13 percent.

I have repeatedly separated my equity through the use of mortgages. I believe in conserving home equity by repositioning it into safe, liquid investments earning a rate of return greater than the net cost of my mortgage interest. The investment vehicle I have used for my liquid side fund, which I will detail in chapters 17 and 18, allows me to "peel off" dollars to invest when opportunities arise. By being in a position to act rather than react to market conditions, I have maintained greater control of my equity. In essence, I have done exactly what conservative banks and credit unions do!

I have a client who is retired and lives in a home valued at more than $1 million. He has a $300,000 line of credit with his bank at 6 percent interest. In the city where he lives, there are several reputable contractors who need money at times for short-term construction expenses. He loans them up to $300,000 at 18 percent interest, which they are happy to pay. Thus, the difference between his borrowing rate and his lending rate equals 12 percent. My client enjoys a $36,000 ($300,000 times 12 percent) a year income as a result of this arbitrage, which he has done for several years!

As an example of investment opportunities I have been able to take advantage of, I have a friend who once came to me wanting a $100,000, short-term loan to secure funding for a large commodity shipment. He only needed the money for thirty days. The money was secured on deposit in my own account in the branch of a bank located in Los Angeles. As a token of appreciation for the use of my $100,000 of capital, he agreed to pay me $10,000. After thirty days, I transferred the money back into my liquid side fund, where I kept my home equity waiting for the next opportunity.

I have used borrowed funds in pursuit of several different investment opportunities, but I have learned that liquidity must be maintained. For example, a mortgage broker once referred me to a developer he knew who had procured, a 2.35-acre piece of property, with a $30,000 earnest money agreement. The property, located in a beautiful area in eastern Salt Lake City, contained nearly 100 mature blue spruce and ponderosa pine trees. The property consisted of two vacant dwellings, both of which were the former residences in the estate of an elderly gentleman recently confined to a rest home. It was a rare, country setting in the middle of the city. His daughter, the trustee of the family trust, was liquidating part of the estate on behalf of her father.

On the last day before his option to purchase the property for $760,000 ran out, the developer pled with me to become a 50 percent partner with him. He assured me the property was on the verge of approval by Salt Lake County to be subdivided into eight quarter-acre lots. He said the subdivision approval would be obtained within thirty days and that the development costs for improvements (sewer, water, gas, electricity, curb, gutter, grading, and road paving) could be easily borrowed. He estimated those costs would likely total around $120,000.

Then he produced copies of five different letters of intent from contractors who wanted to buy the developed lots at a $175,000 to $185,000 fair market price. He believed we could sell all eight lots within three months for a total of $1.4 million. It appeared as though a $500,000 profit could be realized fairly quickly. Thus, a 50 percent share could net me $250,000 to complete the project.

Well, when something seems too good to be true, you definitely want to do your homework. I advise my clients to prepare for worst-case scenarios and make contingency plans after measuring the risks of any venture. Well-intentioned though people may be, most projects take considerably longer to complete than represented.

First, I drafted an agreement with the developer that would protect me and cover the opportunity costs in the event of delays and unanticipated costs. Basically, we agreed that I would become 100 percent owner and the deed would be held strictly by me with no liens or encumbrances. We also agreed that if all eight lots received final approval and sold within ninety days at a sales price agreeable to both of us, the developer would receive 40 percent of the profit realized. For every month over his projected completion of the project, the percent of his profit would drop by 10 percent. For example if he did not complete and sell the lots before four months, I would get 70 percent and he would get 30 percent. If not before five months, I would get 80 percent and he would get 20 percent. If the project took twice as long than he hoped it would, the entire development, as well as any resulting profits, would be in my control; he would relinquish all privileges, rights, and claims to the property and the project.

This developer felt the agreement was more than fair and anxiously signed, knowing that otherwise, he would have lost his $30,000 earnest money that day and with it, a chance to get a return. The opportunity would have gone to other anxious developers waiting to purchase the property. I felt it was fair because, since I was incurring nearly all the risk, I needed to protect my investment. I was borrowing money I considered serious money I couldn't afford to lose. In total, the venture appeared to have a net, after-tax cost of about 5 percent with a potential of about a 30 percent gross return. If the project cost $900,000 to complete, and it took one year to do so, my net cost of using borrowed money would have been $45,000, or 5 percent of $900,000, with a profit potential of $250,000 to $500,000.

Were there risks involved? You bet! But, did the potential return of my money as well as on my money outweigh the risks? I thought so.

So, I moved ahead.

Well, the worst-case scenario ended up becoming a reality. Due to bureaucratic holdups, the project took two years. Nevertheless, at the end of that period, long after I assumed complete control over the entire project (as per the agreement), I was able to develop five lots with a total valuation at the time of $1,385,000. After fees and expenses, I hoped to realize an annual return of about 20 percent on $900,000 of capital invested. This did not include compensation for my time to see the project come to fruition.

Finally two lots sold during the ensuing year that partially recovered my capital investment. The remaining three lots were scheduled to close on September 15, 2001. Due to the terrorist attacks on September 11, 2001, the buyer (a contractor) got cold feet, and the deal fell through. Again, I learned the importance of liquidity in unpredictable times.

GETTING STARTED—IT DOESN'T TAKE MILLIONS

How does a person get to the point of having liquid cash available? In my case, I started with $5,000 of equity from my first home, which I leveraged to net an $18,000 profit. Whether with $5,000 or $1 million in equity, I have used the same concepts to increase my net worth. It's not what you begin with that counts, but what you end up with!

In summary, I want to emphasize three main points:

1. Use debt wisely as a positive lever in equity management, conserving your equity, and enabling you to seize opportunities to use that equity to enhance your net worth.

2. Always protect yourself; prepare for the worst case to ensure in the event of unforeseen delays and costs, by maintaining flexibility, liquidity, and contingency options, you may be able to recover adequately.

3. Don't take unnecessary risks. Conservative, safe returns of only 5 to 9 percent can make you thousands of dollars.

7 | WEALTH-ENHANCEMENT STRATEGY NUMBER SEVEN

- *Use debt wisely as a positive lever for equity management purposes, conserving and compounding equity rather than consuming it.*

CHAPTER 8

The Cost of Not Borrowing

Compare deductible versus non-deductible costs.

Lower mortgages, resulting in lower payments, mean lower costs.

If you take opportunity cost into consideration, low mortgage-to-home value ratios create tremendous hidden costs that increase the time needed to pay off a mortgage.

If you believe lower mortgages (resulting in lower mortgage payments) mean lower costs, maybe you've never been taught the cost of lost opportunity.

There are generally only two ways to separate equity from property into a cash position. The first way is to sell the property. However, this may not be to your advantage, especially if you would like to remain a resident owner. The second way is through a conduit called a mortgage (**fig. 8.1**).

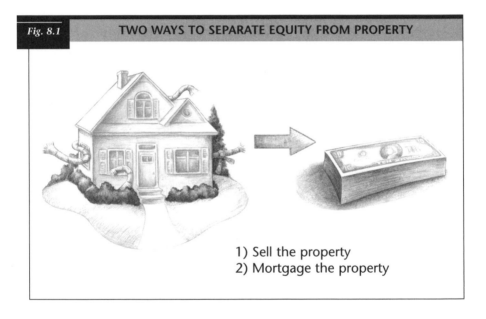

Fig. 8.1 **TWO WAYS TO SEPARATE EQUITY FROM PROPERTY**

1) Sell the property
2) Mortgage the property

EMPLOYMENT COST VS. OPPORTUNITY COST

Let's say $100,000 of equity can be separated from your home. If you borrow that equity through the use of a mortgage you are going to incur interest expense. For the sake of simplicity, let's assume an interest-only loan (different from an amortized loan in that monthly payments only cover interest expense). On such a loan, at an 8 percent annual percentage rate, you would be paying $8,000 in interest expense to separate $100,000 of equity. I consider this interest expense an "employment cost" because, rather than simply separating the $100,000 of equity and burying it in a tin can in the backyard, you are going to put it to work, or employ it.

If I were an employer why would I be willing to hire a secretary for $30,000 per year? Is it because I feel charitable toward that secretary? Perhaps so, but most profitable businesses are not just benevolent institutions. They employ people in order to get a return on the cost of employment. A prudent business owner would calculate the costs of employing each employee and measure the resulting return on those costs. I would be willing to hire a secretary for $30,000 per year if I were confident I would get a return on that cost. Hopefully, by incurring that employment cost, I would not only recoup that cost, but my secretary would help me make more than I could otherwise earn. Smart business owners are most willing to pay for the expense of personnel and equipment, even through borrowing, when the returns surpass the expenses.

In like manner, whenever I separate equity from property, I am going to incur an employment cost—the interest expense on my mortgage. Why am I willing to incur an employment cost on my equity? Because I know I can get a return equal to or greater than the cost of the equity that I employ.

Perhaps surprisingly, if you choose to leave the $100,000 of equity in your home, you incur almost the same cost. The only difference is, instead of referring to that cost as employment cost, it is referred to as opportunity cost. If you choose to leave equity in the property, you give up the opportunity to employ it in some type of investment that would earn, say, an 8 percent return. If you choose to separate the equity and invest it in an instrument that would earn 8 percent, you pay an employment cost. Either way, it costs you (**fig. 8.2**).

Let's take this one step further. If a couple is in a combined federal and state income tax bracket of 34 percent, when they borrow $100,000 against their home at 8 percent interest, the true cost may not be 8 percent because, according to current tax laws, they may be able to deduct $8,000 off their income tax return. The $8,000 is the gross outlay in interest expense, but because of the income tax deduction, they receive 34 percent of the $8,000, or $2,720, in tax savings. The interest expense, or employment cost, of borrowing that $100,000 is, therefore, only $5,280 after they receive their refund at the end of the year. Thus, the

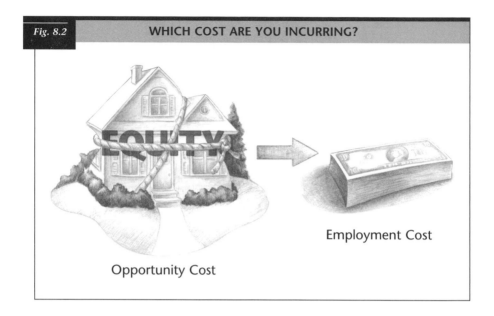

Fig. 8.2 — **WHICH COST ARE YOU INCURRING?**

Employment Cost

Opportunity Cost

true cost of borrowing against your home at 8 percent, in a 34 percent marginal tax bracket, is only 5.28 percent.

If an 8 percent employment cost is tax deductible, but the lost opportunity cost to invest those funds is a non-deductible 8 percent, are they really equal? You have no choice but to pay one or the other—which will you choose? My advice is to choose to incur deductible employment costs rather than non-deductible opportunity costs.

In the seminars I teach, I always make an offer in jest to my audience. If any of them will write a check to me for $100,000, I will sign an agreement to pay a lifetime annuity of 5 percent interest annually on the $100,000. I would be very willing to pay $5,000 a year—$416.67 a month—indefinitely. Why? Because I am confident I can earn more than $5,000 a year by putting the $100,000 to work. That's why banks and credit unions are willing to pay 5 percent for the money they borrow from you, which they then employ.

MOTIVATING LAZY EQUITY

At this point, you may be saying to yourself, "But wait a minute, if I employ my equity in an 8-percent-yielding investment, I'll have to pay tax on that interest and will only net 5.28 percent!"

There are two key elements that should exist as a solution to that problem. First, we can still enhance our net worth because the employed equity is compounding, whereas the cost of the mortgage interest is computed on a simple-interest, tax-deductible, declining-balance basis. Because of compound interest, to make a profit over the long run, it is not even necessary to earn at an interest rate equal to or greater than the net interest rate cost of borrowing those funds (**fig. 8.3**). That is because sooner or later, I will be earning interest, though the rate may be low, on a much greater sum of money than I am paying interest on.

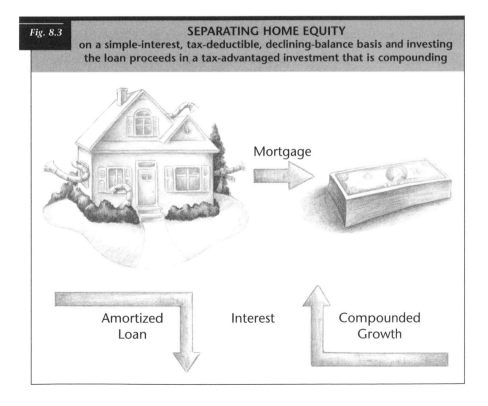

Fig. 8.3

SEPARATING HOME EQUITY
on a simple-interest, tax-deductible, declining-balance basis and investing the loan proceeds in a tax-advantaged investment that is compounding

Mortgage

Amortized Loan   Interest   Compounded Growth

Second, there are tax-free vehicles for investing those borrowed funds, which I will introduce to you later. My separated equity not only is earning tax-free interest during the compounding of the investment, but also, when I realize the gain by withdrawing and using the money, it can remain tax free if I adhere to proper procedures defined in the Internal Revenue Code!

Hopefully, your mind is beginning to open up to the advantages of having some properly managed, preferred debt. If, on one hand, we choose to leave equity sitting dormant in the property, those idle dollars are losing the opportunity of earning a rate of return. If we use a mortgage to separate the equity, because the cost of those funds is deductible, our return is dramatically enhanced.

8

WEALTH-ENHANCEMENT STRATEGY NUMBER EIGHT

- *Choose to incur deductible employment costs rather than non-deductible opportunity costs, since you have no choice but to incur one or the other.*

CHAPTER 9

Home-Made Wealth

Turbo charge your wealth growth rate!

Borrowing funds at a particular interest rate, then investing them at the same or lower interest rate, holds no potential growth returns.

You can earn a tremendous profit—regardless of the relative interest rates—by positioning your money in a tax-free, interest-compounding investment that earns a return greater than the real net cost of obtaining that money.

When I teach educational seminars, I usually ask the question, "Does it make sense to borrow money at 8 percent interest, then put those funds in an investment only earning 8 percent interest?" Most people immediately respond, "No, you can't possibly get ahead financially by doing that!"

In fact, you *can* create tremendous wealth by borrowing money at a particular interest rate and investing it at the same interest rate or even less, provided two conditions are met: the interest paid on the borrowed funds is deductible, and the investment in which we invest those funds earns compound interest. And if the investment earns compound interest in a tax-favored environment, the potential for growth is even greater!

THE EFFECTS OF TAX-PREFERRED BORROWING AND INVESTING

Let's go back to the example we used in the last chapter, in which we assumed ownership of a home from which we separated $100,000 of equity using a mortgage. Remember, separating equity from the home made no difference to the rate of the property's appreciation. The home will likely continue to appreciate regardless of whether it is free and clear or mortgaged. In other words, we are not giving up the opportunity to experience appreciation if we separate our equity through the use of a mortgage. We are simply taking dormant, lazy dollars from the home and providing an opportunity for those dollars to earn a rate of return. Remember, equity has no rate of return while trapped in the property.

First of all, let's use the example of borrowing equity at 8 percent and investing at the same rate. Say a married couple made $60,000 during the year. If those two had paid $8,000 of mortgage interest during that same year, they could deduct that interest from their gross income, thereby reducing their taxable income from $60,000 to $52,000. If a $60,000 gross income puts a married couple filing a joint tax return in a 27 per-cent tax bracket, they thus would enjoy 27 percent in federal tax savings. Assuming a 7 percent state income tax rate, they would also save an addi-tional 7 percent—a total of 34 percent savings on that $8,000. They would have, in effect, saved $2,720 which would have otherwise been paid in income tax had they not had a mortgage in place. Therefore, when you take that deduction on your tax return, your net outlay (net cost) was not really $8,000, but only $5,280.

This principle is illustrated in **figure 9.1**. You will note that if you borrow $100,000 at 8 percent you incur a surface cost of $8,000. But, because that $8,000 is a deductible expense, if you are in a 34 percent marginal tax bracket, the true net cost is only 5.28 percent or $5,280. The other $2,720 was, in essence, paid for by Uncle Sam because of tax benefits.

Let's assume that you separate the $100,000 and put it into an investment earning 8 percent compounded annually, and that this investment is accumulating tax free, or, at least, tax deferred. At the end of the first year your investment would be worth $108,000. Then, because of compounding interest, the next year you would earn 8 percent on $108,000, thereby resulting in a second-year balance of $116,640. The third year, your investment would have compounded to $125,971. The fourth year, it would be worth $136,049. And, in the fifth year it would be worth $146,933. By the sixth year, your initial $100,000 investment would be earning approximately $1,000 a month, or approximately $12,000 a year, in interest! Even if you paid the true employment cost of borrowing that money from a portion of the interest you earned,

| Fig. 9.1 | BORROWING AT 8 PERCENT AND INVESTING AT 8 PERCENT |

END OF YEAR 1

COST OF MORTGAGE	ACCUMULATING ACCOUNT
$100,000	$100,000
x 8%	x 8%
$8,000 = Interest	$8,000 = Interest Earnings
$2,720 = Taxes Saved*	
$5,280 = Real Cost	

END OF YEAR 5

$95,070 = Mortgage Balance	$146,933 = Account Balance
$5,020 = Real Cost for Year 6*	$11,755 = Interest Earnings for Year 6

*assuming a 27% marginal federal tax bracket and 7% state tax rate

the $100,000 of separated equity would still grow, but at a slower pace (**fig. 9.2**). I wish to reiterate the warning I issued earlier. As you read the examples that follow, please don't get overwhelmed trying to comprehend all the details and numbers provided. Focus your attention on grasping concepts rather than exact numbers.

For the sake of simplicity in this chapter, let's assume the mortgage you are using to borrow your equity is an interest-only mortgage rather than an amortized mortgage. Thus, each year, 8 percent interest on $100,000 would be $8,000 (column 1). However, in a 34 percent marginal tax bracket, your net cost would be $5,280 each year (column 2). In year one you earn 8 percent tax free on $100,000, which equals $8,000 (column 3), less the net cost of borrowing (column 2), which equals the net increase in our side fund ($2,720), as shown in column 4. During year two, you earn 8 percent interest on $102,720, which equals $8,218, less the employment cost ($5,280), which equals a net profit of $2,938, bringing your side fund balance to $105,658. As seen, by the end of the fifth year, you are making 8 percent on $115,957, which is nearly $9,280 in interest, less the employment cost of $5,280, resulting in nearly $4,000 realized in profit during year 6. In the tenth year you make $10,717 gross profit, which is more than double the employment cost, resulting in a net profit of $5,437. Over the first ten years, the total employment cost was $52,800 and the gross earnings totaled $92,203—a net profit of nearly $40,000!

Let me put these figures in the proper perspective. If you were the president of a bank or insurance company and reported this year's gross earnings at $9 billion, less the $5 billion cost of interest you had to pay your depositors, resulting in a $4 billion profit, you would be a hero. The board of directors and stockholders would vote to give you a huge bonus, and everyone would be scrambling to buy stock in your profitable financial institution!

As shown, this profit does not stop after the tenth year. It continues to compound and grow, even though you borrowed at 8 percent and only invested at 8 percent interest! If you were able to make a $5,437 profit in year 10 because you made $10,717 on a compounding, tax-deferred balance, while at the same time you paid 8 percent simple interest on your

Fig. 9.2	BORROWING $100,000 AT 8% DEDUCTIBLE INTEREST AND INVESTING THE LOAN PROCEEDS AT 8% TAX-FREE COMPOUND INTEREST USING A $100,000 INTEREST-ONLY MORTGAGE				
YEAR	GROSS INTEREST PAID [1]	NET INTEREST PAID (after tax benefit*) [2]	GROSS INTEREST EARNED [3]	NET PROFIT [3] - [2] [4]	NEW BALANCE [5]
1	$8,000	$5,280	$8,000	$2,720	$102,720
2	8,000	5,280	8,218	2,938	105,658
3	8,000	5,280	8,453	3,173	108,830
4	8,000	5,280	8,706	3,426	112,257
5	8,000	5,280	8,981	3,701	115,957
6	8,000	5,280	9,277	3,997	119,954
7	8,000	5,280	9,596	4,316	124,270
8	8,000	5,280	9,942	4,662	128,932
9	8,000	5,280	10,315	5,035	133,966
10	8,000	5,280	10,717	5,437	139,403
10 YR. TOTALS	$80,000	$52,800	$92,203	$39,403	$109,490
11	8,000	5,280	11,152	5,872	145,276
12	8,000	5,280	11,622	6,342	151,618
13	8,000	5,280	12,129	6,849	158,467
14	8,000	5,280	12,677	7,397	165,865
15	8,000	5,280	13,269	7,989	173,854
15 YR. TOTALS	$120,000	$79,200	$153,054	$73,854	$116,759
16	8,000	5,280	13,908	8,628	182,482
17	8,000	5,280	14,599	9,319	191,801
18	8,000	5,280	15,344	10,064	201,865
19	8,000	5,280	16,149	10,869	212,734
20	8,000	5,280	17,019	11,739	224,473
20 YR. TOTALS	$160,000	$105,600	$230,073	$124,473	$224,473

*assuming a 34% marginal tax bracket 27% federal and 7% state

mortgage balance, which was tax deductible, how much more profit do you think you would realize by year 15 or year 20? How much wider would the spread be?

Look at the results for year 15 in **figure 9.2**. Your net profit is $73,854. Look at the results for the full twenty-year period. The total net employment cost shown in column 2 equals $105,600. Was it worth the cost? Yes, because in column 3 we earned $230,073. The net profit we realized over twenty years by borrowing at 8 percent and investing at 8 percent equals $124,473 (column 4).

Why would I be willing to hire a secretary and pay her $30,000 or more a year? I would do so to get a return on costs. Sometimes it makes sense to spend money to make more money!

ARBITRAGE IN ACTION

This concept—called arbitrage—is really quite simple. We use an asset we possess to borrow funds at a low interest rate, then invest to achieve a higher interest rate. All that is needed is a minimal spread, even as low as 1 percent to 1.5 percent, in order to make a tremendous long-term profit, just as financial institutions do. ("Spread" is defined as the difference between the net investment yield and the net cost of the funds.)

This fundamental practice is exercised by some of the most conservative institutions in America. Banks practice arbitrage when they borrow money from the Federal Reserve Bank. They may borrow at discount rates of 4.5 or 5 percent interest then turn around and loan money (invest it) back out again at 8 or 9 percent interest. After their costs and overhead expenses, they may only net 5.5 to 7 percent interest, which is a spread of .5 to 1.5 percent. Even with such a small spread, financial institutions achieve profitable results. Since we don't have overhead expenses like financial institutions, the spread we can realize by applying the same principles can be even better!

The principle of arbitrage—also defined as borrowing other people's money (OPM) and using it to earn a return—is the basis upon which financial institutions operate. These financial institutions represent the wealth and backbone of America. Insurance companies collectively represent a trillion-dollar industry. Much of their wealth and financial strength can be attributed to this concept. But you do not need to be a large financial institution to practice this principle. Many, if not most, self-made multi-millionaires achieved their financial status through the proper, prudent use of OPM. They learned the power of arbitrage and put it to work in order to create tremendous wealth. Remember, it's not what you begin with that counts, but what you end up with.

Now that we can see how it would be advantageous to apply the principle of arbitrage in our personal finances, let's take a look at a couple of other scenarios. Consider using a mortgage to borrow at 9 percent and invest at only 7.5 percent.

As shown in **figure 9.3** if you borrow $100,000 at 9 percent, your surface cost may be $9,000, but your net cost will only be $5,940. As shown in years 1 through 20, your net cost stays constant (column 2) with an

Fig. 9.3	BORROWING $100,000 AT 9% DEDUCTIBLE INTEREST AND INVESTING THE LOAN PROCEEDS AT 7.5% TAX-FREE COMPOUND INTEREST USING A $100,000 INTEREST-ONLY MORTGAGE				
YEAR	GROSS INTEREST PAID [1]	NET INTEREST PAID (after tax benefit*) [2]	GROSS INTEREST EARNED [3]	NET PROFIT [3] - [2] [4]	NEW BALANCE [5]
1	$9,000	$5,940	$7,500	$1,560	$101,560
2	9,000	5,940	7,617	1,677	103,237
3	9,000	5,940	7,743	1,803	105,040
4	9,000	5,940	7,878	1,938	106,978
5	9,000	5,940	8,023	2,083	109,061
6	9,000	5,940	8,180	2,240	111,301
7	9,000	5,940	8,348	2,408	113,708
8	9,000	5,940	8,528	2,588	116,296
9	9,000	5,940	8,722	2,782	119,079
10	9,000	5,940	8,931	2,991	122,069
10 YR. TOTALS	$90,000	$59,400	$81,469	$22,069	$122,069
11	9,000	5,940	9,155	3,215	125,285
12	9,000	5,940	9,396	3,456	128,741
13	9,000	5,940	9,656	3,716	132,457
14	9,000	5,940	9,934	3,994	136,451
15	9,000	5,940	10,234	4,294	140,745
15 YR. TOTALS	$135,000	$89,100	$129,845	$40,745	$140,745
16	9,000	5,940	10,556	4,616	145,360
17	9,000	5,940	10,902	4,962	150,323
18	9,000	5,940	11,274	5,334	155,657
19	9,000	5,940	11,674	5,734	161,391
20	9,000	5,940	12,104	6,164	167,555
20 YR. TOTALS	$180,000	$118,800	$186,355	$67,555	$167,555

*assuming a 34% marginal tax bracket—27% federal and 7% state

interest-only loan, but the earnings compound and become greater (column 3). This illustrates the second important factor of this wealth building strategy—the compounding of the investment on a tax-favored basis. This will make a substantial difference as years pass. The interest expense is calculated on a simple-interest basis, but your investment accrues interest on a compounding, tax-deferred basis. Thus, for the period of fifteen years, totaling the growth on the separated equity ($129,845) then subtracting the cost of those funds ($89,100), we end up with $40,745 net profit in fifteen years. Over a twenty-year period, our net profit would be $67,555. This is true even though we borrowed at 9 percent and invested at only 7.5 percent! Again, this is possible because of two factors: 1) the 9-percent cost of borrowing is not the actual cost to us due to tax deductibility of the mortgage interest, and 2) while the cost of borrowing is calculated using simple interest, the interest accrued by the investment is compounded and tax deferred or tax free.

Let's study another example (**fig. 9.4**). We borrow $100,000, using a mortgage, at 8 percent and invest at only 6 percent. Again, by borrowing at 8 percent, we are only really incurring costs of 5.28 percent, or $5,280, on a $100,000 loan in a 34 percent tax bracket. By investing that $100,000 at 6 percent, we will make a return of $6,000 the first year, which is greater than the net cost of $5,280. Even with this small margin, because of the compounding effect of the investment, we would realize a net profit of $16,759. By the twentieth year, this profit will have grown to $26,486.

The results of borrowing at 8 percent and investing at 6 percent may not seem that impressive. But, let me now illustrate how to turbo charge your wealth growth rate to make $115,114 rather than $26,486 over the same time period by borrowing at 8 percent and investing at 6 percent. I'll conclude by showing you how to make over $1 million by borrowing at 7.5 percent and investing at 7.5 percent.

HOME EQUITY MANAGEMENT VS. TRADITIONAL INVESTMENTS

Let's assume you currently have some discretionary dollars you are saving for long-term goals, such as retirement or college funding for

Fig. 9.4	BORROWING $100,000 AT 8% DEDUCTIBLE INTEREST AND INVESTING THE LOAN PROCEEDS AT 6% TAX-FREE COMPOUND INTEREST USING A $100,000 INTEREST-ONLY MORTGAGE				
YEAR	GROSS INTEREST PAID [1]	NET INTEREST PAID (after tax benefit*) [2]	GROSS INTEREST EARNED [3]	NET PROFIT [3] - [2] [4]	NEW BALANCE [5]
1	$8,000	$5,280	$6,000	$720	$100,720
2	8,000	5,280	6,043	763	101,483
3	8,000	5,280	6,089	809	102,292
4	8,000	5,280	6,138	858	103,150
5	8,000	5,280	6,189	909	104,059
6	8,000	5,280	6,244	964	105,022
7	8,000	5,280	6,301	1,021	106,044
8	8,000	5,280	6,363	1,083	107,126
9	8,000	5,280	6,428	1,148	108,274
10	8,000	5,280	6,496	1,216	109,490
10 YR. TOTALS	$80,000	$52,800	$62,290	$9,490	$109,490
11	8,000	5,280	6,569	1,289	110,780
12	8,000	5,280	6,647	1,367	112,146
13	8,000	5,280	6,729	1,449	113,595
14	8,000	5,280	6,816	1,536	115,131
15	8,000	5,280	6,908	1,628	116,759
15 YR. TOTALS	$20,000	$79,200	$95,959	$16,759	$116,759
16	8,000	5,280	7,006	1,726	118,484
17	8,000	5,280	7,109	1,829	120,313
18	8,000	5,280	7,219	1,939	122,252
19	8,000	5,280	7,335	2,055	124,307
20	8,000	5,280	7,458	2,178	126,486
20 YR. TOTALS	$160,000	$105,600	$132,086	$26,486	$126,486

*assuming a 34% marginal tax bracket—27% federal and 7% state

children. If those discretionary dollars amounted to at least 10 percent of your $60,000 annual income, you could reallocate $5,280 or $5,940 of that each year to cover the net employment cost in the arbitrage examples illustrated in figures 9.2 to 9.4. This would allow the invested home equity to compound and grow without having to pay the employment cost from our profit each year.

Before studying the enhanced results, let's make sure you thoroughly understand your two options. If you had extra discretionary dollars amounting to $5,280 a year, you could either: 1) save or invest $5,280 a year in an investment earning 8 percent interest compounded annually, or 2) you can reallocate that $5,280 to cover your share of the employment cost of $8,000 of deductible interest each year from separating $100,000 of home equity. Under the first option, you had to allocate $8,000 of gross income and pay $2,720 (34 percent) in taxes in order to have $5,280 left over to invest. You see, if you, as a taxpayer in a 34 percent tax bracket, want to buy a personal automobile that costs $19,800, you have to allocate $30,000 of gross income, then pay $10,200 (34 percent) in taxes, to net $19,800 to purchase the vehicle. In other words, you are forced to use sixty-six-cent dollars (after tax) much of the time in order to spend your money. The same is true when you want to save money in traditional savings accounts and investments.

Figure 9.5 illustrates a traditional savings account or investment, which is taxed as earned, wherein annual deposits are made with sixty-six-cent after-tax dollars. Column 1 shows we had to earn $8,000 gross each year to accomplish this. Column 2 is the annual state and federal income tax we are required to pay on that $8,000 of income. Column 3 shows the net of $5,280 we have left over to invest. Column 4 is the new balance we earn interest on each year after adding the new annual deposit of $5,280 (column 3) to the previous year's balance (column 8). Column 5 reflects the gross interest earned that year at 8 percent. Column 6 shows the tax liability you have to pay that year on the interest earned. Column 7 reflects the true net increase in the account after tax. Column 8 shows the year-end balances (column 4 plus column 7). Column 9 shows the cumulative taxes paid on the interest earned.

As seen, by the end of the tenth year, you have accumulated $70,838 (column 8), but you had a basis of $52,800 (10 years times $5,280 per year), resulting in a net gain of $18,038. However, remember you had to allocate $80,000 of your gross income during that ten-year period to accomplish this, so in essence, you are still in the hole $9,162 ($70,838 - $80,000 = -$9,162)!

Fig. 9.5

TRADITIONAL SAVINGS OR INVESTMENTS, EARNING 8%, TAXED AS EARNED
(Deposits Made with Sixty-Six-Cent After-Tax Dollars)

OBJECTIVE: To Invest $5,280 Per Year

$8,000 — Gross Income Earned in a 34% Tax Bracket
[$2,720] — Tax at 34%
$5,280 — Net Income Available to Invest Each Year

YEAR	[1] GROSS INCOME EARNED	[2] INCOME TAX PAYABLE	[3] NET ANNUAL DEPOSIT [1 - 2]	[4] NEW BALANCE EARNING INTEREST	[5] INTEREST EARNED AT 8%	[6] LESS TAX AT 34%	[7] NET INCREASE	[8] YEAR END BALANCE [4 + 7]	[9] CUMULATIVE TAXES PAID ON INTEREST EARNED
1	$8,000	$2,720	$5,280	$5,280	$422	$144	$279	$5,559	$144
2	$8,000	$2,720	$5,280	$10,839	$867	$295	$572	$11,411	$439
3	$8,000	$2,720	$5,280	$16,691	$1,335	$454	$881	$17,572	$893
4	$8,000	$2,720	$5,280	$22,852	$1,828	$622	$1,207	$24,059	$1,514
5	$8,000	$2,720	$5,280	$29,339	$2,347	$798	$1,549	$30,888	$2,312
6	$8,000	$2,720	$5,280	$36,168	$2,893	$984	$1,910	$38,078	$3,296
7	$8,000	$2,720	$5,280	$43,358	$3,469	$1,179	$2,289	$45,647	$4,476
8	$8,000	$2,720	$5,280	$50,927	$4,074	$1,385	$2,689	$53,616	$5,861
9	$8,000	$2,720	$5,280	$58,896	$4,712	$1,602	$3,110	$62,006	$7,463
10	$8,000	$2,720	$5,280	$67,286	$5,383	$1,830	$3,553	$70,838	$9,293
11	$8,000	$2,720	$5,280	$76,118	$6,089	$2,070	$4,019	$80,137	$11,363
12	$8,000	$2,720	$5,280	$85,417	$6,833	$2,323	$4,510	$89,927	$13,687
13	$8,000	$2,720	$5,280	$95,207	$7,617	$2,590	$5,027	$100,234	$16,276
14	$8,000	$2,720	$5,280	$105,514	$8,441	$2,870	$5,571	$111,086	$19,146
15	$8,000	$2,720	$5,280	$116,366	$9,309	$3,165	$6,144	$122,510	$22,311
16	$8,000	$2,720	$5,280	$127,790	$10,223	$3,476	$6,747	$134,537	$25,787
17	$8,000	$2,720	$5,280	$139,817	$11,185	$3,803	$7,382	$147,199	$29,590
18	$8,000	$2,720	$5,280	$152,479	$12,198	$4,147	$8,051	$160,530	$33,738
19	$8,000	$2,720	$5,280	$165,810	$13,265	$4,510	$8,755	$174,565	$38,248
20	$8,000	$2,720	$5,280	$179,845	$14,388	$4,892	$9,496	$189,341	$43,140
	$160,000	$54,400	$105,600					$189,341	

By the end of the fifteenth year, you are finally gaining some ground. You have accumulated $122,510, less the basis of $79,200 (15 years times $5,280 per year), resulting in a net gain of $43,310. But again, remember you had to allocate $120,000 (15 years times $8,000 per year) of your gross income during that period to arrive at a savings balance of $122,510. So you are now $2,510 ahead.

Let's take a look at the end of the twentieth year. You have accumulated $189,341, less the basis of $105,600 (20 years times $5,280 per year) resulting in a net gain of $83,741. However, this required an allocation of $160,000 (20 years times $8,000 per year) out of your gross income during that period to arrive at a balance of $189,341, so you are now ahead $29,341. This equates to an internal rate of return of 1.6 percent compounded annually on the $8,000 per year of income required to accomplish the result, even though you were earning 8 percent on the net after-tax contribution!

In **figure 9.6** you will notice that $9,000 of gross income needs to be allocated to net $5,940 to invest. Let's assume we can earn 7.5 percent interest that is taxed as earned. In years 10, 15, and 20 we will have accumulated $78,228, $134,016, and $205,048, respectively.

In **figure 9.7** we are assuming we can only earn 6 percent interest taxed as earned. As in figure 9.5, we will allocate $8,000 of gross income to net $5,280 to invest. In years 10, 15, and 20 we will have accumulated $65,780, $109,585 and $162,778, respectively.

COMPARING THE EFFECT OF DIFFERING TAX TREATMENTS

As I will explain in more detail in chapters 15 and 16, an American taxpayer has five basic options with regard to the tax treatment on savings:

1. She can save or invest after-tax dollars (sixty-six-cent dollars in this case) in investments that are taxed as interest is earned, dividends are paid, or capital gains are realized (fig. 9.5-9.7).
2. She can save or invest after-tax dollars in investments that are tax deferred and then pay taxes on the gain when she realizes it later.

Fig. 9.6

TRADITIONAL SAVINGS OR INVESTMENTS, EARNING 7.5%, TAXED AS EARNED
(Deposits Made with Sixty-Six-Cent After-Tax Dollars)

$9,000 Gross Income Earned in a 34% Tax Bracket
[$3,060] Tax at 34%
$5,940 Net Income Available to Invest Each Year

OBJECTIVE: To Invest $5,940 Per Year

YEAR	[1] GROSS INCOME EARNED	[2] INCOME TAX PAYABLE	[3] NET ANNUAL DEPOSIT [1 - 2]	[4] NEW BALANCE EARNING INTEREST	[5] INTEREST EARNED AT 8%	[6] LESS TAX AT 34%	[7] NET INCREASE	[8] YEAR END BALANCE [4 + 7]	[9] CUMULATIVE TAXES PAID ON INTEREST EARNED
1	$9,000	$3,060	$5,940	$5,940	$446	$151	$294	$6,234	$151
2	$9,000	$3,060	$5,940	$12,174	$913	$310	$603	$12,777	$461
3	$9,000	$3,060	$5,940	$18,717	$1,404	$477	$926	$19,643	$939
4	$9,000	$3,060	$5,940	$25,583	$1,919	$652	$1,266	$26,849	$1,591
5	$9,000	$3,060	$5,940	$32,789	$2,459	$836	$1,623	$34,413	$2,427
6	$9,000	$3,060	$5,940	$40,353	$3,026	$1,029	$1,997	$42,350	$3,456
7	$9,000	$3,060	$5,940	$48,290	$3,622	$1,231	$2,390	$50,680	$4,688
8	$9,000	$3,060	$5,940	$56,620	$4,247	$1,444	$2,803	$59,423	$6,131
9	$9,000	$3,060	$5,940	$65,363	$4,902	$1,667	$3,235	$68,599	$7,798
10	$9,000	$3,060	$5,940	$74,539	$5,590	$1,901	$3,690	$78,228	$9,699
11	$9,000	$3,060	$5,940	$84,168	$6,313	$2,146	$4,166	$88,335	$11,845
12	$9,000	$3,060	$5,940	$94,275	$7,071	$2,404	$4,667	$98,941	$14,249
13	$9,000	$3,060	$5,940	$104,881	$7,866	$2,674	$5,192	$110,073	$16,924
14	$9,000	$3,060	$5,940	$116,013	$8,701	$2,958	$5,743	$121,755	$19,882
15	$9,000	$3,060	$5,940	$127,695	$9,577	$3,256	$6,321	$134,016	$23,138
16	$9,000	$3,060	$5,940	$139,956	$10,497	$3,569	$6,928	$146,884	$26,707
17	$9,000	$3,060	$5,940	$152,824	$11,462	$3,897	$7,565	$160,389	$30,604
18	$9,000	$3,060	$5,940	$166,502	$12,475	$4,241	$8,233	$174,562	$34,846
19	$9,000	$3,060	$5,940	$180,502	$13,538	$4,603	$8,935	$189,437	$39,448
20	$9,000	$3,060	$5,940	$195,377	$14,653	$4,982	$9,671	$205,048	$44,430
	$180,000	$61,200	$118,800					$205,048	

Fig. 9.7

TRADITIONAL SAVINGS OR INVESTMENTS, EARNING 6%, TAXED AS EARNED
(Deposits Made with Sixty-Six-Cent After-Tax Dollars)

$8,000   Gross Income Earned in a 34% Tax Bracket
[$2,720]   Tax at 34%
$5,280   Net Income Available to Invest Each Year

OBJECTIVE: To Invest $5,280 Per Year

YEAR	[1] GROSS INCOME EARNED	[2] INCOME TAX PAYABLE	[3] NET ANNUAL DEPOSIT [1 - 2]	[4] NEW BALANCE EARNING INTEREST	[5] INTEREST EARNED AT 8%	[6] LESS TAX AT 34%	[7] NET INCREASE	[8] YEAR END BALANCE [4 + 7]	[9] CUMULATIVE TAXES PAID ON INTEREST EARNED
1	$8,000	$2,720	$5,280	$5,280	$317	$108	$209	$5,489	$108
2	$8,000	$2,720	$5,280	$10,769	$646	$220	$426	$11,196	$328
3	$8,000	$2,720	$5,280	$16,476	$989	$336	$652	$17,128	$664
4	$8,000	$2,720	$5,280	$22,408	$1,344	$457	$887	$23,295	$1,121
5	$8,000	$2,720	$5,280	$28,575	$1,715	$583	$1,132	$29,707	$1,704
6	$8,000	$2,720	$5,280	$34,987	$2,099	$714	$1,385	$36,372	$2,418
7	$8,000	$2,720	$5,280	$41,652	$2,499	$850	$1,649	$43,302	$3,267
8	$8,000	$2,720	$5,280	$48,582	$2,915	$991	$1,924	$50,506	$4,258
9	$8,000	$2,720	$5,280	$55,786	$3,347	$1,138	$2,209	$57,995	$5,396
10	$8,000	$2,720	$5,280	$63,275	$3,796	$1,291	$2,506	$65,780	$6,687
11	$8,000	$2,720	$5,280	$71,060	$4,264	$1,450	$2,814	$73,874	$8,137
12	$8,000	$2,720	$5,280	$79,154	$4,749	$1,615	$3,135	$82,289	$9,752
13	$8,000	$2,720	$5,280	$87,569	$5,254	$1,786	$3,468	$91,037	$11,538
14	$8,000	$2,720	$5,280	$96,317	$5,779	$1,965	$3,814	$100,131	$13,503
15	$8,000	$2,720	$5,280	$105,411	$6,325	$2,150	$4,174	$109,585	$15,653
16	$8,000	$2,720	$5,280	$114,865	$6,892	$2,343	$4,549	$119,414	$17,996
17	$8,000	$2,720	$5,280	$124,694	$7,482	$2,544	$4,938	$129,632	$20,540
18	$8,000	$2,720	$5,280	$134,912	$8,095	$2,752	$5,343	$140,254	$23,292
19	$8,000	$2,720	$5,280	$145,534	$8,732	$2,969	$5,763	$151,297	$26,261
20	$8,000	$2,720	$5,280	$156,577	$9,395	$3,194	$6,200	$162,778	$29,456
	$160,000	$54,400	$105,600					$162,778	

3. She can save or invest after-tax dollars in investments that accumulate tax free, then use that money tax-free later, including the gain she made (i.e., Roth IRAs and insurance contracts properly structured and used).

4. She can save or invest one-hundred-cent pre-tax dollars in investments that accumulate tax-deferred, then later are fully taxable (e.g., traditional IRAs and 401(k)s).

5. She can use one-hundred-cent dollars because of tax deductions and enjoy tax-free accumulation and also tax-free use of the money later. (Proper home equity management can allow you to accomplish option 5).

For now, let's just study the difference between option 1 and option 5 from a capital accumulation standpoint.

In **figure 9.8**, let's do a comparison of traditional savings or investments earning 8 percent taxed as earned, versus home equity management—borrowing 8 percent and investing the loan proceeds at 8 percent compounding tax free. Let's take snapshots of the two situations in years 10, 15, and 20.

Column 1 illustrates the results of traditional savings (taxed as earned) taken from figure 9.5. Column 2 illustrates the results if you separate your home equity and manage it by paying the employment cost from the interest earnings as illustrated in figure 9.2. Column 3 assumes you are doing each of these activities independent of each other and reflects the total. Column 4 illustrates managing home equity by reallocating the savings deposits in column 1 to cover the net employment costs of the mortgage, thus allowing compounding of the full amount of interest. Column 5 reflects the difference between traditional savings versus allocating those dollars to cover the employment costs of equity management. Therefore, in column 4, $100,000 at 8 percent compounded annually for ten years grows to $215,893, meaning you made $115,893 gross gain after subtracting the mortgage of $100,000. This growth would be realized if you paid the annual net employment cost of $5,280 from

Fig. 9.8

COMPARISON OF
TRADITIONAL SAVINGS OR INVESTMENTS EARNING 8% INTEREST TAXED AS EARNED
VERSUS
HOME EQUITY MANAGEMENT - BORROWING AT 8% TAX DEDUCTIBLE AND INVESTING AT 8% TAX FREE

	[1] Traditional Savings Taxed as Earned (From Figure 9.5)		[2] Equity Management Paying Employment Cost from Interest Earnings (From Figure 9.2)		[3] Total of Traditional Savings & Equity Management Independent of Each Other (Columns 1-2)		[4] Equity Management Combined with a Repositioning of Traditional Savings to Cover Employment Costs, Which Allows Full Compounding on Equity	[5] Additional Profit Realized through the use of Equity Management and a Repositioning of Savings to Cover Employment Costs vs. Traditional Savings Alone (Column 4 - 1)
10 Years							($100,000 at 8% for 10 years =)	
Liquid Asset	$70,838	+	$139,403	=	$210,241	vs	$215,893	
Less : Mortgage	0		[$100,000]		[$100,000]		[$100,000]	
Gross Gain	$70,838	+	$39,403	=	$110,241	vs	$115,893	
Less : Basis	[$52,800]		0		[$52,800]		[$52,800]	
Net Gain	$18,038	+	$39,403	=	$57,441	vs	$63,093	$45,055
15 Years							($100,000 at 8% for 15 years =)	
Liquid Asset	$122,510	+	$173,854	=	$296,364	vs	$317,217	
Less : Mortgage	0		[$100,000]		[$100,000]		[$100,000]	
Gross Gain	$122,510	+	$73,854	=	$196,364	vs	$217,217	
Less : Basis	[$79,200]		0		[$79,200]		[$79,200]	
Net Gain	$43,310	+	$73,854	=	$117,164	vs	$138,017	$94,707
20 Years							($100,000 at 8% for 20 years =)	
Liquid Asset	$189,341	+	$224,473	=	$413,814	vs	$466,096	
Less : Mortgage	0		[$100,000]		[$100,000]		[$100,000]	
Gross Gain	$189,341	+	$124,473	=	$313,814	vs	$366,096	
Less : Basis	[$105,600]		0		[$105,600]		[$105,600]	
Net Gain	$83,741	+	$124,473	=	$208,214	vs	$260,496	$176,755

other sources instead of paying it from the interest earned each year like you did in figure 9.2 (also shown in column 2).

You may say, "Well, why should I do that? I could be earning interest by investing $5,280 each year in a savings or investment account!" If you earned 8 percent interest on your annual savings contribution of $5,280, it would grow to only $70,838 (column 1) versus the $115,893 (column 4) you achieved by allocating the money to cover the employment cost! If you subtract the basis of $52,800 (10 years times $5,280 per year) from each result, you would have made a net gain of $18,038 in your traditional savings account versus $63,093 in your equity management account. That's a difference of $45,055, or $3^1/2$ times more profit!

Let's look at the results after fifteen years, illustrated in **figure 9.8**. The net gain in a traditional savings account would have been $43,310 (column 1) versus $138,017 (column 4) in your equity management account. That's a difference of $94,707—three times more profit! After twenty years, you would have a net gain of $260,496 in your equity management account, which is three times more than what you would have achieved in your savings account ($83,741) earning the same interest rate on the same contributions!

Some people may say, "Well, I'll just continue my regular savings and investment plan and do equity management independent from my savings activity." In that case, you would have the results as shown in column 1 plus the results of column 2 shown, which equal the totals shown in column 3 (figure 9.8). By managing your equity independent of regular savings and investment activities (not investing any of your own money or basis to cover the employment cost), you are still substantially ahead after twenty years. You would have accumulated $208,214 (column 3) versus $83,741 (column 1) had you not separated your equity. However, you would have accumulated $260,496, or $52,282 more (which is 25 percent more as shown in column 4), by reallocating the savings contributions to cover the employment cost, thus allowing the interest on $100,000 of separated equity to compound and grow undisturbed.

The difference in results are just as dynamic when you apply the same concept when borrowing at 9 percent and investing at 7.5 percent.

Fig. 9.9

COMPARISON OF
TRADITIONAL SAVINGS OR INVESTMENTS EARNING 7.5% INTEREST TAXED AS EARNED
VERSUS
HOME EQUITY MANAGEMENT—BORROWING AT 9% TAX DEDUCTIBLE AND INVESTING AT 7.5% TAX FREE

	[1] Traditional Savings Taxed as Earned (From Figure 9.6)		[2] Equity Management Paying Employment Cost from Interest Earnings (From Figure 9.3)		[3] Total of Traditional Savings & Equity Management Independent of Each Other (Columns 1+2)		[4] Equity Management Combined with a Repositioning of Traditional Savings to Cover Employment Costs, Which Allows Full Compounding on Equity	[5] Additional Profit Realized through the use of Equity Management and a Repositioning of Savings to Cover Employment Costs vs. Traditional Savings Alone (Column 4 - 1)
10 Years							($100,000 at 7.5% for 10 years =)	
Liquid Asset	$78,228	+	$122,069	=	$200,297	vs	$206,103	
Less : Mortgage	0		[$100,000]		[$100,000]		[$100,000]	
Gross Gain	$78,228	+	$22,069	=	$100,297	vs	$106,103	
Less : Basis	[$59,400]		[$59,400]		[$59,400]		[$89,100]	
Net Gain	$18,828	+	$22,069	=	$40,897	vs	$46,703	$27,875
15 Years							($100,000 at 7.5% for 15 years =)	
Liquid Asset	$134,016	+	$140,745	=	$274,761	vs	$295,888	
Less : Mortgage	0		[$100,000]		[$100,000]		[$100,000]	
Gross Gain	$134,016	+	$40,745	=	$174,761	vs	$195,888	
Less : Basis	[$89,100]		0		[$89,100]		[$89,100]	
Net Gain	$44,916	+	$40,745	=	$85,661	vs	$106,788	$61,872
20 Years							($100,000 at 7.5% for 20 years =)	
Liquid Asset	$205,048	+	$167,555	=	$372,603	vs	$424,785	
Less : Mortgage	0		[$100,000]		[$100,000]		[$100,000]	
Gross Gain	$205,048	+	$67,555	=	$272,603	vs	$324,785	
Less : Basis	[$118,800]		0		[$118,800]		[$118,800]	
Net Gain	$86,248	+	$67,555	=	$153,803	vs	$205,985	$119,737

Figure 9.9 shows that after fifteen years, you could achieve a net gain of $106,788 by reallocating $5,940 a year from other savings contributions to cover the employment cost. This is a substantial increase over the $44,916 of net profit achieved during fifteen years, shown in column 1. As shown in figure 9.9, you would have a net gain of $205,985 after twenty years using equity management versus a net gain of only $86,248 if you saved $5,940 per year in a taxed-as-earned investment, assuming a growth rate of 7.5 percent in both accounts. That's a $119,737 difference, or about $2^1/2$ times more profit. By allocating the $5,940 savings contribution each year to cover the employment cost rather than doing equity management independently, after twenty years, you end up with $205,985, versus $153,803, as shown in column 3.

Remember in figure 9.4 when you made $26,486 over a twenty-year period borrowing at 8 percent and investing at 6 percent? What if you reallocated $5,280 of annual savings contribution to cover the net employment cost (**fig. 9.10**)? In the same twenty-year period, your liquid equity management account could grow to a balance of $320,714 (column 4) instead of $162,778 (column 1). After subtracting the mortgage of $100,000 and the employment cost of $105,600 (column 4), the net gain would be $115,114, versus a net gain of $57,178 (which is what you would have accumulated net after tax by investing $5,280 at 6 percent as shown in column 1)—twice as much net profit!

Figure 9.11 illustrates the summary results from borrowing at 7 percent and investing at 7 percent, assuming the employment cost is covered by reallocating funds from other sources that already had been earmarked for long-term savings. As you study figure 9.11, please remember the liquid assets in column 3 are actually $100,000 greater than shown as long as we keep our equity separated through the conduit of a mortgage. By borrowing at 7 percent interest (tax deductible) and investing at 7 percent (compounding tax free), we are able to accumulate $386,986 in our side fund at the end of year 20. When we subtract the $100,000 mortgage balance (assuming an interest-only mortgage), we end up with $286,968 (column 3). After subtracting our basis of $92,400 (column 1) invested in the equity management plan, we realized a profit or net gain of $194,568!

Fig. 9.10

COMPARISON OF
TRADITIONAL SAVINGS OR INVESTMENTS EARNING 6% INTEREST TAXED AS EARNED
VERSUS
HOME EQUITY MANAGEMENT—BORROWING AT 8% TAX DEDUCTIBLE AND INVESTING AT 6.0% TAX FREE

	[1] Traditional Savings Taxed as Earned (From Figure 9.7)		[2] Equity Management Paying Employment Cost from Interest Earnings (From Figure 9.4)		[3] Total of Traditional Savings & Equity Management Independent of Each Other (Columns 1+2)		[4] Equity Management Combined with a Repositioning of Traditional Savings to Cover Employment Costs, Which Allows Full Compounding on Equity	[5] Additional Profit Realized through the use of Equity Management and a Repositioning of Savings to Cover Employment Costs vs. Traditional Savings Alone (Column 4 - 1)
10 Years							($100,000 at 6% for 10 years =)	
Liquid Asset	$65,780	+	$109,490	=	$175,270	vs	$179,085	
Less : Mortgage	0	+	[$100,000]	=	[$100,000]		[$100,000]	
Gross Gain	$65,780	+	$9,490	=	$75,270	vs	$79,085	
Less : Basis	[$52,800]	+	0	=	[$52,800]		[$52,800]	
Net Gain	$12,980	+	$9,490	=	$22,470	vs	$26,285	$13,305
15 Years							($100,000 at 6% for 15 years =)	
Liquid Asset	$109,585	+	$116,759	=	$226,344	vs	$239,656	
Less : Mortgage	0	+	[$100,000]	=	[$100,000]		[$100,000]	
Gross Gain	$109,585	+	$16,759	=	$126,344	vs	$139,656	
Less : Basis	[$79,200]	+	0	=	[$79,200]		[$79,200]	
Net Gain	$30,385	+	$16,759	=	$47,144	vs	$60,456	$30,071
20 Years							($100,000 at 6% for 20 years =)	
Liquid Asset	$162,778	+	$126,486	=	$289,264	vs	$320,714	
Less : Mortgage	0	+	[$100,000]	=	[$100,000]		[$100,000]	
Gross Gain	$162,778	+	$26,486	=	$189,264	vs	$220,714	
Less : Basis	[$105,600]	+	0	=	[$105,600]		[$105,600]	
Net Gain	$57,178	+	$26,486	=	$83,664	vs	$115,114	$57,936

Fig. 9.11	MANAGING EQUITY SUCCESSFULLY		
	BORROWING AT 7% (Tax Deductible)	EQUITY REPOSITIONED $100,000	INVESTING AT 7% (Compounding Tax Free)
	[1] NET CUMULATIVE ANNUAL COST at 7% ($7,000-34%)	[2] Difference [3 - 1]	[3] NET CUMULATIVE GROWTH at 7% (Less Mortgage of $100,000)
Year			
1	$4,620	$2,380	$7,000
5	$23,100	$17,155	$40,255
10	$46,200	$50,515	$96,715
15	$69,300	$106,603	$175,903
20	$92,400	$194,568	$286,968

You would have to be earning almost 10 percent interest tax free (which is equal to 15 percent in a taxable investment) on annual savings contributions of $4,620 to end up with $286,968 in twenty years!

Think of the wealth you can create, all born of otherwise dormant, lazy home equity dollars. If these dollars had been left in the property, they would have earned a zero rate of return. I like to refer to this application of arbitrage as "Home-Made Money." This ability—taking idle equity and turning it into a substantial profit at conservative rates of return—is truly the key to substantially enhancing net worth!

MORE OPTIMISTIC PROJECTIONS

We've taken a look at some pretty conservative cases. How about more optimistic projections? Let's study **figure 9.12** for a moment. What if you were able to borrow at 7 percent tax deductible and invest the loan proceeds at 8 percent tax free? In the first year we earned $8,000. The net employment cost was $4,620, resulting in a net gain of $3,380. In year 10, $100,000 invested at 8 percent would grow to $215,893, resulting in a gain of $115,893. The net employment cost the first ten years totals $46,200, resulting in a net gain of $69,693. By managing our equity, in fifteen years, our net gain would be $147,917, and in year 20 it would total $273,696!

Fig. 9.12	MANAGING EQUITY SUCCESSFULLY		
BORROWING AT 7% (Tax Deductible)	**EQUITY REPOSITIONED** $100,000		**INVESTING AT 8%** (Compounding Tax Free)
[1] NET CUMULATIVE ANNUAL COST at 7% ($7,000-34%)	**[2]** Difference [3 - 1]		**[3]** NET CUMULATIVE GROWTH at 8% (Less Mortgage of $100,000)
Year			
1	$4,620	$3,380	$8,000
5	$23,100	$23,833	$46,933
10	$46,200	$69,693	$115,893
15	$69,300	$147,917	$217,217
20	$92,400	$273,696	$366,096

Fig. 9.13	MANAGING EQUITY SUCCESSFULLY		
BORROWING AT 7% (Tax Deductible)	**EQUITY REPOSITIONED** $100,000		**INVESTING AT 9%** (Compounding Tax Free)
[1] NET CUMULATIVE ANNUAL COST at 7% ($7,000-34%)	**[2]** Difference [3 - 1]		**[3]** NET CUMULATIVE GROWTH at 9% (Less Mortgage of $100,000)
Year			
1	$4,620	$4,380	$9,000
5	$23,100	$30,762	$53,862
10	$46,200	$90,536	$136,736
15	$69,300	$194,948	$264,248
20	$92,400	$368,041	$460,441

Figure 9.13 illustrates the results that could be achieved through managing equity by borrowing at 7 percent tax deductible and investing the loan proceeds at 9 percent tax free. Please note in just ten years, the net gain is $90,536. The net gain increases to $194,948 by year 15 and $368,041 by year 20! You would have to be earning almost 13.7 percent interest tax free (which is equal to 20.75 percent in a taxable investment) on annual contributions of $4,620 to end up with $460,441 (column 3) in twenty years!

Can you see why I call this strategy "Home-Made Wealth"?

Fig. 9.14	TWO WAYS TO STACK UP $1 MILLION

#1 SEPARATE $100,000 OF EQUITY

	BORROWING AT 7% (Tax Deductible)	EQUITY REPOSITIONED $100,000	INVESTING AT 9% (Compounding Tax Free)
	[1] NET CUMULATIVE ANNUAL COST at 7% ($7,000-34%)	[2] Difference [3 - 1]	[3] NET CUMULATIVE GROWTH at 9% (Less Mortgage of $100,000)
Year			
1	$4,620	$4,380	$9,000
5	$23,100	$30,762	$53,862
10	$46,200	$90,536	$136,736
15	$69,300	$194,948	$264,248
20	$92,400	$368,041	$460,441
25	$115,500	$646,808	$762,308
30	$138,600	$1,088,168	**$1,226,768**

#2 SEPARATE $160,000 OF EQUITY

	BORROWING AT 7.5% (Tax Deductible)	EQUITY REPOSITIONED $160,000	INVESTING AT 7.5% (Compounding Tax Free)
	[1] NET CUMULATIVE ANNUAL COST at 7.5% ($12,000-34%)	[2] Difference [3 - 1]	[3] NET CUMULATIVE GROWTH at 7.5% (Less Mortgage of $160,000)
Year			
1	$7,920	$4,080	$12,000
5	$39,600	$30,101	$69,701
10	$79,200	$90,565	$169,765
15	$118,800	$194,620	$313,420
20	$158,400	$361,256	$519,656
25	$198,000	$617,734	$815,734
30	$237,600	$1,003,193	**$1,240,793**

STACKING UP $1 MILLION

Finally, here are two ways to stack up a million dollars for your retirement (**fig. 9.14**). Based on the last example, if you can achieve a net gain of $368,041 on $100,000 over twenty years, then you can achieve well over $1 million in thirty years by borrowing $100,000 at a tax deductible 7 percent and investing the loan proceeds at 9 percent in a tax favored environment. In fact, your liquid equity management account would be

$1,326,768 by that time. You would realize a net gain of $1,088,168 *after* deducting the $100,000 mortgage and the $138,600 of employment costs (30 years times $4,620 per year). If you had invested $4,620 per year in a tax-deferred investment earning 9 percent, it would have grown to only $686,418 less the basis of $138,600, resulting in a net gain of $547,818. In other words, we achieved almost twice as much by allocating those same dollars to equity management!

Another way to stack up a million dollars would be to employ $160,000 of home equity by separating it at 7.5 percent and investing the loan proceeds at the *same* rate of 7.5 percent for thirty years. Your liquid equity management account balance would be $1,400,793 at the end of thirty years ($1,240,793 after deducting the $160,000 mortgage). The net gain would be $1,003,193 after deducting the mortgage balance of $160,000 and the cumulative employment cost of $237,600. In contrast, only a net gain of $642,743 would have been achieved in a tax-deferred investment ($7,920 per year at 7.5 percent for 30 years = $880,343, less the basis of $237,600). In this case, managing your equity provides 56 percent more net gain! Either way, you could end up with over $1 million in your retirement account using the principle of arbitrage to manage your home equity.

In summary, there are two key elements to remember as you apply the principle of arbitrage to turbo charge your wealth growth rate.

1) Borrow funds at the most attractive rate possible. An interest-only home mortgage is by far the most desirable vehicle because you can maximize the deductibility of the interest, fully using Uncle Sam as your partner. Amortized loans also work well, but they slowly trap your equity in the home again, possibly requiring more frequent refinancing.

2) Invest in a safe environment, yet earn the highest rate of interest possible. Invest in a tax-favored—or even tax-free—low-risk vehicle, as will be introduced in Section III. Moderate returns in a safe environment will yield excellent results! It is not worth incurring

high risks on serious money like home equity to try to earn higher returns. This is not a get-rich-quick scheme; let common sense and compound interest create your wealth safely and slowly. Patience will pay.

The twofold power of this strategy is the compounding of your investment in a tax-favored environment and the tax benefit achieved through borrowing funds in a deductible environment.

I hope you are getting excited about some of the opportunities you may not have been aware of before. Keep your seatbelt on—more dynamic concepts lay ahead on the road to financial independence!

9 WEALTH-ENHANCEMENT STRATEGY NUMBER NINE

- *Learn to apply the fundamental principle that highly profitable financial institutions use to accumulate and create wealth—arbitrage.*
- *Employ equity to earn a rate of return higher than the net cost of separating that equity*
- *By doing so, you will create tremendous wealth and substantially enhance your net worth.*

CHAPTER 10

Strategic Refinancing

Increase your net worth by separating your home equity
and putting those idle dollars to work.

Equity in your home enhances your net worth.

*Equity in your home does not enhance your net worth at all.
Separated from your home, however, it has the ability to
dramatically enhance your net worth over time.*

Hopefully, it is now clear that by separating your home's equity and repositioning it into a liquid and safe side fund, it can compound and grow, especially at a net rate of return that is greater than the net cost of those funds. Using this method, you will not only experience growth from the appreciation on the property, but you will also experience growth from the invested funds. Indeed, the home itself is a valuable asset, but much more wealth can be attained by managing equity rather than by leaving it idle in the property.

WHY SEPARATE EQUITY?

Figure 10.1 illustrates the full effect of separating $100,000 of equity from a home and repositioning it into a conservative side fund. Let's assume the home has a fair market value of $200,000 and a previous mortgage balance of $60,000. Thus, the new mortgage is $160,000 ($60,000 needed to pay off the previous mortgage and $100,000 cash out). Column 1 illustrates the value of the home each year if it were to appreciate at an average of 5 percent each year. At this rate, using the Rule of 72, this home would double in value approximately every fifteen years.

By studying column 1 and column 6 in figure 10.1, you will clearly see how a home continues to appreciate, regardless of whether it carries a mortgage. By separating the equity and diversifying it into two separate funds for the initial four to five years (for purposes I will explain in chapter 17), represented by columns 2 and 3, we can calculate the value of those investments as they compound and grow. By separating the equity we can add the value of the assets in columns 2 and 3 to the appreciating value of the home in column 1. So the sum of columns 1, 2, and 3 equals our total assets in column 4—the home value and the value of the side funds in which we invested the separated equity.

Column 6 illustrates the mortgage balance over a thirty-year amortization. Because we separated the funds using a mortgage, we incurred an employment cost (interest expense). The mortgage balance is a liability which will decrease very slowly, assuming an amortized loan, over the entire thirty-year period. Column 7, then, is figured by subtracting

Fig. 10.1	PLAN NET WORTH ILLUSTRATION						
	[1]	[2]	[3]	[4]	[5]	[6]	[7]
END OF YEAR	PROPERTY VALUE	SUPPLEMENTAL FUND VALUE	YEAR-END ACCUMULATION VALUE	PLAN ASSET VALUE (1+2+3)	DEATH BENEFIT	TOTAL MORTGAGE BALANCE	PLAN NET WORTH (4-6)
1	$210,000	$85,838	$21,554	$317,392	$293,051	$158,525	$158,867
2	220,500	65,957	45,004	331,461	293,051	156,936	174,525
3	231,525	45,058	70,515	347,098	293,051	155,223	191,875
4	243,101	23,091	98,268	364,460	293,051	153,377	211,083
5	255,256	0	128,461	383,717	293,051	151,388	232,329
6	268,019	0	136,690	404,709	293,051	149,245	255,464
7	281,420	0	145,642	427,062	293,051	146,935	280,127
8	295,491	0	155,381	450,872	293,051	144,446	306,426
9	310,266	0	165,976	476,242	293,051	141,763	334,479
10	325,779	0	177,502	503,281	293,051	138,873	364,408
11	342,068	0	189,868	531,936	293,051	135,758	396,178
12	359,171	0	203,162	562,333	293,051	132,401	429,932
13	377,130	0	217,497	594,627	293,051	128,783	465,844
14	395,986	0	233,035	629,021	293,051	124,885	504,136
15	415,786	0	249,878	665,664	293,051	120,684	544,980
16	436,575	0	268,350	704,925	293,051	116,157	588,768
17	458,404	0	288,585	746,989	303,014	111,278	635,711
18	481,324	0	310,502	791,826	326,027	106,021	685,805
19	505,390	0	334,026	839,416	350,727	100,355	739,061
20	530,660	0	359,259	889,919	377,222	94,250	795,669
21	557,193	0	386,324	943,517	405,640	87,671	855,846
22	585,052	0	415,350	1,000,402	436,118	80,581	919,821
23	614,305	0	446,469	1,060,774	468,792	72,940	987,834
24	645,020	0	479,815	1,124,835	503,806	64,707	1,060,128
25	677,271	0	515,606	1,192,877	541,387	55,834	1,137,043
26	711,135	0	554,021	1,265,156	581,722	46,273	1,218,883
27	746,691	0	595,126	1,341,817	624,883	35,969	1,305,848
28	784,026	0	639,080	1,423,106	671,034	24,865	1,398,241
29	823,227	0	686,044	1,509,271	720,346	12,899	1,496,372
30	864,388	0	736,369	1,600,757	773,187	0	1,600,757

mortgage liability (column 6) from total assets (column 4), resulting in our net worth on those assets.

As you can see, our net worth grows each year at a substantial appreciation and growth rate all the way through year 30 because we separated the equity out of the property in column 1. Had we chosen to leave our equity in the property, all we would have realized is the value of the home (column 1), plus the value of saving the employment cost incurred by separating $100,000 of equity, had we disciplined ourselves to invest it faithfully every year. However, as illustrated in chapter 9, equity management can achieve far greater results than traditional savings. By separating our equity and allowing it to grow through the magic of compound interest, we have unleashed the potential of that equity to earn a handsome rate of return. Likewise, if we were purchasing a new home and had just sold the home in this example for $200,000, we should keep as much equity separated from the new home as feasible by taking out the maximum mortgage possible. There are important reasons for doing this I will explain in chapter 12.

One of the safest and most conservative investments many clients choose for equity management is a life insurance contract because it allows for growth in a tax-favored environment. The guidelines for using life insurance contracts are explained in detail in chapter 17. If this type of investment were used as the primary side fund, column 5 of figure 10.1 shows a hypothetical example of the resulting life insurance death benefit that would accompany that investment. This benefit would be sufficient for a 60-year-old male to pay off the mortgage and substantially increase the estate in the event of an untimely death. The total estate value is thereby enhanced through the years, depending upon the types of financial instruments (in this case, life insurance) in which we reposition the home equity to increase liquidity, safety, and growth.

By keeping the equity separated, we can achieve growth on a greater asset base. Think of the goblet and pitcher of water analogy in chapter 5. The goblet, or property, can continue to appreciate regardless of whether it is filled to brim with equity (filled with water) or mortgaged to the hilt (empty)—the equity having been separated from it for investment purposes (poured over to the pitcher).

Remember our perceptions influence greatly the way we view life? Hopefully, instead of viewing a mortgage as a great negative in your life, you have begun to view it as a positive lever to help catapult you to a greater net worth. This positive leverage allows people to tie up little of their own capital in acquiring properties and allowing those properties to appreciate and grow to a substantial value. ("Leverage" is the use of a small amount of your own cash in conjunction with the use of OPM to control a much greater value of assets.) A 5 percent return per year on $200,000 may not seem like a very attractive rate of return, but if you tied up only 20 percent or even none of your own capital in acquiring that $200,000 asset, then you've created substantial leverage for yourself!

For example, 5 percent appreciation on $200,000 is $10,000. However, if you only tied up 20 percent of the value of the property ($40,000) using your own money, the $10,000 of appreciation represents a 25 percent return on your invested money. This positive leverage can generate a return on appreciating property, in addition to the profit we can make on the $160,000 of equity separated from the property (as explained in chapter 9). If you only tied up 10 percent of your own money in the property ($20,000), then $10,000 of appreciation represents a 50 percent return! If you tied up none of your own money in the property, then $10,000 of appreciation represents an infinite return! However, some people may argue that the interest on the borrowed equity diminishes the property owner's return. That's true, but with mortgage payments approximately equal to rent for similar living accommodations, the cash outlay is about the same. If the home were rented to tenants, the rental income should at least cover the mortgage payments plus property expenses.

By borrowing to conserve rather than to consume your equity, and by keeping the money liquid, you are protecting yourself against down markets when it may be critical to meet the liabilities created by separating the equity. The primary reason people get into trouble from leveraging property is they have either consumed the capital they borrowed or have not kept the money in a liquid environment to access in case of financial hardship. It is also important to earn a rate of return on leveraged capital that is greater than the net cost of those funds, as explained in chapters 7 to 9.

Through managing and controlling their home equity, many homeowners not only substantially increase their net worth, but also they get out of debt the quickest, smartest way possible. By refinancing as often as feasible and properly managing the excess equity accruing within the home during that time, you, as a homeowner, could achieve the enviable position of having substantial assets that far exceed your liabilities. You should consider refinancing your home every time the interest rate is even slightly better than your current rate or your current mortgage balance is 60 percent or less than the fair market value of your home.

Let's calculate the future value of just $10,000 of separated equity. Assume we are borrowing home equity at 7.5 percent interest in a 33.3 percent (I am using exactly one-third to keep the example simple) marginal tax bracket, so the net cost of borrowing is approximately 5 percent. Let's also use interest-only loans rather than amortized loans for the sake of simplicity. Every year the net after-tax cost of separating $10,000 of equity would be $500 (**figure 10.2**). In column one, separating $10,000 of equity for five years would cost us approximately $2,500, for ten years $5,000, fifteen years $7,500, and for twenty years $10,000. Column 2 shows what $10,000 earns at 7.5 percent interest (deducting the mortgage) each period: $750 in one year, $4,356 in five years, $10,610 in ten years, $19,589 in fifteen years, $32,479 in twenty years, $50,983 in twenty-five years, and $77,550 in thirty years. Column 3 shows the net profit we would realize after subtracting employment cost in column 1. The net profit would be: $1,856 in five years, $5,610 in ten years, $12,089 in fifteen years, $22,479 in twenty years, $38,483 in twenty-five years, and $62,550 in thirty years.

Using this example, if you were able to borrow dormant equity from your home at 7.5 percent interest in a 34 percent marginal tax bracket and invest the loan proceeds to earn 7.5 percent interest tax free, you could calculate approximately what your growth potential would be. If you separated $100,000 of equity (10 times $10,000), you could realize a profit of $18,560 in five years, $56,100 in ten years, $120,890 in fifteen years and $224,790 in twenty years! (10 times each number shown in Column 3, **fig.** 10.2) In fact, as I illustrated in chapter 9, if you separated $160,000 of equity for thirty years at 7.5 percent tax-deductible interest and invested the loan proceeds at 7.5 percent interest compounding tax free, you would realize a gain of $1,000,800 (16 times $62,550).

Fig. 10.2	NET WORTH ENHANCEMENT POTENTIAL FROM SEPARATING $10,000 OF HOME EQUITY		
	BORROWING $10,000 AT 7.5% (Tax Deductible in a 33.3% Bracket)		INVESTING $10,000 AT 7.5% (Compounding Tax Free less the $10,000 Mortgage)
	[1]	[2]	[3]
END OF YEAR	NET COST TO BORROW	YEAR END ACCUMULATION VALUE	NET PROFIT [2] - [1]
1	$ 500	$ 750	$ 250
5	2,500	4,356	1,856
10	5,000	10,610	5,610
15	7,500	19,589	12,089
20	10,000	32,479	22,479
25	12,500	50,983	38,483
30	15,000	77,550	62,550

So, as seen from **figure 10.2**, every time you can separate an additional $10,000 of equity from your home you could accumulate a liquid fund worth $32,479 twenty years from then, which is more than triple the value of that equity when it was first separated. Again, this assumes you borrowed at a tax-deductible 7.5 percent and invested at a tax-free 7.5 percent and covered the employment cost by reallocating other dollars earmarked for savings or investments. If you were to pay the employment cost from the interest you earned each year, thereby not allowing the $10,000 of equity to compound undisturbed, you can still enhance your net worth as explained in chapter 9. In that case, the net profit would be $1,452 in five years, $3,537 in ten years, $6,530 in fifteen years, and $10,826 in twenty years. These results can be achieved even if your home didn't appreciate at all during that twenty-year period! Of course, it is highly likely your home will appreciate during that time period, which provides more opportunities to separate more equity.

FINDING THE RIGHT OPPORTUNITY

How often do opportunities arise to do this? Let's look at three scenarios. Let's assume you have a home valued right now at $200,000 with an 80 percent loan-to-value of $160,000 for a thirty-year amortized mortgage at 7.5 percent. After five years, your mortgage will have only reduced to $151,388. However, if your home appreciated an average of 5 percent during those five years, it would be worth $255,256. At that point, you could probably qualify for an 80 percent loan-to-value cash-out refinance in the amount of $204,204, which would allow you to separate an additional $52,816 of equity ($204,204 less $151,388). By going to the chart in figure 10.2, you know that for every $10,000 of equity, you can enhance your net worth twenty years down the road by an additional $22,479. So, by separating $52,816 of equity you could enhance your net worth an additional $118,725 over twenty years (5.2816 times $22,479).

If your home appreciates an average of 7.5 percent those five years, it would be worth $287,126. An 80 percent loan-to-value cash-out refinance would allow a mortgage of $229,700, separating an additional $78,312 of equity after paying off the previous mortgage of $151,388. By employing that equity at 7.5 percent, you could enhance your net worth by $176,038 (7.8312 times $22,479) over the next twenty years.

If your home appreciates an average of 10 percent during those five years, it would be worth $322,102. An 80 percent loan-to-value cash-out refinance would allow a mortgage of $257,681, separating an additional $106,293 of equity after paying off the previous mortgage of $151,388. By employing that equity at 7.5 percent interest you could enhance your net worth by $238,936 (10.6293 times $22,479) over twenty years!

I usually find it advantageous to refinance my home, as often as every two to five years, and every time I do so, I shorten the timetable to pay off my home. In other words, I give myself the ability to accumulate enough funds to pay off the new, higher mortgage sooner than I would have been able to pay off the former, lower mortgage. This can be true even if I have to borrow at a higher rate of interest than my previous mortgage rate. The last time I refinanced, I had just invested $160,000 into home improvements. I was not only able to recoup my $160,000 but also separate an additional $100,000 of equity from my home and place it into my liquid side fund. I did not improve my interest rate through this refinance; however, I was able to put an additional amount of newly created equity to work. Continually refinancing my home or purchasing new homes in order to take advantage of accumulated equity has allowed me to substantially increase my net worth on that asset by as much as double every five to ten years. This was possible, after I reached the crossover point— the point at which I had the liquid funds needed to pay off my property.

AFTER THE CROSSOVER POINT

Let's study two examples of how you can substantially enhance your net worth on home-equity-generated assets every five to ten years after you have reached the crossover point. When I have enough money in my liquid side funds to totally pay off my mortgage, rather than actually paying them off, I continue to keep my equity separated for liquidity, safety, rate of return, and tax benefits.

Say I have a home valued at $200,000 and have kept all but $40,000 of my equity ($160,000) in a liquid, safe environment from which it could be accessed to pay off the mortgage. So let's assume that I obtain or retain a $160,000 mortgage on the home at 7.5 percent interest. Again, for the sake of simplicity, let's use an interest-only loan rather than an amortized loan. Thus, I really have a net worth on this asset of $200,000; $40,000 of which is in the home and the remaining $160,000 of which is separated from the home.

Let's say the home appreciates an average of 13 percent a year for five years, just like mine did in Salt Lake City, Utah, during the 1990s. The $200,000 home would be worth $368,487 after five years. Let's also assume that the $160,000 of equity I kept separated from the property grows at 8.5 percent interest. At the end of five years it will have grown to $240,585. After deducting the mortgage balance and the employment cost on $160,000 (which would have been approximately $8,000 per year assuming 7.5 percent deductible mortgage interest in a 33.3 percent tax bracket), I would have realized a net profit of $40,585. (For the sake of using round numbers, 7.5 percent gross interest in a 33.3 percent tax bracket equals a net of 5 percent.) I would have realized an enhanced net worth of $209,072. This is the sum of $168,487 of the home appreciation plus the net profit of $40,585 from managing my equity (**fig. 10.3**).

In this first example, the net worth on these assets more than doubled in five years, but this is attributable primarily to phenomenal real estate appreciation.

Let's study a second example (**fig. 10.4**). Let's assume now that the home only appreciates an average of 5 percent a year for ten years. The $200,000 home would be worth $325,779 after ten years—a 63 percent gain. However, after just five years, it would be worth $255,256. At 80 percent loan-to-value, at that point I could borrow approximately an additional $44,000 ($255,256 times 80 percent less the $160,000 existing loan). Therefore, at the start of the second five years I would have $240,585 from managing my equity the first five years in my side fund plus an additional $44,000 of newly separated equity for a total of $284,585 earning interest at 8.5 percent. In the sixth year, I would earn $24,190 in gross interest. If I subtract the new net after-tax employment cost of $10,200 (5 percent of the new loan balance of $204,000), I would realize a net profit that year of $13,990.

By the end of the tenth year I would be earning 8.5 percent on a balance in my side fund of $427,918, which would generate gross earnings that year of $36,373. After deducting the employment cost of $10,200, my net profit that year would be $26,173.

Fig. 10.3	ENHANCEMENT OF NET WORTH THROUGH EQUITY MANAGEMENT						
	[1]	[2]	[3]	[4]	[5]	[6]	[7]
End of Year	Property Value*	Repositioned Equity Accumulation at 8.5%	Employment Cost	Mortgage Balance	Net Profit on Equity	Net Home Appreciation	Enhanced Net Worth
					[2] - [3] - [4]	[1] - 200,000	[5] + [6]
Beginning Values	$200,000	$160,000	Interest Only at 7.5% in 33.3% Tax Bracket	Interest Only			
1	226,000	$173,600	$8,000	$160,000	$ 5,600	$26,000	$31,600
2	255,380	188,356	16,000	160,000	12,356	55,380	67,736
3	288,579	204,366	24,000	160,000	20,366	88,579	108,945
4	326,095	221,737	32,000	160,000	29,737	126,095	155,832
5	368,487	240,585	40,000	160,000	40,585	168,487	209,072

*assuming a 13% appreciation rate

Fig. 10.4

ENHANCEMENT OF NET WORTH THROUGH EQUITY MANAGEMENT

End of Year	[1] Property Value*	[2] Equity Accumulation Balance at 8.5%	[3] Employment Cost Balance	[4] Mortgage Balance	[5] Net Profit on Equity [2] - [3] - [4]	[6] Net Home Appreciation [1] - 200,000	[7] Enhanced Net Worth [5] + [6]
Beginning Values	$200,000	$160,000	Interest Only at 7.5% in 33.3% Tax Bracket	$160,000 Interest Only			
1	$210,000	$173,600	$ 8,000	$ 160,000	$5,600	$10,000	$15,600
2	220,500	188,356	16,000	160,000	12,356	20,500	32,856
3	231,525	204,366	24,000	160,000	20,366	31,525	51,891
4	243,101	221,737	32,000	160,000	29,737	43,101	72,838
5	255,256	240,585	40,000	160,000	40,585	55,256	95,841

*assuming a 5% appreciation rate

2nd Re-Finance End of Year 5

$255,256 at 80% LTV = approx. $204,000 - 160,000 = $44,000
$240,585 + 44,000 = $284,585

End of Year	[1] Property Value*	[2] Equity Accumulation Balance at 8.5%	[3] Annual Increase on Repositioned Equity	[4] Employment Cost Balance	[5] Annual Net Profit [3] - $10,200	[6] Mortgage Balance	[7] Cumulative Net Profit on Equity [2] - [4] - [6]	[8] Total Assets [1] + [2]	[9] Total Assets Minus Liabilities [8] - [6]
Beginning Values	$255,256	$284,585		Interest Only at 7.5% in 33.3% Tax Bracket		$204,000 Interest Only			
6	$268,019	$308,775	$24,190	$10,200	$13,990	$204,000	$ 94,575	$576,794	$372,794
7	281,420	335,021	26,246	20,400	16,046	204,000	110,621	616,441	412,441
8	295,491	363,497	28,476	30,600	18,276	204,000	128,897	658,988	454,988
9	310,265	394,395	30,898	40,800	20,698	204,000	149,595	704,660	500,660
10	325,779	427,918	33,523	60,000	23,323	204,000	163,918	753,697	549,697

From managing my equity for ten years, the liquid side fund in the amount of $427,918 less the mortgage owing of $204,000 results in my side fund's net profit of $223,918. This money accumulated in addition to the house's appreciation realized during that period from $200,000 to $325,779. So my balance sheet would show assets comprised of my home valued at $325,779, plus the cash in my side fund valued at $427,918 for total assets of $753,697. When the liability of the $204,000 mortgage is subtracted from the total assets, it results in a net worth of $549,697. That is more than $2^{1}/_{2}$ times the net worth I had ten years earlier!

If I would have paid the employment cost from the interest earnings each year, rather than leaving my side fund undisturbed, I would have accumulated a net of $417,980. That is more than double the net worth I had on those assets ten years earlier. If I had left my equity dormant in the home, I would have only realized a net worth on that asset of $325,779 strictly from the home appreciation. Instead, by having my equity separated, I was able to realize a 109 percent gain in my net worth on that asset instead of just a 63 percent gain!

Please note if I could have separated and employed 100 percent of my home equity, not just 80 percent, I would have had an additional $40,000 to employ the first year and $55,000 instead of $44,000 after five years. This could have additionally enhanced my net worth during that time period.

SOURCES AND TYPES OF HOME FINANCING

Perhaps by now you're consider refinancing. Let's explore various finance options.

If you own your home free and clear or have a substantial amount of equity, you may consider obtaining a conventional mortgage or home equity loan. An amortized loan provides for repayment of the debt over a specified time period (term) by means of regular payments at specified intervals. A portion of each payment is applied toward principal reduction and the remainder to interest. On the other hand, interest-only loans require that for a certain time period, only the interest that accrues on the loan is payable until the original principal becomes due then requiring either a balloon payment, a refinance, or conversion to an amortized loan.

The mortgage or deed of trust is the written instrument that provides security for payment of a specified debt. A deed of trust transfers title of the property to a third party who holds it until the loan is repaid. The lender has the right to request the property be sold should the borrower default. When the debt is secured by a mortgage, the borrower signs a document that provides the lender a lien against the property. The mortgage note is the borrower's contract with the lender to repay the loan. This promissory note sets the terms and conditions of repayment.

A senior mortgage is the first mortgage recorded, providing the holder with a lien against the property. The senior mortgage has priority over all other liens against the property. The liens held by junior mortgages are subordinate (of a lesser priority) to those which have been filed ahead of them. The lender's risk is directly related to the priority of the mortgage. With greater risk, the lender will demand a higher interest rate.

Mortgage insurance protects the lender against loss should the borrower default and foreclosure become necessary. With conventional loans, the lender will require Private Mortgage Insurance (PMI) on most loans with a loan-to-value ratio greater than 80 percent. FHA loans require Mortgage Insurance Premiums (MIP) on all loans. The VA charges a funding fee on all VA loans rather than mortgage insurance. The insurance is generally purchased by the homeowner at closing. The premium may be paid at closing, over a scheduled time period, or added into the loan amount.

Mortgage companies (mortgage bankers and brokers) include individual investors, banks, insurance companies, and other institutional sources of capital. The mortgage companies generate mortgages and are paid a fee for their services. Historically, commercial banks have been in the business of making short-term loans. Recently they have been making more long-term loans such as mortgages. Credit unions, created for the benefit of their members, also may be a good source for a mortgage. Loan fees and interest rates of credit unions are generally more favorable than those offered by traditional lenders. However the loan terms and the ability to offer first mortgages may be limited with some credit unions. Loans from private sources, such as family members and controlled loans from employers or private pension plans, are considered non-conforming loans that provide additional flexibility.

CONVENTIONAL LOANS

Mortgage loans are divided into two groups: conventional mortgage loans and government loans. A conventional mortgage loan is one that is neither insured, guaranteed, nor funded by the government. Conventional financing is a transaction which takes place strictly between the borrower and the lender. Conventional loans may be obtained from many sources, including banks, credit unions, and mortgage companies. Private loans may also be considered conventional loans.

Most conventional loans allow a maximum loan-to-value of 80 percent to purchase a primary residence. They are also available at 85 to 100 percent loan-to-value when PMI is purchased.

FHA LOANS

The Federal Housing Administration was created by the National Housing Act of 1934 and has since become an integral part of America's housing industry. The FHA has been an innovative force in the mortgage industry with the objective of putting more people into better housing. The FHA does not actually make loans, but rather insures loans made by banks, credit unions, or mortgage companies. Anyone with the ability to repay the loan is eligible. Maximum loan limits are set by the FHA according to the cost of housing within a given area.

All FHA loans must contain mortgage insurance, which is payable as cash in advance or can be financed into the loan. At the time of this book's publication, this one-time premium was approximately equal to 1.5 percent of the loan amount for single family homes, plus an annual mortgage insurance premium of approximately .5 percent of the loan amount, paid monthly.

Closing costs of FHA loans may be financed when a borrower adds a portion of the closing costs to the sales price, or acquisition cost. The actual mortgage is computed on the lesser of acquisition cost or appraised value on any type of loan. The FHA permits the financing of a percentage of "acceptable closing costs" when the buyer pays these costs. Some acceptable closing costs may include:

- origination fee
- appraisal fee
- document preparation fee
- title insurance
- test and treatment required by FHA
- survey
- termite report
- credit report
- home inspection
- recording fees on the mortgage

A homeowner intending to use the cash proceeds on a refinance for purposes unrelated to the property may obtain a mortgage of up to 85 percent of the FHA appraised value of a property occupied by the owner.

VA LOANS

The VA loan benefit program was created by Congress in 1942 to help veterans who have given service to our country. As with the FHA program, the Veteran's Administration does not make loans, but guarantees loans made by private lenders to eligible veterans. A veteran may borrow 100 percent of the purchase price, up to a specified limit. The federal government determines how much a veteran may borrow through the use of "entitlement." Entitlement is determined by length of time spent in the service and is adjusted by the VA periodically as housing prices increase. The maximum loan amount is determined by multiplying the amount of entitlement by four. Veterans may reinstate previously used entitlement by paying the loan in full or selling the property and having the VA loan assumed by a qualified eligible veteran who will occupy the property, and who agrees to substitute his own entitlement. When a portion of but not all entitlement is used to purchase a home, remaining entitlement may be used to purchase subsequent homes used as primary residences.

Veterans desiring to secure a VA loan must have served a predetermined number of days on active status. If you are a veteran interested in a VA loan, see your lender or contact the Veteran's Administration for more information. The form required to obtain a Certificate of Eligibility is VA-DD214. Unremarried veteran surviving spouses are eligible for a VA loan if the veteran died while on active duty (service-related), or after a service-connected discharge. Regular refinancing mortgages permit the veteran to borrow up to 90 percent of the Certificate of Reasonable Value (CRV). The home must be owner-occupied in order to obtain cash proceeds. A VA loan is sometimes referred to as a G.I. loan.

FEDERAL MORTGAGE ASSOCIATIONS

While investigating or securing a mortgage, you may have heard terms such as "Fannie Mae," "Ginnie Mae," or "Freddie Mac." Fannie Mae is a nickname for the Federal National Mortgage Association (FNMA) which is a private organization (originally chartered by the federal government) that purchases mortgages, predominantly from mortgage bankers. Ginnie Mae is a nickname for the Government National Mortgage Association (GNMA), a government program that assists in the financing of homes by purchasing mortgages from primary lenders. GNMA's purchase of these loans provides primary lenders additional money to lend for other home purchases. Freddie Mac is a nickname for Federal Home Loan Mortgage Corporation (FHLMC), an organization that was created to purchase mortgages, primarily from savings and loans.

I will briefly explain three general types of mortgage programs: 1) fixed-rate mortgages, 2) adjustable-rate mortgages, and 3) balloon mortgages. I will discuss reverse mortgages in detail in chapter 14.

FIXED-RATE MORTGAGES

Fixed-rate mortgages are quite simple. The interest rates are fixed and the payments are fixed. Fixed-rate mortgages are usually amortized over either fifteen or thirty years. For example, a $150,000 loan at 8 percent over a thirty-year amortization has a fixed monthly principal and interest payment of $1,100.65. The monthly principal and interest payment does not vary unless late payment interest and/or penalties are incurred. If the lender wants to make sure taxes and home insurance are always current, the payment required by the mortgage company will include those in escrow. The tax and insurance portion of the monthly mortgage may vary each year depending upon those rates. However, the sum of the principal and interest (PI) will be constant with a fixed rate mortgage.

ADJUSTABLE-RATE MORTGAGES

Adjustable-rate mortgages are loans on which the interest rate may adjust over the life of the loan. ARMs were created during periods of high interest rates in an attempt to make housing more affordable. ARMs allow for lower qualifying incomes because of the initially lower interest rates. Lenders are not risking being locked into long-term fixed loans at interest rates which could be well below their cost of funds. Therefore, they may offer ARMs at rates below the current fixed-rate mortgages. As a trade-off for the lower initial interest rate, the borrower bears the burden of increasing rates in the future. In order to determine the amount of adjustments, interest rates in ARMs are tied to one of many interest-rate adjustment indexes that represent the general movement in interest rates. Lenders then add percentage points, referred to as the "margin," to the index to determine the adjustable rate.

Interest-rate caps limit the changes in the interest rate. The periodic rate cap limits the adjustments during a stated time period. For example, the period rate cap might limit the rate change within a year to 2 percent. If the initial rate was 7 percent, the second year rate could not exceed 9 percent after adjustment. The aggregate (total) rate cap limits the rate changes over the entire life of the loan. For example, the loan might have an aggregate rate cap of 5 percent. If the initial loan rate was 6 percent, the highest interest rate the loan could ever reach would be 11 percent.

The payment cap limits the changes in the monthly payment amount. Even though the interest rate can increase, the increase in the monthly payment amount may be limited by the loan's payment cap. If this occurs, the monthly payments will not increase to the level necessary to fully repay the loan within the agreed term. This deficiency may be made up by either increasing the term of the loan, making additional lump sum payment(s), or increasing future monthly payments. The payment cap in some loans must be adequate to pay at least the interest owed on the outstanding loan balance. This prevents the loan balance from actually increasing during periods of high interest rates.

The conversion option allows an ARM to be changed to a fixed rate mortgage without the normal expenses of refinancing. A flat fee, or a certain number of points, is usually charged to exercise this option, and it must be exercised during a specified time period—usually between the thirteenth and sixtieth month. (Note: Be sure to check with your lender to determine how the fixed rate is calculated *before* securing this type of loan for the conversion option feature.)

The Federal Trade Commission suggests careful consideration of the following when shopping for an adjustable-rate mortgage:

1) initial interest rate;
2) how often the rate may change;
3) how much the rate may change;
4) initial monthly payments;
5) how often payments may change;
6) how much payments may change;
7) mortgage term;
8) how often the term may change;
9) index to which the rate, payment, and term changes are tied;
10) and limits, if any, on negative amortization.

BALLOON-PAYMENT MORTGAGES

Balloon payment mortgages usually have interest rates that are fixed. The payments are also fixed and may apply only to the interest. After a specified period of time, a substantial payment of principal, called the balloon, is due. The balloon is typically the final payment of a loan and may include both accumulated interest and principal. Loans with a balloon payment provision may be amortized over a traditional mortgage term (fifteen or thirty years) for the purposes of determining the monthly payment amount. However, the payments may be smaller than a traditional mortgage payment until the balloon payment comes due. Homeowners using a mortgage with a balloon payment feature need to prepare well in advance for the balloon payment due date.

Let me now briefly address two other considerations: buy-downs and a negative amortization. A buy-down is a sum of money paid to the lender at closing in exchange for a reduction in the interest rate of the mortgage loan. As a result, the monthly payments will be lower, allowing the borrower to qualify for a loan. Buy-downs may be temporary or permanent. A temporary buy-down decreases the interest rate for only a short time period—usually the first one to three years—after which the interest rate will return to its original amount for the duration of the loan. A permanent buy-down will reduce the interest rate over the entire term of the loan. Negative amortization is the process of adding unpaid interest to the principal balance of the loan. Negative amortization can occur over the entire term of the loan, or it may occur at unspecified intervals, depending on the mortgage. Negative amortization occurs when the payment is not sufficient to cover the interest being charged.

DETERMINING THE BEST TYPE OF MORTGAGE TO USE

Whether it's to reduce monthly payments, consolidate monthly payments, free up equity to conserve rather than consume, or manage equity as described in this book, homeowners face a variety of options for tapping into available equity. Borrowers can choose to refinance their existing mortgage, apply for a second mortgage or establish a home equity line of credit. Depending on the option selected, you will need to decide whether to opt for a fixed-rate or a variable-rate mortgage.

The best financing plan for a homeowner using the equity management strategies contained in this book will depend on factors such as:

- ability to make monthly payments;
- amount of equity available;
- interest rate on the current mortgage;
- and expected length of residence in the current home.

Those with mortgages at below-market interest rates may not want to refinance that debt. A second mortgage or home equity loan might be more appropriate. In addition to preserving an attractive interest rate on the first mortgage, this strategy usually results in lowering or even eliminating closing costs.

Homeowners with above-market rates of interest on their first mortgages may choose to refinance with a new first mortgage at current rates. This reduces the cost on the balance of their existing mortgage and allows them to obtain a lower interest rate on the additional equity they may be accessing.

Fixed-rate mortgages have been more appealing for many homeowners due to the certainty of monthly payment amounts. However, this can be the more expensive route for those homeowners who move within four or five years. Adjustable-rate mortgages offer lower interest rates than fixed mortgages, and due to their annual and lifetime interest rate caps, will likely be more economical during the first few years even if interest rates increase dramatically. Interest-only balloon payment mortgages might also be considered by those desiring lower payments, wanting to maximize tax deductions, and planning to relocate within a few years. For individuals planning to remain in their homes for longer than five years, a fixed-rate mortgage can offer greater certainty and protection against high interest rates.

Here I have only given some general items to consider when choosing a particular type of mortgage. The financing option most appropriate for a specific homeowner will vary depending on these and other factors. Consultations with competent professional financial services representatives and mortgage loan officers can assist you with the mortgage selection process.

DETERMINING WHEN IT IS WISE TO REFINANCE

Often, homeowners perform a simple exercise to determine whether it is wise to refinance their homes. The old rule of thumb used to be if you can improve your interest rate by 2 percentage points or better, then it is wise to refinance. **Figure 10.5** illustrates a typical three-step exercise often used by homeowners considering a refinance. Step A is designed to

Why is this common exercise invalid?

Fig. 10.5	SHOULD YOU REFINANCE YOUR HOME?

$100,000 30-year fixed mortgage, refinancing from 9.0% to 7.0%

STEP

A *What will it cost?*
Call a mortgage company or banking institution

		Example	Your Mortgage
Total Points	0.5 pts	$ 500.00	_____
Appraisal Fee		350.00	_____
Title Insurance		363.00	_____
Other Fees		2,287.00	_____
Add for TOTAL		3,500.00	_____

STEP

B *What will your monthly savings be?*

	Example	Your Mortgage
Current Monthly Payments *Principal and Interest*	$804.62	_____
New Mortgage Monthly Payments *Principal and Interest*	665.30	_____
Subtract for TOTAL	$139.32	_____

STEP

C *How long will it take to recoup refinancing costs?*
(Divide step A total by step B total)

	Example	Your Mortgage
TOTAL COST of Refinancing *Step A*	$3,500.00	_____
TOTAL Monthly Savings *Step B*	139.32	_____
ANSWER:	25	_____

help you decide what a new mortgage will cost. Step B is designed to help you calculate what your monthly savings will be. Step C is supposed to determine how long it will take to recoup your closing costs by dividing step A by step B.

Let's assume you are considering a refinance of your current mortgage in the amount of $100,000 from 9 percent interest down to 7 percent interest. All of the refinance costs—discount points, appraisal fees, title insurance, origination fees, and other costs—are totaled up. Let's say they total $3,500. A current thirty-year amortized mortgage of $100,000 at 9 percent interest would have a monthly payment of $804.62, whereas a new thirty-year mortgage of $100,000 at 7 percent interest would have a monthly payment of $665.30. The difference between the two monthly payments equals $139.32. Thus, $3,500 divided by $139.32 equals twenty-five months. This supposedly means that it will take twenty-five months to recoup your closing costs.

After learning about opportunity costs, true after-tax interest costs, and the power of positive leverage, is this exercise valid? Absolutely not! If this were the only formula used to determine whether a homeowner would be wise to refinance, the homeowner would be missing out on opportunities to accelerate the process of getting out of debt and dramatically enhancing net worth.

Let's assume this person was tempted to refinance the current mortgage of $100,000 to lower the interest rate and to accelerate the payoff. He decides to refinance using a fifteen-year mortgage term (**fig. 10.6**). A fifteen-year $100,000 amortized mortgage at 7 percent would have a monthly payment of $898.83 (principal and interest). This equals total house payments of $10,786 per year. His mortgage interest for the first year is $6,876. In a 34 percent marginal tax bracket, he would save $2,338 in taxes. The difference between the total annual mortgage payments and the tax savings results in a net annual mortgage payment of $8,448. Therefore, using a fifteen-year mortgage, he is not using his partner (Uncle Sam) to the fullest extent.

Let's assume his home appraises for at least $187,500 so he can also qualify for a cash-out refinance of a $150,000 thirty-year mortgage

Fig. 10.6	15-YEAR MORTGAGE ANALYSIS					

Principal $100,000   *Rate* 7.00%
Balance $100,000   *Type* Amortized
Payment $898.83   *Years* 15

END OF YEAR	[1] LOAN BALANCE	[2] PRINCIPAL PAYMENT	[3] INTEREST PAYMENT	[4] TOTAL PAYMENT	[5] TAX SAVINGS	[6] NET PAYMENT AFTER TAX
1	$96,090	$3,910	**$6,876**	**$10,786**	**$2,338**	**$8,448**
2	91,898	4,192	6,593	10,786	2,242	8,544
3	87,402	4,496	6,290	10,786	2,139	8,647
4	82,582	4,821	5,965	10,786	2,028	8,758
5	77,413	5,169	5,617	10,786	1,910	8,876
6	71,870	5,543	5,243	10,786	1,783	9,003
7	65,927	5,943	4,843	10,786	1,646	9,139
8	59,554	6,373	4,413	10,786	1,500	9,286
9	52,720	6,834	3,952	10,786	1,344	9,442
10	45,392	7,328	3,458	10,786	1,176	9,610
11	37,535	7,857	2,929	10,786	996	9,790
12	29,109	8,425	2,361	10,786	803	9,983
13	20,075	9,035	1,751	10,786	595	10,190
14	10,387	9,688	1,098	10,786	373	10,41
15	0	10,387	398	10,785	135	10,650
TOTAL	**$100,000**	**$61,789**	**$161,789**	**$21,008**	**$140,781**	

Notes:
a. Tax Savings [5] assumes a state and federal marginal tax bracket of 34.00%
multiplied by the interest payment [3].
b. Mortgage interest is generally tax deductible, however, certain limitations are applicable.
Please review with your tax advisor.
c. Net Payment After Tax [6] equals Total Payment [4] less Tax Savings [5].

(**fig. 10.7**). Its monthly payment would be $997.95, which appears to be about $100 more per month. His annualized house payments would be $11,975. His mortgage interest for the first year would be $10,452 using a thirty-year amortization. In a 34 percent tax bracket, he would save $3,554 in taxes. The difference between the total annualized mortgage payments and the tax savings results in a net annualized mortgage payment of $8,422. This is no more than the fifteen-year $100,000 mortgage he was considering!

By having an additional $50,000 of dormant equity separated from his home, he has increased the liquidity, safety, rate of return and maxi-

Fig. 10.7	30-YEAR MORTGAGE ANALYSIS

Principal	$150,000	Rate	7.00%
Balance	$150,000	Type	Amortized
Payment	$997.95	Years	30

END OF YEAR	[1] LOAN BALANCE	[2] PRINCIPAL PAYMENT	[3] INTEREST PAYMENT	[4] TOTAL PAYMENT	[5] TAX SAVINGS	[6] NET PAYMENT AFTER TAX
1	$148,476	$1,524	$10,452	$11,975	$3,554	$8,422
2	146,843	1,634	10,342	11,975	3,516	8,459
3	145,091	1,752	10,223	11,975	3,476	8,499
4	143,212	1,879	10,097	11,975	3,433	8,542
5	141,198	2,014	9,961	11,975	3,387	8,589
6	139,038	2160	9,815	11,975	3,337	8,638
7	136,722	2,316	9,659	11,975	3,284	8,691
8	134,238	2,484	9,492	11,975	3,227	8,748
9	131,575	2,663	9,312	11,975	3,166	8,809
10	128,719	2,856	9,120	11,975	3,101	8,875
11	125,657	3,062	8,913	11,975	3,030	8,945
12	122,374	3,283	8,692	11,975	2,955	9,020
13	118,853	3,521	8,455	11,975	2,875	9,101
14	115,078	3,775	8,200	11,975	2,788	9,187
15	111,029	4,048	7,927	11,975	2,695	9,280
16	106,689	4,341	7,635	11,975	2,596	9,380
17	102,034	4,655	7,321	11,975	2,489	9,486
18	97,043	4,991	6,984	11,975	2,375	9,601
19	91,691	5,352	6,623	11,975	2,252	9,723
20	85,952	5,739	6,237	11,975	2,121	9,855
21	79,798	6,154	5,822	11,975	1,979	9,996
22	73,200	6,599	5,377	11,975	1,828	10,147
23	66,124	7,076	4,900	11,975	1,666	10,309
24	58,537	7,587	4,388	11,975	1,492	10,483
25	50,402	8,136	3,840	11,975	1,306	10,670
26	41,678	8,724	3,252	11,975	1,106	10,870
27	32,324	9,354	2,621	11,975	891	11,084
28	22,293	10,031	1,945	11,975	661	11,314
29	11,537	10,756	1,220	11,975	415	11,561
30	0	11,537	442	11,980	150	11,829
TOTAL		$150,000	$209,266	$359,266	$71,151	$288,116

Notes:

a. Tax Savings [5] assumes a state and federal marginal tax bracket of 34.00% multiplied by the interest payment [3].

b. Mortgage interest is generally tax deductible, however, certain limitations are applicable. Please review with your tax advisor.

c. Net Payment After Tax [6] equals Total Payment [4] less Tax Savings [5].

mized his tax deductions. What will his financial picture be in fifteen years? If he achieved an average annual return of 8.5 percent on his $50,000, it would grow to $169,987! His mortgage balance would be $111,029. Therefore, he would have made an extra $58,958 without increasing his monthly outlay. Keep in mind this example assumes that he never refinances again during that fifteen-year period to manage the equity that accrues by virtue of his home appreciating. Even if he had to pay tax in the amount of $40,796 on the gain from $50,000 to $169,987 (a total of $119,987) he would have ended up with $129,191 of liquid cash with only a mortgage balance owing in the fifteen-year example of $111,029, leaving him a net of $18,162 profit!

Finally, let's study the scenarios of two couples, the Smiths and the Clarks, who each received $160,000 of equity from the sale of their previous homes (**fig. 10.8**). The Smiths took $160,000 and applied it as a down payment into a new home purchased at $200,000, because they had the misconception equity from a former home had to be invested into the new home to avoid capital gain tax (see chapter 12). They took out a $40,000 interest-only mortgage. Ten years later let's assume the house only has appreciated at about 4 percent a year on average. So it's worth $300,000 in the tenth year. The home value of $300,000, less the

Fig. 10.8	FINANCE OPTIONS	
SMITHS		**CLARKS**
$ 200,000	Home Value	$ 200,000
- 160,000	Down Payment	- 40,000
$ 40,000	Mortgage	$ 160,000
	10 YEARS LATER	
$ 300,000	Home Value	$ 300,000
- 40,000	Mortgage	- 160,000
$ 260,000	New Equity	$ 140,000
- 160,000	Less Down Payment	- 40,000
$ 100,000	Gain	$ 100,000

outstanding mortgage balance of $40,000, less the down payment or original equity of $160,000, results in a $100,000 gain.

On the other hand, the Clarks buy a $200,000 home, only put 20 percent down ($40,000), and take out a $160,000 interest-only mortgage. Ten years later, in the same circumstances as the Smiths, their home is also worth $300,000, less the mortgage balance of $160,000, less the down payment or original equity of $40,000. That equals the same $100,000 gain!

Why are the answers the same? Because we learned in chapter 5 that equity has no rate of return. However, let me ask the question: "Who had the better net internal rate of return?" The Clarks did, because they only tied up $40,000 of their own money to make $100,000. The Smiths tied up $160,000 of their own money to make the same $100,000.

Let's consider the many other differences between the two couples. First of all, let's address the seemingly negative aspect head on. What do the Clarks have that the Smiths don't have? A higher mortgage payment! The Clarks have a principal and interest mortgage payment of $1,174 a month (assuming 8 percent fixed interest on a thirty-year amortization) whereas the Smiths only have a mortgage payment of $293.51. That's a difference of $881 per month! However, what else do the Clarks have that the Smiths do not have? A larger tax deduction! The Clarks have $12,800 in tax deductions. The Smiths only have $3,200 in tax deductions. The difference is that the Clarks have $9,600 more tax deductions, meaning they will save $3,264 more in taxes in the first full year (and each subsequent year thereafter) than the Smiths. (The Smiths only save 34 percent of $3,200, which equals $1,088, while the Clarks save 34 percent of $12,800, which equals $4,352). That equals an average of $272 per month they can get back from Uncle Sam. So, the Clark's real net house payment is only about $900 a month, not $1,174 a month. The true difference between the monthly mortgage of the Smiths and the Clarks is approximately $700 a month. As explained in chapters 7, 8, and 9, why would I be willing to pay $700 more? Because the $160,000 that I have employed is working for me and has the ability to compound and grow to a much greater value than the net monthly cost of $700.

The very first year, at 8 percent interest, the Clarks can earn an average of $1,066 a month on $160,000 while paying only a difference of $700 a month higher payment. The net profit is $366 a month or $4,400 per year!

Can you begin to see why the Clarks will have enough money to pay off or cover their $160,000 mortgage much sooner than the Smiths will be able to pay off their $40,000 mortgage using the same dollars? The Clarks have $160,000 of liquid cash to use as an emergency fund, to put in a yard or finish their basement, thereby increasing the value of their home without having to qualify to borrow to perform these improvements. What are some other advantages? The Clarks have greater safety of principal in down markets because a larger portion of equity is separated. The Clarks also have greater property portability by being able to possibly sell their home more quickly and for a higher price in a soft market (see chapter 11). They can also convert some of their non-preferred debt to preferred or deductible debt, thereby increasing the return on their money using that strategy.

The Clarks also may qualify for other benefits by virtue of having a larger mortgage and less equity trapped in their home. For example, there have been instances in the past where parents applied for college grants for their children and were rejected—not because they earned too much income, but because they had too much equity in the home, deemed as discretionary dollars. They were told to borrow on their home to pay for their children to attend college. When home equity is separated, depending on where it is repositioned, parents may qualify for certain benefits and grants because those equity dollars may not be classified as discretionary after repositioning.

Of all these benefits, however, probably the greatest and most dynamic benefit the Clarks have over the Smiths is the ability to establish a home equity retirement plan, which can increase their net spendable retirement income by as much as 50 percent over their IRAs and 401(k)s (see chapter 19).

By now, you should see there are more factors to consider when refinancing a home than just interest rates and closing costs. A homeowner can effectively reduce the time to achieve a "debt-free" home on his balance sheet and dramatically enhance net worth through strategic refinancing and proper management of his home equity.

Remember the purpose of managing equity is to conserve and enhance it, not to consume it. The primary reason to consider refinancing every two to five years is always to separate as much equity as possible in order to:

1) increase its liquidity
2) enhance its safety
3) increase its rate of return
4) keep the home more portable
5) maximize tax deductions

10 WEALTH-ENHANCEMENT STRATEGY NUMBER TEN

- *Set the stage to substantially increase the net worth on your assets.*
- *Refinance your home as often as feasible to separate equity and accelerate the process of accumulating the resources to cover all your debts.*

CHAPTER 11

Selling Your Home Effectively

Keep your mortgage balance high to sell your home
more quickly—and for a higher price!

The amount of equity you have in your home has no bearing
on how marketable it is.

REALITY

*Your home may likely sell much more quickly and for a higher
price if it has a high mortgage balance (low equity)—rather than
a low mortgage or no mortgage balance (high equity)—especially
in soft real estate markets.*

S ince beginning my financial and estate planning practice in 1974, I have found the overwhelming majority of American home-owners believe the amount of equity in a home has no bearing on how marketable it is. In reality, a home may likely sell more quickly and for a higher price if it has a high mortgage balance, especially in a soft real estate market. In such markets, you may find yourself very frustrated if you are trying to sell a home with a low mortgage balance. You may not even realize how trying to sell such a home may limit your market of potential buyers. This is probably one of the most difficult concepts to understand about home selling and buying, and it is directly affected by the real estate market at the time of sale.

THE SELLER'S PERSPECTIVE

Let's say there are two people, each with identical homes valued at $200,000. All amenities and features of these two homes are fairly equal. These two homeowners live on the same street in the same neighbor-hood. One day, because each is relocating to another state, these indi-viduals need to sell their homes within sixty to ninety days. Both mis-takenly believe they need to use the equity out of their current homes for a down payment on a new home. The market they are trying to sell their homes in has gone soft—buyers rule the roost because the supply of homes is greater than the demand.

These individuals' situations differ only in one respect: Hal has a $40,000 mortgage balance and all the remaining $160,000 of equity trapped in his home; Rosa has a $160,000 mortgage on her home, (she refinanced recently at 80 percent loan-to-value and invested $120,000 of the net mortgage proceeds—$160,000 less the former mortgage of $40,000—in a liquid side fund, leaving the remaining $40,000 of equity in her home). Really, each homeowner has the same $160,000 of equity at this point, but it is located in different places. Rosa has $120,000 in a liquid side fund with the remaining $40,000 in the property. Hal has $160,000 of equity in the property itself.

Several prospective buyers may come to look at both homes and realize they are almost identical. Many among those buyers may themselves be relocating and looking to purchase a home without having established employment—either with a firm or as self-employed business owners—long enough to be able to secure a mortgage. (Keep in mind many mortgage lenders will not loan money until a client has been established in a new job for at least six months to a year.) Some potential buyers may be financially able to handle a mortgage payment, but might be waiting for their former homes to sell in the area from which they have moved.

If you were the homeowner who only had a $40,000 mortgage, you would most likely feel comfortable selling your home to buyers who had already sold their previous homes or who had the ability to borrow enough money to cash you out. However, there would likely be many other qualified homebuyers willing to buy your home on contract if you could take some type of down payment or deposit, say at 10 or 20 percent the value of the home. They may even be willing to rent or lease it from you (with an option to buy) for a six- or twelve-month period until they are able to come up with the balance by qualifying for a mortgage or selling their previous home. You would be eliminating these potential buyers, restricting yourself to only those who had the ability to cash you out of your property at the time of sale.

Why are banks and investors that supply funds for loans so willing to invest in mortgage contracts? It's because these investments are deemed safe. In addition, FHA and VA loans are insured by the federal government. As I indicated before, homes generally appreciate in value over time, and thus a lender's investment becomes more and more secure as time passes. If a mortgage banker feels secure loaning you 80 percent of the value of your home, shouldn't you be thrilled at the chance to receive, from a buyer, some or all of the remaining 20 percent of the value of your home? You should, especially if that person made a contractual promise to either pay off your mortgage within a certain time frame, or allow you to keep the money they had already paid you. The money the borrower gave you as a down payment would be legally yours should they default (not make the agreed upon monthly payments) on this $200,000 asset!

Furthermore, during the life of the contract, *you* could then be receiving some of the interest instead of a mortgage company.

THE BUYER'S PERSPECTIVE

Up to now, we have been discussing the seller's perspective. For a moment, imagine you are in the market to buy, instead of to sell, a home. If you were self-employed and relocating to a new state, you would discover that because of your change in employment, it would be difficult to obtain a mortgage for at least six months, maybe even two years. You might have a lot of capital but would probably need to use it in the establishment of your new business. You may be waiting for your previous home to sell before being able to finalize a deal for a new home.

If you were to come across the two identical homes described earlier, you might first approach Hal who had only a $40,000 mortgage with all of his equity tied up in his property. You might offer that homeowner a $20,000 or even $40,000 down payment and ask if he would be willing to carry a contract or allow you to rent or to lease with an option to buy. He would probably be hesitant to do so, preferring to be cashed out on all his equity to buy a new home in the new location. Thus, he would probably turn down your offer.

You could next go to the other homeowner—Rosa who had a $160,000 mortgage. You might ask Rosa to consider accepting a $20,000 or $40,000 down payment with a contract to pay the balance in six months to a year, or perhaps to allow you to lease with an option to buy. That homeowner would likely be much more willing to accept the $20,000 to $40,000 down payment because she already had the other $120,000 of her equity in a side fund! She would have already received all, or nearly all, of her equity out of the home. Moreover, if you were to move into the home, then, at some point later, happen to default, she would have the right to foreclose on the home as per the trust deed note. In the event of foreclosure, she would be able to turn around and sell the property again, having pocketed a $20,000 to $40,000 profit! Not that anyone would wish someone else to lose a home, but this example vividly illustrates a lender's position of security when able to use a home as collateral for a loan.

If you were to default on a payment, would Rosa worry? No, not if she didn't make the mistake of putting all of her equity into her new home rather than keeping it separate in a liquid side fund. She could easily peel off a monthly payment out of the side fund to cover the mortgage until she foreclosed on you.

To conclude, Rosa with a $160,000 mortgage balance may accept the earnest money and sell the home to you. You may be willing to pay not only top dollar for the home, but perhaps a premium because she was willing to carry the contract for a while. In the meantime, Hal may get so discouraged because of his restrictions on potential homebuyers, he may lower the price of his home—first to $190,000, then to $180,000, then $160,000 or even $150,000—whatever necessary to find someone to cash him out of the home.

PUTTING IT ALL TOGETHER

Once, I owned a condominium as a rental income property, which I had purchased using a lease with an option-to-buy contract. When I put it in the newspaper to sell, I had only one or two inquiries the first thirty days. Then I realized the existing mortgage was an assumable loan. So, I changed the ad to read "assumable loan at 7.5 percent interest with 10 percent down payment." I received over twenty calls from interested parties in the next thirty days!

Let me illustrate this concept further using another personal example. In 1990 I negotiated the purchase of a beautiful, 7,600-square-foot home on a half-acre piece of property in a nicely wooded subdivision. The home had been built by the owners four years previously, and they had invested over $450,000 into its construction, including improvements and beautiful landscaping. The home's neighborhood was an affluent planned-unit development with large, mature trees. It boasted a community park, which included a common-area swimming pool and a tennis court. Only 5,000 square feet of the home was finished, nonetheless, in a strong real estate market two years earlier, the home had appraised for $505,000. Then, an interstate freeway was constructed adjacent to the south boundary of the property. The homeowners had known the interstate would be constructed when they built the home, but because of the forest and mature trees, they could not imagine the freeway would eliminate all of that serenity. Nevertheless, after the freeway's construction, the home and its neighborhood experienced a property devaluation with the resulting noise pollution.

At the time I began negotiating a purchase of the home, these homeowners were anxious to move back to a neighborhood close to where they had once lived, allowing them to reunite with former friends. In this new neighborhood, they had planned, designed, and wanted to build a beautiful new home with a private swimming pool and landscaped yard. They were anxious to see their plans come to fruition.

Unfortunately, because of the construction of the interstate and a soft real estate market, larger homes were not selling for the values they had appraised for only a year or so earlier. Worse, these homeowners had put the equity from their former homes into this home and had been making triple mortgage payments to rapidly pay down the mortgage. The mortgage balance owing at the time I entered the picture was approximately $105,000; about $400,000 of equity was tied up in the property (based on the $505,000 valuation at the highest peak in the market). When the homeowners first put the home on the real estate market, they had tried to sell it for $450,000 to $500,000 and had been unable to find any qualified buyers who were willing to pay that price, with the exception of those who had offered to buy the home on some type of contract with a small or low down payment.

If you were the seller of this home, would you be anxious to sell the property on contract with $400,000 of equity tied up in the property? I wouldn't. If I needed the equity to build a new home, I would not be comfortable selling a current home on contract for only $50,000 or $100,000 down, then face the burden of carrying that individual through the contract.

My understanding is that many offers were made but rejected because the homeowners would not or could not carry a contract with so much equity trapped in the home. They instead kept the home on the market and continued lowering the selling price of the home in hopes of attracting a qualified buyer to purchase it outright.

When I came across the property in early 1990, it was advertised in a local real estate magazine found in many grocery stores. I noticed the home had been reduced drastically in price in order to sell. The home owners were asking approximately $319,000 so they could net $300,000 after realtor's fees. The ad also stated the home had earlier been appraised at $505,000. I could tell the sellers were highly motivated to sell their home.

My wife and I toured the home and found it to be in excellent condition—well built and well maintained. The home definitely was worth the $505,000 valuation, but only after the market recovered again. In the backyard, the interstate noise was irritating. The homeowners were anxious to sell the property because of this noise, but I felt we could take care of the problem with strategic improvements. (As a side note, a few years after we purchased the home, we built a 100-foot stream along the freeway fence, complete with five waterfalls and two fishponds. The stream recycled 365 days a year and the waterfalls drowned out the freeway noise. This improvement required an investment on our part of approximately $10,000, whereupon our home immediately went up in market value $50,000.)

At that time, my wife and I had been set on constructing a new home. The house plans were all ready. However, it was apparent in the soft market, an expenditure of $300,000 or $400,000 in the construction of a new home might exceed the final appraisal. Because the supply was so much greater than the demand, prices on existing homes had plummeted lower than the cost of constructing new ones. So, my wife and I set aside our desire to build a new home and resigned ourselves to finding a good deal on an existing home.

I made an offer on the home for $300,000, including a condition allowing the homeowners to continue living in the home for the nine months they were constructing their new home, saving them the unpleasant hassle of having to move twice.

The homeowners accepted and my wife and I purchased the home for $300,000 with no down payment (see chapter 13). I had the home appraised in that soft market with two separate appraisals (one was SRA certified and the other MAI certified). One appraisal came in at $382,000 and the other at $382,500 in spite of the bordering interstate freeway.

I am grateful to the seller because of the beautiful home we acquired at an excellent price. In turn, I was able to cash out the homeowners using OPM, which money they received gratefully, as their home had been on the market for a year and a half. With money in hand, they were able to move ahead in building their new home; however, as a result of the market, a great deal of the sellers' equity was relinquished to and eventually realized by the subsequent owners (my wife and me).

The former homeowners were also grateful we allowed them to stay and rent the home from us for the nine-month period in which they constructed their new home. For us, that rent made the monthly house payment in full.

The point I want to make here is because they had all their equity tied up in the property, these homeowners had not been able to sell their home as they wished. Much higher offers had previously been made before mine, but because of the lack of liquidity in their home equity, they lowered the price of the home dramatically. Neither was this experience unique. During 1990, in Salt Lake City, Utah, many other homes were for sale in the soft market. Often, the large homes that sold more quickly and for higher prices were those with a high mortgage balance and little equity, rather than vice versa.

Many people have come to me in frustration because they couldn't sell their homes quickly enough for what they have felt they were worth. Often I have advised them to take out brand new mortgages with the maximum cash out on their refinance. Then they advertise their homes much more attractively by stating "owner will carry contract," or "seller financing," or "assumable loan." These people can't believe the response they get from potential homebuyers interested in purchasing their homes. They are able to get their equity out of their homes and the closing costs of the mortgage are usually more than compensated because they didn't have to lower the selling price. Each of these carrots that can be dangled when selling a home comes with the caveat the buyer needs to make a 10 to 20 percent down payment or possibly be required to qualify under an assumption. Also, the seller needs to be aware of such things as "due on sale" clauses that may exist in some mortgage contracts. In those cases, creative sales and financing arrangements may need to be used.

When refinancing your home, consider loans that have assumption options. An assumable loan is one that may allow a subsequent purchaser of your house to "take over" or assume the loan obligation of the seller. However, the original borrower (seller) usually remains liable for the debt unless the lender agrees to a release. The reasons why you may sell your home easier with an assumable loan are:

- the assumable mortgage could be below market interest rates;
- it will likely be for a reduced term;
- there will likely be reduced closing costs;
- it may require a lower down payment;
- and buyers with poor credit may more easily purchase a home.

A non-qualifying assumption (also called a blind or simple assumption) occurs when the purchaser is allowed to assume the mortgage obligation without the lender's investigation of the buyer's income, credit, and financial status. The lender will generally charge a processing fee to transfer an assumable loan. The most common non-qualifying mortgages are older loans insured by either the Federal Housing Administration or Veteran's Administration (FHA loans made prior to December 15, 1989 and VA loans made prior to March 1, 1988).

In order to assume a qualifying loan (FHA loans originating after December 15, 1989 and VA loans made after March 1, 1988), the buyer must apply to the lending institution. The buyer is allowed to assume the loan only if the mortgage holder approves the application. The buyer will then be charged a processing fee, which may be as high as $1^{1}/_{2}$ percent of the remaining loan balance.

The original mortgage borrower may remain financially responsible for the loan even after a new buyer has assumed the loan. However, a seller can often obtain a release of liability from the lender. The original borrower applies to the lender and upon acceptance is released from any liability in the event the subsequent borrower defaults.

Non-assumable loans may have a "due on sale" clause which requires the seller to repay the loan in full upon the actual sale of the property. Therefore, leasing your home to someone with an option for them to buy it later may be an alternative solution.

11 WEALTH-ENHANCEMENT STRATEGY NUMBER ELEVEN

- *Always maintain as high a mortgage—with flexibility—on your home as feasible to keep it marketable at the highest possible price should you want to sell the property.*

Freeing Yourself From

Traditional Money Traps

and Tax Traps

CHAPTER 12

What Is the IRS Really Saying?

Don't lose out on thousands of dollars—understand what
the IRS is actually saying!

COMMON MYTH-CONCEPTION

To avoid capital gains tax, you have to use as much as
possible of the cash proceeds from the sale of a previous
residence in purchasing a new home.

REALITY

*Under the Taxpayer Relief Act of 1997, a married taxpayer may
exclude up to $500,000 (up to $250,000 if unmarried) of the gain
on the sale of a principal residence. This exclusion can be used
once every two years. Not one dime of equity from the former
home needs to be put into the newer home to avoid taxation.*

For years I have taught seminars on the topic of successfully managing equity. Invariably, when asked how many think as much equity as possible from the sale of a previous home needs to be put into a new home to avoid a long-term capital gains tax, the vast majority of attendees raises their hands. Even after the Taxpayer Relief Act of 1997, this continues to be a common misconception.

Occasionally, I find homeowners who hold back $10,000 or $20,000 of equity from the sale of their previous homes and feel like they are "getting away with something." They hope they are not caught, thinking they would otherwise have to pay a capital gains tax on the portion they held back. Let's look at a number of issues regarding tax law misconceptions.

THE PRE-1997 LAW

Even prior to the 1997 Taxpayer Relief Act, to avoid immediate payment of a capital gains tax, the Internal Revenue Code only required a homeowner to purchase or exchange a new home at a cost equal to or greater than the previous home. The tax was simply deferred until a point at which a homeowner decided to sell a home of greater value and move into a home of lesser value. In the meantime, never did even one dime of equity from the former home have to be put into the newer home in order to avoid the payment of a long-term capital gains tax.

Before the 1997 law was passed, a homeowner needed to keep records from the sale of his first home, indicating its cost basis and any resulting capital gain from the sale. Each time a gain was rolled into a new home by virtue of the new home's purchase price being greater than the sale price of the older home, those records also needed to be maintained.

The cost basis of a home is basically computed by taking the amount paid for the home, adding the cost of home improvements, and subtracting any depreciation that might have been taken on the property if it was ever used as a rental property. Ever since purchasing my first home, I have kept a file of the amount I originally paid for each home purchased, and all the costs associated with home improvements while I resided in those homes.

Here we might note the importance of not confusing home-improvement costs with money spent on home maintenance and repairs. Replacing the roof because the old one has worn out does not qualify. However, if at the same time you were to upgrade from your previous roof of asphalt shingles to a 100-year, bar-tile roof, a portion of the replacement costs could be added to the basis of your home as a home improvement, along with any other substantial home improvements.

Prior to the 1997 Taxpayer Relief Act, at the time of sale, the difference between the net sales price (after costs such as realtor's commission) and the basis would equal the taxable capital gain. If the new home purchase price were equal to or greater than the previous home, the taxpayer would roll the gain over into the newer home by deferring the tax (not necessarily eliminating it) to a possible future sale of the new home.

Many did not understand this pre-1997 law regarding long-term capital gains on a personal residence. Because of this rollover provision, many had the misconception that the homeowner actually had to roll the money into the new home. Not true! He was only required to buy a new home at a price equal or greater than the sale price of the old home. He could have taken his equity gain and spent it, invested it, or given it away. However, if he were to have sold his home and not buy a new one within eighteen months, the capital gains tax would have been due and payable, not only on the difference between the purchase price and sales price of his last home, but also on all capital gains he had rolled over from previous homes he had sold. The only exception to this rule was a provision offering some relief to retiring couples: a couple wanting to downsize their home could take a once-in-a-lifetime exclusion of up to $125,000 in gains without tax after age 55.

Because I understood this law, I never took any equity from the sale of any of my former homes and invested it in my newer homes, not even for a cash down payment (see chapter 13). Instead, all the equity I realized when I sold a previous home was kept separate from the new property. Not only did this establish the highest acquisition indebtedness possible for tax deduction purposes, but also it allowed me to manage my equity to increase my liquidity, safety, and rate of return.

Even for those who understood it, there were a number of downsides to this law—first, the whole process was very complicated because homeowners did not keep accurate records of the basis in their homes. Most people haven't kept records of the sales transaction closing documents of every previous home in which they have lived, let alone long-term records of home improvements. Not only that, but Congress began to realize due to inflation, a once-in-a-lifetime exclusion of only $125,000 was not a significant amount.

Capital gains have often been an unfair target for shots taken by the tax revenuers. For instance, homes often appreciate in value largely as a function of inflation. Capital gains taxes penalize homeowners for such gains, which are simply a by-product of keeping up with the cost of living! As such, I have always felt the capital gains tax is one of our most unfair taxes. It almost discourages people from investing, which is critical for stimulating economic growth.

THE TAXPAYER RELIEF ACT OF 1997

Fortunately, the Taxpayer Relief Act of 1997 changed the rules for the recognition of gain on the sale of a principal residence. It repealed the rules allowing a homeowner to sell his home and roll over the gain into a new home. Also repealed was the one-time $125,000 exclusion for taxpayers over age 55. Under the new law, a married taxpayer may exclude up to $500,000 ($250,000 if unmarried) of gain on the sale of a principal residence. This exclusion can generally be used only once every two years. In the case of a sale of a principal residence due to a change in employment, health, or other unforeseen circumstances, a homeowner is eligible for a reduced exclusion even if the two years have not passed.

These rules are even flexible enough to accommodate second marriages. For example, if one spouse owns a home from a prior marriage, the $500,000 exclusion is still available. In that case, both spouses must meet the two-out-of-five use requirement. In other words, each spouse must have used his or her respective home as a personal residence (by living in it) for at least two of the five years prior to taking the gain. Also, neither spouse may have used the exclusion within the last two years. But, if one spouse has used the exclusion and the other has not, the $250,000 exclusion may be claimed by the non-using spouse. The new rules have been effective for sales that occurred after May 6, 1997.

Because of the 1997 law, homeowners no longer need to worry about keeping records of rollover gains from one home to the next. Of course, a homeowner still needs to keep track of the basis in his current home (purchase price, plus home improvement costs, minus any depreciation). When he sells his property, the capital gain is calculated as the difference between its basis and the net sales price. Then the $500,000 exclusion ($250,000 if unmarried) is applied.

What a significant change! In most cases, this is an improvement over the old law because it frees up additional cash for investments. In some cases, particularly if the sale of a home results in a large gain, the old law may have been more beneficial because the gain could have been rolled over indefinitely. Now, large gains may be subject to tax. This result may limit the amount that can be spent for a new house because some of the gain must be paid in taxes.

TAX AVOIDANCE VS. TAX EVASION

What is the difference between income tax avoidance and income tax evasion? I usually tell people the difference is about ten years—in jail! There are many legitimate tax deductions and strategies that purposely exist in the tax code for our benefit. If they are leveraged, they can generate thousands of extra dollars in your personal net worth, which in the long run can trigger future taxable events for the government to reap its fair share.

I don't like referring to tax strategies as "loopholes." This term carries the connotation of a taxpayer getting away with something until the IRS and Congress plug it up. If a person were to live on Long Island and pay a toll to drive into Manhattan every day to work, that's his choice. But if he knew about it, he might take an alternate route and avoid paying a toll. That would also be his legitimate choice. But if he chooses one day to break through that tollgate, he is evading the payment of the toll. That's the difference between avoiding taxes using legitimate tax strategies and evading taxes illegally. I recommend you do the former, and I am giving you the knowledge to make a sound choice as to how to do so. Many homeowners end up paying a substantially greater amount of tax than is really their fair share, simply because they were not aware of the legitimate avenues.

It is up to the taxpayer to research and understand all legitimate deductions that may be taken or else hire someone who will. I believe that if a thorough audit analysis were done on most Americans' taxable circumstances, it would be discovered some deductions taken on the tax return were probably not legitimate. But I also believe a good CPA or tax preparer could find more legitimate deductions not taken than illegitimate deductions taken. For those who lack the expertise or time to do their own research, perhaps the assistance of a professional CPA is the answer.

I think an aggressive, thorough, certified public accountant can be well worth the investment. Of course, by "aggressive" I don't mean a CPA who crosses the line into the gray area of tax preparation. I mean someone who acts as more than the tax preparer who plugs the numbers into the proper blanks. A good CPA will meet with you a few times a year to assess your situation for that year and discuss strategies to alleviate unnecessary tax.

So often, people stumble on a tax strategy that may apply to them—perhaps in an airline magazine article—then go to their respective CPAs and ask, "Hey, I've read about this tax strategy. Can I do this in my set of circumstances?"

"Yep, you sure can."

"Well, why didn't you tell me about it?"

"You never asked!" comes the reply. There are so many parachutes professionals are aware of, yet sometimes they become too lazy to watch out for what's best for all of their clients. Occasionally I've observed the attitude, "What they don't know won't hurt them!" (**fig. 12.1**)

I am convinced there are only two ways to approach an IRS audit:

either extremely organized or extremely disorganized. Anywhere in between could prove to be a long visit!

I once used a home contractor who was one of the nicest guys you could ever meet. During the process of building our home, I gave him a Pratt and Lambert paint number for a cream-colored paint for our master bedroom. He lost it and our bedroom was painted Poi Gray! Our daughter's room color was supposed to be "cantaloupe," and it ended up "pumpkin!" Well, his expense receipts were just as mixed up. All of his tax-deductible receipts for construction jobs were wadded-up, wrinkled, and faded from being put through the washing machine in his coverall pockets. When he went to an IRS audit, he walked into their office with shoeboxes full of illegible, disorganized receipts. After about ten minutes, they excused him and said they would accept the numbers on his tax return!

On the other end of the spectrum, when I was audited, I chose to be organized. I had every category of deduction itemized on a computer printout and subtotaled. Each expense item was filed both alphabetically and chronologically by month. I had check vouchers in chronological order by check number and also a separate voucher stapled to every receipt or invoice filed in the same way. You should never volunteer any information not asked for during an audit. However, when the auditor asked for verification of any item, I could cross-reference and find the check receipt immediately. It took just a few minutes to audit an entire category for one year. An adding machine wasn't even necessary because I had the tape totaled in order of all the receipts that were attached to the records. Because of this meticulous record keeping, I got in and out of the audit quickly and painlessly.

WHAT TAX STRATEGIES CAN I USE?

Having said all that, let us now explore legitimate avenues homeowners can use to avoid the payment of unnecessary income tax. Under the old law, homeowners could roll over gains from previous homes indefinitely, and if the final home purchased were never sold, it would have received a stepped-up basis (in other words, the heir would not have had to pay capital gains tax on the difference between the grantor's basis and the value of the home at the grantor's death). Thus the capital gains tax could be completely avoided. The heir then only had to calculate the capital gain from the stepped-up basis, calculated on the value of the home on the date it was inherited or received, and the ultimate price for which it was later sold by the heir.

Under the Taxpayer Relief Act of 1997, homeowners can still pass a home to heirs with a stepped-up basis. This strategy could avoid the payment of capital gains taxes, but the home equity could still be subject to estate tax. In 2010, the step-up in basis is scheduled to be repealed along with the repeal of the estate tax.

ESTATE TAX ISSUES

Estate tax, often referred to as the inheritance tax, is the tax liability owing on assets when they are transferred to non-spousal heirs. Prior to the Economic Growth and Tax Relief Reconciliation Act of 2001, federal estate, gift, and generation-skipping transfer taxes had a deathtime transfer exemption of $675,000. For estates valued in excess of $675,000, the estate tax basically started at 37 percent on estate value over that amount and topped out at 55 percent for assets in excess of $3 million. The applicable credit amount (exemption) was scheduled to increase gradually until the exemption level reached $1 million in 2006.

However, the Economic Growth and Tax Relief Reconciliation Act of 2001 was passed by the Senate and House on May 26, 2001 and made substantial modifications to estate taxes, retirement arrangements, and individual taxes (as explained in chapter 1). Even though the 2001 Act was signed into law by President George W. Bush, at the time of this book's publication, there is still considerable debate as to whether all of the changes will stay in effect. Many factors, such as the complexity of the new law and issues regarding the expending of tax revenue to finance the war on terrorism could change some portions of the new law back to the old law if legislation successfully passes.

The most important thing to understand under the Economic Growth and Tax Relief Reconciliation Act of 2001 is that all the tax changes in the act will "sunset," or end, on December 31, 2010. In other words, the "sunset" restores the law in 2011 to the law as it existed before the act was signed. That is why it is important for us to understand the laws as they existed for 2001!

Under this act, the unified credit exemption amount is increased to $3.5 million over an eight-year period until repeal of the estate tax in year 10. The highest marginal estate tax rate from 2002 to 2007 is reduced to 45 percent until repeal of the estate tax in 2010 (**fig. 12.2**). In 2010, the estate and generation-skipping transfer taxes will be repealed. The gift tax rates, however, will remain in effect with a $1 million lifetime gift exclusion and gift tax rates at the highest individual income tax rate (35 percent). Also, except as provided in regulations, a transfer to trust will be treated as a taxable gift unless the trust is considered a grantor trust under the grantor trust provisions of the Internal Revenue Code.

| Fig. 12.2 | THE ESTATE AND GIFT TAX RATES UNIFIED CREDIT EXEMPTION AMOUNT FOR ESTATE TAX PURPOSES* | |

Calendar Year (January 1)	Estate & GST Tax Deathtime Transfer Exemption	Highest Estate and Gift Tax Rates
2000	$675,000	55% + 5% Surtax
2001	$675,000	55% + 5% Surtax
2002	$1 Million	50%
2003	$1 Million	49%
2004	$1.5 Million	48%
2005	$1.5 Million	47%
2006	$2 Million	46%
2007	$2 Million	45%
2008	$2 Million	45%
2009	$3.5 Million	45%
2010	Repealed	Top Individual Tax Rate Under the Act (Gift Tax Only)
2011	2000 Tax Law Reinstated on 1/1/2011	2000 Tax Law Reinstated on 1/1/2011

as set forth in the Economic Growth and Tax Relief Reconciliation Act of 2001

As a trade-off, after repeal of the estate and generation-skipping transfer taxes, the current law providing a step-up in basis to fair market value will be repealed. A modified carryover basis system generally will take effect that provides recipients of property transferred at the decedent's death with a basis equal to the lesser of the decedent's adjusted basis or the fair market value as of the date of death. The exception to the carryover in basis is an increase in basis for $1.3 million of inherited assets and an additional $3 million of basis increase for assets passing to a surviving spouse. This means that inherited appreciated assets may be subject to increased capital gains taxes when sold.

It is estimated that only about 1 percent of American taxpayers will directly benefit from the repeal of the estate tax. However, the repeal of the current law providing a step-up in basis to fair market value is estimated to generate far more tax revenue than will be given up with the repeal of the estate tax. This would come at the expense of a much broader base of taxpayers rather than just the top 1 percent comprised of the wealthiest individuals.

DOWNSIZING YOUR HOME

What if a retired couple wants to downsize their home? Before the 1997 Taxpayer Relief Act they were often trapped. But the 1997 Act significantly expanded their options. Say a couple built a home twenty-five years ago, now worth $700,000 with a basis of $200,000. They could sell their home and take the $500,000 exclusion resulting in no capital gains tax, whereas before, they would have had to pay 20 to 28 percent in capital gains taxes.

I had a couple use this downsizing strategy to buy a beautiful two-bedroom condominium with a fully-maintained yard in Park City, Utah—twenty minutes from metropolitan Salt Lake City. They were also able to purchase a condominium in the warm climate of St. George, Utah, ninety minutes from Las Vegas, Nevada, as their winter home. The nice thing is they still had $300,000 of their $700,000 home proceeds left to invest! That remaining $300,000 generates $2,000 a month of tax-free income because of where it is invested, which they use to supplement their other retirement income. In addition, they used the equity management strategies introduced in this book by taking 80 percent loan-to-value mortgages on both of their retirement condominiums (valued together at $400,000). They use the separated equity to generate an additional $2,133 per month in tax-free income, which easily covers their mortgage payments on both condominiums, and which totals $2,129 a month on the surface. As outlined before, the $2,129 per month in mortgage payments results in $22,000 of tax deductions they would not have received had they owned their condos free and clear. Instead, they save nearly $8,000 each year in taxes! Thus the $2,129 a month combined mortgage payment on their condominiums is really only costing them a net of about $1,479 a month.

By implementing money-saving income tax and equity management strategies, this couple saved all the capital gains tax on the sale of their home, acquired two new retirement condominiums, and are now enjoying nearly $2,650 a month of additional retirement income. As a side benefit, the tax deductions resulting from the mortgages totally offset the tax liability on their annual IRA withdrawals!

Yes, there is a way to downsize your home, avoid capital gains tax, simplify your life, increase your net spendable income, and save unnecessary tax on IRA distributions. Chapters 14 and 21 will explain other alternatives for those who choose to remain in their homes and still wish to avoid capital gains tax while generating additional retirement income through the use of a reverse mortgage or a charitable remainder trust. Chapter 19 will show you how to offset some or all of the tax liability owed on IRAs and 401(k)s when beginning distributions through the use of these strategies.

TAX BRACKET MISCONCEPTIONS

Besides the capital gains tax, let me discuss other examples of common misunderstandings people have with regard to the IRS tax code.

Taxpayers often complete their tax returns and the tax preparer may say, "Well, you are on the verge of moving into the next higher tax bracket." In other words, their taxable income is about to cross the threshold from 15 to 27 percent or from 27 to 30 percent on federal tax. This alarms the taxpayer because of the misconception that all income up to that threshold, as well as any over that threshold, will be taxed at the higher rate. Not so! You only pay the higher rate on dollars earned in excess of each tax threshold.

How has this misunderstanding gotten people into trouble? I know of several people who get caught in the trap of thinking that "deferred taxes" means "saved taxes." Their tax preparers might have told them something like, "Well, if you don't pull $10,000 out of your IRA this year, you'll save $3,400 in tax." What should have been said was, "Well, if you want to postpone your tax on your IRA—which inevitably needs to be paid—and compound it to a larger sum, paying tax later at likely a higher rate, you can do so." How many people would put off IRA distributions if it were phrased that way?

As you will learn in chapter 16, deferred taxes are usually taxes that have simply been postponed. You are delaying the inevitable and may be compounding the liability! I know of several people in the 2000 tax year who put off taking some of their IRA or 401(k) distributions because those distributions would have sent them to the next tax threshold. In the year 2000, taxable income in excess of $105,950 up to $161,450 was the third bracket (31 percent), only an increase of 3 percent over the second bracket (28 percent), which itself started at incomes in excess of $43,850. So, in order to save 3 percent of $55,500, or a measly $1,655 in tax, they postponed their distributions. Then, due to the extreme market correction in the later part of the year 2000 through 2001, many of these people lost 30 percent or more of the account values in their IRAs and 401(k)s. In other words, they postponed a withdrawal to save $1,655 in additional tax and ended up losing ten times that much in some cases because of the market!

LOAN PROCEEDS ARE NOT TAXABLE

Remember the old Fram and Autolite commercials? A mechanic would hold up a Fram oil filter and say, "You can pay me now—or pay me later (in major car repairs)!" Likewise, it may well be better to pay the IRS now rather than wait and pay it later.

One of the key elements of equity management is the use of the mortgage conduit. Let me clarify here that whenever a person borrows any money, the loan monies are not taxable as income to the borrower. This concept—borrowed money not being subject to tax—is of critical importance in generating tax-free income (see chapter 17).

THE THREE KINDS OF INCOME SUBJECT TO INCOME TAX

In 1986 Congress passed the Tax Reform Act, which was supposed to reduce and simplify taxes. In reality, although about twelve tax brackets were reduced to only two brackets (resulting in only two marginal rates— 15 and 28 percent), after the elimination of several deductions, the effective tax Americans paid went from 12 percent on the average to about 18 percent! Under the Tax Reform Act of 1986, Congress clearly defined the existence of only three types of income when it comes to taxation— earned income, passive income, and portfolio income.

- **Earned income** is the money you physically go out and earn as a result of providing goods and services. This income is subject to income tax, FICA (Social Security tax) and Medicare tax.
- **Passive income** usually comes in the form of passive financial activities such as rental income from property, or lease income. It is subject to income tax but generally not to FICA or Medicare.
- **Portfolio income** is usually realized through the receipt of interest or dividends on savings and investments. It is also subject to income tax, but not FICA or Medicare.

All of these income types are classified as "ordinary income" and are taxed as such.

A capital gain is not subject to tax until it is realized, which isn't until an asset is sold. At that point, the difference between the original purchase price and the net sales price of that asset is considered the capital gain. In 1997 the maximum tax rate on capital gains was reduced from 28 percent to 20 percent (10 percent for taxpayers in the 15 percent tax bracket) for sales after May 6, 1997. This new tax rate only applies to assets held over eighteen months. For assets held more than five years, there is also a further reduction of the maximum capital gains tax gain rate to 18 percent (8 percent for taxpayers in the 15 percent bracket). This reduction only applies to assets whose holding period began after December 31, 2000. There are also provisions allowing certain assets previously purchased to be treated as having been purchased on January 1, 2001 if the owner so chooses. The act also changed the recapture rules. Previously, gain on a sale that resulted purely from depreciation from capital assets was "recaptured" and taxed at ordinary income tax rates. Under the new law, the amount of gain attributed to depreciation is now taxed at 25 percent.

Remember that earned, passive, and portfolio incomes are the only ones subject to income taxes. If we can generate cash flow to meet our needs and wants, especially during retirement, that is not deemed earned, passive, or portfolio income, then we may realize and enjoy tax-free income in full compliance with IRS guidelines (see chapter 17).

LIQUIDATING INVESTMENT REAL ESTATE INCOME PROPERTIES

When real estate is purchased and used as an investment for both rental income and future gain upon its sale, it's important to understand a few basics. Many clients have come to me in retirement feeling their money is trapped—not only in their IRAs and 401(k)s but also in their investment real estate income properties. They feel trapped because if they liquidate the assets they've avoided tax on for years, they'll have to pay those taxes. They want a way out! But the time of reckoning must come.

Unfortunately, because of the stage of life in which I meet most clients for the first time, I spend much of my financial planning process helping them cure their financial and tax problems rather than preventing them. If you also are in the "cure" phase, don't give up! I will explain powerful strategies in forthcoming chapters that can alleviate some or perhaps all of your tax liability on IRAs and 401(k)s and other highly appreciated assets (**fig. 12.3**). On the other hand, if you are in the "prevention" phase of your life, pay close attention to these strategies.

When you purchase a rental income property, hopefully you will be able to produce positive cash flow quickly. The gross rental income you receive is subject to tax under the passive income category. It will be taxed as ordinary income during each year unless you opt to offset the

Fig. 12.3

Don't Ever Give Up!

income with deductions. Deductions on income property come in three basic areas:

- mortgage interest expense (another reason to maintain as high a mortgage as is feasible);
- depreciation allowed to be taken on the property;
- legitimate expenses related to maintenance and repairs to the property.

A word about depreciating property: Your tax preparer may strongly suggest that you depreciate the property. This can do two things: Combined with the interest-expense write off, it may be adequate to off-set all taxable rental income, and it may result in a loss that can be used to offset other income on your tax return, saving you otherwise payable income tax. However, the depreciation you take each year reduces your basis in the property. So, in actuality, you may not be really saving all of those taxes—instead you're probably deferring and converting them to a capital gains tax. The problem is, when it comes time to sell, the capital gain is computed as the difference between the price for which the property was purchased (less the accumulated depreciation) and the net selling price. This way, taxpayers get wonderful tax breaks for years, then when it's time to realize the gain, they go out screaming!

So, if you bought a rental duplex for $250,000 and twenty-five years later you sell it for $750,000 and your basis is down to $0 through depreciation write-offs, your taxable capital gain is $750,000—not just $500,000. This must be paid unless you choose to once again postpone your tax by rolling over your gain into an equivalent piece of rental property. Then under Section 1031 of the Internal Revenue Code, an exchange can be made and the capital gains tax again deferred until the new property is sold and the capital gains tax paid or deferred again through another 1031 exchange. I have had many clients come to me who have used this strategy for years, thinking they would retire peacefully with several real estate properties that had been paid for and had depreciated down to nothing. What many of them find is these properties are management intensive.

If you don't want to deal with the headaches of being a landlord, you either must be willing to pay the cost of property management performed by someone else, or you need to convert the real estate to low-maintenance, income-producing investments. If you do the latter you'll have to bite the bullet and pay the capital gains tax or avoid it altogether through the use of a charitable remainder trust (see chapter 21).

Beware—real estate investments may appear to be wonderfully flawless and risk free, but the postponed obligation of taxes on the gain eventually realized could disappoint you down the road.

THE IRS IS NOT A GOOD SAVINGS OR ACCUMULATION VEHICLE

Let's talk about another tax misconception. Many new clients come to my firm with copies of the tax returns they've filed the previous three years. In studying these returns, we find they may be getting tax refunds of, say, $3,000. I ask them, "Why do you continue to overpay the IRS $3,000 each year just to get it refunded?" You won't believe their answers! They say, "Well, this is our forced savings account! Then every April we splurge, buy something and go on a vacation!" Perhaps you have the same frame of mind, but I hope not! Maybe you haven't noticed something about the IRS. If you owe them money, there are interest charges and penalties accruing from the time you should have sent them the taxes owed. The statute of limitations never seems to run out for money owed to the IRS. However, if the IRS owes you money, how much interest do they pay for using your money? None! Worse yet, if you don't make a claim within three years for the money they owe you, the statute of limitations is up, and they don't have to pay you a dime!

Let me give you a personal example. In 1984 I received a letter from the IRS notifying me because I did not respond to an audit request for my 1982 tax return, they redid my tax return and all of my deductions and most of my exemptions were eliminated. This resulted in a tax liability of over $15,000! Including penalties and interest, they requested that I immediately pay them approximately $25,000!

To my knowledge, this was the first notice I'd received regarding an audit on my 1982 tax return. Where the previous notices were mailed is still a mystery to me. Yes, I had moved during that tax year. But the post office had my forwarding address. Because I did not respond to the initial audit request, they chose to throw out all of my mortgage deductions (which were substantial)! They disallowed my charitable contributions. Also, all medical, property tax, and business deductions were nixed. They only allowed my wife and myself as exemptions. The four children we had at the time were eliminated from the tax return. (Interestingly enough, they allowed me to have those children in the years before and after 1982, but according to the IRS, in 1982 we mysteriously didn't have them!)

Finally, I was able to speak to an IRS supervisor in Denver, Colorado. She granted me an "audit reconsideration." It took three more years before the Salt Lake office finally scheduled to see me regarding the audit reconsideration. In the meantime, the penalties and interest continued to accrue. The IRS filed three different liens against my home and other assets for updated amounts each time. Even after several letters of correspondence, the three credit agencies—TRW, CBI-Equifax, and TransUnion—would not recognize the three separate liens as being in fact the same lien. So my credit report showed that I owed over $75,000 of federal taxes to the IRS. Thank goodness my bankers and creditors knew me well enough and ignored these negative items on my credit report. When I finally got my day in court, I met with the IRS with a preponderance of meticulous records showing all of my deductions and exemptions. In the process, I discovered an error where I had overpaid my tax and the IRS in fact owed me about $3,000. Their reply was, "Well, if you had owed us money it would be due now with interest. However, since you don't and we owe you, the statute is up and we are not able to refund your overpayment!"

If the IRS will not pay you interest for the use of your money, why pay them any more than necessary? You could be using that money to make more money! As long as you pay the IRS an estimated tax or withholding in the amount each year that you owe, at least based upon the previous tax year's liability, they will not assess a penalty. To knowingly overpay tax for the sake of establishing a forced savings account is to me a ridiculous notion. My goal with my clients is to plan their tax situations carefully enough so when they file their return each year, they will either get a refund of no more than $1,000 or have to pay no more than $1,000 in unplanned tax liabilities. I want them to have the greatest use of their money rather than use the IRS as a non–interest bearing savings account.

UNDERSTANDING TAX WITHHOLDINGS

Some wage-earning taxpayers don't know how to adjust their withholding. The purpose of the form W-4 Employee's Withholding Allowance Certificate is so your employer can withhold the correct federal income tax from your pay. The form is comprised of a personal allowances worksheet. You may be under the impression you can only claim as many withholding exemptions as there are dependents in your household, plus yourself. Not true! That is just a guide. Sometimes, wage earners may claim fewer exemptions because they know if they don't, they will have to cough up more tax on April 15. The actual exemptions you can claim on your 1040 tax return and the number of exemptions you may claim for withholding purposes can be two totally different numbers. In fact, if I am sure I will not owe any federal tax in a given year because of my deductions and exemptions, then I can claim as many as thirty to forty exemptions on my withholding if I am taking a salary or wage. This avoids unnecessary tax collection that would be refunded to me upon the filing of my tax return. I may still have to pay maximum FICA and Medicare tax, but I can claim as many exemptions as I need to avoid the overpayment of income tax.

Therefore, if a couple had consistently been receiving a $3,000 annual tax refund, and they saved an extra $2,500 in taxes by taking out an additional $100,000 mortgage on their home for a full year, they would likely receive a refund of $5,500 that next year. Rather than wait until April 15 of the following year to receive their $5,500 refund with no interest, I would advise them to change their exemptions on their withholding tax to avoid overpaying $5,500 in the first place. This amount—about $450 per month—would come back into their monthly budget to help meet their higher house payment.

A word of care: Before changing the exemptions on your withholding, it is best to meet with a personnel payroll manager and hypothetically enter in different numbers of exemptions to see how your withholding tax will be reduced. This is so you will not underestimate the amount you should be paying and owe too much tax at year's end.

DEDUCTIBILITY OF INTEREST ON INDEBTEDNESS

The deductibility of home mortgage interest is yet another common misconception. Remember a homeowner can deduct mortgage interest expense on Schedule A of an itemized tax return on loans up to $100,000, over and above acquisition indebtedness. This is true unless the loan proceeds are used to increase the acquisition indebtedness by doing home improvements. I have often seen people take other cash from investments such as IRAs and spend $40,000 on home improvements. Then they turn around and use consumer debt to buy an automobile! Using proper planning, they should have borrowed on their homes to complete home improvements to get a lower, deductible interest rate, increasing the acquisition indebtedness or basis in their homes. They should have paid cash for the autos from other sources.

The same principle applies if you owned a business, as a sole proprietor (or an S-Corporation), and passed your net business profits through as gross income to your personal tax return. If you feel the need to borrow $20,000 to buy a personal automobile (which is not a deductible business expense), it may be smarter to justify taking money out of the business in the form of a bonus or personal draw and purchase your automobile. The IRS would receive income tax revenue on the bonus that you took, but they would have received that anyway, since net business income converts to gross personal income. This could create a shortfall and a need for more cash in the business. Then you could borrow cash for business needs, in order to deduct the interest on the loan as a business expense. Any such transaction must be in full compliance with the Internal Revenue Code and proper documentation kept. You would also want to check with your CPA to make sure you met all guidelines for tax deductibility of business interest expense.

Internal Revenue Code Section 163 defines the deductibility of interest paid or accrued within a taxable year on indebtedness. After the 1986 Tax Reform Act, according to Section 163(h), there is a disallowance of deduction for personal interest paid or accrued during a taxable year. However, there are a few exceptions, such as interest paid or accrued on indebtedness properly allocable to a trade or business, any investment interest (within the meaning of subsection (d)), and any qualified residence interest.

- **Qualified residence interest** means any interest which is paid or accrued during the taxable year on acquisition indebtedness with respect to any qualified residence of the taxpayer or home equity indebtedness with respect to any qualified residence of the taxpayer. The determination of whether any property is a qualified residence of the taxpayer is made as of the time the interest is accrued.

- **Qualified residence** means the principal residence of the taxpayer (within the meaning of Section 1034), and one other residence of the taxpayer which is selected by the taxpayer for the deductibility of interest for the taxable year, and which is used by the taxpayer as a residence (within the meaning of Section 280A(d)(1)).

- **Acquisition indebtedness** means any indebtedness which is incurred in acquiring, constructing, or substantially improving any qualified residence of the taxpayer, and is secured by such residence (how much you borrowed when you bought, built, or fixed up your house). However, there is a $1 million limitation. In other words, the aggregate amount treated as acquisition indebtedness for any period cannot exceed $1 million ($500,000 in the case of a married individual filing a separate return).

- **Home equity indebtedness** means any indebtedness (other than acquisition indebtedness) secured by a qualified residence to the extent the aggregate amount of that indebtedness does not exceed the fair market value of the qualified residence, reduced by the amount of acquisition indebtedness with respect to the residence (money you borrow out of your house to use for purposes other than improving your house).

There is also a limitation for deducting interest on home equity indebtedness. The aggregate amount treated as home equity indebtedness for any period cannot exceed $100,000 ($50,000 in the case of a separate return by a married individual).

The key element of Section 163(h)(3) is that according to Temporary Regulation 1.163-8T(m)(3), qualified residence interest is allowable as a deduction *without regard* to the manner in which such interest expense is allocated under the rules of this section. It is important to understand these tax implications when implementing the strategies contained in this book. A taxpayer should always seek advice and confirmation as to the deductibility of interest from a competent tax advisor regarding his particular set of circumstances.

POSTPONING TAXES OFTEN INCREASES YOUR LIABILITY

Many people have the misconception the total amount of money made from smaller amounts combined results in greater interest earnings than the smaller amounts divided up can earn. It's true that more money can qualify you for investments that pay higher interest. It is also true that more money at a given interest rate generates higher volumes of money. However, one account worth $200,000 earning 10 percent compound interest does not earn one dime more than the total of two accounts each with $100,000 dollars earning 10 percent interest (**fig. 12.4**). Likewise, $1 million earning 10 percent does not earn any more money than ten $100,000 accounts earning 10 percent interest. The results are identical.

The same basic concept applies to tax-deferred earnings that are later taxable, versus after-tax contributions to tax-free investments, when all other variables are equal. For instance, $150,000 taxed at 33.3 percent nets $100,000. If that after-tax amount were invested tax-free at 7.2 percent interest and it doubled in ten years, it would be worth $200,000. If

Fig. 12.4	TWO $100,000 ACCOUNTS WILL GROW TO THE SAME AMOUNT AS ONE $200,000 ACCOUNT	

	Year One Totals	
$200,000	$100,000	$100,000
X 10%	X 10% +	X 10%
$20,000	$10,000	$10,000

	10 Years of Compounding	
$220,000	$110,000	$110,000
$242,000	$121,000	$121,000
$266,200	$133,100	$133,100
$292,820	$146,410	$146,410
$322,102	$161,051	$161,051
$354,312	$177,156	$177,156
$389,743	$194,872	$194,872
$428,718	$214,359	$214,359
$471,590	$235,795	$235,795
$518,748	$259,374	$259,374

$518,748 = $259,374 + $259,374

$150,000 were put into a pre-tax investment and it doubled in ten years to $300,000, then was taxed at 33.3 percent, the net result is $200,000. Both scenarios result in the same amount. The problem is other factors usually do not remain constant. Tax rates usually increase, rather than decrease, as time passes. The key, then, is to earn interest tax free, not just tax deferred, or in other words, to be able to earn interest that will not be treated as earned, passive, or portfolio income.

Perhaps you do not yet fully realize the dramatic difference between taxable investments and non-taxable investments. Investments subject to tax leave you with the option of having to incur greater risks in order to achieve the same net after-tax rate of return as tax-free investments. To whet your appetite for what follows, let me illustrate. Let's say at the beginning of a time frame consisting of twenty periods, you have one dollar invested in a tax-free account that doubles every period for the twenty periods. One dollar grows to $2 during period 1, then to $4 during period

Fig. 12.5	A DOLLAR DOUBLING EVERY PERIOD FOR 20 PERIODS TAX FREE VERSUS A DOLLAR DOUBLING EVERY PERIOD FOR 20 PERIODS TAXED AS EARNED*	
Periods	**Tax Free**	**Taxed as Earned**
	$1	$1.00
1	$2	$1.73
2	$4	$2.99
3	$8	$5.18
4	$16	$8.96
5	$32	$15.50
6	$64	$26.81
7	$128	$46.38
8	$256	$80.24
9	$512	$138.81
10	$1,024	$240.14
11	$2,048	$415.44
12	$4,096	$718.71
13	$8,192	$1,243.37
14	$16,384	$2,151.02
15	$32,768	$3,721.27
16	$65,536	$6,437.80
17	$131,072	$11,137.40
18	$262,144	$19,267.70
19	$524,288	$33,333.12
20	**$1,048,576**	**$57,666.30**

*assuming a 27 percent tax bracket

IN WHICH ENVIRONMENT WOULD YOU PREFER TO ACCUMULATE YOUR WEALTH?

2, $8 during period 3, $16 during period 4 and so on (**fig. 12.5**). At the end of twenty periods the account would be worth $1,048,576.

Now let's say you are in a 27 percent federal tax bracket and there is no state income tax where you live. Your money is taxed as earned. With an account under the same terms as before, at the end of the first period, instead of having $2 you would only have $1.73. That's $1 profit less 27 percent tax equals $.73. The next period you would double $1.73 and then pay 27 percent on that profit and so on until the twentieth period.

At the end of the same twenty periods your investment would only be worth $57,666.30, not $1,048,576!

What I recommend to my clients is they invest in low-risk, moderate-yielding investments that are tax free. Some may also have money in IRAs and 401(k)s. When they choose to strategically roll their money out of their IRAs and 401(k)s to get the tax liability over with, this money can be positioned to earn tax-free income from that point forward. During the process they learn how to dramatically offset some or all of the tax liability on IRAs and 401(k)s by using proper equity management. These strategies with accompanying references to the applicable sections of the Internal Revenue Code are explained in chapters 17 and 19.

12 WEALTH-ENHANCEMENT STRATEGY NUMBER TWELVE

- *If feasible, do not use more equity than necessary, (none, if possible) from the sale of a previous home to purchase a new home.*
- *Position yourself to take advantage of up to $500,000 of capital gains tax free on the sale of a personal residence as often as every two years.*
- *If you have more home than you need, downsize and take the difference, free of capital gains tax, and generate tax-free retirement income.*
- *You may also create additional savings by virtue of mortgage interest deductions on a new home.*

CHAPTER 13

Pay No Money Down

Alleviate cash down payments when purchasing real estate.

COMMON MYTH-CONCEPTION

You must always pay cash down when you purchase
real property.

REALITY

*There are many ways to purchase real property without paying
cash down.*

Traditionally, whenever personal or real property is purchased in our American economic system, a down payment is expected. By making a down payment, the buyer demonstrates she is financially prepared to purchase the property. This practice is common but not necessary. In reality, there are many methods of purchasing homes or other real estate property without paying a cash down payment. (In this chapter I will not attempt to cover all strategies that may be used to accomplish this goal. For additional resources, many publications, books, videos, and audio programs explain different methods by which successful real estate investors have purchased property with no money down.)

I have never regarded myself as a major real estate investor. During the first twenty-five years of our marriage, my wife and I purchased and lived in six different homes to accommodate our family of six children. In every case, we were able to acquire the property without a cash down payment, although we incurred some costs associated with closing or title work. I also have been able to avoid down payments or using my own cash when purchasing investment real estate and recreational property. Don't misunderstand me—paying a cash down payment when purchasing property is not an irreversible mistake. But I believe by paying no more money down than necessary, I can keep the equity in a liquid side fund that will maintain safety of principal and can earn a rate of return greater than the cost of those funds. I never want to tie up equity unnecessarily.

Let me reiterate what I have taught thus far in the book—it is vital I remain liquid. I also want to maintain safety of principal in my home. Then if real estate markets temporarily go soft, I can keep my options open in case I am forced to liquidate. Interest rates are relative. When interest rates are up, they are up for borrowing as well as for investing. When interest rates are down and my return on investments drops, employing equity still makes sense because borrowing rates are also low. Tax benefits allow us to further enhance our rate of return. This widens the margin between borrowing rates and investment rates so we can earn a rate of return on the idle dollars that were tied up in property.

USING FHA OR VA LOANS

Let us now discuss some of the ways by which homebuyers can avoid making a down payment. Many homebuyers are required to pay little or nothing down if they can qualify for a FHA loan or a VA loan. As explained in chapter 10, through the Veteran's Administration, veterans are allowed to purchase property under certain conditions with no money down. I have recommended to clients who qualify for such VA benefits to take advantage of that opportunity, even if they have cash they can use to pay down on a home. Those who use the FHA loan process may be able to pay as little as 2.5 to 3 percent of the purchase price in a down payment rather than the minimum 5 to 20 percent usually required by conventional lenders. As previously explained, a 20 percent down payment is most common because it acts as a buffer for lenders in case they must foreclose and resell the property in a soft market. Paying 20 percent down appears appealing because the buyer avoids the expense of mortgage insurance.

Remember that FHA loans require Mortgage Insurance Premiums (MIP) on all loans. The VA charges a funding fee on all VA loans rather than mortgage insurance. Mortgage insurance protects the investors funding the loan against loss should the borrower default and foreclosure become necessary.

Whether or not you have the capital to put a down payment on a home, I believe it is in your best interests to pay little or nothing down when purchasing property. You thus keep equity outside the property in a position of liquidity so funds are available in case of emergencies, financial setbacks, or conservative investment opportunities. Also, I believe homeowners should keep as much equity separate as possible at the initial purchase of a home. This way you start with the highest mortgage possible, establishing the highest amount of acquisition indebtedness possible. This gives you more to deduct from income taxes, as well as a chance to tap into that equity and employ it elsewhere.

BUYING A HOME ON CONTRACT

Another method of acquiring property with little or nothing down is to purchase it through an assumable contract. There may be some older mortgages on the market that allow for simple, non-qualifying assumptions that do not require any type of approval or qualification on the part of the new buyer. As explained in chapter 11, a buyer is allowed to assume a qualifying loan only if the mortgage holder approves the application. The difference owing between the balance of the mortgage that is assumed and the sales price of the home can then be negotiated in a variety of ways.

Property can also be purchased with little or nothing down when a real estate sales contract is used. This method is very workable with property that is owned outright by the seller. If there is an existing mortgage on the property, selling on contract is an option only if the mortgage contract allows for such a sale and there is no "due on sale" clause in the contract. Otherwise, the seller may be able to rent or lease the property to an interested buyer, giving them an option to buy. Such a contract can allow for the rental payments or lease payments to accrue as part of an eventual down payment when the purchase option is exercised. The buyer is not required to come up with a lump sum down payment in this case, but can allocate rent or lease payments toward a down payment— payments that otherwise would have gone down the drain. If the seller is willing to create such a contract, it may be a better method for the buyer than trying to save for a down payment while renting. (Trying to save that much money on top of a rent payment has been the frustration of many would-be home buyers.) I have discovered many people are willing to use a contract sale that allows them to stretch out the realization of the long-term capital gain on a property they own but do not occupy.

One of the best methods for buying a new home with little or no cash down is to free the land on which the home is going to be built of any loans or liens. Most lenders will allow the building lot to qualify as the down payment if the lot appraises for a certain ratio of the home's projected value. So, if the home builder or buyer can show a free and clear title to the property to pledge as collateral, that is often enough to satisfy the down payment required by the lender. This can sometimes be accomplished without actually paying for the building lot up front, as I will explain.

Sometimes there are golden opportunities whereby people can buy property for nothing down. I have learned you have to help create the opportunities rather than wait for them to come your way. Someone once said there are three types of people in the world: those who make things happen, those who watch things happen, and those who wonder what happened!

If you are buying a home from someone who is retired or who has experienced a high amount of appreciation in her property, she may be amenable to selling the home on a contract that requires little or no cash for a down payment, and thus carry the contract. Look for situations where people may not want or need to be cashed out of their property. I have had clients come to me who have found homes occupied by elderly people. When those people passed away, the home transferred to the estate of that individual. On many occasions, the heirs were willing to sell the property on some type of contract for a little higher price than normal, allowing the buyer to avoid coming up with a down payment. The surviving family received a monthly income through the use of a mortgage contract.

A mortgage contract as described above may contain an attractive interest rate for both parties concerned. The seller of a non-owner-occupied house will often have to pay a long-term capital gains tax and then invest the net after-tax proceeds in an attempt to generate a monthly income from the return. Given typical market conditions, most conservative, safe investments only earn 5 or 6 percent, while at the same time mortgage contracts might pay as high as 7 or 8 percent. Both the buying and selling parties need to understand the safety of a mortgage that is backed, or collateralized, with a piece of property that will probably continue to appreciate. Simply carrying the contract and letting the buyer make monthly payments rather than paying a cash down payment may prove to be one of the most prudent and stable investments. Selling a home on contract is usually most comfortable when it is the seller's personal residence. However, selling on a contract may also be a good option—even for a non-owner-occupied seller—rather than selling the house outright, which leads to paying a capital gains tax and trying to invest the rest of the money at a rate as attractive as the mortgage rate.

HOW I HAVE NEVER PAID MONEY DOWN FOR A HOME

I have used several ways to acquire property with nothing down, including the purchase of my most recent home, which appraised for over $500,000 prior to my purchase. Because I bought the home in a soft market, I was able to purchase it for $300,000 (see chapter 11) and pay no cash down payment. Many good deals in the real estate market are found by methodically searching for homes worth more than their selling prices. I have often had to be patient for up to eighteen months while watching for these kinds of opportunities. The best deals are homes that are worth more than or will appraise for greater than the amount for which you are buying it. These opportunities tend to exist more in a soft real estate market where homes are temporarily lower in marketability.

The first home my wife and I purchased was a small, two-bedroom rambler with 900 square feet on the main floor and an unfinished basement. It sat on a one-third acre fenced lot. It was what you would call a "fixer-upper." We wanted to purchase the home through the use of a FHA loan, which would only require about a 2.5 percent down payment. Rather than spend cash for a down payment, we opted to put that money into improving the property. We got acquainted with the sellers and, through the negotiation process, they became our good friends. Both parties felt very comfortable, and a sense of trust was established. We agreed to spend about $3,000 to improve the property.

This was more or less a private loan arrangement through which we made improvements to the property we knew would enhance its appraised value by about $5,000 or $6,000. We completed those improvements and had the home appraised. Sure enough, the home appraised for about $5,000 more than the original asking price. We were thus able to establish a higher selling price and obtain a FHA loan that was high enough to pay off the sellers at their original asking price and reimburse us for the money spent fixing up the property. After the loan was closed, the sellers paid us the money used to fix up their property. When everything was said and done, we obtained this home with nothing down because the money we put into the home was set aside for improvements after the purchase anyway. Under this method, we got the capital back to use for other investments. We lived in this home for about nine months before we acquired our next property, on which we decided to build a home.

OUR SECOND HOME—WITH NO MONEY DOWN

After looking at several different plans, we decided to build a townhouse duplex that could either be used as a duplex or sold as two separate condominiums. After selecting the property, a one-third acre lot, I proposed to the property owner that we become partners in constructing the townhouse duplex. He owned the property free and clear, and we decided to build a townhouse duplex that had a three-bedroom, split-level plan with 1650 square feet of living space per side. I knew that if the owner of the property would supply the free and clear deed to the property, we could secure the construction loan, as well as the long-term take-out financing for the final thirty-year mortgage without having to come up with a cash down payment. Based on this arrangement, we qualified for and signed the mortgage documents. We agreed that one-half of all the equity in the duplex plus the original value of the property would be reimbursed to my partner on the future sale of the duplex. I was able to not only use the duplex for my own personal residence, but I was also able to substantially offset the monthly mortgage payment with the rental income generated from the other half of the duplex.

While we were living in the duplex, another friend and I were able to purchase four other duplex lots close to a development that was about to begin. We were able to obtain the four lots for a price of $10,000 each. We simply signed an offer putting $250 earnest money on each of the four lots. The $1,000 earnest money agreement was held in escrow until closing, which was set for about thirty days out. During the process, we secured a buyer for all four lots. The buyer was a construction company doing development in the area. We turned around and sold each of the duplex lots for $16,000 apiece at the same time we closed our purchase of the property. We paid virtually nothing down during this transaction and were able to make a $24,000 profit in the process by searching for property in high demand because of development underway in that area.

OUR THIRD HOUSE—WITH NO MONEY DOWN

The next year, we were introduced to a beautiful development in its infancy stage. It was located on a canyon rim overlooking all of Utah Valley in central Utah. The developer had subdivided this property into one-acre parcels. In an attempt to get the property sold and obtain financing from the bank to complete improvements, the developer was motivated to sell the initial properties on uniform real estate contracts. My wife and I found two prime-view lots, each containing over one acre of land. The lots were located in an area that did not yet have a paved road, however, we knew with the completion of the improvements, they would become some of the most prime building lots in the entire community.

We purchased the two lots with only a $100 earnest money agreement on each. Additionally, we agreed to pay $75 per month on the property with the balance due in a balloon payment in five years. We purchased one lot for the price of $7,000 and the other lot for the price of $8,000. The uniform real estate contracts were at interest rates of 7 percent and 8 percent respectively, which meant that with our $75 per month we were only reducing the principal about $25 to $35 per month. However, through the principle of positive leverage, we obtained two pieces of property we were confident would become valuable in a short time period, enhancing our rate of return.

Within one year we found a contractor who specialized in building unique rustic homes with cathedral beam, wood-decked ceilings. We designed two different homes, one for each lot, and were prepared to live in either of the homes when completed. The floor plan we preferred included 6,400 square feet of finished living space. The other home had over 5,000 square feet of living space and was also a very attractive design.

I made arrangements with the contractor and a savings and loan institution to take out a construction loan on the 6,400 square-foot home in my name. The contractor took out a construction loan under his company's name for the 5,000 square-foot home, which we designated as the speculation property in hopes of selling that one first.

We realized that, in this new community, many people preferred lots that were not so large and spacious. Through the proper process, we obtained approval to subdivide each of the lots into four lots of over half an acre each. I then went to the developer from whom I had purchased the property and laid out my plans to build my home and a speculation home.

To construct these two homes with no cash down payment, I needed to have two of the four lots free and clear to satisfy the down payment. So I asked the developer if he would be willing to transfer the two liens against the two one-acre descriptions over to two of the new lots with one-half acre descriptions. This would leave the two one-half acre lots we wanted to build on free and clear. By doing this, I showed the developer I would be able to build both my home and the speculation home within six to nine months. That way, after taking out long-term financing on my home and selling the speculation home, I would have the funds necessary to pay off the uniform real estate contract held by the developer on an accelerated basis. This arrangement was truly a win-win situation for both of us. He gave me free and clear deeds for the two lots that I decided to build on.

We went to work, and over a period of eight months we built two absolutely beautiful homes on the one-half acre view lots. I obtained the construction financing on my home, and the contractor easily obtained construction financing on the speculation home. I also arranged for long-term take-out mortgages on our home and the speculation home, in case it became necessary. However, my hopes were to sell the speculation home before it was completed, which it did. I was able to take the profits derived from the sale of the speculation home and not only pay off the developer in full for the land, but also keep capital to furnish and obtain needed amenities for our own home. When our home was completed, we had incurred costs on the property of approximately $180,000 and it appraised immediately for over $250,000!

Over the next two years, the other two subdivided pieces of property sold—at a substantial profit because of the area's growth and the excellent lots' location.

We enjoyed our new home immensely, and our intentions were to stay in that home for quite a while. After just three years, our home had appreciated to a value of $300,000, with only a $150,000 mortgage balance owing on the property. We thus had $150,000 of equity. However, due to the recession of the early 1980s, and some external influences beyond our control, we were forced into circumstances in which I began to learn why it is so important to establish and maintain liquidity on home equity.

WHEN THE UNEXPECTED HAPPENS...

From 1974 until 1982 I built my financial planning practice into a large agency organization, hiring and training in excess of 150 independently contracted representatives throughout a thirteen-state region. Then two of my business associates and I discovered our regional director had been misappropriating and routing compensation to himself—money that should have been paid to us over the previous six-year period. He refused to reimburse us according to our original understanding and agreement. Unfortunately, all of our cash flow and compensation from the financial institutions we represented was frozen until the situation could be resolved through litigation or arbitration.

Even though I had substantial receivables accruing and accumulating in an escrow account, I could not convince the mortgage company to give us the time to coast even a little while. As described in chapter 2, my wife and I tried everything in our power to borrow on the $150,000 of equity we had in our property, but it was to no avail.

Needless to say, this particular experience is not a fond memory. However, it taught us to separate as much equity from our property as possible and to remain liquid to weather the tough times.

Shortly thereafter we settled the litigation out of court. Even though I received all my accrued compensation, it was too late—we had lost the property. Next we faced the challenge of needing to purchase a new property with a home foreclosure on our credit report, as well as three back-to-back ninety-day delinquencies. Even though my income could have justified a new mortgage, the credit reports would have prevented me from qualifying for a new mortgage. I knew that probably the only way we could obtain our next home was to use some type of creative financing and assume a contract that wouldn't require qualifying.

We discovered that many opportunities were available for us to purchase with no cash down payment. We decided on a beautiful home in a nice neighborhood, close to schools, shopping malls, the community college, and other amenities attractive to homebuyers. It was owned by a couple who have since become two of our dearest friends. This home had a FHA loan on it for the first mortgage, which contained a simple assumption provision. It also had a second mortgage, carried by the developer.

We purchased this home in a buyer's market for $98,000. The FHA loan balance was $49,000 and was available under a simple assumption. Therefore, we did not need to qualify for this mortgage; we simply went to the title company and signed the appropriate documents. The developer was willing to carry us with a negative amortization for a while to help us with the second mortgage of $49,000. We were then able to move into the property with nothing down because we had financing on the entire purchase price!

I have told this story numerous times because there are many people who feel all is lost when their credit is ruined or when they do not have cash for a down payment. That is the exact situation we found ourselves in, yet we were able to buy and immediately move into a late-model home.

We ended up finishing the entire basement and landscaping the entire yard. This allowed us to recoup our investment with a nice profit as we moved from that property to another property a few years later.

To increase the value of a property to make it more attractive to prospective buyers, certain improvements will enhance its value more than others. Be careful, because often, redecorating a home will not allow the seller to recoup the amount of money invested in the new décor. This is especially true if the home décor does not appeal to the new homebuyer. However, finishing additional square footage in a home or adding square footage can enhance the value of the property.

For instance, this home had a double-car garage, but we enhanced its value by adding an RV parking area cement pad that provided off-street parking. We also invested about two thousand dollars in ornate landscape accoutrements, such as an archway with a bridge, accent lighting areas, and a nature path to our back yard—for which we were nominated for one of the most beautiful yards in the community. This small investment, in addition to some "sweat equity" (the landscape work done by us), helped us to sell our home for approximately 20 percent ($20,000) more than the appraised value of the home just a year earlier.

As I related to you in chapter 11, the sellers of our next home had approximately $450,000 of actual costs invested in the property, which had appraised for $505,000 two years earlier. But the recent construction of a nearby interstate freeway had made the neighborhood less appealing. The advertised asking price at that point was $319,000. We made an offer of $300,000 with the condition the sellers could continue to live in the home for up to nine months while they built their new home. The sellers accepted the offer.

In order to purchase the home for $300,000, I first had it appraised with two different professional appraisers. Both appraisals came in at about $382,000. Next, I opened up correspondence with my mortgage lender—a major insurance company. It is important to understand that mortgage loans are not just available through traditional mortgage bankers.

It doesn't really matter with whom you deal, only that you understand their requirements, and that you are honest with your disclosure and negotiations with them. I understood from the insurance company it would only loan 80 percent of the home's worth. My first question was, "Is that 80 percent of the home's appraised value or is that 80 percent of the home's purchase price?" Because most mortgage institutions are quite conservative, they will usually only loan 80 percent of either the purchase price of the home or the appraised value, whichever is less, until the loan is seasoned (meaning you've made mortgage payments on it for six months to a year). After having both appraisals come in at $382,000, I felt comfortable knowing the purchase price and earnest money offer I had made in the amount of $300,000 was well within their guidelines to justify the mortgage.

After a day or so of scratching out numbers on a pad of paper, I met with the sellers to complete a sales contract based on a sales price of $350,000. The $350,000 sales price would normally require a 20 percent down payment of $70,000, leaving a mortgage amount of $280,000 I would need to qualify for with my mortgage lender. Next I drew up an agreement in which the down payment would be carried by the seller and would be due and payable after thirteen years with no interest—a balloon payment of $70,000. However, the contract provided the debtor of the note (myself) the option to pay off the $70,000 note at a discount prior to the maturity of the no-interest note. A schedule was put forth showing the amount of the discount each year retroactive from the beginning of the fourteenth year back to the first day. On the very first day, the $70,000 note could be paid off in the amount of $20,000 because of the discount. (This was calculated based on approximately a 10 percent interest formula, meaning the $20,000 at 10 percent compounded annually would grow to $70,000 shortly after the end of the thirteenth year.) This "early-out" provision, or discount option, allowed me as the buyer to exercise said option as early as the home purchase date. By so doing I would be paying off a $70,000 note due in fourteen years at 0 percent discounted to $20,000! In effect, this would result in my purchasing the home for $300,000 instead of $350,000.

In disclosing this arrangement with my mortgage company, they left it to the seller to determine down payment conditions. The mortgage lender accepted and approved our loan in the amount of $280,000.

My next hurdle was to figure out a way to come up with the $20,000 to exercise the option at closing. I did not want to expend any of my own money, as explained earlier. Never underestimate the value of establishing dialogue with people to build relationships of trust. I began asking questions of the home seller on how we might create a win-win situation to accomplish both of our goals.

I discovered he had a self-directed pension retirement plan because he was a self-employed dentist. I inquired as to what his average return was on his retirement portfolio. I next asked if he would be interested in a transfer of capital from his self-directed pension plan into an investment that would qualify as "prudent"—one that would earn a return of 10 percent interest on a fixed, guaranteed basis and would be secured through a substantial piece of property. He indicated this would be attractive. I proposed he transfer $20,000 from some of his conservative investments in his pension into another conservative investment using a trust deed note with a second mortgage lien on the home he was selling to me. This would put him in a second position behind a $280,000 first mortgage on a home that conservatively appraised for $382,000. In other words, he had at least $100,000 of collateral protecting his $20,000 investment! He agreed.

What took place on the day of closing was quite simple. We bought the house first for the stated price of $350,000. We signed a mortgage contract with the mortgage lender for a thirty-year mortgage in the amount of $280,000 (80 percent of $350,000). A check for $280,000 less his outstanding mortgage balance was handed over to the seller in exchange for the property. At that moment, the remaining $70,000 "down payment" would not be due until fourteen years from then at 0 percent interest.

The next transaction that occurred was a $20,000 loan made payable to me from the seller's pension plan. The $20,000 was at 10 percent interest and required an annual payment of at least $2,000 each year and was due at the end of five years with a balloon payment requiring the principal to be paid in full.

The third transaction that took place involved me taking the $20,000 check, endorsing it, and handing it back to the seller. In other words, I exercised my option to pay off the $70,000 "down payment"—at a discount—for $20,000 fourteen years earlier than its due date as provided in our real estate sales contract. I did this using $20,000 of the seller's money that otherwise was trapped in a pension and not accessible to them without incurring a penalty. Because I had arranged my loan through an insurance company's mortgage department, I did not have the usual closing costs and origination fees. However, I had agreed to reimburse the lender for preparing the legal documents and the title insurance and appraisal fees. These fees totaled less than $2,000.

On that day, I walked into a title company and walked out twenty minutes later having purchased a home that was worth between $380,000 and $500,000, having paid nothing as a down payment. I began to make my regular mortgage payments. The second mortgage trust deed note to the seller only required an annual payment of $2,000 on each anniversary thereafter until the fifth year.

During the ensuing eight months, the sellers remained in the home while they constructed their new home and paid rent to me in an amount equivalent to my new mortgage payment. I was grateful to them for the opportunity I had to purchase a beautiful home with nothing down. They were grateful to me for having received the cash necessary to allow them to build their next home despite the soft real estate market. It was a win-win situation.

Only nine months later, the market began to strengthen again. I was pleasantly surprised one day to receive an offer in the mail from a couple relocating from Newport Beach, California, who wanted to purchase our home for $600,000! They had sold their California home for that price. To avoid realizing a taxable capital gain—and because they liked the home's location and design—they were willing to pay $600,000 for our home.

We turned down their offer and still reside in the home as of the publication of this book. As I mentioned earlier, we have finished an additional 3,000 square feet of living space and enhanced our yard with two recycling streams that have waterfalls and fishponds in the front and rear yards. Our home valuation was over $1 million just over ten years after we purchased it for $300,000.

Let's go back and analyze what would have happened had I sold the home to the couple from Newport Beach, just nine months after I had purchased the home. Had I gone ahead and sold it for $600,000, what would have been the rate of return? It would have been infinite because, technically speaking, no money was invested beyond the house payments I had made during those nine months, which had been covered by the rental income from the seller! With no cash expended, I would have sold the home for twice what I had paid for it. This is not a 100 percent return because no cash was actually invested for a down payment. Therefore, it would be deemed an infinite rate of return! Possibly the only costs that could be attributed to calculate such a rate of return would have been the closing costs, including appraisal fees, title report, and insurance fees.

Three-and-a-half years after purchasing the home, I refinanced it with a different first mortgage lender. I also obtained a second mortgage, thereby separating $120,000 of excess equity from our home for home improvements and equity management. One year during the past ten years we actually put an additional $160,000 into major home improvements. As soon as we completed our remodeling, we were able to separate an additional $240,000 of equity from the property in order to exercise the equity management concepts taught thus far in the book.

FINDING MORE OPPORTUNITIES

The next example I would like to relate concerns a house that I nearly purchased a few years ago. Although it was valued at over $700,000, I would have been able to acquire the house with no down payment. I share this example to illustrate how easy it is to find such opportunities.

Many of my friends and clients are home contractors especially skilled in building beautiful, award-winning custom homes. One such home had been constructed by a friend two years before. We had fallen in love with its architecture, design, and decorating. My wife and I toyed with the idea of moving back to central Utah, even though we loved our current home. We debated whether to move or to spend the money fixing up our current home. We began negotiations for the purchase of this other home. Even though we decided to stay in our existing home, had we decided to go ahead with the purchase of the new home, we could have acquired it with no down payment. In fact, the same opportunity was presented six years earlier through the same contractor—we could have purchased a $300,000 home without a down payment. How can a homebuyer do that?

Often, sellers of homes are willing to sell their property on a contract. Perhaps they may be motivated to sell their home for a higher price and then require the buyer to take out a long-term mortgage within a five-year period to cash them out. Remember, the best opportunities exist where a home has a purchase price less than the appraised value. While this home was worth well over $700,000, our purchase price would have been $620,000. The negotiation and arrangement for the purchase of this home with no down payment took all of five minutes.

Again, I began by asking questions of the seller. I asked the seller, "If I were to buy the home for $620,000, what would you do with the money?" In other words, did he absolutely need the money from the property in order to purchase his next home? He indicated he did not. I then asked what rate of return he could average on his invested funds if I were to write him a check for $620,000. He indicated the rate of return would likely be around 7 to 7.5 percent. I then asked, "What if you could earn 8 percent on a fixed basis and secure that investment with a legal document that would protect your funds with an asset worth $700,000? Would that seem like a reasonable and prudent investment to you?" He said, "Yes, it would." Then he wanted to know what investment I was referring to.

I explained that simply carrying a mortgage contract with a trust deed note for the first lien on his home would likely be one of the safest investments he could ever make. Rather than taking the proceeds from selling his house and plowing them into a new home without a mortgage—missing out on some of his only available tax deductions—he could instead benefit from a brand new mortgage. Furthermore, when he bought his next home, he could establish the highest acquisition indebtedness possible, thus creating the greatest tax deduction possible.

Why wouldn't he be willing to carry a mortgage with me on a piece of property very familiar to him? He would secure his $620,000 investment with the home such that, if I were to default, he could foreclose on it and sell the property for at least the $620,000 I was to pay. In fact, every month and year that passed, his investment would become more and more secure because as the home appreciated and the mortgage went down, his position of security would become stronger and stronger. He immediately understood and said this would be attractive to him. Of course, had I purchased the home on contract, I would have had the option of paying him off, refinancing the home, or selling the home anytime during the mortgage term.

Even though I decided not to purchase that property, had I done so, I would have easily purchased a $700,000 home without having made any type of down payment. This is because the seller was willing and able to carry the contract under the terms and conditions outlined once he understood the safety behind carrying a personal mortgage contract.

I have seen this opportunity arise many, many times—not only for myself but also for many of my clients. They have been able to take advantage of the opportunity both from the buyers and seller's end of the spectrum. They have experienced a tremendous rate of return in a very secure investment while doing so.

SELLING ON CONTRACTS TO FAMILY MEMBERS

If selling real estate on contract is done between family members, I would caution the parties involved to make certain the arrangement is made at arm's length. When children purchase property from parents, they tend not to make timely payments on mortgage contracts because they feel that mom and dad will understand. This becomes a sensitive situation because the parents do not want to foreclose on children! I would not deem such an arrangement a safe investment, as it would otherwise be, because parents can be left with the turmoil of sporadic payments. Thus, they may not be able to sufficiently plan their own retirement or accomplish other objectives. You may wish to consider this technique, whenever the possibility exists, by using private mortgage lenders. You can create a win-win situation between the buyer and the seller if the proper conditions are met, agreed on, and implemented.

BUYING INVESTMENT PROPERTIES WITH LITTLE DOWN

There are also many opportunities to purchase investment income properties with little or nothing down. On several occasions, I have purchased property for which the seller was willing to carry the contract. This has allowed the seller to either spread out the capital gain or to generate income.

I purchased rental properties on two occasions where I leased them with an option to buy. Look for deals where the sellers are highly motivated. For example, one seller was highly motivated to sell because she had purchased a new 1,800-square-foot condominium and then received a job transfer to California just thirty days afterward. When this happens, the new employer will sometimes provide a cash moving allowance or cash incentive that allows the seller to discount her house for quick sale. These bonuses help the seller feel okay about giving up the small amount of equity she might have had in the home.

If the mortgage loan has a "due on sale" clause, usually the lender will still allow the owner to rent or lease the home. I have executed a lease with an option to buy wherein I technically took over the monthly mortgage by paying a lease payment sufficient to cover the mortgage payment for a period of time—about three years. Then I turned around and subleased it to another tenant for an amount equal to the monthly obligation. In this situation, I had the option to buy the home at any point in the three-year period for the price of the then-owing mortgage balance. If I purchased the property at a discount price to begin with and the property appreciated at 5 percent a year, I could then possibly sell the property for, say $180,000, by exercising my option to purchase it for $150,000 under the "lease with option to buy" agreement. Under these circumstances, the home would net me a $30,000 profit having paid no cash down and hopefully having expended little cash during the three years for maintenance and repairs, or for covering the mortgage during months when the home might be vacant of tenants.

I have not explained the myriad of other "no money down" methods by which real property may be acquired because many other instructional materials explain how to do this. I hope only to have opened your mind to opportunities you might not have been aware of. Use your own creativity to seize the abundance of opportunities to acquire properties with little or nothing down.

13 WEALTH-ENHANCEMENT STRATEGY NUMBER THIRTEEN

- *As your budget allows, when acquiring a home or other properties, pay little or no cash down.*

House Rich, Cash Poor

Elderly homeowners can annuitize the equity in their homes to generate tax-free retirement income using a reverse mortgage.

Financial security is, to a large degree, achieved when your home is paid for.

Financial security is usually obtained with adequate liquid assets in a safe environment to cover any liabilities and generate positive cash flow to cover living expenses indefinitely.

The American dream for many families is to obtain home ownership. In fact, most Americans believe they will have arrived at a position of financial security when their home is totally paid for. The reality is that financial security is not achieved when the home is paid for. I have had many clients whose homes were free and clear. But then they realized that even though debt-free home ownership had been a lifelong goal, that free and clear home was housing not only them but also a ton of idle cash. Their homes would probably just transfer down to their heirs upon their deaths unless there was some way to tap into this resource they had spent a lifetime putting money into.

TAKING ADVANTAGE OF YOUR EQUITY IN RETIREMENT

I believe financial security is really obtained when there are enough liquid assets in a safe environment to not only wash any liabilities, including a home mortgage, but also to have enough cash flow generated from those assets to meet living expenses—and have our needs and wants satisfied. Today there are over 20 million Americans over the age of sixty-two who own their homes totally free and clear. This represents over $2 trillion in home equity. However, if you were to interview most of those people, I doubt the majority would feel they were financially secure. In fact, at least 5 million of those Americans, or about one-fourth of them, are under the national poverty level as far as income is concerned. They are what I call "house rich, cash poor." You may know someone in this category, or you, yourself, might be in this category. You are living in an asset that is free and clear, but find yourself with too much month left at the end of the money!

Unfortunately, many elderly homeowners could not afford to make a mortgage payment if they wanted to. Their Social Security or other retirement income is hardly sufficient to meet their minimum living expenses. Perhaps they can barely afford to pay the property tax on their homes, let alone the utilities, grocery bills, and other necessities of life. Senior citizens are concerned about their health and quality of life. They are also concerned about money or the lack of money. Retired seniors with few assets face serious issues, especially when they realize they may have to downgrade their lifestyle just to fill prescriptions.

A 1998 *New York Times* survey indicated only 11 percent of the population over age 64 live in retirement communities, while 84 percent of all older Americans would prefer to stay in their own homes and never move. Seniors also do not want to be a burden on their children.

My advice to couples preparing for retirement is they should always retain the key to unlocking the value of one of the most important assets—their home equity. Too many people enter retirement and throw away the key to one of the most golden opportunities they have to remaining financially secure. At the least, these people ought to obtain an equity line of credit that will be good for possibly five, ten, or fifteen years. By doing so, they will have the option of simply writing a check in the event of an emergency and using that dormant equity in the home. It's much better to qualify for a second mortgage or equity line of credit before you retire and still have an income than to try to qualify afterwards and have to verify the income and cash flow to meet the bank's lending guidelines. There are usually no fees associated with establishing an equity line of credit. Most banks and credit unions will pay for the appraisal and closing costs. The only time you pay interest is when you actually write out a check to use the line of credit. (Some banks and credit unions may charge a nominal annual fee to maintain an equity line of credit.)

I have observed several couples who anticipated a possible layoff from their employments. While they were yet gainfully employed, they qualified for equity lines of credit on their homes. A few months later, after being laid off, they were able to use those equity lines of credit to get them through the tough times until they found new jobs. Their banks and credit unions were not concerned because they qualified at the time they applied for the equity line. However, I have observed other couples who waited to apply for equity lines of credit until after being laid off. Almost without exception, the banker refused to extend the equity line of credit—no matter how much equity they had in their homes—because at the time of application they did not satisfactorily possess the ability to repay. Again, it is much better to have access to equity and cash before you need it than to need it and not be able to obtain it. This is particularly true as people enter retirement.

The *Chicago Tribune* published an article by Robert Bruss on February 20, 1988 headlined "Large Equity In Your Home Can Be A Big Disadvantage." The article stated, "By having cash available for emergencies and investment opportunities, most homeowners are better off than if their equity is tied up in their residences." It also said, "...large idle equity, also called 'having all your eggs in one basket,' can be risky if the homeowner suddenly needs cash. While employed and in excellent health, borrowing on a home is easy. Most people, especially retirees, unexpectedly need cash when they are sick, unemployed, or have insufficient income. Obtaining a home loan under these circumstances can be either impossible or very expensive."

REVERSE MORTGAGES

During the last decade, there have been more opportunities for retirees to convert the equity from their homes into income during this critical time in their lives. There are actually ways by which you can convert the equity in your home into monthly income. These strategies allow people to annuitize the equity in their homes. The most common way is through a reverse mortgage.

A reverse mortgage is a safe and easy way for seniors to turn their home's equity into an additional source of income to meet any financial need. A reverse mortgage is a loan available to senior homeowners who are at least 62 years of age. It turns home equity into cash with no out-of-pocket closing costs. So, instead of the homeowner making a mortgage payment to the mortgage company, it works in reverse. The mortgage company makes a payment to the senior homeowner. Loans through federal programs can offer seniors up to $275,000 in either a lump sum, a monthly payment, or a line of credit. The money they receive through the reverse mortgage is tax-free, and the senior never has to make a payment on the loan. In fact, the loan only comes due when

the borrower decides to move from the home permanently, decides to sell the home, or dies. Also, the amount of the loan can never exceed the value of the house.

The reverse mortgage concept is gaining momentum as baby boomers begin to retire. Let's take a look at a couple of typical "house rich, cash poor" situations that benefited from using a reverse mortgage. The first example was published in the September 9, 2001, *Deseret News* in Salt Lake City, Utah, in an article entitled "Reverse Mortgages" by Max Knudsen, Executive Business Editor.

> Retired West Valley residents Hal and Barbara Potter were just squeaking by on Social Security last year, and their "savings" were tied up in the equity of their home.
>
> They could have sold it, of course. It was paid for, and the proceeds would have likely been tax-free, allowing them to rent an apartment and bolster their income.

But like many retirees, they didn't want to go through the hassles—both physical and emotional—of selling and moving. After doing some research, the couple celebrated their sixtieth wedding anniversary by taking out a reverse mortgage, which pays them $400 a month while allowing them to stay in their home as long as they want or until circumstances, such as ill health, require them to move.

We were at the senior center one day and some people were talking about them (reverse mortgages)," Hal Potter said. "I asked a young lady who works at the bank about them and we ended up going that way. I can tell you that the extra cash every month really helps us."

The second example is about a widow named Lilian Hunter. Lilian isn't a real person, but her situation is. It was published in the September 2001 edition of the magazine, *Senior Market Advisor,* in an article entitled, "Home Equity on Tap," by MariJo Harding, a senior loan advisor with Financial Freedom Senior Funding Corporation in Houston:

Lilian Hunter's life hadn't been the same since her husband Henry died last year. As a housewife for 42 years, Lilian's career was raising their three children while Henry worked at one of the big oil companies in Houston. Unfortunately, he wasn't one of the privileged few executives. During their retirement years they had come to rely upon Henry's pension checks to help them make ends meet.

It was only after he died, and the pension checks went away, that Lilian realized that they hadn't developed a very effective retirement plan. To make matters worse, Lilian's HMO had shut down in her area last year. She suddenly was faced with high Medicare supplement premiums. She was also struggling with drug prescription costs and even began to skip a few doses to stretch her dollars. Every little penny counted now, so the cherished "girlfriends only" weekend tradition looked impossible to attend this year. In fact, Lilian began taking steps toward selling her house as a last-ditch effort to try to live the rest of her retirement years with grace and dignity. She would never ask the children for help because she knew they had financial concerns and responsibilities of their own.

One morning, while having coffee, Lilian was reading the newspaper when she glanced at an article about reverse mortgages. Because Lilian had been considering selling the house, the article caught her attention. Lilian read how a widow much like herself

watched her retirement income dwindle. To solve this income problem, the lady took a lump-sum reverse-mortgage payment and used
it to fund an immediate annuity. That solved her cash flow problem.
The woman could continue living in her house.

Lilian made a few calls, and by the end of the day, a loan officer
gave her sixty-five thousand reasons why she shouldn't cancel her
girlfriend's weekend. Without hesitation, she picked up the phone.
"Darling? Count me in for this weekend. I'll be there!"

How do you qualify for a reverse mortgage? Qualifying for a reverse
mortgage is simple. Seniors can qualify for reverse mortgages if they are
62 or older and own their homes or condominiums free and clear, or
have a very small mortgage left to pay. There are no medical or income
requirements, although the age of the applicant does affect the amount
of the loan (the older the applicant, the higher the loan, usually). Based
on the retired couple's combined ages, their mortality is calculated by the
mortgage company in much the same way a life insurance company calculates it. Specifically, criteria that determine the loan amount are age,
type of reverse mortgage chosen, the home's value, current interest rates,
and location. Also, a credit report is not required.

Those who qualify may choose from a variety of ways to receive
funds from a reverse mortgage. The loan proceeds can be paid in any
combination of the following:

- A lump sum
- Monthly (tenure) payments for the life of the loan
- Term payments for a specific period of time
- A line of credit with possible growth
- A modified tenure, which is a combination of a monthly
  payment and a line of credit

Reverse mortgage borrowers may use the proceeds for whatever they
wish.

Possible uses of the money may include:

- paying off debts, including mortgage and credit cards;
- making needed home repairs;
- paying for home health care;

- purchasing long-term health insurance;
- making additional retirement investments;
- traveling, or helping a grandchild with college expenses.

There are three types of reverse mortgage programs typically available. The first one is the FHA home equity conversion mortgage, or HECM. The maximum lending limit for the HECM (at the time this book was published) is $239,250. The second program is offered by the Fannie Mae HomeKeeper mortgage. This has a maximum lending limit at the time of publication of $275,000. Some lending institutions also offer a line of credit or cash account. Financial Freedom Senior Funding Corporation offers a financial freedom cash account with a maximum lending limit of $1 million or more. Each of these reverse mortgage products has a different interest rate.

There are certain property requirements for a reverse mortgage. In most cases, the property must be a single-family dwelling. However, the HECM reverse mortgage option is also available for one to four units. The borrower must occupy the property as his or her primary residence. Condos and PUD's are eligible if they are FHA- and Fannie Mae-approved. Also, all properties must meet the minimum FHA/Fannie Mae guidelines.

There are also responsibilities required of reverse mortgage borrowers. They are required to attend a free counseling session by an FHA- or Fannie Mae-approved counselor. The reverse mortgage borrower must also continue to maintain the property. The borrower is also required to continue to pay property taxes and insurance on the property.

There are several misconceptions surrounding a reverse mortgage. A common misconception is the lender can take the home. This is incorrect—the reverse mortgage is simply a lien, so the homeowner retains full ownership of the home. Another misconception is the homeowner can be thrown out of his home. This is also untrue—the homeowner can stay in his home for as long as he wishes. A third misconception is the homeowner can end up owing more than his home is worth. In reality, the homeowner can *never* owe more than the value of the home under a reverse mortgage program.

Although reverse mortgages are considered a relatively new product, according to Peter Bell, President of the National Reverse Mortgage Lenders Association, the concept can be traced back to the nineteenth century. In the September, 2001 issue of *Senior Market Advisor*, MariJo Harding gives us a brief history of reverse mortgages in her article, "Home Equity on Tap."

> Records dating back to the 19th century show European investors purchasing homes from aging individuals and then permitting them to live in the home rent free. During the 1920s in Great Britain, the business of home-equity reversion, a precursor to the current reverse mortgage, gained popularity, although it took 50 years for the concept to catch on in the United States. Even then, these loans usually were sponsored by local government agencies and were available only for property taxes and home repairs.
>
> In 1988, President Ronald Reagan signed legislation to launch the Federal Housing Administration's reverse mortgage program, known as the Home Equity Conversion Mortgage. In 1995, the Federal National Mortgage Association (Fannie Mae) entered the scene with its HomeKeeper program. Currently, both programs are available in all 50 states and, according to the National Reverse Mortgage Lender's Association, about 90 percent of all reverse mortgage loans are processed through the Department of Housing and Urban Development. NRMLA also lists Financial Freedom Senior Funding Corporation as the nation's primary private lender of jumbo loan sizes.

Jeff Ludwick, a CPA with Matthews, Ludwick & Follender, P.C. in Temple, Texas, stated, "We believe that the reverse mortgage is one of the best-kept secrets in estate and retirement planning. If used correctly, a reverse mortgage can assist many mature Americans, and in doing so, often removes a financial burden from their children by providing immediate monthly income in what sometimes appears to be a hopeless situation."

Harding also explains the method for obtaining a reverse mortgage.

> Most mortgage lending companies can facilitate a reverse mortgage, so call around to find one you feel comfortable working with.

A loan officer will then be able to coordinate the required HECM or Fannie Mae counseling with your client. Once the client receives a counseling certificate, the application and certificate can be submitted through the lender. The lender discloses the estimated cost of the loan, which usually is financed as part of the loan. The lender will then process the loan and set up an appraisal of the house. The borrower has three business days to rescind after closing. After this period, the loan is disbursed at the beginning of the following month. The borrower never has to make any monthly payments to repay the loan; the loan will be fully repayable when the last co-borrower leaves the home (usually the heirs selling the home). The loan also is nonrecourse, meaning the loan to be repaid will never exceed the value of the home. Interest rates normally are competitive with regular mortgage rates, but a few offer fixed interest rates.

So why should senior homeowners consider a reverse mortgage? It can unlock the equity trapped in the home. There are no income or credit qualifications. The loan proceeds are received as tax-free income. Reverse mortgages are FHA-insured or Fannie Mae-guaranteed. There are several flexible payment options available. Growth can be achieved on a line of credit using a reverse mortgage. None of the debt passes on to heirs. Also, reverse mortgage proceeds do not affect Social Security or Medicare benefits. Hence, reverse mortgages can be used as an effective financial planning tool, helping retirees to augment their monthly incomes and to purchase life insurance or long-term care insurance if needed. Some retirees have used reverse mortgage proceeds for charitable gifts. Others have used the reverse mortgage proceeds to purchase a second retirement home. Reverse mortgage proceeds can also be used for any type of investment funding the borrower desires.

A typical reverse mortgage might work this way: A seventy-year-old homeowner with a property appraised at $200,000 could get a monthly income payment of $540 for as long as he lives in the home, or a lump sum or open credit line of $80,017. An eighty-year-old homeowner with a property appraised at $200,000 could get a monthly income payment of $790 or a lump sum or open line of credit of $100,897—about half the home's value. One of the best user-friendly web sites I have found to help people determine possible options for a reverse mortgage in a

Fig. 14.1

FINANCIAL FREEDOM
A Subsidiary of Lehman Brothers Bank, FSB

REVERSE MORTGAGE CALCULATOR

Age Information:

04/22/1932 Nearest Age: 70

Additional Information:

City/State: Salt Lake City, UT
County: Salt Lake
Home Value: $200,000
Liens: $0

	FHA/HUD	REVERSE MORTGAGE PROGRAMS Fannie Mae HomeKeeper	Freedom Cash Acct.
CASH AVAILABLE			
Cash Available	$80,017	$58,222	$45,076
OR MONTHLY INCOME			
Monthly Income Available	$540	$421	*$0
OR LINE OF CREDIT			
Creditline Available	$80,017	$58,222	$45,076
Annualized Growth Rate	4.51%	N/A	5.00%
Creditline Value in 5 Years	$99,766	$58,222	$57,529
Creditline Value in 10 Years	$124,391	$58,222	$73,423
OR ANY COMBINATION OF THE ABOVE			

For example: 1/2 Cash Available, 1/4 Monthly Income and 1/4 Line ofCredit.

*Monthly Income Available under the Freedom Cash Account is created via the purchase of an optional full refund annuity.

All numbers listed above are ESTIMATES ONLY. This is not an offer to make you a loan, nor does this qualify you to obtain a loan. If you would like more information or would like to speak to a qualified loan advisor, please click the "More Information" button below. Interest rates vary by product.

<Back   Print

particular set of circumstances is www.financialfreedom.com. By entering the ages of the homeowners, the value of the home, the zip code, and other necessary information, this web site quickly calculates three different options that may be available (**fig. 14.1**). Another helpful web site is www.kendalltodd.com. **Figure 14.2** contains a simplified Reverse Mortgage Estimate Table to quickly calculate approximate reverse mortgage lump sum payments available to borrowers.

The NRMLA has two booklets available, "The Consumer Guide to Reverse Mortgages" and "Using Reverse Mortgages for Health Care." Other helpful information is listed below.

Fig. 14.2

REVERSE MORTGAGE ESTIMATE TABLE

Select the age (or year of birth) of the youngest living person in the home for which the reverse mortgage may be utilized. Then select the estimated value of the home and follow across to the estimate of current lump sum payment available to the borrower at closing net of all closing costs. For an exact estimate, please visit kendalltodd.com for a Mortgage Plan Request.

BIRTH YEAR	1940	1938	1936	1934	1932	1930	1928	1926	1924	1922	1920	1918	1916	1914	1912	
AGE	62	64	66	68	70	72	74	76	78	80	82	84	86	88	90	OVER 90
VALUE $ 50,000	$20,682	$21,574	$22,478	$23,395	$24,327	$25,325	$26,343	$27,431	$28,494	$29,634	$30,804	$31,959	$33,152	$34,339	$35,525	
$ 70,000	32,742	33,954	35,178	36,415	37,667	39,005	40,363	41,811	43,214	44,714	46,244	47,739	49,272	50,779	52,265	
$ 90,000	44,802	46,334	47,878	49,435	51,007	52,685	54,383	56,191	57,934	59,794	61,684	63,519	65,392	67,219	69,005	
$ 110,000	56,662	58,514	60,378	62,255	64,147	66,165	68,203	70,371	72,454	74,674	76,924	79,099	81,312	83,459	85,545	
$ 130,000	68,322	70,494	72,678	74,875	77,087	79,445	81,823	84,351	86,774	89,354	91,964	94,479	97,032	99,499	101,885	
$ 150,000	79,982	82,474	84,978	87,495	90,027	92,725	95,443	98,331	101,094	104,034	107,004	109,859	112,752	115,539	118,225	
$ 170,000	91,642	94,454	97,278	100,115	102,967	106,005	109,063	112,311	115,414	118,714	122,044	125,239	128,472	131,579	134,565	
$ 190,000	93,277	96,134	99,003	101,885	104,781	107,868	110,973	114,272	117,422	120,773	124,153	127,396	130,677	133,829	136,857	
$ 210,000	93,277	96,134	99,003	101,885	104,781	107,868	110,973	114,272	117,422	120,773	124,153	127,396	130,677	133,829	136,857	
$ 230,000	93,277	96,134	99,003	101,885	104,781	107,868	110,973	114,272	117,422	120,773	124,153	127,396	130,677	138,664	139,796	
$ 250,000	93,277	96,134	99,003	101,885	104,781	107,868	110,973	114,272	117,422	120,773	124,153	133,190	142,115	151,095	152,315	
$ 270,000	93,277	96,134	99,003	101,885	104,781	107,868	110,973	114,272	117,422	124,735	134,281	144,192	153,828	163,527	164,834	
$ 290,000	93,277	96,134	99,003	101,885	104,781	107,868	110,973	114,272	117,422	134,312	144,558	155,194	165,541	175,958	177,353	
$ 310,000	93,277	96,134	99,003	101,885	104,781	107,868	110,973	114,272	117,422	139,435	150,056	161,081	171,807	182,609	184,050	
$ 330,000	93,277	96,134	99,003	101,885	104,781	107,868	110,973	114,272	117,422	139,435	150,056	161,081	171,807	182,609	184,050	
$ 350,000	93,277	96,134	99,003	101,885	104,781	107,868	110,973	114,272	119,794	139,435	150,056	161,081	171,807	182,609	184,050	
$ 400,000	93,277	96,134	99,003	101,885	104,781	107,868	110,973	124,604	137,124	150,644	165,044	180,044	191,004	199,564	208,204	
$ 500,000	93,277	96,134	99,003	105,834	116,734	128,734	141,834	156,134	171,784	188,684	206,684	225,434	239,134	249,834	260,634	
$ 600,000	93,277	99,424	112,924	127,804	140,884	155,284	171,004	188,164	206,944	227,224	248,824	271,324	287,764	300,604	313,564	
$ 700,000	102,244	116,664	132,414	149,774	165,034	181,834	200,174	220,194	242,104	265,764	290,964	317,214	336,394	351,374	366,494	
$ 800,000	117,424	133,904	151,904	171,744	189,184	208,384	229,334	252,224	277,264	304,304	333,104	363,104	385,024	402,144	419,424	
$ 900,000	132,604	151,144	171,394	193,714	213,334	234,934	258,214	284,254	312,424	342,844	375,244	408,994	433,654	452,914	472,354	
$ 1,000,000	147,784	168,384	190,884	215,684	237,484	261,484	287,684	316,284	347,584	381,384	417,384	454,884	482,284	503,684	525,284	
OVER $1M																

Property Location and current Interest Rates will adjust these numbers up or down. Home values provided in $20,000 increments—use lowest value for conservative estimate. Ages provided in 2-year increments—use lowest age of youngest borrower living in home for conservative estimate.

1. Department of Housing and Urban Development (888-466-3487, www.hud.gov): They provide details on Home Equity Conversion Mortgage (HECM), a list of agency approved counselors, and a series of helpful FAQs.

2. The National Federal Mortgage Association (Fannie Mae) (800-732-6643, www.homepath.com, www.fanniemae.com): They offer details on the HomeKeeper and HECM programs as well as a list of lenders nationwide.

3. Financial Freedom Senior Funding Corporation (800-500-5150, www.financialfreedom.com, www.ffsenior.com): Here you can learn about Financial Freedom's Equity Guard and Cash Account Plans.

4. National Reverse Mortgage Lender's Association (202-939-1765, www.reversemortgage.org): They provide a state-by-state listing of the NRMLA members and detailed reverse mortgage information.

5. The American Association of Retired Persons (800-424-3410, www.aarp.org): They provide a step-by-step process on how reverse mortgages work and eligibility.

6. Kendall Todd (919-309-9078, www.kendalltodd.com): They provide a comprehensive mortgage planning analysis in harmony with the concepts contained in this book.

CASE STUDY #1

Let's look at three simple case studies to see how a reverse mortgage might help you or someone you know. If a couple, ages 70 and 68, owned a home valued at $200,000, the eligible proceeds might be $75,000 as a lump sum. One of their options could be to put the $75,000 into an immediate annuity. The annuity could generate an annual income of $4,000. In addition, they could purchase long-term care insurance if necessary. Another option would be to put the $75,000 to work in a real estate investment trust. Their cash flow could then possibly reach 7.5 percent, or about $5,625 annually. They could purchase life insurance or long-term care insurance with some of the proceeds. A third option might be to leave the $75,000 as an open line of credit. A fourth option would be to pay off a first mortgage and then use the savings to improve quality of life.

CASE STUDY #2

Let's look at a second case study. If a homeowner was age 76 and single, he could qualify for a reverse mortgage. Let's assume the value of the home is $300,000. This person might be able to fund some savings plans for three grandchildren. He could put the entire proceeds strategically into a life insurance contract to achieve a tax-advantaged rate of return and leave behind a greater amount should he die. He could also fund long-term care insurance. He could give it to his church or charity for an endowment, or he could invest it in a real estate investment trust for cash flow and appreciation.

CASE STUDY #3

In case study number three, let's assume the homeowners are ages 82 and 80. Let's also assume their home is valued at $1.4 million. In this case, the eligible proceeds might be as much as $400,000 under the lump sum option. They could place the $400,000 in a survivorship life insurance contract with a single payment. The death benefit could be $1,889,661 with a policy designed to likely maintain life insurance coverage until they both attained age 95. Let's assume they have both died by the fifteenth year. If the home appreciated at an average of 4 percent a year the home would be worth approximately $2,521,320 at the time of their deaths. Let's assume the interest on the loan averaged 8 percent. Therefore, the loan amount will have accrued to $1,268,868. The death benefit at that point is $1,889,661, which would redeem the loan balance and leave the heirs with the option of having a free and clear home and a remaining $620,793 of tax-free life insurance proceeds. They could also choose to keep the tax-free proceeds from the insurance and let the lender have the home in the event it was not worth more than the loan balance.

Reverse mortgages do have their disadvantages, though. The first is the couple may be spending down their equity gradually. Second, they may be slowly disinheriting their heirs. Remember, the loan does not become due until the home is sold, the borrower permanently moves from the primary residence, or both the husband and the wife have passed away. At that point, the mortgage and its accrued interest will become due based solely on the collateral of the home. In the event of the borrowers' deaths, the heirs to the home then have the option of paying off the mortgage (probably from the sales proceeds of the house) or allowing the mortgage company to take over the property. Many retired couples are concerned about spending down that equity because they do not want to disinherit their children. Actually, I have found many children do not really care about inheriting their parents' home! They would rather see their parents enjoy life during the golden years of their retirement. Thus, if there were a feasible way to live in the home during their lifetimes and still use the idle equity dollars, it would be wise to consider annuitizing the equity in their home to create a tax-free supplemental retirement income.

SECOND-TO-DIE LIFE INSURANCE

I feel the best way to pass down your home free and clear to your heirs if a reverse mortgage is taken out is to use a portion of the reverse mortgage proceeds to purchase an inexpensive second-to-die life insurance policy. A second-to-die life insurance policy is less expensive than a normal life insurance policy because it covers two lives and only pays one death benefit after both individuals have passed away. The insurance proceeds are payable to the beneficiary upon the second death of the two insureds.

If an eighty-year-old couple had a home worth $200,000, had taken out a reverse mortgage generating monthly income of $790, and had both passed away after ten years, their mortgage may have accrued to $145,491 (assuming an 8 percent interest rate) during that time period. If they had reserved a portion of the tax-free cash flow each month generated by the reverse mortgage, they could have possibly qualified to purchase a second-to-die life insurance policy with a $150,000 death benefit for a monthly premium cost of about $232. Thus, they would have realized a net monthly tax-free income of $558 after deducting the insurance premium of $232 from the $790 of monthly mortgage proceeds. If their home had appreciated during that ten-year period at 5 percent per year, it would then be worth $329,401. Therefore, it would behoove the heirs to pay off the mortgage in order to retain the equity growth that had occurred in the home. The $150,000 of life insurance proceeds would pass down income tax free to the heirs upon the deaths of the owners. The heirs would then have the option of taking the tax-free insurance proceeds and relinquishing the house to the mortgage company. They could also take the insurance proceeds and pay off the mortgage balance with accrued interest at the time of death, then keep both the house and the remaining cash. The latter is usually the most desirable choice for the heirs, depending upon the circumstances.

LEASE-BACK

Other options are available for retirees who are house rich and cash poor. A retired couple could sell their home to their children and then lease it back. In that case, the retirees could realize up to $500,000 of tax-free capital gains (see chapter 12). Using this method, the home can be sold to their children and leased back so they could use some of the cash tied up in their property while they remain living in the home.

Under current tax law, as explained in chapter 12, a home that is properly transferred to heirs upon death receives a step-up in basis. This means the heirs who inherit the asset do not have to pay capital gain taxes. For example, if the house had a basis of $70,000 and it had appreciated in value to $250,000 at the time of their deaths, the new basis for the heirs would be stepped up to $250,000. Therefore, the children would only have to pay capital gains tax on the difference between what they later sold it for and the new $250,000 basis. This is true unless it had been their personal residence for at least two of the previous five years.

As explained in chapter 12, the current law providing a step-up in basis to fair market value is set to be repealed in the year 2010, but could be reenacted again under the sunset provision in 2011.

LIFE ESTATE

Another option would be a life estate. According to *Black's Law Dictionary*, Revised Fourth Edition, a life estate is "an estate whose duration is limited to the life of the party holding it, or some other person." Therefore a life estate provides the right to the use of the property or asset for one's lifetime. This could give the person all the income from the asset during his life.

As an example, if a child purchased his parents' home but the parents retained a life estate in the home, then the child would pay a reduced price for the home. Thus, the child is only buying the remainder interest that is left after the life estate. The parents would live in the home during their lifetimes. When the parents die, the home would be the child's home. The child could either purchase the home with a fully cashed out payment or could purchase it in installments. Once committed, the child would have to fully pay the agreed upon amount. The amount of the life estate and remainder interest are set by the Internal Revenue Code, Reg. 25.2512-5(f). For example, for a seventy-year-old individual, the factor for the life estate is .60522, so the remainder interest would be .39478 (the combined total equals 1.00000). For an eighty-year-old individual, the factor for the life estate is .43659, so the remainder interest would be .56341. If a child purchased his eighty-year-old parents' home and the home was worth $100,000 at the time of purchase, the life estate is valued at $43,659, and the remainder interest would be $56,341. So the child could buy the home for $56,341, but the parents would retain the right to live in the home for the rest of their lives.

Whatever method is used, my advice to retiring couples is to retain access to the greatest amount of available equity on their property. Two clients once came into my office who were three years from retirement and owned a home free and clear. They told me throughout their entire lives, their goal had been to have their home paid for. After attending my seminar on successfully managing equity, they came in for a comprehensive analysis. They then refinanced their home to 80 percent loan-to-value and separated the equity into a conservative side fund. By doing so, we not only gave them additional tax benefits for the next several years, but we also created a nest egg they used for retirement income. We met their after-tax mortgage payment easily with the interest generated from their side fund. We also generated an additional $300 of monthly income after the mortgage payment to supplement their retirement. A wonderful side benefit was that the tax benefits from this strategy dramatically offset the tax liability on some of their IRA distributions. I will explain more about this in chapter 19.

I consulted with another couple who owned their home free and clear. They were about to sell their home and build a new retirement home. As we analyzed their situation, they realized their home had appreciated substantially during the past twenty years. They sold their existing home and avoided the capital gains tax through the exclusion and built a new retirement home. Their first temptation was to pay cash for the retirement home. This would still allow them to have plenty of cash left over. However, I illustrated how using a maximum mortgage of 80 percent loan-to-value on their new retirement home and employing as much equity as possible from the sale of their former home could create a substantial liquid side fund. The side fund now generates enough monthly tax-free income to meet the newer mortgage payment and give them over $500 a month more retirement income than if they had paid cash for their new retirement home!

These strategies usually require people to "change their seat" and accept a new perspective on equity management and proper debt management. Please keep in mind that at any time, those couples who choose to retain equity in a liquid side fund have the ability to take the money from one pocket (their liquid side fund) and pay off the mortgage in the other pocket. Their newly created asset can wash out the mortgage liability and put them back with the free and clear home if they so choose, provided they conserve that equity and only consume the excess interest they are earning. The key is they can generate more cash for retirement needs by using this strategy than if they had combined all of their assets together into a free and clear piece of property.

14 WEALTH-ENHANCEMENT STRATEGY NUMBER FOURTEEN

- *Retain the key to one of the most important assets you have —the value of your home equity.*

CHAPTER 15

IRAs and 401ks—Do You Know "The Rest of the Story"?

Retirement affects the amount of income taxes you pay.

COMMON MYTH-CONCEPTION

You will be in a lower tax bracket when you retire than when employed.

REALITY

With the 1986 Tax Reform Act and subsequent tax reform, most retirees in America will find themselves in a tax bracket at least as high—if not higher—than during their earning years. Why? Fewer deductions and exemptions.

Most Americans concerned about preparing for retirement are lured into contributing pre-tax dollars into 401(k) plans or tax-deductible contributions into IRAs. Such "qualified plans" only give you tax-favored advantages during the contribution and accumulation (growth) phases of your retirement account. What about the most important phases—when you withdraw the money for retirement income, or transfer any remaining funds to your heirs? As Paul Harvey would put it, "Has anyone ever told you the rest of the story?"

DECONSTRUCTING QUALIFIED RETIREMENT PLANS

A couple filing a joint income tax return with a taxable income above $46,700 in 2002 (the threshold between the second and third brackets) would have been in a 27 percent marginal federal tax bracket plus the applicable state income tax rate (let's assume the state tax rate is 7 percent). If each spouse qualifies for deductible contributions to their IRAs, they would save approximately $1,360 a year in taxes if they were to contribute $4,000 per year. However, most retirees will pay back every dollar to Uncle Sam they saved in taxes during the contribution phase of their retirement account during the first eighteen to twenty-four months of their actual retirement. In fact, the average retired couple will pay eight to twelve times more in taxes on their IRAs and 401(k)s during their retirement years than they saved during their contribution and accumulation years.

In 1989, *US News and World Report* published an article written by Leo Weidner entitled, "How Congress Is Peddling IRA and 401(k) Snake Oil." In the article, Mr. Weidner stated, "One of the original IRA and 401(k) tenets held that deferring tax until retirement was advantageous because funds would likely be taxed at a lower rate. That is no longer axiomatic. You may well spend retirement in the same or higher bracket if you accumulate a respectable retirement nest egg. In fact, tax rates will likely rise in the future to cover budget deficits." So, my question is, "Why postpone the inevitable and compound the tax problem?"

Americans are not to blame for believing they will be in a lower tax bracket when they retire because this is how retirement accounts are generally sold to people. Many financial planners, investment counselors, and insurance agents show people that by making tax-deductible retirement contributions to their retirement accounts with pre-tax dollars, they will have the full amount (let's say $4,000) working for them instead of a net after tax of $2,640 working for them (in a 34 percent tax bracket).

Most people understand that at a given rate of return, $4,000 a year will grow to a larger sum of money than $2,640 a year will grow to. The theory is you not only accumulate a larger nest egg this way, but also you will be in a lower tax bracket upon retirement. Because of the changes that took place with the 1986 Tax Reform Act, we found the top marginal bracket in the United States dropped from 70 percent down to 28 percent. However, the average effective rate for Americans rose from approximately 12 percent up to 18 percent! In other words, people paid effectively more in tax after the 1986 Tax Reform Act because of the exemptions and deductions reduced or eliminated.

This is especially true for retirees. As many people approach retirement, they find themselves with a free and clear home. So, they no longer have the mortgage interest expense deduction. Their children have matured into adults, so they can no longer claim them as dependents. No longer are people entitled to double exemptions when they retire as they were entitled to before 1986. Even though many retirees have a lower amount of cash flow or income, they find themselves in at least as high a bracket as they were throughout their earning years. All of the deductions and exemptions that were helping them during those earning years have either been eliminated or they can no longer qualify for them.

I know many retirees who have begun to draw on their retirement income and almost curse the day they ever began their qualified plans. They find they are now paying back everything they saved in taxes during their accumulation and contribution years within the first two years of their retirement. And they will continue to pay it back over and over again! Qualified plans may be one of the best savings bonds the government has ever instituted as a way to generate future tax revenue.

Let's clarify what is meant by the term "qualified plan." Who qualifies the plan? Uncle Sam, right? Under the Internal Revenue Code, a retirement plan that is established in compliance with the rules and guidelines outlined by the IRS has tax-favored benefits to make it appear attractive. Generally, a qualified plan allows the individual to either contribute money with pre-tax dollars or receive a tax deduction for the amount she contributes. The account generally is allowed to grow tax deferred. Qualified plans include, but are not limited to, IRAs, 401(k)s, TSAs, 403(b)s, 457s, pension, and profit-sharing plans.

THE FOUR PHASES OF RETIREMENT PLANNING

To have a clear understanding of the tax trap people get themselves into, let's break up retirement planning into four general phases. The first phase of retirement planning is the contribution phase. This is when we make contributions or deposits into some type of an investment or savings vehicle to accumulate it for future use during retirement. If we contribute money into an investment vehicle that is considered a qualified plan under the Internal Revenue Code, we may deduct those contributions from our gross income on our tax return or contribute money with pre-taxed income. This reduces our gross income, and we are able to use 100-cent dollars on the front end. Some qualified plans, although they are less prominent, allow you to put in after-tax dollars for your seed money. As an example, we will discuss the Roth IRA that was introduced under the 1997 Tax Payer Relief Act in chapter 16.

The second phase of our retirement planning overlaps the first phase. In this phase we can accumulate money with compound interest, appreciation, or through the reinvestment of dividends and capital gains. Depending on the investment vehicle the investor chooses, capital gains may be realized or unrealized as the account grows. The accumulation takes place free of tax under qualified plans because any dividends, capital gains, or credited interest stays and compounds with the account, and is not reportable as a taxable event on your annual tax return. Therefore, the compounding that takes place in a tax-deferred

Fig. 15.1	FOUR PHASES OF RETIREMENT PLANNING			
	CONTRIBUTION	ACCUMULATION	WITHDRAWAL	TRANSFER
		IRA/401(k)		
	Tax Favored	Tax Favored	Taxed	Taxed

environment allows greater growth because the children of the investments (the interest) also help your account to blossom and grow without being taxed during the accumulation phase.

On the surface this would seem like an ideal arrangement—to be able to contribute 100 percent of your dollars before being taxed and have them continue to compound and grow without being taxed on the gain during the growth process. In most mathematical figures shown by sales people, this is as far as they go—contribution and accumulation. I ask, "What about the most important phase: the point when you will use that money the most (the withdrawal phase)? Or, if you do not use all of the money before you pass away, what happens to your retirement funds during the transfer of those monies to a spouse or to non-spousal heirs (the transfer phase)?" As shown in **figure 15.1**, this is when these accounts become taxable.

Money that has grown inside qualified plans is not only subject to income tax as it is withdrawn, but also, in the transfer phase, an estate tax (see chapter 12) may be due upon the second death of two spouses' deaths, as the remaining money passes down to non-spousal heirs. Therefore, retirement plan assets may be essentially taxed twice.

HOW CONGRESS TAXES QUALIFIED PLANS

I have discovered Congress and the IRS have held to the attitude that money accumulating in retirement accounts is fair game after the account holder dies, and then it's open season (**fig. 15.2**)! The government has found one of the least painful ways to gather revenue is to tax assets as they are passed down from one generation to another, partly

Fig. 15.2

Open Season

because the least resistance arises in that phase. In other words, the people who accumulated the money are no longer here to protest the tax. Many children and heirs are anxious to inherit whatever they can. They often do not protest the amount of income tax levied on their parents' accounts and the tax on inheritance as the estate transfer takes place. I know of many heirs who inherited a qualified plan from their parents but ended up with only about twenty-two cents on the dollar. I have actually witnessed retirees whose qualified plan assets were nearly all lost between the estate tax and income taxes due at their deaths.

This happened more often with affluent individuals in the top income tax and estate tax brackets prior to the 1997 Taxpayer Relief Act when the excess accumulation "success tax" of 15 percent was in effect. The "success tax" was an additional 15 percent excise tax that became due on any distributions in excess of approximately $150,000. In other words, if you were too successful saving for your retirement, you were penalized an additional 15 percent on top of your normal income tax rate! Such a tax could be reintroduced again in the future.

As you can appreciate, I believe it is important that all financial planning strategies contain flexibility to accommodate unexpected, uncontrollable changes. If you begin a qualified plan and need to dip into the funds for emergency purposes before age 59^1/$_2$, there is a 10 percent penalty.

Many 401(k) plans allow individuals to borrow on their 401(k)s. However, certain conditions must be met in order to avoid a 10 percent penalty. One of those conditions is the loan must be paid back systematically, according to a schedule that starts immediately. The interest charged on borrowing from a 401(k) can be credited back to the person's 401(k), so you are in effect paying interest to yourself. This can be an attractive feature. If timely payments are not made or deducted from your paycheck, then any of those funds that were received in the form of a loan convert to a distribution and are taxed in the year it was converted. A 10 percent penalty tax may be assessed on top of that if you are under age 59^1/$_2$.

THE BENEFITS OF A STRATEGIC ROLL-OUT

Many postpone the transfer of any qualified funds into a non-qualified status until age 59^1/$_2$ in order to alleviate the 10 percent tax penalty. What they don't realize is the only thing they may be saving by postponing a transfer is the 10 percent penalty. The normal income tax will still be due. Sometimes, by postponing the tax and penalty, people will find themselves in a higher tax bracket after age 59^1/$_2$ due to either Congress raising tax rates over the interim period or the individuals earning more money. Understand you often will not save taxes by postponing the tax liability. You may be simply delaying the inevitable!

LEVERAGE TAX-YEAR FLUCTUATIONS

Sometimes couples experience a year in which they have a large tax deduction. Maybe through a job change their gross income drops dramatically for one year. For example, their taxable income might be $20,000 below the third tax bracket, where the federal rate jumps up 12 percent from 15 percent to 27 percent. These couples should seize the opportunity to convert some of their qualified accounts to non-qualified accounts that could provide tax-free growth and access during retirement. If they took advantage of the low taxable income year, they could possibly pull out and reposition $20,000 of IRA/401(k) monies and pay the tax they would otherwise pay at a higher rate later on. Even with a 10 percent penalty, their total tax might be 15 percent plus a 10 percent penalty, which equals 25 percent. That is 2 percent less than the next bracket they might be in if they postpone!

Many older couples fail to take advantage of a low tax bracket to reposition qualified funds. For instance, they may be in a 15 percent bracket with their taxable income $10,000 below the 27 percent threshold. This means they can add $10,000 of income, while still remaining in the lower bracket. In this case they could reposition $10,000 of qualified funds at the low 15% tax rate. Their tax rate may be higher in the future; if they don't reposition now, that opportunity may be lost forever. It is usually advisable to get qualified money out, taxed, and repositioned into a tax-free environment rather than leave it there to continue to compound the problem.

A seventy-year-old couple came to me feeling so proud that during the previous ten-year period, they had reduced their taxable income, by virtue of other deductions, to zero. In other words, they had incurred no income tax liability for an entire decade, from ages 60 to 70. However, this couple had substantial assets that were growing, tax deferred, in their IRAs. When I showed them they could have transferred about $450,000 out of their IRAs during the previous decade and enjoyed the lowest tax rate of 15 percent federal tax, they were heartsick. Because they continued to postpone their tax and delay the inevitable, the minimum distribution requirements at age 70$1/2$ forced them into paying some tax as high as the third bracket (31 percent at that time), which was 16 percent higher!

MINIMUM DISTRIBUTIONS

If an individual does not begin withdrawing money by the age of $70^1/2$ in accordance to the Internal Revenue Code's minimum distribution formula, the IRS will penalize that individual for not withdrawing those funds. The IRS would like to have some of the money out and taxed each year before the couple passes away so they can receive revenues during the couple's lifetime. It may be taxed a second time, if not consumed, as it transfers to non-spousal heirs. If an individual leaves the money in a qualified plan and does not make the minimum withdrawal based upon the minimum distribution formula, a 50 percent penalty is assessed to the taxpayer on the amount that should have been withdrawn!

Let's use a simple example, illustrated in **figure 15.3.** For a couple in which the husband is age $70^1/2$ and a younger wife is within ten years of his age (or any age older), the divisor is shown for a period of twenty-one years. This assumes he began minimum distributions on April 1 of the year following 2002, which in this example is the year he reached $70^1/2$ years of age. Thus, on April 1, 2003, he must take the total of all his qualified accounts and divide by 25.3 to arrive at the minimum distribution required to avoid a 50 percent penalty. If his qualified accounts totaled $100,000, that means he would have to withdraw $3,952.57 ($100,000

Fig. 15.3	MINIMUM DISTRIBUTION CALCULATOR					
[1]	[2]	[3]		[1]	[2]	[3]
AGE	DATE	DIVISOR		AGE	DATE	DIVISOR
$71^1/2$	Apr. 2003	25.3		82	Dec. 2013	16.0
72	Dec. 2003	24.4		83	Dec. 2014	15.3
73	Dec. 2004	23.5		84	Dec. 2015	14.5
74	Dec. 2005	22.7		85	Dec. 2016	13.8
75	Dec. 2006	21.8		86	Dec. 2017	13.1
76	Dec. 2007	20.9		87	Dec. 2018	12.4
77	Dec. 2008	20.1		88	Dec. 2019	11.8
78	Dec. 2009	19.2		89	Dec. 2020	11.1
79	Dec. 2010	18.4		90	Dec. 2021	10.5
80	Dec. 2011	17.6		91	Dec. 2022	9.9
81	Dec. 2012	16.8				

divided by 25.3). If his qualified accounts totaled $1 million, he would have to withdraw $39,525.70, whether he needed the money or not. The next year, he would have to recalculate the total value of all his qualified accounts and divide by 24.4 to arrive at the minimum distribution. As seen from figure 15.3, the divisor changes each year as he gets older until by age 90, he must be withdrawing a minimum of approximately 10 percent of the value of his qualified accounts to avoid a penalty.

The best user-friendly website I have found to help you calculate this is found at www.tiaacref.org (or tiaacref.com). Just search under the calculators for the minimum distribution calculator. You may need to register before using the minimum distribution calculator, but all you need to calculate minimum distributions is your and/or your beneficiary's date(s) of birth, the value of your accounts and the growth rate you feel you'll be earning during your retirement years.

Couples must pull out the fractional amount required each year so the money is generating tax revenue before they die. At first, this seems like a very gentle distribution process and the taxes may not seem significant. But as the couple continues their minimum distributions, they end up paying extensive taxes when all the years are totaled together, and the remainder left behind at death gets taxed, as well.

I have repeatedly found instances in which a retired couple may pay more than twice the amount of taxes on their retirement plans if they string them out using the government's minimum distribution formula, rather than if they simply "bite the bullet" and pay the tax on a systematic withdrawal plan or strategic transfer over five to seven years. Often, after careful analysis, they may only pay 40 percent of the taxes they would have paid had they strung the withdrawals out over their lifetimes and transferred the remainder to their heirs. This is especially true if they reposition their after-tax distributions into a tax-free environment from that point on.

Upon the death of the first spouse, the surviving spouse may inherit or be the beneficiary of qualified plans. At that point, there are certain rules that allow a beneficiary under the age of 59 1/2 to receive those funds and not be subject to a 10 percent penalty. The funds could also be converted to an IRA under the beneficiary's name, but the distribution and subsequent tax would then be postponed. This option seems to be the temptation of most survivors or beneficiaries after inheriting a qualified account. They want to continue to defer or postpone the tax. In many instances it may be better for them to take out the money, and pay the tax at today's rates, and be done with it if they can without increasing their tax bracket. They could then reposition those after-tax funds into a non-qualified status possibly accumulating tax free from that point forward.

TRANSFERRING RETIREMENT FUNDS TO NON-SPOUSAL HEIRS

If there are still funds remaining in a qualified retirement plan such as an IRA or 401(k) upon the death of the second spouse, the value of the account is included in the estate of the deceased and must be calculated into the total value of the estate assets. Form 706, "United States Estate (and Generation-Skipping Transfer) Tax Return," comprised of over thirty pages, must be filed, and any estate taxes owed must be paid within nine months after death. If the estate is valued over the unified credit exemption illustrated in chapter 12, figure 12.2, the estate tax rate starts at 37 percent and eventually tops out at 45 to 50 percent depending on the year. Remember that if the 2001 Act is not changed, the unified credit exemption amount is increased to $3.5 million by 2009, then repealed in 2010, being replaced on January 1, 2011, by the estate tax law in effect in the year 2001!

In addition to possible estate tax liability, the income tax will have to be paid on those qualified funds at the tax rate of the beneficiary if the funds are not rolled over to another IRA. Such a transfer will generally move the beneficiary to a higher federal tax bracket. Let's assume she also has a 7 percent state income tax rate. Based on those distributions, a tax rate of over 32 percent will likely need to be paid on top of any estate tax due. Many people are not aware of tax impact on qualified plans during the withdrawal and transfer phases. Maybe that is why it is called the "withdrawal" phase—because so many people go into withdrawal when they realize the tax liability they have postponed and compounded!

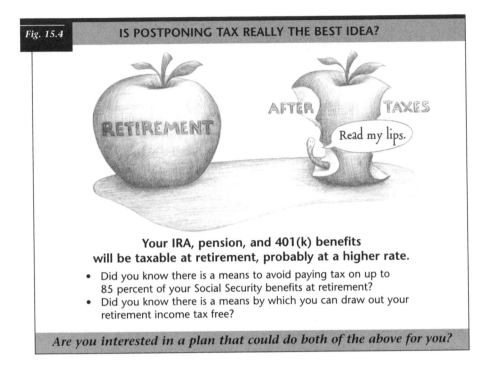

Fig. 15.4   **IS POSTPONING TAX REALLY THE BEST IDEA?**

AFTER   TAXES

RETIREMENT

Read my lips.

**Your IRA, pension, and 401(k) benefits
will be taxable at retirement, probably at a higher rate.**

- Did you know there is a means to avoid paying tax on up to
85 percent of your Social Security benefits at retirement?
- Did you know there is a means by which you can draw out your
retirement income tax free?

Are you interested in a plan that could do both of the above for you?

As shown in **figure 15.4**, often a person's retirement apple looks like plump, juicy fruit. Unfortunately, it often looks like an apple core after all the taxes are paid during the withdrawal years.

Let me illustrate with a simple example (**fig. 15.5**). If a couple contributed $4,000 a year for thirty years from age 35 into qualified plans, that would equal total contributions of $120,000. If their combined federal and state marginal income tax bracket was 34 percent, they actually achieved tax savings, each year they made a contribution, in the amount of $1,360. If you multiply $1,360 by thirty years, you end up with $40,800 of total tax savings achieved during the thirty-year contribution phase of their retirement plan. Their net outlay each year was only $2,640. This was attractive to them because they had a full $4,000 working for them when in actuality they only experienced $2,640 coming out of their pocket. In effect, Uncle Sam was paying the other $1,360 by not charging them the tax on $4,000 of annual income.

For the sake of simplicity, let's say that $4,000 grew at a rate of 10 percent for the thirty years. Their account balance at the end of thirty

Fig. 15.5	WHY DIDN'T SOMEBODY TELL ME "THE REST OF THE STORY?"

Annual IRA/401(k) Contribution = $4,000 x 30 yrs = $120,000 Total Contribution
Tax Bracket (income > $46,700) = 34%
Tax Savings   = $1,360 x 30 yrs = $40,800 Total Tax Savings
Net Outlay   = $2,640 per year

$4,000 year at 10% for 30 yrs = $723,774

At Age 85½ $500,000 Taxes Paid in Retirement Years VERSUS $40,800 Taxes Saved During Contribution Years	x 10% 72,000
	x 34% Tax Bracket
	(-24,480) Annual Tax
	= **$47,520** Net Income

In the first 20 months of retirement, every dollar of taxes saved during 30 years of deductions will be paid back. In fact, a person living a normal life expectancy will pay over 10 times the taxes on a qualified retirement plan during the retirement years than the taxes saved during the contribution years.

years would be $723,774. If they continued to earn a 10 percent return, they theoretically should be able to withdraw $72,377 per year or about $6,000 per month and never reduce the principal because they would simply be withdrawing the interest. If they were fortunate enough to be in the same tax bracket as during their earning years, they might pay 34 percent on $72,000 each year. They would pay an annual tax on the $72,000 of income in the amount of $24,480, leaving them a net spendable income of $47,520. If you study the annual tax liability of $24,480 you will realize in the first twenty months of retirement, every dollar of tax saved during thirty years of deductions was paid back! In fact, a person living a normal life expectancy may pay well over ten times the taxes saved during the contribution years on qualified retirement plan distributions during the retirement years. In this example, this retired couple at age 85½ will have paid over $500,000 in taxes during their retirement years, versus the $40,800 of taxes they saved during the contribution phase of their retirement plan! Depending on which average rate of return you achieve on your retirement plans, you may end up paying back every dime of taxes you saved during the contribution phase in the first eighteen to twenty-four months of your withdrawal phase. Not only that, but you will continue to pay taxes for the remainder of your life on those distributions!

SOCIAL SECURITY BENEFITS

Take a moment to recall the three different types of income the IRS taxes on our federal tax return: earned income, passive income, and portfolio income. Most qualified plans are funded with some type of investment that generates portfolio income. In retirement, if you receive income from a traditional qualified plan, it will be taxed as distributions are made. Roth IRAs are an exception. Having portfolio or passive income currently does not directly reduce the amount of your Social Security benefits. Could that change in the future?

The plight of the federal government regarding Social Security is when it was first established, there were approximately sixty workers to every one recipient of Social Security benefits. Not many years later, with expanded benefits, there were about fifteen workers to every recipient of Social Security. About fifteen years ago, we were down to six workers to every recipient. Currently, there are approximately three workers to every recipient of Social Security! It is projected that, starting in the year 2006, we will begin to arrive at the point of two people pulling the wagon for every one riding in it. In other words, two-thirds of American workers will be providing for the other third of America receiving Social Security or welfare benefits!

Our maturing work force, affectionately called the baby boomers, is now approaching retirement. The younger generation, which will replace that workforce, is smaller. The smaller workforce will have to earn the income taxed for Social Security so it can provide the same benefits for an expanding group of retired individuals. We may witness the Social Security Administration in serious trouble.

Just a few years ago, a recipient of Social Security benefits between the ages of sixty-two and seventy experienced a reduction in benefits if she had earned income that exceeded a certain amount (approximately

$8,000). However, a couple could have had unlimited passive or portfolio income and still could have qualified for full Social Security benefits. This rule always bothered me as I witnessed elderly people working hard to earn money at such jobs as cleaning tables at restaurants to make ends meet, sometimes losing some Social Security benefits as a result! At the same time, very wealthy individuals, with an abundance of passive and portfolio income, received full Social Security benefits! It was unfair. The law has since changed. Now, retiree Social Security recipients between the ages of sixty-two and sixty-five are the only group that has limits on what they can earn before experiencing a reduction in benefits. After age sixty-five, Social Security recipients can have unlimited earned, passive, or portfolio income without experiencing a direct reduction in benefits.

However, a portion of Social Security benefits may be subject to income taxation, depending on a beneficiary's tax filing status and "provisional income." For most people, provisional income is adjusted gross income, plus tax-exempt income, plus one half of Social Security benefits.

- Under the 2001 tax rates, for married persons filing jointly, Social Security benefits were taxable only if provisional income exceeded $32,000.
- Between $32,000 and $44,000, up to 50 percent of benefits were taxable.
- Above $44,000, up to 85 percent of benefits were taxable. For singles, the 50 percent tier applied between $25,000 and $34,000.
- The 85 percent tier applied above $34,000.

For married persons filing separately, the 85 percent tier applied from the first dollar of provisional income. Taxation of Social Security benefits will likely continue in the future in a similar manner when a person has other sources of income.

Thirty years ago, the Bureau of Labor and Statistics released revealing statistics. They gathered extensive data on American males who worked throughout their lives an average of forty years from age 25. They found out of every 100 males who worked for forty years, only one was wealthy. Four had sufficient income and didn't have to work. Five were still working after age 65 just to provide the basic necessities. Thirty-six were dead—they didn't even make it to age 65! The majority— 54 percent—were completely dependent on Social Security, welfare, charity, or their own children. This happened in America, the richest nation on earth! Today we have better mortality rates and somewhat better saving habits. However, by age 65, 16 percent of Americans are dead, 46 percent have incomes less than $15,000, and 26 percent have incomes between $15,000 and $35,000. The largest combined group remains the same—those who are either dead or financially dependent on others!

FINANCIAL INDEPENDENCE

So, how do we become one of those who are financially independent? Remember in chapter 5 I explained how to quickly calculate what the cost of living may be at your retirement age by using the Rule of 72. Let's assume you are retiring today and could make ends meet with a $3,000 a month income. If you want to know how much you would need thirty years from now to buy the same loaves of bread or gallons of gasoline at a 5 percent average inflation rate, you divide 5 into 72. That tells you that the cost of living will double approximately every fifteen years. So, assuming a 5 percent average inflation rate, you would need $6,000 a month fifteen years from now and $12,000 a month thirty years from now to buy the same amount of goods and services you can get today for $3,000 a month.

So, how much would I need to accumulate in a retirement nest egg to generate $12,000 a month in tomorrow's dollars? Simply take $12,000 per month times twelve months, which equals $144,000 in annual income. Assuming you could earn an average 8 percent interest on your retirement accounts, you would need $1.8 million ($144,000 divided by 8 percent) to generate $12,000 a month. This is an interest-only solution, where you would not deplete your principal of $1.8 million, which might be helpful to hedge against cost-of-living increases.

The next question is how much would you need to set aside each year if you were earning an average of 8 percent interest in order to accumulate

$1.8 million in thirty years? A financial calculator comes in handy here. You simply enter $1.8 million as the future value, 8 percent as the interest rate, and 30 as the number of years, and then solve for the annual payment. The answer is $14,712. That is how much you would need to invest earning 8 percent per year to accumulate $1.8 million by year 30. Assuming you could earn 10 percent interest, you would only need to set aside $9,948 a year. And at 12 percent interest you would only need to set aside $6,660 per year.

As a general rule of thumb, I usually counsel my younger clients, who have at least thirty-five years in which to contribute to retirement plans, to set aside a minimum of 10 percent of their income annually. If they manage their investments and savings wisely, 10 percent of their income set aside annually at a moderate rate of return (8 to 10 percent) should produce a retirement income thirty-five years down the road that would be comparable to the same standard of living enjoyed during their earning years. This assumes inflation treats their increases in income throughout the years the same as it does other goods and services. If they only have twenty-five years left in which to contribute to a retirement plan, they ought to set aside at least 20 percent of their income to enjoy the same standard of living during retirement. Let's look at it in another way: A thirty-five-year-old couple who wants to retire at age sixty rather than at the usual age of sixty-five ought to set aside 20 percent or more of their income for twenty-five years to enjoy their current lifestyle without fear of outliving their money. If they set aside 20 percent of their income for thirty years, they could likely enjoy a higher standard of living than they did during their earning years, or they could be philanthropic and benefit charitable organizations, which is also fulfilling.

I have actually had couples come to me who were setting aside 60 percent of their income into savings and investments! They disciplined themselves to live on only 40 percent of their earnings! This is truly admirable. However, I counsel my clients there needs to be a balance. I believe that you need to smell some roses as you go through life's journey, building priceless memories! (See chapter 23, which addresses the optimization of the human, intellectual, and financial assets comprising "true wealth.")

Let's shift now to the plight of those who save and invest in qualified plans to augment their retirement income over the Social Security benefits they plan on receiving. If you saved and invested in a qualified plan, in your retirement years you may very well have disqualified yourself from your fair share of Social Security. In truth, if the tax revenue for funding Social Security were to cease, the system would probably be bankrupt within nine months because of the rate of benefits being paid out. Unfortunately, we have created a huge problem for our children tomorrow because of the benefits we want to provide people today. Hence, Congress may have to allocate more Social Security benefits to those who don't have any form of earned, passive, or portfolio income, penalizing those who saved in alternative plans for their retirement. Congress realizes this and is now trying to create more incentives for people to prepare for their own retirement rather than rely on Social Security.

As I will explain in the following chapters, I advise most people to position their retirement savings primarily in investment vehicles that will generate income-earning cash flow—and does not fall under the definition of earned, passive, or portfolio income. By doing so, their savings should not disqualify them from their fair share of Social Security benefits. I'm afraid people who save too much in traditional IRAs and 401(k)s may end up feeling cheated out of something to which they have contributed so faithfully during their entire working lives.

The following is an excerpt from an article, published on May 27, 2001, in the *New York Times*, entitled "A Study Dares to Question the 401(k)," by James Schembari, an editor at the *Times*.

> At a time when Congress is considering raising the annual investment limits on 401(k) plans to $15,000 from $10,500, a new study suggests that many people should invest less or not at all. For some low- to moderate-income-workers, investing in these tax-deferred retirement accounts may actually raise their taxes and reduce the amount of money they have available to spend over their lifetimes.
>
> My father would have been shocked. When I was in my 20s and in my first job out of college, he preached to me about the benefits of tax-deferred savings. He then asked if I had opened an individual retirement account. "I don't have $2,000," I said, referring to the

annual investment limit. "I'll loan it to you," he said. "But I'd still have to pay it back," I said. "Take your time," he said.

For my normally frugal father this was an extraordinary offer, and I took it. When my employer later offered a 401(k) plan, I had learned my lesson and signed up.

Millions of baby boomers have done the same thing. Of the 39.6 million people invested in 401(k) plans at the end of 1999, the latest year for which numbers were available, 21.5 million, or 54 percent, were held by baby boomers, according to the Employee Benefit Research Institute in Washington.

But Laurence J. Kotlikoff, an economics professor at Boston University, who wrote this new study with Jagadeesh Gokhale and Todd Neumann, economists at the Federal Reserve Bank of Cleveland, said many households with incomes of $50,000 or less that invest in 401(k) plans could lose the full benefit of their mortgage deduction as the contributions lower their tax bracket. The study, which used theoretical examples, said families would be pushed into a higher bracket when they withdraw money from the plan.

Even worse, he said the withdrawals will increase their income so much that a larger percentage of their Social Security benefits will be taxed by the federal government. (He said richer households do not have that problem because their Social Security benefits are already taxed at the upper limit.)

According to the study, which is expected to be published next month, a married couple earning $50,000 combined at age 25 will indeed do well in a 401(k) if it returns a steady 4 percent a year. Their lifetime taxes will go down; the money they have available to spend will go up. But if the return increases to 6 percent, their taxes increase 1.1 percent and their available money falls by 0.39 percent. With an 8 percent return taxes rise 6.38 percent and available money falls 1.73 percent.

And that leads to the question: Why get into an investment at all if you have to hope it does not do too well? (The authors also discovered that IRAs generally do not share the same problems as 401(k)s, but they will if Congress increases the IRA investment maximum to $5,000, a move it is considering.)

"A lot of people don't take advantage of 401(k) participation," Dr. Kotlikoff said. "They may be smarter than their employers."

He said he and his co-authors were surprised by the findings and ran the numbers again and again in ES planner, a personal finance program he and his colleagues created. (www.esplanner.com).

"We discovered this by accident," he said. "Then we started scratching our heads wondering if we did something wrong."

Well, I can assure you that after nearly thirty years of doing retirement plan analysis, I know these authors did not do something wrong!

If I could show you a way to generate a retirement income that was, in fact, tax free—not only on the gain you achieved during the accumulation years but also on the income you receive during the withdrawal years—and if the receipt of that income would not affect your Social Security or Medicare benefits under current laws, would you be interested? The true reality is that after the 1986 Tax Reform Act, most retirees in America are finding themselves in at least as high, if not higher, an effective tax bracket as during their earning years. This is primarily because they have fewer deductions and exemptions, especially if they accumulated any type of respectable retirement nest egg.

15 WEALTH-ENHANCEMENT STRATEGY NUMBER FIFTEEN

- *Position yourself to retire with the highest possible net spendable income stream.*
- *Minimize, even eliminate, the payment of unnecessary taxes on your retirement income-generating assets.*

CHAPTER 16

Why Delay the Inevitable?

Deferred taxes equal compounded taxes.

COMMON MYTH-CONCEPTION

Tax deductible or pre-tax contributions to qualified plans such as IRAs, 401(k)s, TSAs, 403(b)s, and 457 plans provide the most attractive retirement benefits.

REALITY

Other non-qualified retirement vehicles may provide greater net spendable retirement income. Proper equity management can provide indirect deductions that may be comparable to qualified retirement plan contributions. More important, this strategy allows tax-free retirement income.

A long with the misconception that a person will likely be in a lower tax bracket when he retires than he was during his earning years, there is a related misconception people have regarding retirement plans. The general consensus, even among financial planners, investment brokers, and insurance agents, is that tax-deductible or pre-tax contributions to qualified plans such as IRAs, 401(k)s, TSAs, 403(b)s, and 457 plans will provide the greatest retirement benefits because of tax-deferred growth.

Let me give my view with an analogy: If you were a farmer, would you rather save tax on the purchase of your seed in the springtime then pay tax on harvest sales in the fall, or would you rather pay tax on the price of the seed but sell your harvest without any tax on your gain?

I would prefer to purchase the seed with after-tax dollars and later sell and enjoy my harvest, assuming my harvest represented a gain on a tax-free basis. The actual dollar amount of the tax due on the seed money would be so much less than paying tax on the money realized during the harvest.

Yet we as Americans do exactly the opposite. We contribute thousands of dollars to traditional qualified retirement plans to give ourselves a tax break on the seed money. We enjoy tax-deferred growth, but then, during the harvest years of our life, we're subject to the payment of income tax on our harvest sales. We are led to believe we would not need to worry—we could deal with those taxes down the road, when we would likely be in a lower tax bracket. As explained earlier, this is generally not true.

ARE TAX RATES DECREASING?

It doesn't make sense, then, to continue to compound and grow an investment into a huge nest egg so you can pull it out in the future when you are most likely in a higher tax bracket (due to the size of your nest egg) or when Congress has nudged up the rates. When I teach public seminars, I usually ask the question, "Do you feel that future tax rates will likely be *lower*?" I don't believe I have ever received an affirmative response to that question. I then ask the question, "Does anyone in the audience feel like future tax rates will be the *same*?" Once in a great while, someone raises a hand at this question. But when I ask the third question, "How many people feel future tax rates will likely be *higher*?" Almost all raise their hands in agreement.

Does this tell us something about the history behind what Congress has done? We have no faith Congress will do anything about lowering tax rates in the future! If it does attempt to give any tax back, it seems to take it away again somewhere else. Why then do we think putting money into vehicles that defer and postpone tax will be beneficial to us? Yet Americans do it every single pay day because they want a tax deduction today.

You can see on the graph in **figure 16.1** that by accumulating money in a qualified account such as an IRA, the tax liability is compounded and shifted into the future. At the end of the growth period on an IRA, it is substantially greater than before. That's why I refer to qualified plans as the savings bond the government has developed for itself. When retirees withdraw those funds, they will pay taxes on them that quite possibly could be as much or more than if they had just paid taxes on them in the first place.

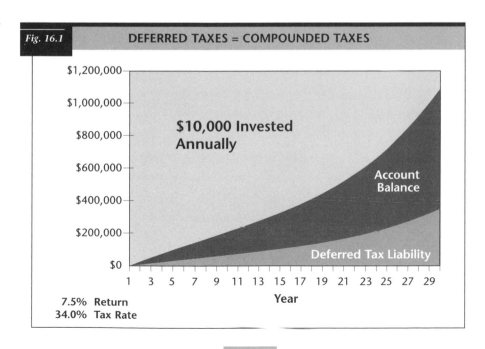

Fig. 16.1 — DEFERRED TAXES = COMPOUNDED TAXES

$10,000 Invested Annually

Account Balance

Deferred Tax Liability

7.5% Return
34.0% Tax Rate

Year

REVISITING THE FIVE SAVINGS OPTIONS

In chapter 9, I briefly explained five basic options American taxpayers have with regard to tax treatment on savings. Let's now study them in more depth.

OPTION #1

You can save or invest after-tax dollars (sixty-six-cent dollars in a 34 percent tax bracket) in financial instruments that are taxed as interest is earned, dividends are paid, or capital gains are realized. Traditional savings accounts that are non-qualified such as passbook savings, money market accounts, and certificates of deposit usually fall into this category of taxation. Also, non-qualified mutual fund accounts may fall into this category. If you invest into stocks and bonds or even real estate, under a non-qualified situation, it is usually done with after-tax dollars and the dividends, interest, capital gains, or rental income are taxed as earned or realized.

The tax liability due on the increase is either on income categorized as portfolio (interest and dividends) or passive (rents and leases) income. As explained earlier, under the Taxpayer Relief Act of 1997, capital gain tax is calculated at a lower rate than income tax and is not payable until the gain is realized by selling the asset and actually realizing a profit over the cost or basis.

As was illustrated in chapter 9, figures 9.5 to 9.7, depending on the rate of return, it may take fifteen years before we break even with what we have to earn or allocate when using sixty-six-cent after-tax dollars on the front end and paying tax on the increase as we go. In other words, we had to earn a gross amount of $8,000 a year for fifteen years (equaling $120,000) before our annual net after-tax investment of $5,280 growing at 8 percent taxable interest finally exceeded the true before-tax basis (fig. 9.5)!

Likewise, in figure 9.6, we had to earn a gross income of $9,000 a year for fifteen years (equaling $135,000) before our annual net after-tax investment of $5,940 growing at 7.5 percent taxable interest finally exceeded the true before-tax basis.

In figure 9.7, we allocated $8,000 a year of our gross income for savings, resulting in $5,280 left after tax to invest. If we only earned 6 percent interest, it took us twenty years before our savings account balance exceeded the before-tax basis of $160,000!

Therefore, option 1 can be a discouraging approach. Unfortunately, it is a common approach to saving and investing.

To make a comparison between all five options, let's use a uniform, simple example. Let's assume we have a cumulative total of $151,515 of our gross income over a certain number of years to allocate to long-term savings. For the sake of simplicity, I'm going to assume we have all $151,515 at the very start as a one-time lump sum. We have the choice of either using 66-cent after-tax dollars or 100-cent before-tax dollars, depending upon which of the five savings options we choose. We'll assume a 7.2 percent return on all investments.

Under option 1 (**fig. 16.2**), our $151,515 is gross income, so we have to pay tax on the front end in the amount of $51,515 (34 percent) in order to net $100,000 to save or invest. We know by the Rule of 72 that if we earn 7.2 percent interest, our account will double in ten years. However, if we have to pay tax on our yearly increase, we will only end up with a net of $159,083 (column 4, year 10). After ten years, we want to begin taking out our annual interest earnings to supplement our other income. If we keep earning 7.2 percent taxable interest, we would have $11,454 of annual interest income. However, we would have to pay 34 percent tax on that interest income each year in the amount of $3,894. So we would only realize a net of $7,560 in spendable annual income.

OPTION #2

You can save or invest after-tax dollars on investments that accumulate tax deferred and pay taxes on the gain when later realized. Typical investments in this category may include real estate that is not leveraged,

Fig. 16.2	$151,515 OF CUMULATIVE GROSS INCOME ALLOCATED TO LONG-TERM SAVINGS

OPTION 1:

Invest After-Tax Dollars (Sixty-Six-Cents in a 34% Tax Bracket) in Financial Instruments Earning 7.2% that are Taxed as Earned

Gross: $151,515
- [$51,515] Less: 34% Tax
$100,000 Net to Invest

Year	Gross Interest Earned [1]	Tax Liability at 34% [2]	Net Interest Earned [3]	Year End Balance [4]
1	$7,200	$2,448	$4,752	$104,752
2	$7,542	$2,564	$4,978	$109,730
3	$7,901	$2,686	$5,215	$114,944
4	$8,276	$2,814	$5,462	$120,407
5	$8,669	$2,947	$5,722	$126,128
6	$9,081	$3,088	$5,993	$132,122
7	$9,513	$3,234	$6,279	$138,400
8	$9,965	$3,388	$6,577	$144,977
9	$10,438	$3,549	$6,889	$151,866
10	$10,934	$3,718	$7,216	$159,083

Convert to Annual Income:

$159,083   10 Year Total Account Value
x   7.2%   Annual Interest Income
$11,454   Annual Taxable Income
[$3,894]   Less: Annual Tax Liability at 34%
$7,560   **Net Spendable Annual Income** .

or perhaps some stocks or mutual funds for which there are no dividends, but only grow through unrealized capital gains until the asset is sold. Non-qualified deferred annuities also fall into this category.

Under option 2 (**fig. 16.3**) we invest the net $100,000 (sixty-six-cent after-tax dollars) in an investment that is tax deferred. So the $100,000 doubles to $200,000 at 7.2 percent in ten years. If we now realize our profits, we may owe $20,000 in capital gains tax on the $100,000 gain we made. This would leave us a net of $180,000. If this were now invested in an account earning 7.2 percent taxable interest, it would generate an interest income of $12,960 each year. With tax liability each year on that interest in the amount of $4,406, we would only realize a net spendable income of $8,554.

If the $100,000 grew to $200,000 in a non-qualified deferred annuity and it generated 7.2 percent of annual income, the gross annual interest would be $14,400 ($200,000 x 7.2 percent). This income would be fully taxable because annuities receive LIFO tax treatment, as I will explain in chapter 17. After paying a 34 percent tax of $4,896 each year, the net income would be $9,504.

Fig. 16.3	$151,515 OF CUMULATIVE GROSS INCOME ALLOCATED TO LONG-TERM SAVINGS

OPTION 2:

Invest After-Tax Dollars (66 Cents in a 34% Tax Bracket) in Financial Instruments that are Tax Deferred

Gross: $151,515
- [$51,515]   Less: 34% Tax
$100,000   Net to Invest

$100,000 Growing at 7.2% for 10 Years = $200,000

Capital Gain Example:

$200,000	10 Year Total Account Value
[$20,000]	Less: Capital Gain Tax of 20%
$180,000	Net Balance to Re-Invest
x 7.2%	Annual Interest Income
$12,960	Annual Taxable Income
- [$4,406]	Less: Annual Tax Liability at 34%
$8,554	Net Spendable Annual Income

Non-Qualified Annuity Example:

$200,000	10 Year Total Account Value
x 7.2%	Annual Interest Income
$14,400	Annual Taxable Income
- [$4,896]	Less: Annual Tax Liability at 34%
$9,504	Net Spendable Annual Income

OPTION #3

You can save or invest after-tax dollars in investments that accumulate tax free and use the money tax free later, including the gain you made. These types of investments include Roth IRAs and insurance contracts that are properly structured and used (chapter 17).

Under option 3 (**fig. 16.4**), we invest the net $100,000 (sixty-six-cent after-tax dollars) in an investment that is tax free during the accumulation phase and withdrawal phase. So the $100,000 doubles to $200,000 at 7.2 percent interest in ten years. However, now we also get to enjoy the gain and income it can generate tax free. Therefore, $200,000 earning 7.2 percent annually gives us a tax-free, net spendable income of $14,400 a year!

OPTION #4

You can save or invest 100-cent pre-tax or tax-deductible dollars in investments that accumulate tax deferred, then later when you use the money, it is fully taxable, including the basis. Investments such as traditional IRAs, 401(k)s, and other qualified plans fall into this category.

Under option 4 (**fig. 16.5**), now we get to use 100-cent dollars. So the full $151,515 can be invested on the front end. At 7.2 percent interest,

Fig. 16.4	$151,515 OF CUMULATIVE GROSS INCOME ALLOCATED TO LONG-TERM SAVINGS

OPTION 3:

Invest After-Tax Dollars (66 Cents in a 34% Tax Bracket) in Financial Instruments that are Tax Free and Remain Tax Free When You Withdraw the Money Including the Gain

Gross: $151,515
- [$51,515]   Less: 34% Tax
$100,000   Net to Invest

$100,000 Growing at 7.2% for 10 Years = $200,000

$200,000   10 Year Total Account Value (tax free)
x   7.2%   Annual Interest Income
$14,400   **Net Spendable Annual Income**

Fig. 16.5

$151,515 OF CUMULATIVE GROSS INCOME ALLOCATED TO LONG-TERM SAVINGS

OPTION 4:

Invest Pre-Tax or Tax-Deductible Dollars in Financial Instruments that are Tax-Deferred and then Later are Fully Taxable

Gross: $151,515
[$0]   No Tax
$151,515   Net to Invest

$151,515 Growing at 7.2% for 10 Years = $303,030

Lump Sum Distribution Example:

$303,030   10 Year Total Account Value
- [103,030]   Less: Tax of 34%
$200,000   **Net After-Tax Value**

Interest Only Example:

$303,030   10 Year Total Account Value
x   7.2%   Annual Interest Income

21,818   Annual Taxable Income
- [7,418]   Less: Annual Tax Liability @ 34%
$14,400   **Net Spendable Annual Income**

this investment doubles to $303,030 in ten years. However, if we withdraw that money, we now have to pay tax on the full $303,030. If we were still in a 34 percent tax bracket, we would only net $200,000 ($303,030 - $103,030 = $200,000). Instead, if we decided to take 7.2 percent (our annual interest earnings) of income each year thereafter from our IRA account worth $303,030, it would generate $21,818 of taxable income, leaving us a net of $14,400 after tax ($21,818 less 34 percent).

Wait a minute, did you notice all things being equal, there is *no* difference between the net results of option 3 and option 4? Because I am not confident that in real life, all things will be equal— in fact, I think tax rates will be higher later, especially if I accumulate a respectable nest egg—I would rather go with option 3 rather than option 4. Let me have my money tax free during the harvest years of my life! In chapters 17 to 20, I will show how you can have your cake and eat it too!

OPTION #5

You can use 100-cent dollars because of indirect tax-deductions and enjoy tax-free accumulation and also tax-free use of the money. Not only that, but you can transfer any remaining funds to your heirs tax free if you use properly structured insurance contracts.

Under option 5 (**fig. 16.6**) we may use up to 100-cent dollars because we may be able to get indirect tax deductions due to mortgage interest offsets. If we succeeded in offsetting all our contributions with this strategy, the full $151,515 would be available to save or invest on the front end. By using tax-advantaged capital accumulation vehicles such as explained under option 3, we can have tax-favored treatment for all four phases of our non-qualified retirement plan (**fig. 16.7**). Thus, $151,515 would double to $303,030 at 7.2 percent interest for ten years. If we now can take tax-free income at 7.2 percent on $303,030, it generates $21,818 of net spendable income (fig. 16.6).

In this example, option 5 almost tripled the net spendable income that option 1 generated. It more than doubled the net spendable income

Fig. 16.6	$151,515 OF CUMULATIVE GROSS INCOME ALLOCATED TO LONG-TERM SAVINGS

OPTION 5:

Invest 100-Cent Dollars Because of Indirect Tax Deductions in Financial Instruments that Accumulate Tax-Free and Remain Tax Free When You Withdraw the Money, Including the Gain

Gross: $151,515
- [$51,515]   Less: 34% Tax
$100,000   Adjusted Net
+ $51,515   Plus Tax Savings as a Result of Indirect Deductions
$151,515   **Net to Invest**

$151,515 Growing at 7.2% for 10 Years = $303,030

Equity Management Example:

$303,030   10 Year Total Account Value / Tax Free
x 7.2%   Annual Interest Income
$21,818   **Net Spendable Annual Income**

Fig. 16.7 — **FOUR PHASES OF RETIREMENT PLANNING**

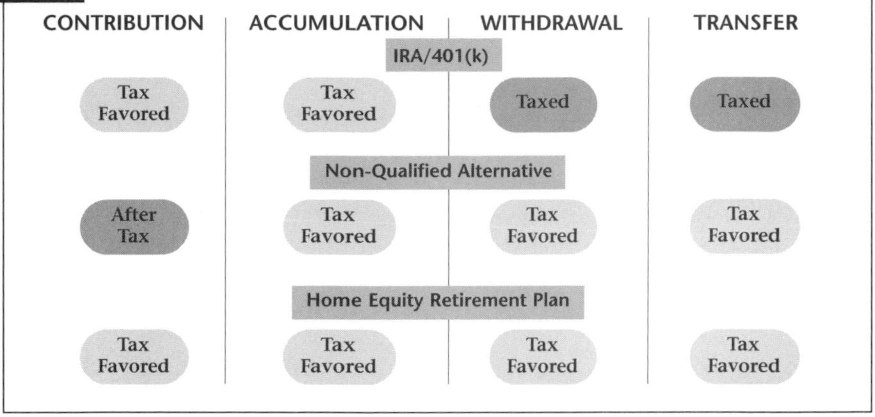

CONTRIBUTION	ACCUMULATION	WITHDRAWAL	TRANSFER
	IRA/401(k)		
Tax Favored	Tax Favored	Taxed	Taxed
	Non-Qualified Alternative		
After Tax	Tax Favored	Tax Favored	Tax Favored
	Home Equity Retirement Plan		
Tax Favored	Tax Favored	Tax Favored	Tax Favored

option 2 generated. Option 5 also generated 50 percent greater net spendable retirement income than options 3 or 4. Now, having illustrated these dynamic differences, let me emphasize the several factors that relate to each of these options that create real-life dilemmas. Once people understand these dilemmas, they need to conduct a careful analysis to determine whether it is wise to participate in a qualified plan. There is no simple "yes, you should" or "no, you shouldn't" answer.

EMPLOYER MATCHING BENEFITS

A potential qualified plan participant should closely analyze the possible benefits that may be afforded to him from an employer who does not offer an alternative to a qualified plan. Perhaps there are matching benefits offered by the employer the employee can receive by participating in a qualified plan. The reason an employer is motivated to match funds on contribution dollars on a qualified plan is to encourage an employee to save for his own retirement. If he participates in a 401(k), the employer may match that participation to some degree to help him stay loyal to the company and create "golden handcuffs." These golden handcuffs are designed to help keep the employee attached to the company and help him prepare for his future retirement.

According to traditional thought, the responsibility of planning for an individual's retirement rests with the employer. On the contrary, I believe this responsibility should rest solely with the individual. True security should be found in the individual and his unique abilities—not in the job provided by an employer. If more employers would help educate their employees through retirement planning seminars and explain the difference, as illustrated in the seed versus harvest analogy, perhaps they would be willing to match retirement savings whether the employee was contributing to a qualified or a non-qualified plan. But until employers are educated on this, we will predominantly see matching funds only on qualified plans. The fact of the matter is, contributions made by employers to employee retirement plans can be deductible for the employer whether or not they are to qualified plans.

Often people will come to me who are currently contributing the maximum amount allowable under law on their 401(k)s or other qualified plans (limits were revised under the 2001 Act, as illustrated in **figure 16.8**). Many are contributing 10 percent or more of their income, and their employer may be matching 50 cents on the dollar or perhaps 100 cents on the dollar, but only on the first 4, 5, or 6 percent. Sometimes an employer will contribute a portion to a 401(k), regardless of whether the employee is contributing anything. Schoolteachers in the state of Utah have enjoyed such an arrangement. This is technically not an employer match, but an additional contribution of a certain percentage of employees' incomes to their 401(k)s.

A true matching arrangement is one in which the employer agrees to match, dollar for dollar on a certain percentage, such as 50 percent, an employee's contributions up to a specified limit or percentage of his income. In order to take advantage of matching, many employees will contribute at least the amount required to get the full matching benefit. I have found many employees contribute beyond that into their qualified accounts thinking that it is the best way to enhance their future retirement.

The answer to the question of whether an employee should contribute up to and over the amount being matched by the employer is

Fig. 16.8

CONTRIBUTION AND BENEFIT LIMITS FOR
INDIVIDUAL RETIREMENT ARRANGEMENTS AND QUALIFIED PENSION PLANS

Calendar Year (January 1)	Elective Deferrals	SIMPLE Contribution	Defined Benefit $ Limit	Limit for Defined Contribution	Qualified Plan Comp Contribution	Eligible 457 Plans Limit
2000	$10,500	$6,000	$135,000	$30,000	$170,000	$8,000
2001	$10,500	$6,500	$140,000	$35,000	$170,000	$8,500
2002	$11,000	$7,000	$160,000	$40,000	$200,000	$11,000
2003	$12,000	$8,000	$160,000	Indexed	Indexed	$12,000
2004	$13,000	$9,000	$160,000	Indexed	Indexed	$13,000
2005	$14,000	$10,000	$160,000	Indexed	Indexed	$14,000
2006	$15,000	Indexed	$160,000	Indexed	Indexed	$15,000
2007	Indexed	Indexed	$160,000	Indexed	Indexed	Indexed
2008	Indexed	Indexed	$160,000	Indexed	Indexed	Indexed
2009	Indexed	Indexed	$160,000	Indexed	Indexed	Indexed
2010	Indexed	Indexed	$160,000	Indexed	Indexed	Indexed
2011	2000 Tax Law Reinstated on 1/1/2011	2000 Tax Law Reinstated on 1/1/2011	2000 Tax Law Reinstated on 1/1/2011	2000 Tax Law Reinstated on 1/1/2011	2000 Tax Law Reinstated on 1/1/2011	2000 Tax Law Reinstated on 1/1/2011

*as set forth in the Economic Growth and Tax Relief Reconciliation Act of 2001

really a function of yield and performance on the particular portfolio in which the 401(k) or qualified plan is invested. Assuming the same general yield can be achieved in a non-qualified, private retirement account that is tax free during the harvest, I would generally advise the employee only to contribute to a qualified plan up to the amount matched by the employer. It is most advantageous when at least 50 percent matching is offered by the employer. Again, this is only my general rule of thumb and does not apply to all sets of circumstances.

Simply speaking, if an employee contributes a dollar and it is matched 50 cents on that dollar, the employee now has a $1.50 working for him. The illusion is that he is receiving a 50 percent return on his money. The principal is increased by 50 percent, but the interest rate from that point on is whatever is earned. As the account continues to compound and grow, he doesn't continue to receive an annual repeated 50 percent enhancement of the retirement account. The 50 percent increase is only on the seed money going into the account. If the individual were capable of pulling out that money without incurring a 10 percent penalty immediately after it was contributed, and the matching was immediately vested in a 34 percent tax bracket, he would essentially be paying back the 50 cents the employer matched—only in the form of taxes. In other words, on $1.50 you would pay about 50 cents in taxes. The employer is more or less paying the portion that you will end up having to pay back in tax. If the account continues to compound and grow, the tax liability will also compound and grow. Still, employer matching can be attractive if used properly and understood.

I generally recommend that, all other things being equal, a person should not contribute any funds beyond the amount required to receive matching contributions by the employer. If you contribute to a plan such as this, you must go into it with the complete understanding that any distributions on the back end, or in the "harvest years" of your life, will be fully subject to income tax both at a federal and a state level. You need to plan on giving up somewhere between 20 and 40 percent of your distributions in some type of tax liability. You should also be aware if you tap into those funds before the age of $59^1/2$ there will be a 10 percent penalty. There will likely be limits as to what percent of your income you can contribute, no matter what qualified plan you choose. You must withdraw a certain amount of money based upon minimum distribution rates beginning at age 70^1/$_2$, whether you need the income or not; otherwise, you will be subject to a 50 percent penalty.

I hate having all of those restrictions and strings attached! If you are like many of my clients who are self-employed and whose businesses are seasonal, you want flexibility. During a banner year of business profits, they may want to contribute a sizeable sum of cash to a tax-advantaged investment or retirement account. In other years, they may not have any money to contribute. In fact, in the tight years, my clients like the flexibility of being able to tap into their non-qualified retirement fund for temporary use of that capital without any penalty imposed by the IRS. Then they like to be able to replenish their retirement savings without restriction on the percent of income they can contribute that year. They don't want to be penalized should they withdraw money before age 59^1/$_2$ or be required to withdraw a certain amount beginning at age 70^1/$_2$.

Using a non-qualified retirement planning strategy, you are not restricted on the amount of money you can contribute. There are also no discrimination clauses, so as an employer you are not required to cover any employees under the same rules and ratios of contribution-to-income you are investing. On the other hand, the qualified retirement plan requires certain amounts to be contributed for all eligible employees based upon their income and vesting schedule, if you as an employer have established and are contributing to a qualified plan.

If I conduct an in-depth analysis of whether a client should contribute to his qualified plan, depending on the rates of return he has achieved, I often suggest he discontinue making new contributions to his qualified plan. Continuing may result in possibly too much taxable income in retirement. I usually redirect new contributions to a non-qualified private retirement account, unless he is being matched so handsomely he can't refuse contributing the percentage needed to qualify for the match. In such cases, though, I make sure he is aware of the tax impact that qualified plans will have on the back end. For example, if he were contributing 10 percent but only being matched on the first 6 per-cent, I would have him pull back to only a 6 percent contribution. I would have him redirect the remaining 4 percent into a non-qualified private retirement account funded with after-tax dollars. This can then grow tax free and continue to be tax free during the withdrawal phase of his retirement planning, assuming he uses the vehicles that provide those tax advantages.

STRATEGIC CONVERSIONS

Sometimes individuals have me illustrate the effects of a strategic con-version of their qualified accounts to a non-qualified retirement planning strategy or pension alternative. We begin a strategic conversion out of their qualified accounts by making annual withdrawals and subjecting those withdrawals to taxes each year, perhaps even incurring a penalty if they are under age 59^1/2. By doing that, we strategically plan to withdraw that money and keep them in an equal or lower bracket than they would be in at retirement if they chose to postpone and compound the tax lia-bility. If we wait until age 59^1/2 to begin a strategic conversion qualified plan roll-out (*not* roll-over), we save the 10 percent penalty.

Sometimes I show people who are under age 50 why they should consider rolling their money out under a strategic plan, even if they incur the 10 percent penalty, because the amount of the penalty could be recouped with better interest during a ten- to fifteen-year period before retirement. If the individual is close to age 59^1/2, though, it is usu-ally better to wait to begin this strategic conversion. Otherwise, we would need to use other tax planning strategies that would offset the 10 percent penalty. I have witnessed many individuals who postponed doing a strategic conversion and found themselves only a few years later in more damaging taxable circumstances than they would have been in if they hadn't waited—even considering the 10 percent penalty.

Remember you can either pay the government now or you can pay later. Thus, if you can get the same rate of return in a non-qualified account as you can in a qualified account, and enjoy tax-free growth and access to your account, I would recommend the discontinuance of new contributions to any type of qualified plans—unless an attractive matching percentage is available and you understand the consequences of tax postponement. You should strongly consider redirecting your contributions to non-qualified retirement vehicles funded with after-tax dollars on the front end that are tax free on the back end.

THE ROTH IRA

Many Americans have been intrigued with the recently introduced Roth IRA under the Taxpayer Relief Act of 1997. However, it may not be all it is cracked up to be! The concept of the Roth IRA is definitely a step in the right direction. However, as I will illustrate in the next few chapters, there is a better way to have tax-free retirement income without all of the strings attached!

The Roth IRA does contain a critical feature of which I am a proponent. Again, it may prove better to pay taxes on the seed money contributed to a retirement fund and later enjoy a tax-free harvest than to contribute tax-favored seed money to a traditional IRA or 401(k) and pay taxes during the harvest years, in a higher tax bracket. The problem with a Roth IRA is that there are still too many government restrictions. The Roth IRA has been referred to as a "back-loaded IRA." Contributions to a Roth IRA are not deductible. But all the earnings are tax free as long as withdrawals meet certain requirements. One requirement is that a distribution may not be made until at least five years after the first contribution is made. In addition, a distribution can only be made:

- on or after the owner attains the age of 59$1/2$;
- due to the owner's death;
- for the purchase of a first home with a limit of $10,000;
- or due to the owner's disability.

When they were first introduced, the maximum yearly contribution an individual could make to a Roth IRA was $2,000, which remained the limit until the Economic Growth and Tax Relief Reconciliation Act of 2001. Under the 2001 Act, the annual contribution limit became $3,000 for the years 2002 to 2004 and increases to $4,000 for the years 2005 to 2007 (**fig. 16.9**). (This also applies to annual contribution limits for traditional IRAs.) Under the provisions of the 1997 Act, Roth IRA limits are reduced for couples whose income exceeds $150,000 ($95,000 for single filers). The eligibility to contribute the full annual contribution limit is phased out between $150,000 and $160,000 for married taxpayers filing jointly (between $95,000 and $110,000 for single filers). After those limits, a person is not eligible for a Roth IRA. The annual contribution limit is also reduced by the amount of contributions made to any other IRAs. There is a 6 percent tax on excess contributions to a Roth IRA.

Roth IRAs can be rolled-over tax free to other Roth IRAs. The roll-over is subject to the roll-over rules for an ordinary IRA. Also, an ordinary IRA can be rolled-over to a Roth IRA, but only if the taxpayer meets the following conditions: The taxpayer's adjusted gross income for the tax year cannot not exceed $100,000, and the taxpayer cannot be married filing separately. Roth IRAs are not subject to the age $70^1/_2$ required distribution rules that apply to traditional IRAs. In my opinion, there is a better approach to achieve tax-free income, as well as create indirect

Fig. 16.9	IRA AND ROTH IRA PROVISIONS*	
Calendar Year (January 1)	Annual Contribution Limit	Catch-up Contribution Limit for Individuals Age 50 or Older
2000	$2,000	$0
2001	$2,000	$0
2002	$3,000	$500
2003	$3,000	$500
2004	$3,000	$500
2005	$4,000	$500
2006	$4,000	$1,000
2007	$4,000	$1,000
2008	$5,000	$1,000
2009	Indexed	$1,000
2010	Indexed	$1,000
2011	2000 Tax Law Reinstated on 1/1/2011	2000 Tax Law Reinstated on 1/1/2011

*as set forth in the Economic Growth and Tax Relief Reconciliation Act of 2001

tax-favored benefits on the contribution amounts without all of the restrictions and rules.

When I contribute money to my non-qualified retirement fund, there is virtually no restriction on how much I can put in. During good years, I can contribute generously; during not-so-good years, I don't have to contribute anything! In fact, I can withdraw money if needed, without IRS penalties, and not be obligated to put the money back. As a homeowner, I also structure my retirement planning to get indirect tax deductions on my contribution amounts. Most important, my retirement funds accumulate tax free, and I can access the funds whenever I want on a tax-free basis (including the interest or gain) without having to wait until I am 59$^{1}/_{2}$! If I don't use up my retirement funds before I pass away, they blossom and transfer income tax free to my heirs! The growth on such an account can look like the graph in **figure 16.10** in contrast to the graph in figure 16.1.

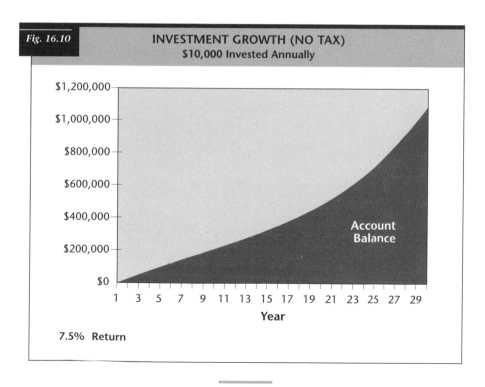

Fig. 16.10

INVESTMENT GROWTH (NO TAX)
$10,000 Invested Annually

Account Balance

7.5% Return

To understand how to receive tax-favored benefits during all four phases of retirement planning—contribution, accumulation, withdrawal, and transfer—please be sure to carefully study chapters 17 to 20.

USE IT OR LOSE IT

Many readers of this book may already be heavily into qualified plan accumulations. If you are in this category, it may be in your best interest to analyze what a strategic conversion from your qualified plan to a non-qualified situation could achieve for you in the long run, even though it may hurt tax-wise in the short run. I prepare many of my clients so that as early as age 59$^{1/2}$ they can begin the strategic conversion process, even if they are not ready to retire yet. The idea is to create a plan where they can begin to withdraw money strategically out of their retirement plan over a five-, six- or seven-year period and get the money taxed at today's rates rather than tomorrow's probable higher rates. They may especially want to take advantage of any room they have in their current tax bracket before crossing the next threshold.

For example, for a married couple filing a joint tax return (under the tax brackets that existed in the year 2002), there is $66,150 of room for taxable incomes between $46,700 and $112,850. Taxable income is the net income after all deductions and exemptions. So, if you had $100,000 in gross income but had itemized deductions comprised of $18,000 of mortgage interest, $10,000 of charitable contributions, $6,000 in taxes, plus two exemptions (a husband and wife) totaling approximately $6,000, your taxable income would be only $60,000—not $100,000. Therefore, you could withdraw $52,850 from a qualified account ($112,850 threshold less a taxable income of $60,000) and probably pay no higher income tax rate on that money than you would if you postponed withdrawing the money until later. If you miscalculated and withdrew $5,000 more ($57,850), which put you into the next higher bracket, remember, you would only pay the higher tax rate (3 percent more) on the $5,000 overage, which would be $150, not on the entire $57,850 (chapter 12). In fact, it may behoove this couple to transfer or withdraw up to another $59,100 per year out of a qualified account to take their taxable income up to $171,950, because income taxed in that bracket is only 3 percent higher than the previous bracket.

As explained earlier, I have witnessed many people who postponed and waited, trying to "save" inevitable tax on their qualified money. They were trying to avoid moving themselves from the 28 percent bracket into the 31 percent bracket before the year 2000 stock market crash. They were motivated to save just 3 percent on $59,100, which would have been $1,773. By postponing a withdrawal, they lost 30 percent of $59,100, which equals $17,730, or ten times as much because they left it in the market during a downturn! To add insult to injury, they then were forced, because of lack of liquidity, to pull their money out and still pay tax. If they could do it over, they would gladly trade paying $1,773 in extra tax to have an extra $17,730 in retirement funds. If you do not use the available room between your current taxable income and the next tax bracket threshold for possible withdrawals, you will lose it for that tax year. You cannot go back and amend a return to retroactively withdraw qualified money.

Hopefully, between the ages of 59$^{1}/_{2}$ and 64$^{1}/_{2}$ and no later than 70$^{1}/_{2}$, couples can have most or all of their qualified plans repositioned and the taxes over with. They then can be in a tax-free environment from that point forward and enjoy tax-free income the remainder of their lives, provided they reposition their after-tax distributions into the appropriate investment vehicles. When retiring couples do this they have generally been able to save as much as 60 percent of the tax they would have paid had they strung out the tax liability over the remainder of their lives. In addition, they can enhance the value of those funds when they are transferred down to non-spousal heirs at the second death and replenish some of the money they gave up in taxes during the roll-out or conversion process.

In the next four chapters, I describe how this can be done so as to maximize a person's net spendable retirement income, as well as the amount transferred down to surviving heirs. There is no question the IRS will require income tax not only during the distribution or withdrawal phase of a traditional qualified plan account, but also during the transfer phase. As qualified money is transferred to beneficiaries, the tax liability is not alleviated—it will still loom out there to some future day of reckoning. Also, remember that if a person's estate is sizeable, the IRS may perform a major "cashectomy" on all estate assets. That includes qualified plans. Estate tax may end up cutting into the overall value of your estate with tax rates at 37 to 50 percent. In case you haven't noticed the common reference, "THE IRS" when combined together spells THEIRS.

16 WEALTH-ENHANCEMENT STRATEGY NUMBER SIXTEEN

- *Periodically evaluate repositioning some or all of your qualified plan contributions or distributions to a non-qualified private retirement fund. This will reduce tax liability, and help you achieve the highest net spendable income in your retirement years.*

Understanding Which

Investment Vehicles Are

Best to Use for Safe

Accumulation of Wealth

CHAPTER 17

Accumulating, Accessing, and Transferring Your Money Tax Free

Properly structured life insurance contracts are the only investment vehicles that accumulate money tax free, allow access to the money tax free, and blossom tax free upon transfer to heirs.

COMMON MYTH-CONCEPTION

Life insurance is not a good place to accumulate and store cash, and is a poor investment.

REALITY

Modern cash-value life insurance can be designed to accumulate and store cash safely, provide tax-favored living benefits, and deliver tax-favored death benefits—all while safely maintaining liquidity and earning an attractive rate of return.

By now you should be somewhat convinced separating equity from your property can be a wise strategy for increasing its liquidity and safety. Managing equity properly also increases the rate of return on what would otherwise be idle dollars. Also, you should be somewhat convinced that possibly repositioning some or all of your qualified plan contributions or distributions to a non-qualified private status can be a wise strategy for achieving the highest net spendable retirement income. Having gained this insight, the only question remaining should be: "Which investment vehicles are the best choices in which to reposition serious cash?"

SERIOUS CASH

What type of an investor are you with regard to "serious cash" such as home equity or repositioned retirement funds? Which of the following categories of investments would you be more inclined to invest in:

1) high risk, high potential yield investments,

2) moderate risk, moderate yield investments,

3) or low risk, safe investments?

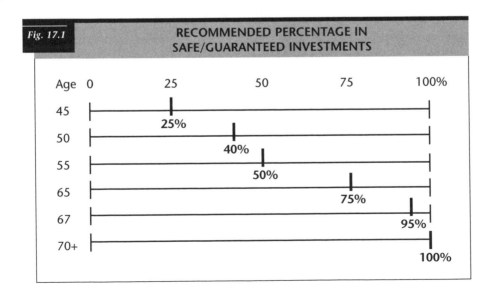

As shown in **figure 17.1**, the closer we approach retirement, the greater the percentage of our assets that should be invested in safe and/or guaranteed investments.

Let's go through a risk versus return model to determine which categories of investments are most advantageous for capital accumulation or the repositioning of serious cash such as home equity and IRA and 401(k) monies. In **figure 17.2**, I have listed sixteen general categories of investments ranging from highest risk at the top of the pyramid to lowest risk at the bottom. When choosing a place in which to save, invest, or store cash for conservative, stable returns, we want to ask ourselves the four same questions we ask with regard to our home equity:

- Is it liquid?
- Is it safe (guaranteed or insured)?
- What rate of return am I likely to get?
- Are there any tax benefits associated with this investment?

You see, I regard my home equity and my retirement funds as serious cash! I don't want to hinder their liquidity, safety, and rate of return; I want to enhance these features!

Fig. 17.2   **THE RISK-RETURN MODEL**

1. Commodities
2. Business Ventures
3. Limited Partnerships
4. Raw Land
5. Speculative Common Stocks
6. Lower Quality Bonds
7. Investment Real Estate
8. Blue Chip Stocks
9. High Grade Bonds
10. Mutual Funds
11. CDs
12. Investment-Grade Insurance
13. Money Market Funds
14. U.S. Treasury Bills
15. Annuities
16. Equity in House

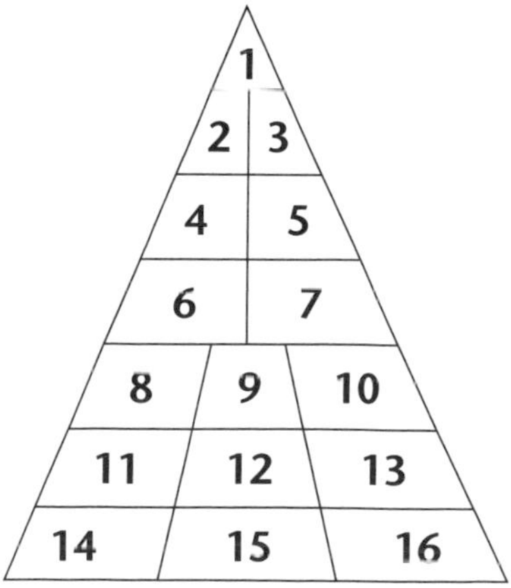

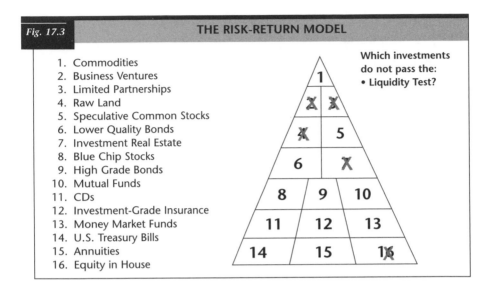

Fig. 17.3 — THE RISK-RETURN MODEL

1. Commodities
2. Business Ventures
3. Limited Partnerships
4. Raw Land
5. Speculative Common Stocks
6. Lower Quality Bonds
7. Investment Real Estate
8. Blue Chip Stocks
9. High Grade Bonds
10. Mutual Funds
11. CDs
12. Investment-Grade Insurance
13. Money Market Funds
14. U.S. Treasury Bills
15. Annuities
16. Equity in House

Which investments do not pass the:
• Liquidity Test?

When we apply the liquidity test, you can see in **figure 17.3** we must eliminate several of the investments. They do not pass the liquidity test because we may not be able to obtain cash when we may need it (within the time frame we would define for a liquid investment). As seen from the chart, investments such as business ventures, limited partnerships, raw land, investment real estate and equity in your home do not allow a quick conversion into cash under normal circumstances.

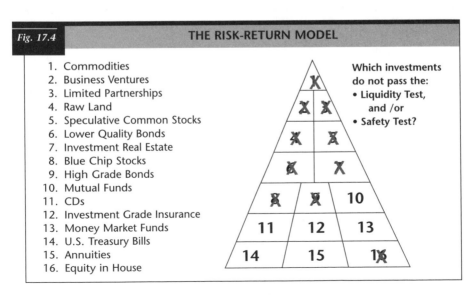

Fig. 17.4 — THE RISK-RETURN MODEL

1. Commodities
2. Business Ventures
3. Limited Partnerships
4. Raw Land
5. Speculative Common Stocks
6. Lower Quality Bonds
7. Investment Real Estate
8. Blue Chip Stocks
9. High Grade Bonds
10. Mutual Funds
11. CDs
12. Investment Grade Insurance
13. Money Market Funds
14. U.S. Treasury Bills
15. Annuities
16. Equity in House

Which investments do not pass the:
• Liquidity Test, and /or
• Safety Test?

When we apply the second test—safety—we eliminate five more of the investments (**fig. 17.4**). Most financial planners agree that commodities, speculative common stocks, lower quality bonds, and even blue-chip stocks and high-grade bonds are not adequately safe investments because they lack some type of guarantee with regard to monies involved (principal or interest).

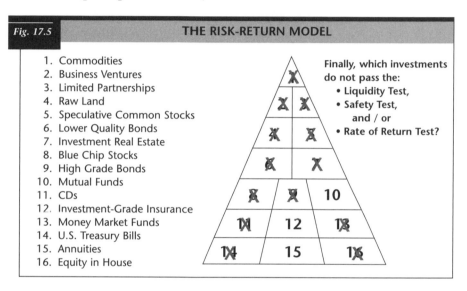

Fig. 17.5   **THE RISK-RETURN MODEL**

1. Commodities
2. Business Ventures
3. Limited Partnerships
4. Raw Land
5. Speculative Common Stocks
6. Lower Quality Bonds
7. Investment Real Estate
8. Blue Chip Stocks
9. High Grade Bonds
10. Mutual Funds
11. CDs
12. Investment-Grade Insurance
13. Money Market Funds
14. U.S. Treasury Bills
15. Annuities
16. Equity in House

Finally, which investments do not pass the:
• Liquidity Test,
• Safety Test,
and / or
• Rate of Return Test?

In applying the third test, remember we must earn a rate of return, net after tax, that will be in excess of the net cost of the funds used, in order to maximize their growth potential. Applying the third test, we eliminate three more possible investments (**fig. 17.5**). You may ask why I have eliminated certificates of deposit. The main problem with CDs is interest is taxed as earned. Thus, a CD with a 6 percent yield in a 34 percent tax bracket only nets a 4 percent after-tax return. Also, CDs generally do not have a very high rate of return relative to interest rates charged on mortgages. Money market accounts have the same drawbacks. A money market account may only credit 2 or 3 percent after-tax yield (assuming about a 4 percent before-tax interest rate in a 30 to 40 percent tax bracket) while net after-tax mortgage rates are around 4 or 5 percent (assuming a 7 or 8 percent mortgage in a 30 to 40 percent tax bracket). If the side fund containing your separated equity were a money market or CD, it would be hard pressed to earn a net after-tax return that would exceed the net cost of the tax-deductible, simple-interest, declining mortgage balance. U.S. Treasury bills fall into the same category; the net return cannot be deemed sufficient to pass the rate of return test.

Thus we are left with three remaining possibilities in which to consider investing our serious cash: annuities, some mutual funds, and investment-grade life insurance contracts. Let's go through a simple analysis of each of these remaining investment alternatives.

ANNUITIES

Today, most annuities are simply savings accounts with insurance companies. When you deposit premium dollars into an annuity, you accumulate your money in a tax-favored environment. Even if it is not a qualified plan, money inside of an annuity accumulates tax deferred. But, because of the 1984 Deficit Reduction Act, even though any money that accumulates inside an annuity is tax deferred, when money is withdrawn from the annuity, it is taxed. If funds are accessed from a deferred annuity before age 59$^{1}/_{2}$ there is also an additional 10 percent penalty on the distributions. This is similar to the early withdrawal penalty assessed on an IRA, 401(k) or any other qualified plan. In order to avoid a 10 percent penalty when accessing funds from an annuity, it should be done after age 59$^{1}/_{2}$. When money is withdrawn from an annuity, it is taxed LIFO.

LIFO is an acronym for Last In First Out. This means the last money you earn in an annuity is the interest credited most recently on your annuity account. When you begin to withdraw money from your annuity, the IRS regards your distribution as being the last money you earned and treats it as the first money you are withdrawing. Thus, you are taxed on 100 percent of your distributions (assuming interest-only withdrawals) from the first day you start distributions. You can't avoid it. Even if you make principal and interest withdrawals, you must still count the interest earned each year as the first money you withdraw for tax purposes. A single premium immediate annuity (SPIA) is a type of annuity in which one lump sum payment is made and the annuitant begins to receive immediate income distributions. Under a SPIA, the taxable portion of the annual distribution is averaged during the period the annuity is calculated to pay out.

For the sake of simplicity, let's assume a person deposits $100,000 into an annuity. If that annuity were to pay 10 percent interest, theoretically, she ought to be able to pull out $10,000 of interest a year without depleting the corpus of the annuity, which would be the basis, or original principal amount, if she purchased an immediate annuity. The $10,000 of interest that person earns is reported on her tax return as an interest withdrawal rather than a withdrawal of any principal. In other words, it is 100 percent taxable income. Only when she begins to deplete the principal will she get a tax break, because the basis was created with after-tax dollars (assuming the annuity is a non-qualified annuity). If she could live off only the interest throughout her entire retirement years, although she would incur tax on that income, she would be able to transfer the principal to her heirs income-tax free.

During the last twenty years, fixed annuities have usually credited interest at a rate between 5 to 9 percent, averaging somewhere in the 7 percent range. There are also variable annuities that participate directly in the market and indexed annuities which credit interest at rates linked to an index such as the Standard and Poor's 500 Index. Annuities are deemed a safe and prudent investment under most circumstances because they are only obtainable through insurance companies, which have legal reserve requirements more stringent than do banks or credit unions. Insurance company assets also usually have higher solvency or higher capital and surplus ratios than do many banks or credit unions. If an annuitant of a deferred annuity (the owner of the annuity) should die before withdrawing the funds in her annuity, the remaining annuity balance is then paid at face value—the exact amount remaining in the annuity—to the surviving beneficiary. Annuities do not blossom into a higher death benefit as life insurance does.

A person may choose to "annuitize" her annuity by converting it to an immediate annuity, which means she can choose between several different options to create a set income based on her life expectancy. For instance, she can opt to designate a certain number of years for which she and her beneficiary want to receive income, whether she is living or not. Under a period-certain option, the beneficiary would receive income, even in the event of the death of the annuitant, for a set number of years. Under a life-only option, the annuity only pays throughout the annuitant's lifetime. Should the annuitant pass away before her mortality-calculated age (all annuity benefits are calculated based on mortality risk), the insurance company retains the balance of the annuity. But if she should live beyond her life expectancy, the insurance company must still pay benefits up until her eventual death. Annuities also carry several options with regard to survivor benefits.

Until the last fifteen to twenty years, many people would choose one of these annuitization formulas. Since then, more people have been using annuities simply as savings accumulation vehicles, similar to saving money at a bank or credit union, only, in the case of an annuity, the money is held by an insurance company. With flexibility in how much can be deposited and the timing and amount of withdrawals, annuities generally pass the liquidity test. They also generally pass the safety test and the rate of return test. Remember, though, an annuity will become subject to tax on the withdrawal phase, and it is taxed under LIFO tax treatment.

MUTUAL FUNDS

A wide variety of mutual funds meet the liquidity, safety, and rate of return tests. Even so, not all mutual funds pass all three tests. Depending upon their most recent experiences in the market place, individual investors will either praise or condemn mutual funds. Many individuals were apprehensive about investing in mutual funds in the 1980s when the unstable stock market made fixed money markets and other interest-bearing accounts attractive. During the 1990s, money market accounts, CDs, and bonds reached a twenty-year low, while stocks soared to twenty-year highs. By the time the bullish market experienced its correction in late 2000, investors had witnessed an unprecedented period of continual prosperity and growth in stock market history. Investors need to under-stand when the stock market is up, bonds, money markets, and interest rates will generally be down. Conversely, in an economy free from gov-ernment intervention (through Federal Reserve manipulation of interest rates or tax rebates), when the stock market goes down, bonds, money markets, and fixed instruments tend to gradually go up.

While the market generally goes up over the long term, there are also many ups and downs in the short run—much like a person with a yo-yo walking up a flight of stairs. Americans have never experienced an extended period of time in which the stock market went up without some fluctuations along the way. Likewise, bond interest rates may drop tomorrow, but they won't stay down forever. In the long run, the inter-est rate and bond history will traditionally be less than the same return achieved in a ten- or twenty-year period in the stock market. It all depends on a particular investor's risk tolerance as he decides what per-centage of assets to put into a growth environment, versus an income environment. A growth environment would be investments such as stocks predicted to appreciate in value over the long term. An income environment would be investments such as bonds, money markets, and other financial instruments that primarily generate needed income or dividends for use in the short term.

Series 1 of **figure 17.6** shows an example of a typical mutual fund for a ten-year period reflecting seven gain years and three loss years. Only one of the loss years was a substantial reduction in value of the portfo-lio. The percentage reduction wasn't as significant as many of the gain years. The other two loss years represent relatively small losses when compared to the gain years. Remember when you experience a 16 per-cent loss in a portfolio, you are experiencing a 16 percent reduction on the entire portfolio! Thus, just a 16 percent or even a 3 percent loss after the account has grown to a sizable amount in eight or nine years repre-sents a significant dollar loss because of the account's worth when the loss was incurred.

When I have asked investors what the average return appears to be in series 1 as shown in Figure 17.6, the response is typically, "Oh, about

Fig. 17.6	STARTING WITH $100,000 If You Were Approaching Retirement, Which Series Would You Prefer?	
Year	SERIES 1 – Taxable + or -	SERIES 2 – Tax-Free + or -
1	+20%	+8%
2	+21%	+8%
3	+10%	+8%
4	-16%	+8%
5	+12%	+8%
6	-2%	+8%
7	+22%	+8%
8	- 6%	+8%
9	+11%	+8%
10	+15%	+8%
A Taxable SERIES 1 Fund Value at the End of 10 Years = $215,571 A Tax-Free SERIES 2 Fund Value at the End of 10 Years = **$215,892**		

12 to 14—maybe 15—percent." In actuality, the $100,000 investment shown in the example would have grown to $215,571 at the end of ten years. If you calculate your true average compounded annual interest rate by applying the Rule of 72, you will realize the rate of return was really only about 8 percent. In fact, if you started out with $100,000 and received a consistent, stable return of 8 percent compounded annually during the same ten-year period, you would end up with slightly more, $215,892!

Which investment would you prefer in figure 17.6 —a taxable ten-year gain from $100,000 to $215,000, or a ten-year gain from $100,000 to $215,000 tax free not only during the accumulation phase, but also during the withdrawal phase and the transfer phase? Let me ask another question: Which of the two scenarios would give you more peace of mind —a consistent, stable return of 8 percent or a model of returns including some great gain years, along with some unfavorable, uncertain loss years?

One of the problems with a mutual fund environment is if you want or need to convert mutual fund shares into cash for living expenses, you may need to pay close attention to the timing and strategic liquidation of the portfolio. It is always a temptation to hold off in a down market until you can recapture some of your previously attained paper profits. I have found this creates tremendous turmoil for people in retirement who are trying to take a stable, consistent income out of their volatile mutual fund portfolios. If you could achieve a similar average return over the same time period, knowing you can withdraw the money tax free on the back end without much regard for market timing, wouldn't that make a significant difference? Most people want to free themselves from having to read the *Wall Street Journal* and worry all the time about managing their investments—what to buy when and what to sell when. I, for one, would prefer to put my money in a more stable, tax-free environment, knowing that if I can achieve a conservative rate of return of 6 to 8 percent, I have earned the equivalent of a more aggressive, less certain 10 to 12 percent in a taxable portfolio.

Sometimes the risk of certain investments is simply not worth the reward. Dr. Denis Waitley puts this in perspective beautifully. He uses an example of someone walking a two-inch-thick, twelve-inch-wide wood plank for 100 feet to obtain a $100 bill at the other end. If this plank were laid on the ground, very few people could not accomplish the task. But, if that same plank were stretched across the top of two skyscrapers, how many people would be willing to perform the identical feat for a measly $100? The risk is definitely not worth the reward!

When we talk about serious cash—cash we separate from our homes to accomplish the goals outlined in this book, or the cash we set aside for long-term goals such as our retirement, or cash we reposition out of life savings, IRAs or 401(k)s—there are certain investments wherein the associated risk may not be worth the reward. We want to nail that plank to the floor because we can accumulate wealth without that high of a return. We only need to leverage safely and get conservative returns. I will illustrate this in the next chapter.

ADVANTAGES AND DISADVANTAGES OF MUTUAL FUNDS

There are some distinct advantages to mutual funds. Small investors can use a mutual fund because it pools money together with other small investors, thereby allowing small amounts of money to be diversified over perhaps 100 or more food, machinery, electronics, mining, metals, oils, computer, and communication technology companies throughout America. As we are busy doing what we do best, we can afford, through pooling money together with others, to hire professional managers who study what to buy when and what to sell when as a full-time pursuit. By reading their prospectus and choosing mutual funds that parallel our particular investment objectives, we can go about our own business, letting professional managers "tend" our money. With mutual funds, if ten or fifteen companies don't do as well as the managers had anticipated, you will probably have eighty to ninety other companies in the mutual fund portfolio that will hold you up. Spreading your money around through diversification and using professional money managers help to dramatically reduce the risk of personally investing a small amount of capital otherwise limited to perhaps just one or two stocks.

The disadvantage of mutual funds, whether they are qualified for tax-favored retirement funding or not, is the taxation must occur either on the front end (the contribution and accumulation phases) or at the back end (the withdrawal and transfer phases), or possibly both ends. Tax advantages are not available on the back end except in the case of Roth IRAs or in certain tax-free or tax-exempt bond mutual funds.

INVESTING IN INSURANCE

Many investors in America don't realize many major life insurance companies are really not much different from a mutual fund type of asset management company. Insurance companies are experts in managing risks. As they bank and hold money set aside for future needs, they are responsible for investing that money to achieve a safe rate of return. I believe many life insurance companies, when properly managed, could almost be regarded as conservative mutual funds in and of themselves because they usually invest their capital in a conservative portfolio primarily consisting of high-grade bonds. A small percentage of the assets are usually also invested in mortgage loans on real estate, and sometimes in common stocks and other like investments. The annual reports and financial statements of many insurance companies show they are structured similarly to conservative, income-oriented mutual funds with some growth potential. Because the portfolio of an insurance company is more conservative and is likely less volatile than most mutual funds, it will likely earn a lower rate of return—only 7 to 9 percent on the average, versus the 10 to 12 percent growth rate in an average mutual fund.

Ask yourself this question: How does achieving an average 7 to 9 percent, tax-free return over a ten- or twenty-year period compare with earning a 10 to 12 percent return and having to pay tax on that gain? Frankly, I would prefer to have the more stable, less volatile investment and have it grow tax free in addition to being tax free on the back end —during the harvest period of my life. With that kind of investment, I would probably achieve my goals with a higher net spendable income and greater accumulation value than other investments that are taxed on the back end. For this reason, wise investors are turning more to insurance companies for tax-favored, long-term savings and capital accumulation.

Prior to the 1980s, life insurance policies were not considered a very attractive investment because the typical whole life insurance policy may have only credited about 2.5 percent to 3.5 percent return on the cash values that would accumulate. A participating policy with dividends reinvested may have performed two or three percentage points better. During the 1970s and early 1980s, I was a big proponent of buying term insurance and investing the difference in mutual funds. In fact, for eight years, I recommended that my clients purchase a special product that consisted of a term-to-65 life insurance policy with an annuity rider. A conservative investor could choose to leave two-thirds of her dollars in an annuity which earned approximately 7 to 8 percent interest. However, most of my clients opted to assign their annuity cash values each quarter to a mutual fund of their choice. Even today, that concept may still be a good alternative to traditional life insurance products. However, mutual fund accounts are still subject to taxation during the accumulation phase on dividends and capital gain distributions, as well as the capital gain that may be realized during the withdrawal phase.

E. F. Hutton is often credited as the brainchild behind the emergence of non-traditional, interest-sensitive life insurance, which has predominantly come to be called universal life insurance. The insurance industry in America is a trillion-dollar industry and is probably one of the most stable factors in the American economy. In fact, I believe the insurance industry represents the financial backbone of our country.

During the Great Depression of the 1930s, for instance, a large percentage of banks failed and never opened their doors again. Even some real estate dropped as much as 80 percent in value. Many stocks took a long time to recover, if they did at all. However, research shows that some of the most stable and safe investments during that time were in life insurance contracts. Well-managed and highly rated life insurance companies, as a general rule, are some of the best money managers in the world. Their track record over the past 100 years would be the envy of some of the wealthiest, most profitable individuals and business entities in the world.

If you study the portfolio of an insurance company and feel its philosophies and management history are in harmony with your objectives, you might choose that company to manage your money. By doing so, you would be putting your faith in their managers' ability to earn future rates of return similar to those they had achieved in the past. You would be, in effect, investing your money into the life insurance company just as you would invest in a mutual fund. To qualify for this sort of investment, your accumulation account would of course have to carry a death benefit. Instead of trying to get the greatest death benefit for the lowest premium possible, you would purchase the lowest death benefit required by tax law and pay the highest premiums you could afford. This enables you to invest the greatest amount of excess cash beyond the true cost of the insurance into the policy. You would reverse your approach in order to use your life insurance policy primarily as a living benefit rather than a death benefit!

This unique approach is contrary to that of most buyers of life insurance. If your life insurance insures your life, but only benefits those you leave behind at death, it might more appropriately be called "death insurance." Focusing on the tax-favored living benefits afforded by life insurance better befits the name "life insurance."

INVESTMENT-GRADE INSURANCE CONTRACTS

Until the introduction of investment-grade life insurance in the 1980s, many people viewed life insurance only as a necessary evil—an instrument into which you would try to pay the smallest premium possible to buy the greatest insurance protection should an untimely death occur. There were basically two broad categories of life policies. Those that provided only a death benefit were classified as term insurance. Those that provided some type of equity build-up in addition to the death benefit were classified as cash-value or permanent insurance.

All life insurance—term and cash-value—is based on the concept that each individual pays a premium based on the desired coverage. Life insurance is priced per $1,000 of coverage per year. The cost per $1,000 varies with factors such as age, insurability, health of the insured, type of policy purchased, and mortality, usually calculated using the 1980 Commissioners' Standard Ordinary Mortality Table.[1]

Let me illustrate how the CSO Table is used. According to this table, out of 1,000 thirty-year-old males in America, 1.93 will likely die in a particular year. Thus, if 1,000 thirty-year-old males got together in a fraternal organization and decided to create a death benefit of $1,000.00, to be awarded to the beneficiaries of the (approximately) two who would die, each of the fraternal members might have to deposit $2 into a box. Assuming no interest is credited on the amount in that box, at the end of the year, when those two people died, $1,000.00 would be paid out to each beneficiary.

In this example the box represents an insurance company, with one significant difference—the insurance company takes those funds and invests them in order to earn a rate of return, thus allowing them to charge lower insurance premium rates than the mortality table might indicate. They also improve their risk, potentially further lowering premium rates, by screening potential deaths—using physical exams,

---

[1] For years the 1958 Commissioners' Standard Ordinary Mortality Table was used. Then it was later upgraded to the 1980 CSO Table. You may ask, "Why doesn't the National Association of Insurance Commissioners (NAIC) come out with a newer, updated mortality table?" They may do so. However, just because the CSO table is based on mortality rates from 1980 doesn't mean that you are paying insurance premiums based solely on that table of statistics for your particular insurance policy. Insurance companies charge the insurance rates based upon their actual mortality with the approval of each of the state's insurance departments.

doctors and hospital records, and inspecting lifestyles. This pure cost of insurance is called the true mortality cost. In addition to the pure mortality cost of insurance, there are also other expenses related to the administration of the insurance benefits. To profitably operate an insurance company, the administration and sales expenses also need to be deducted from the amount of money contributed by each insured person. Insurance premiums also cover sales and administration expense charges associated with the establishment of a life insurance policy.

TERM VS. CASH-VALUE INSURANCE

Term insurance premiums generally increase with age. That's because mortality rates increase each year as people get older. Because of this, when purchasing insurance, you would have to pay a higher premium each year (or, in actuality, every month) because your chances of dying increase as you age. Some people do not want to pay a higher premium each month, so instead pay a level premium based upon the average premium required to cover mortality and expense charges over a five-, ten- or twenty-year period, or perhaps for an entire lifetime. The company's actuarial department calculates the amount that needs to be collected, then credits the time value of the money invested to arrive at the necessary premium figures. Otherwise, a level premium can also be maintained if the insured elects to purchase decreasing term insurance, in which the death benefit goes down as the person gets older. Term insurance may be a good way to meet specific, short-term needs, but it has no cash accumulation value or living benefits. Coverage will lapse or expire the moment premiums are no longer paid into the policy.[2]

Cash value life insurance, on the other hand, was designed to accommodate an overpayment of insurance premiums during the early years, thus allowing an underpayment of premiums in later years. This approach creates an average premium paid into the policy over its lifetime. The

---

[2] This may happen if the premiums become unaffordable. If you would like to get an idea of pricing for competitive term life insurance, feel free to visit my web site at www.improtected.com to get a quote comparing up to 150 different plans with top-rated companies. Simply click on "Term Quotes." This interactive web site will also help you determine how much insurance you may need.

excess premium paid over and above the mortality and administration expenses creates equity in the policy similar to equity in a home. The excess money accumulates with interest, then begins to accrue the cash values that can be used for living benefits. If death occurs, cash values are absorbed into the life insurance death benefit, or they can be added on top of the face amount of the insurance policy.

The principal objective of life insurance originally was to create an immediate estate in the event of a premature death to help cover the economic loss suffered by the beneficiary(s). Along with this immediate estate, "whole life insurance" or any type of cash-value insurance also provides equity build-up inside the policy, which provides a liquid fund that can be used at will—in the event of an emergency, for investment opportunities to supplement other retirement income. Whole life insurance can be an effective method of purchasing insurance on a long-term basis. The excess premiums are invested by the life insurance company in a long-term portfolio, thus creating additional cash accumulation or dividends that can be reinvested or left with the insurance company for further growth. Newer whole life policies, especially those of the last two decades, contain lower costs due to upgraded mortality rates.

Generally speaking, mortality rates continue to improve as modern medicine strives to prolong life. Even the insurance industry became progressively lenient on the minimum underwriting guidelines as inflation made money worth less and less over the years. For example, in the 1980s an insurance company would often accept a life insurance application based upon "non-medical declarations," meaning no medical exam was required, up to certain limits. Blood and urine analysis was sometimes not required for an application of up to $500,000 of life insurance, depending upon the age and lifestyle of the applicant. After a long period of continually rising "non-medical" limits, the AIDS epidemic became a worldwide concern. At the same time, blood and urine lab tests had been perfected to such a degree that all kinds of life-threatening conditions could be detected—harmful drug use, heart, kidney, liver, other vital organ diseases, etc. Suddenly, insurers began requiring blood and urine tests in order for people to prove insurability on insurance amounts as low as $100,000.

Insurance companies try hard to keep their risks at a minimum to be more profitable and reward those who live healthier lifestyles. Unfortunately, those who don't live healthy lifestyles are penalized with substandard premium ratings, or they may even be declined altogether. In other words, people may be rated "standard" or substandard" who lead somewhat "normal" American lifestyles—perhaps including tobacco, alcohol, excessive caffeine, or even occasional drug use; common health problems such as obesity, high blood pressure, or a family medical history of heart disease; hazardous occupations, sports activities, or other interests. People who do not use tobacco or alcohol, whose heights and weights are within certain guidelines, and who are fortunate enough to enjoy a fairly active, healthy lifestyle are rewarded by being rated "preferred" or even "ultra preferred." The difference in true mortality cost for life insurance on a person who smokes tobacco compared to the cost associated with someone who does not should be enough to motivate someone to stop smoking! Earning a conservative rate of return on the difference in premium over a thirty-year period could mean the difference between a barely adequate retirement nest egg and a more than adequate retirement account!

The most unique feature of permanent life insurance is that under Sections 72(e) and 7702 of the Internal Revenue Code, the accumulation of cash values inside the insurance contract are tax advantaged. Not only can the cash values accumulate tax free, but they can also be accessed tax free under certain provisions of the contract. Life insurance death benefit proceeds are also income-tax free under most circumstances as provided under IRC Section 101, no matter how large they are, although they may be included in the total valuation of the deceased's estate. (Upon the death of the second spouse, a large estate comprised partially of life insurance proceeds could be taxable under estate tax unless specifically excluded from the estate through the use of an irrevocable life insurance trust.) Insurance proceeds are not subject to the claims of creditors of the deceased unless they were assigned or pledged as such, or unless the beneficiary was jointly responsible. If the beneficiary of an insurance policy is the estate of the insured rather than the spouse, children, trust, or other party, then the creditors may have a claim.

Hence, the beauty and magic of life insurance: It is a unique investment that allows you to accumulate your money tax free, allows you to access your money tax free, and, when you die, blossoms in value and transfers income tax free!

Provided the required premiums are paid, a permanent life insurance policy contract contains guaranteed cash values. These values are supported by company monetary reserves. They also contain maximum guaranteed premium schedules designed to keep the life insurance in force until a certain age under a guaranteed interest rate. Of course, most life insurance contracts credit more than the guaranteed rate stated in the contract.

As one highly regarded insurance professional, the late John Savage, pointed out, "Contrary to belief, rate of return is generally not the main factor in accumulating wealth." He illustrated this concept by using the following example: If an average American had $10,000 in a bank account earning 5 percent interest, another $10,000 in a different investment vehicle earning 8 percent interest, and a third $10,000 buried in a tin can in the back yard, initially you might think that, ten years down the road, the greatest amount of money would actually have accumulated in the investment earning 8 percent interest. However, if the investment earning 8 percent were highly visible and had easy accessibility, convenience, and maybe even the temptation of a drive-up window, many people would likely end up dipping into that account, regardless of its earning the highest rate of return. If the tin can were soldered shut and buried in the backyard so the person could not easily access it until the end of ten years, I daresay most Americans would have the most money in the tin can at the end of the ten years, even though it would not have earned a dime of interest.

Life insurance contracts function as an ideal tin can wherein money can be stored "out of sight, out of mind." Cash-value life insurance policies were in fact designed with that idea in mind—to store cash just like the tin can in Mr. Savage's example. Money in a life insurance contract tends to stay put, allowing it to compound and grow, whereas money in banks and mutual funds tend to be accessed more often, becoming depleted more quickly.

The real secret to accumulating wealth is not the rate of return, but instead, the ability to: 1) put money aside, 2) keep it aside, and 3) put it to work for you. We would have the best of all worlds if we could find a tin can that accumulates interest! That way, rather than losing value because of inflation, it would grow at a rate of return equal to or greater than the possible net rate of return achieved by higher, more risky, and more volatile taxable investments. This was the idea behind the creation of universal life in the early 1980s. By structuring a life insurance contract with a minimum death benefit, then filling the policy full of cash, the result would be a dramatic overpayment of the premiums normally required to cover mortality and expense charges, and a build-up of equity in the policy. This tremendous excess of cash, stored in the insurance company's internal portfolio, would earn interest, continuing to compound through the years. As you continue to over-fund the contract, the mortality and expense charges associated with the death benefit usually drain out a small portion of the overall interest earned on the cash values.

Everyone recognizes a wonderful product common to American households—baking soda (**fig. 17.7**). A roomful of people, when asked what baking soda can be used for, usually reply, "It removes odors from my refrigerator," or "We use it as toothpaste," or "It's a laundry freshener," or "It's an excellent cleaning agent," or "I use it to relax when soaking in the bathtub!" Then finally the obvious, "Oh, yeah, it can be used when baking!" Baking soda manufacturers have done an excellent job of educating the American public as to how their product can be used for purposes beyond its namesake. Life insurance is the same way. Properly structured life insurance contracts can be used for tax-favored capital accumulation and tax-advantaged retirement income as living benefits, in addition to providing income tax free death benefits.

TEFRA AND DEFRA

The Internal Revenue Service challenged this concept in 1982 and 1984, arguing the insurance contracts we've discussed were not really insurance policies but, in fact, investments. They wanted to redefine a life insurance policy. They felt the need to set certain parameters so people would not abuse a life insurance contract that allows for tax-free death benefits, as well as tax-free accumulation of cash values. These parameters were passed as part of the Tax and Fiscal Responsibility Act of 1982 and also the Deficit Reduction Act of 1984. In the insurance industry, these two acts are commonly referred to as TEFRA and DEFRA.

The TEFRA and DEFRA citation, or tax corridor, basically dictates the minimum death benefit required in order to accommodate the ultimate desired aggregate premium basis, based on the insured's age and sex. In other words, if a person wanted to use a cash-value life insurance policy for tax-free capital accumulation purposes, TEFRA and DEFRA rules would dictate the amount of the minimum death benefit required.

If someone wanted to purchase a universal life policy with a $100,000 death benefit, the TEFRA/DEFRA corridor would dictate the amount of money she could invest in premiums without exceeding the definition of a life insurance contract. This would make the accumulation of cash values and the death benefit not subject to tax. This is what I call a front-door approach.

Most people who come to me as a financial planner do not want or even need life insurance. What they want, instead, is an investment vehicle that contains liquidity, safety, and a nice rate of return in a tax-favored environment. They want to create the greatest amount of future net spendable income with investments that are tax free during the harvest years. I show them several options. But most do exactly what I do with my own money after they understand the advantages: They choose a properly structured investment-grade life insurance contract designed to accommodate the amount of capital they wish to transfer or reposition from other inferior investments.

They might choose an investment-grade insurance contract to reposition some of their IRA and 401(k) contributions or distributions under a strategic conversion (roll-out). They may choose to reposition some or all of their home equity into a life insurance contract. The long-term performance of a properly funded universal life insurance contract, from the standpoint of a cash-on-cash, after-tax, internal rate of return, is usually much better than many IRA and 401(k) investments, mutual funds, annuities, CDs, and money market accounts. In addition, a death benefit comes along for the ride! So, instead of using a front-door approach, I use the TEFRA/DEFRA corridor to calculate the minimum death benefit required using what I refer to as a "back-door" approach.

THE BACK-DOOR APPROACH

First I determine how much the client wants to invest (how much they are going to reposition over a given time period) and feed that data into a computer program. The software then tells us how much life insurance the client gets in accordance with TEFRA/DEFRA parameters. For example, if a person's planned ultimate investment were to total $100,000, she would create a policy which could potentially hold up to $100,000 of new cash contributions or premium payments. Let's compare a life insurance policy structured this way to a bucket (**fig. 17.8**).

In this example, $100,000 is the maximum basis allowed during the first eleven to twelve years of the policy, during which time the investor could put in new cash premium contributions into the bucket (policy). If a person wanted to fill her bucket in one fell swoop or in one lump sum, she would be allowed to do that and still benefit from tax-free accumulation and tax-free death benefit proceeds. However, tax-free access of the cash values, including the interest earned, could be jeopardized unless certain other guidelines are met (I will explain these later). Alternatively, an investor could choose to spread out her premium contributions over a longer time frame and fill up her bucket over an eleven- or twelve-year period.

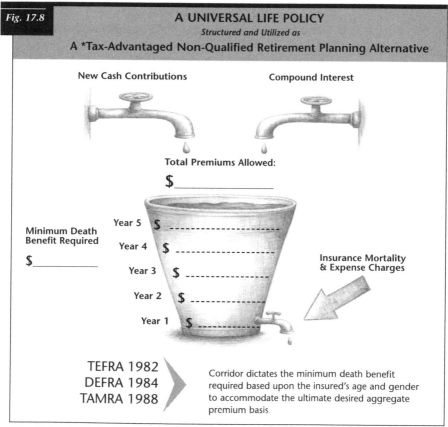

Fig. 17.8

A UNIVERSAL LIFE POLICY
Structured and Utilized as
A *Tax-Advantaged Non-Qualified Retirement Planning Alternative

New Cash Contributions   Compound Interest

Total Premiums Allowed:
$_____

Minimum Death
Benefit Required   Year 5 $- - - - - - - - - - - - - - - - -
$_____   Year 4 $- - - - - - - - - - - - - -   Insurance Mortality
                       Year 3 $- - - - - - - - - - - -   & Expense Charges
                       Year 2 $- - - - - - - - -
                       Year 1 $- - - - - - - -

TEFRA 1982
DEFRA 1984   Corridor dictates the minimum death benefit
TAMRA 1988   required based upon the insured's age and gender
                  to accommodate the ultimate desired aggregate
                  premium basis.

* *Tax Citations: IRC Section 101, IRC Section 72(e), Rev. Rul 66-322, 1966-2 CB 123, TEFRA Section 266, DEFRA Section 221*

In reality, if all we're after is death benefits, it may not be necessary to fill the bucket to the brim with new cash contributions under the maximum amount allowed under TEFRA and DEFRA rules. This is because once the excess cash in the policy grows to a certain amount, the insurance company's investment performance on that excess money should allow an investor to deposit relatively little money (pay small premiums)—or perhaps no further money—and yet continue to have life insurance benefits.

However, if death benefits are the secondary objective and the primary objective is to accumulate cash and receive the highest net rate of return on premiums paid, it would behoove the investor to structure a life insurance policy that accommodates the ultimate desired investment she wants to make over time. The objective is to create a bucket that is just big enough, under TEFRA and DEFRA rules, to accommodate the amount of money you will likely put in it. By doing so the policyholder is not obligated to fill the bucket to the brim with premiums, but has thus set a maximum allowable contribution to the bucket within a given time frame. This figure is referred to as the guideline single premium.

If the premiums paid into a policy reach that limit before the eleventh year, the policy holder must stop putting any additional money into the policy to avoid exceeding the definition of life insurance under TEFRA and DEFRA, excluding herself from the opportunity for tax-free accumulation and tax-free access to her funds. In such a situation, she could simply open another bucket (enroll in a new universal life policy, assuming she passes the physical exam and is approved by the insurance company). This second policy would have the same advantages as the first, provided the tax laws were the same as they were at the time she started her first bucket. Keeping this in mind, many people begin early to choose well-managed insurance companies, just as a person might choose a conservative mutual fund, with whom they can load buckets with cash as soon as possible, thus achieving a handsome net rate of return over time.

This kind of policy, of course, is not free of costs. The costs associated with a universal life policy most closely resemble those for term insurance, but with a significant difference: If premiums are paid that are far greater than the actual pure term insurance premium, the policy accumulates an excess cash value. Over time, the interest and compounding of that cash can more than compensate for the continuing costs of owning that policy. The costs can be compared to a spigot draining cash out of your policy from the bottom of the bucket (**fig. 17.8**). These costs, which allow the investment to qualify as life insurance and, therefore, remain tax free, are an absolutely critical component for achieving the most attractive results. And in the long run, the spigot potentially may only consume approximately .5 percent to 1.0 percent of the interest percentage credited during the life of the policy.

Over a twenty- or thirty-year experience, an investor could very well achieve a net rate of return, cash on cash, of 7 to 7.5 percent on a life insurance policy crediting an average of 8 percent interest. If this were the case, only .5 percent to 1 percent of the interest rate would have gone to pay for the insurance. I would rather have a tax-free return averaging 7 percent over a taxable return of 10 or even 12 percent any day! The small portion of my accumulated cash which is paying for my life insurance is money that would have otherwise gone to Uncle Sam in taxes on a taxable investment. I think of it as Uncle Sam indirectly paying for my life insurance.

To me, achieving a net rate of return on a tax-free basis on an investment that will perform as well or better than an investment in a taxable alternative, with the bonus of an insurance benefit, means the insurance was more or less free. Yes, I know that the reality is there's no such thing as free life insurance; however, if the insurance costs can be paid for out of a portion of the interest earned on the cash values during the life of the policy, and that small portion of interest is equivalent to or less than the money you would have otherwise spent on taxes in another investment, then wouldn't we be justified in thinking of it as free?

The nice thing about the TEFRA/DEFRA guidelines is it doesn't matter much how old you are—the spigot on the bucket can be designed to drain out about the same percentage of your interest regardless. In other words, a sixty-five-year-old qualifying for an insurance policy can structure it to achieve close to the same net rate of return on premium dollars paid into the bucket as a twenty-year-old. The difference is the twenty-year-old simply gets more life insurance. For example, if a policy were designed to accommodate $100,000 of basis (the maximum of cash premiums allowed in the policy under TEFRA/DEFRA) a twenty-year-old male might be required to have about $1,450,000 of life insurance, whereas a sixty-five-year-old male would be required to only have about $210,000 of insurance. But, over a twenty-year period, based upon an average gross interest rate credited on the policy of 8 percent, the net rate of return after deducting the cost of insurance required could be approximately 7 percent for both the twenty-year-old and the sixty-five-year-old.

DEALING WITH MARKET FLUCTUATIONS

Since the early 1980s, when universal life first emerged, interest rates credited on traditional fixed universal life insurance policies with some companies have been as high as 13 percent and as low as 5 percent. I believe an investor need not be concerned about the interest rate fluctuations because they are all relative. During the 1980s when insurance contracts were crediting as much as 11 to 13 percent interest, a person would be rowing upstream, so to speak, at thirteen miles per hour. However, the current of inflation at that time was coming downstream at, say, ten miles per hour (10 percent inflation). The actual margin in that case would only be 3 percentage points.

In recent years, interest rates have been lower. However, if you row upstream at five miles per hour, and the current of inflation is only going against you at two miles per hour, you still have the same margin of 3 percentage points! If our long-term goal is to accumulate enough capital to have the same purchasing power as we do today, we simply need to continue along a path with a consistent rate of return—after taking into account varying inflation rates along the way. Hopefully by doing so, we'll be able to buy as much gas and groceries in the future as today—maybe more.

In comparing this kind of return to the 15 to 25 percent returns stock buyers hope for periodically in the stock market, remember that due to fluctuations in the market, investors do not always experience earnings that average in the 15 to 25 percent range. Smart investors analyze the long-term average rate of return based upon fluctuating markets, discount any cost of loads and management fees, and consider tax effects on the back end. If a universal life policy is structured to perform at its optimal level, it requires the bucket be filled with cash as soon as possible in compliance with IRS guidelines. Then the net rate of return, after discounting mortality and expense charges, may come close to within the gross rate of return over time, even to within 1 percent.

Unfortunately, there are some life insurance agents who are not as concerned with the investment performance as they are with the commissions they might earn. Many universal life policies have been sold that were structured to benefit agents' spouses and children more than the clients' spouses and children. If the amount of death benefit is higher than needed in order to accommodate the ultimate amount you want to invest under TEFRA and DEFRA guidelines, then the net rate of return will not be as attractive (i.e., the spigot is larger than it needs to be, and is draining out cash faster than is desirable).

ESTABLISHING GOALS AND PRIORITIES

An investor needs to remember his priorities by asking himself, "What is the real purpose for establishing the insurance contract?" As I said, the vast majority of my clients do not come to me wanting or particularly needing life insurance death benefits. But they are thrilled when they realize by investing money into an insurance policy, they can possibly achieve a safe net rate of return that is as good or better than an annuity. Not only can they access funds on a tax-free basis, which they can't do with an annuity, but should they die, their investment will actually blossom by as much as double or triple—and still transfer to their heirs on an income-tax free basis! Generally, through structuring a universal life insurance policy correctly to accommodate only the maximum capital invested, a universal life policy will outperform an annuity during the transfer, accumulation, and withdrawal phases.

When purchasing a universal life policy, it is important to determine needs and long-term goals. Is the primary goal to accumulate cash and the highest net rate of return in a tax-advantaged environment? Or is the goal also to obtain a certain amount of death protection in addition to some moderate capital accumulation? If the goal is unclear, and because the creation of a universal life policy is so flexible, a new policy owner should take care not to make the bucket too large or too small (too much or too little death benefit). A policy that is too large may accommodate a schedule of lower premium payments that will not fill up the bucket to the guideline single premium as it should to achieve a maximum investment return. (It would be fine, if you determined you wanted to meet certain insurance needs and realize a conservative investment return, and therefore took out additional insurance above TEFRA and DEFRA requirements.)

THE FLEXIBILITY OF UNIVERSAL LIFE INSURANCE

Universal life has become a flexible insurance product. It is not considered term insurance because it accumulates cash values. It is not considered whole life insurance because premium payments can be varied, fluctuated, and adjusted according to circumstances (universal life is also referred to as flexible-premium life insurance). The policy holder is not forced into non-forfeiture options when premium payments need to be adjusted or halted for a while, provided there is already sufficient cash in the policy to cover insurance costs. Thus, the term "universal life" is used because it is applicable to so many situations.

Perhaps someone you know owned a universal life policy which didn't perform the way he had understood it. Concluding, that universal life is an unwise investment would be foolish. During the high interest rate era in the 1980s, many life insurance agents began to sell universal life policies as a low-cost permanent life insurance policy. They structured universal life policies for their clients with minimum premium funding that provided death benefits with nominal cash value build-up. In a high interest rate environment, clients could deposit a much lower premium into a universal life than a whole life policy and the contract carried itself over the long haul, provided interest rates remained high. However, many policy holders became disgruntled when they were required to pay additional premiums as interest rates dropped. This cause and effect relationship had not been explained to them. This resulted in numerous negative articles and publicity about universal life policies.

On the other hand, universal life policies can be structured to perform as an excellent capital accumulation vehicle by being loaded as full of cash as IRS rules allow. Even in a fluctuating interest rate environment, people who have structured their universal life policies to perform as a means of capital accumulation (funding them at maximum levels with the minimum life insurance required) have done extremely well. Their policies have outperformed other traditionally stable and conservative investments.

Considering that mortality and expense charges for universal life policies are pretty much equal among most competing companies, the key to a successful universal life policy is to first determine what the goal is and then structure the policy accordingly. Again, if your goal is to accumulate the greatest amount of capital at the highest net rate of return possible, you should only take the minimum death benefit required to fund it, then fill the bucket to the maximum level as soon as possible. The guideline single premium represents the maximum that you can put into your bucket during the first eleven years. Of course, over that period, your circumstances may change. If you one day find you may never be able to fill that bucket to the brim, you may want to maximize the return and minimize the costs. So rather than maintain the original life insurance death benefit, you can easily reduce its size by reducing the face amount of the insurance with the stroke of a pen.

Say you cut the insurance in half. In essence, you would also cut your bucket in half. Some care must be taken in doing this because you could well have violated IRS guidelines regulating how quickly you may fund your bucket, causing your policy to become taxable when you withdraw your money. There may also be some surrender charges incurred when reducing the death benefit. Also, remember, this is a permanent change. The only way to increase it again would be to requalify, with a physical exam, for new coverage.

The introduction of universal life policies has led to a remarkable chain of events. Insurance companies offering whole life have since created more interest-sensitive products yielding higher dividends based on the earnings. In this way, if a whole life policy was over-funded, it could also perform in a similar fashion to universal life. The emergence of interest-sensitive life insurance products resulted in quite a revolution in the life insurance industry in the 1980s. Since then, the insurance industry has continued to evolve with the introduction of variable and indexed products both in the universal life and whole life arena.

GRANDFATHERING TAX LAWS

In the past, whenever Congress has made far-reaching changes to the tax code, especially regarding life insurance, it has grandfathered policyholders who already had a policy in force. It may behoove a person to establish a universal life policy now that will accommodate the amount of capital she will eventually like to sock away in case Congress decides to change the rules again. The hope is the existing policies will be grandfathered. No guarantee can be made by an insurance company or life insurance agent that the client will, in fact, be grandfathered. But because of this precedent, and because of the ex-post-facto provision in the Constitution wherein new laws are not supposed to adversely affect things that were established under old laws, grandfathering is a likely scenario.

As an example, between 1982 and 1988, properly structured universal life policies were attractive when compared to other investment alternatives—especially conservative investments such as CDs, money markets, or even stock portfolios. A massive exodus of funds left banks and stock brokerage firms in favor of tax-favored insurance contracts. Many of my clients filled up their buckets in one single premium payment. Some transferred money in lump sums from CDs, money market accounts, and mutual funds in amounts ranging up to as much as $500,000, all in accordance with TEFRA/DEFRA guidelines.

Say a person created a bucket that accommodated a $100,000 guideline single premium at a time when interest rates were crediting as high as

11 percent. An individual could begin filling the bucket to the brim, and immediately after her first premium payment, she would be entitled to a death benefit anywhere between $200,000 to $1,500,000 (remember, this varies depending on age and gender). In the long run the policy would use approximately 1 percent or less of that 11 percent interest for mortality and expense charges, thus resulting in a net 10 percent rate of return. Assuming interest rates remained stable over several years, policyholders theoretically could pull out about $10,000 a year on a tax-free basis, thereby enjoying an income far greater than having the same amount of money in a taxable CD, money market, or stock portfolio.

Let's say you had the choice of two certificates of deposit in which to deposit $100,000. One offered you 6 percent interest, which was taxable. If you happened to die, that CD transferred to your heirs in the amount of the money that you had accumulated in it. The other CD offered you 6 percent interest, this time tax free. If you happened to die, the second CD would blossom into $200,000 or more. Which of the two CDs would you choose, all other factors (think safety and liquidity) being equal? The choice is obvious. (In actuality, the safety of most insurance companies is considered greater than the safety of many commercial banks.)

One of the beauties of a universal life policy is it can be structured to accommodate the amount of capital you will eventually put into the bucket. You can nurse it along with minimum premiums that barely cover the spigot until impending capital comes in that is needed to fill the bucket—perhaps from the planned sale of a home or other piece of real estate. This is a strategy often used to prepare a policy to accept large lump sums—and still hopefully be grandfathered should Congress pass any laws in the interim.

In 1988, it became apparent that banks and stock brokerage firms were suffering because of this massive transfer of capital out of their institutions into life insurance companies. The public was selecting greater safety, better return, more favorable tax treatment, and better transferability of their conservative investments. The banks and brokerage firms lobbied Congress to make the transfer of money to tax-favored insurance contracts less damaging to them. As Congress debated the creation of a new law,

I warned several clients who wanted to invest more than their existing buckets would allow under DEFRA that a change might be coming down the pike. I alerted them to the possibility of establishing another insurance contract that would hopefully be grandfathered if a new law were passed. Unfortunately, many of those clients said, "Well, let us know if Congress passes anything; surely, a law wouldn't go into effect until the following calendar year!" I warned them against waiting until the new law was passed; nonetheless, most of them tried to postpone the day of reckoning.

TAMRA

In 1988 a change was in fact proposed under a section of the Technical and Miscellaneous Revenue Act (TAMRA). The proposal was directed at the tax treatment of life insurance policies if they were maximum funded (the bucket was filled to the brim) in less than seven years. Interestingly enough, one body of Congress passed the act in the summer; the other body of Congress did not pass it until later in the fall. Rather than making it effective the following January 1, the law was made effective retroactive to June 21, 1988, the day the first body approved the bill. Many people who had been waiting to purchase a policy had to comply with the new TAMRA law after June 21, 1988. Those who already had policies in existence were grandfathered under the old rules.

The new law still allows for a policyholder to pay one large single premium. Such a policy is classified as a Modified Endowment Contract under Section 7702A of the Internal Revenue Code, referred in the industry as a MEC. If this is done, the cash values still accumulate inside the policy tax deferred and the death benefit is tax free. However, if any money is withdrawn out of the policy before the age of $59^1/2$, it will be subject to a 10 percent penalty much like an IRA or 401(k). Also when money is withdrawn, the gain is taxable under LIFO (Last In First Out) tax treatment, just like an annuity.

If a policyholder instead decides to fill the bucket in increments of a certain maximum size, it will still fall under the old rules by which money can be accessed before the age of 59^1/$_2$ on a tax-free basis. It can provide tax-free distributions for retirement income or other purposes. To comply with the new law under TAMRA, the policy has to pass what is known as the Seven-Pay Test.

SEVEN-PAY TEST

The Seven-Pay Test means a whole life insurance policy cannot be funded any faster than seven equal installments. Under the existing provisions, if the policy is maximum funded no faster than seven relatively equal installments, then it complies with the TAMRA Seven-Pay Test and cash values can be accessed tax free at any time. However, there has been a tremendous misunderstanding, even among insurance agents, because the Seven-Pay Test is a misnomer with regard to universal life. Because of the TEFRA and DEFRA limits that dictate the amount of life insurance required to meet the definition of a life insurance policy, a universal policy can be maximum funded in as little as three years and one day (four annual installments) by an individual under the approximate age of fifty, and four years and one day (five annual installments) for someone over the approximate age of fifty. If a universal life policy is funded and filled to the maximum level in essentially five annual installments, it will likely outperform a policy that requires seven annual installments in order to fill it to the brim. As long as a policyholder does not exceed the TAMRA premium limit, she is allowed to access cash values on a tax-free basis.

The idea was that by having to spread out the premium payments with four to seven annual installments, the public would be more prone to liquidate their bank accounts or stock portfolios over an equivalent period, rather than transfer the whole amount of capital in one fell swoop. This would result in a more gentle blow to those financial institutions.

The insurance industry responded immediately to the TAMRA law and began to offer temporary side buckets such as single premium immediate annuities (with a term certain of four or five years) or advanced premium deposit funds. These temporary side buckets park the excess funds that would violate TAMRA had they been paid into the main policy. The insurance companies usually credit these accounts with interest equal to or greater than what a bank may be paying. The interest is taxable, but the side buckets can pour one-quarter or one-fifth of the total money over into the universal life bucket automatically each year until the side bucket is empty at the end of five years and the universal life policy is full and in total compliance with TAMRA.

For example, if an investor wants to put $100,000 into her bucket and comply with TAMRA, about $20,000 to $25,000 (depending on her age) can be paid into her universal life policy the first year. The remaining $75,000 to $80,000 can be deposited into a single premium immediate annuity (SPIA). The annuity is established for a term certain of four or five years. It can earn an attractive interest rate; however, the interim interest would be reportable as taxable interest. The annuity would automatically send over to the insurance policy approximately $20,000 to $25,000 a year at the beginning of each subsequent year. At the end of four or five years, the annuity would be empty of cash and expire. The universal life policy would then be maximum funded under TEFRA/DEFRA guidelines, avoid being classified as a MEC, in full compliance with TAMRA, and thereby qualify for tax-favored access to cash values. Even though temporary alternative side buckets were provided by the insurance industry, the law was not repealed, because the law made it just complicated enough that some people opted to keep their money in banks and stock brokerage firms while filling up their buckets over the allotted period.

As I will further explain in chapter 19, the Internal Revenue Code allows a policyholder to over-fund an insurance contract in excess of the TAMRA premium and then "perfect" the contract within sixty-days of the end of the first policy anniversary. To avoid the policy being classified as a MEC, thus preserving the tax-free accessibility of cash values, the policy owner could request a refund of the overage that was paid into the contract in violation of TAMRA, and redeposit it during the first sixty-days of the second year.

MATCHING THE INVESTMENT WITH THE OBJECTIVE

One advantage of the TAMRA law is it helps ensure people who invest in insurance policies for the accumulation of cash values are aware that tax-favored results require a long-term commitment. In order to make the policy perform at its optimum level, a policyholder needs to understand a universal life insurance contract is best used as a long-term investment to meet long-term objectives. One of the biggest mistakes I find people make in financial planning is that of choosing short-term investments for long-range objectives, or vice versa.

To structure a cash-value life insurance policy as an investment to be used primarily for living benefits, it should be clearly and thoroughly understood. Understand if only 20 percent of the bucket (guideline single premium amount) is filled after one year, the spigot will drain out a much higher percent of the bucket than when it is full. You must be patient as you fill your bucket, adhering to TEFRA/DEFRA and TAMRA guidelines, and not become discouraged when the net rate of return is not within one percent of the gross rate of return after only a few years into the contract. Then you must be patient as you let the compounding of interest do its job over time.

Policyholders who understand these concepts do not worry about the net rate of return achieved in the early years of an insurance contract because they know the tremendous benefits they will achieve down the road that will, retroactively back to the first day of the contract, generate a handsome net rate of return that can far outperform other investment alternatives. The success or failure of an investment can only be measured against is intended time frame. You should choose investments based on which ones will provide the most when you will likely use the most. Remember, when you will need that money the most, you will enjoy advantages that far outweigh the disadvantages on the front end.

Unfortunately, many life insurance agents do not totally understand the TEFRA/DEFRA and TAMRA guidelines. Subsequently, they are not competent in how to structure a life insurance policy to perform at its optimum level for living benefits rather than just death benefits. That is why I use the term "properly structured, investment-grade, cash-value life insurance."

DEFINING "INVESTMENT GRADE"

In review, if an investor wants to use a life insurance contract to accumulate capital on a tax-free basis under Sections 72(e) and 7702 of the Internal Revenue Code, it must meet several criteria before I would regard it as "investment grade." The first criterion is the policy must be structured properly to allow it to perform as an investment rather than just a life insurance policy. This is done by taking the minimum death benefit we can get by with within TEFRA/DEFRA parameters for the total premiums that are planned to be paid into the policy. This can be easily calculated through the use of various computer programs. It also needs to be structured so it can be filled to the brim (maximum funded) as soon as possible under TAMRA guidelines—and yet maintain flexibility in case circumstances change. Structuring an insurance policy that will allow it to perform as an attractive investment compared to other conservative investments is one of the reasons I feel it can fit into a category that is worthy of the designation "prudent investment" or "investment-grade contract."

The second criterion that allows an insurance contract to be deemed a prudent investment is the due diligence that must be exerted in researching the insurance companies selected. Insurance companies can be rated investment grade by several different rating agencies. If I were purchasing a life insurance policy for the sole purpose of providing a death benefit, I could probably choose any of a thousand or more legal-reserve life insurance companies in America, all of whom could be counted on to pay a claim upon my death.[3]

However, if I am selecting an insurance company for the purpose of capital accumulation and to achieve the best internal rate of return possible, I get very picky about companies. I generally use three broad guidelines when selecting a life insurance company.

---

[3] Legal-reserve life insurance companies more or less cross-insure each other. If a company were to become insolvent, the National Insurance Guarantee Association insures each life insurance policy up to $100,000 of cash values and $300,000 in death benefits much like FDIC or NCUA insures banks and credit unions. So, in the case of a company's insolvency, the other solvent insurance companies would be required to help pay the claims or benefits. This helps maintain integrity and confidence in the entire insurance industry.

The first of the guidelines is the insurance company's actual track record and philosophy. I study interest rate histories and performance when making the selection of an insurance company. I want to make certain I choose an insurance company that is well managed and generous in its rates of return. I have found many life insurance companies are rather stingy and have the attitude they will pay the least they can while staying competitive. They are more concerned about building up company coffers than policyholders' coffers. Other insurance companies are quite generous and credit the maximum amounts to their insurance policies, after covering their administration and expense charges and retaining a modest profit. The latter type can perform much like a conservative mutual fund.

The second guideline is to choose insurance companies based upon the ratings that various rating agencies assign to these companies. There are several rating agencies. Among those most used are Standard and Poor's, AM Best, Fitch, Moody's, and Weiss. These rating agencies use different methods and scales for rating companies, often confusing the general public, Congress, and the General Accounting Office. For instance, the highest rating that can be assigned by Standard and Poor's is an AAA rating. On the other hand, the highest rating assigned by AM Best is an A++ rating. Fitch, Moody's, and Martin Weiss have their own rating systems also (**fig. 17.9**).

In order to make comparisons, there are some organizations that combine the various rating agencies' data and create a method or "Comdex score" to help the public understand which companies are best. This is helpful because sometimes an insurance agent will tell a prospective client the company he represents is rated "A." What he may not tell you is that the "A" rating was from Standard and Poor's. An "A" is six notches down from the top rating of "AAA." The insurance company may still be deemed "investment grade" or "secure" by Standard and Poor's (usually ratings "BBB" or higher), but the illusion may have been intentionally created by the insurance agent that the company had the highest rating. One of the services I use is called Vital Signs. Vital Signs assigns a Comdex score between 1 to 100 based upon the combined data gathered from various

Fig. 17.9		**THE U.S. GENERAL ACCOUNTING OFFICE'S (GAO) SCALE OF INSURANCE RATINGS***				
RATINGS	**BANDS**	**A.M. BEST**	**STANDARD & POOR'**	**MOODY'S**	**FITCH**	**WEISS**
Secure	1	A++, A+	AAA	Aaa	AAA	A+, A, A-
	2	A, A-	AA+, AA, AA-	Aa1, Aa2, Aa3	AA+, AA, AA-	B+, B, B-
Vulnerable	3	B++, B+, B, B-	A+, A A-, BBB+, BBB, BBB-	A1, A2, A3 Baa1,Baa2,Baa3	A+, A, A- BBB+, BBB, BBB-	C+, C, C-
	4	C++, C+, C, C-	BB+, BB, BB- B+, B, B-	Ba1, Ba2, Ba3 B1, B2, B3	BB+, BB, BB- B+, B, B-	D+, D, D-
	5	D, E, F	CCC, (CC,C), (D), R	Caa, Ca, C	CCC+, CCC, CCC- DDD, DD, D	E+, E, E-, F

according to the GAO's 1994 study

rating agencies and the insurance company. A Comdex score of ninety or higher is an extremely high score. For the establishment of investment-grade contracts, generally I recommend companies that score at least seventy or higher on the Vital Signs Comdex, and I prefer those that score ninety or higher.

The third guideline I use to select an insurance company is its capital and surplus ratio (solvency). I feel it is necessary for an insurance company to maintain liquidity, just as I feel it is necessary for an individual to maintain liquidity. In other words, in order to minimize risk, there needs to be sufficient capital. Generally speaking, an insurance company will have a much greater surplus or solvency ratio than other financial institutions such as banks and credit unions. If times really got tough in the economy, I would prefer my money be positioned in an investment likely to remain somewhat stable. I would also prefer having money in an investment that would be easily accessible if I chose to liquidate my funds. If a financial institution has a capital and surplus ratio of only 4 or 5 percent, it should have about $4 or $5 left over for every $100 of assets if it had to use all its assets to liquidate all of its liabilities. This could prove to be a fairly narrow cushion. However, if the financial institution has a 10 to 15 percent capital and surplus ratio, it should be able to more readily liquidate its liabilities with substantial assets left over. Remember the size of an insurance company does not determine its strength. (As I have always said, "If bigger were better, Miss America would be an elephant!") An insurance company can be very large and yet have a lot of liabilities and poor investments.

PARTIES TO AN INSURANCE CONTRACT

It's essential to understand there are four different roles filled by individuals or entities, in addition to the insurer (insurance company). An individual (or individuals, under joint life) needs to fill the role of the *insured.* When the insured dies, a death benefit is paid to *the beneficiary* (usually a spouse or children of the insured, sometimes an entity such as the insured's business or a charitable organization). There must be an insurable interest between the insured and the beneficiary at the time of the life insurance application. In other words it must be determined the beneficiary would suffer an economic loss if the insured died. Or in the case of a charitable beneficiary the insurable interest is the bestowal or endowment of a gift the insured desires to bequeath the charity. The insurance contract must have *an owner,* who is the only one who has power to make changes to the contract (such as renaming a beneficiary, lowering the insurance amount, changing premium schedules, changing death benefit options, or taking out withdrawals and loans on the contract). The owner also owns all the cash values in a policy and the interest earned on those cash values, assuming all tax liability and enjoying all the tax benefits of a properly structured investment-grade policy. Finally, the insurance contract must also have a *premium payor.*

A single person or entity often plays multiple roles; however, they can be played by as many as four different parties. A grandfather could be the premium payor on a policy in which the insured is his son-in-law, the beneficiaries are his grandchildren, and the owner is his daughter (the insured's wife) or a trust for the purpose of a perpetual college fund for the grandchildren. When the premium payor is someone other than the owner, premiums paid into a contract may be deemed a gift and subject to gift taxes if over $10,000 a year per recipient.

When using a life insurance policy for the primary purpose of cash accumulation in a tax-favored environment for retirement or equity management objectives, the beneficiary is usually the spouse or children of the insured, or a family revocable living trust. Under most circumstances, it is preferred the insured is also the owner and the premium payor. This is because as the owner, (who also acts as the insured), accumulates cash values and uses those monies for retirement income or other purposes, it is advantageous to leave some money in the policy at the time of death to keep a death benefit in force and avoid a taxable event (I will explain this later). The death benefit has the ability to convert the remaining cash in the policy and blossom it into a tax-free death proceed for the benefit of those the insured leaves behind.

When a person dies, she usually leaves behind some assets that were to sustain her had she lived longer. Those assets may include bank accounts, CDs, money markets, stocks, bonds, real estate, or cash values of life insurance. Life insurance is the only asset that instantaneously blossoms from the cash values previously used for living benefits into tax-advantaged death benefits. So, if possible, it usually is best to try to insure the individual in a relationship who will likely pass away first, so the remaining money (cash values) left in the insurance contract can blossom and transfer to the next person in the relationship. The insurance proceeds have the effect of replenishing some of the money that was used for retirement income so the surviving spouse may have a rejuvenated retirement resource to use the remainder of her life.

I have had many client couples who have established investment-grade life insurance contracts for the purpose of enhancing their retirement income. The procedure I use is to strategically reposition their IRAs and 401(k)s and manage the equity in their current homes (or former home if the couple sold or downsized it), to maintain liquidity, safety, and earn a rate of return. When possible I establish two buckets (insurance policies)—one for each—to accommodate the repositioned assets. As a result, I minimize their tax and maximize their net spendable retirement income dramatically. They enjoy retirement with a simple, low-maintenance investment portfolio comprised primarily of two universal life contracts.

Typically, the husband dies first. There might be $200,000 left in his bucket at the time of his death, but it may blossom into $500,000 by virtue of the life insurance death benefit. Thus, his widow gets $500,000 tax free instead of taxable IRAs containing $200,000 or less! I would then advise her to take the $500,000 of tax-free insurance proceeds and keep it tax free. She could open a new bucket (take out a new universal life policy) and, in full compliance with TAMRA, use a side bucket (a SPIA). She can begin accessing tax-free income from the new bucket when she needs it. Then, when she dies, the remaining cash in her bucket may blossom to as much as $1 million and transfer to her children or family trust as a legacy for future generations!

What happens if the owner who wants to take advantage of tax-free accumulation and tax-free retirement income cannot qualify for insurance? In that case, it may become necessary to use the spouse as the insured. You can use a surrogate or substitute insured as long as there is an insurable interest between the insured and the beneficiary.

For example, when I have a client who wants to establish a life insurance contract for investment purposes but is not insurable due to health history or age, we "borrow" someone else's life to insure. My first recommendation is to use a spouse, children, or grandchildren, in that order. You do not need to be insurable to be the owner of a universal life policy that provides tax-advantaged growth and access for your own money.

One time I had an elderly couple, neither of whom were insurable. Rather than place the insurance on their children, they chose to insure all twenty-seven of their grandchildren. They have since added five more buckets with the addition of five more grandkids! At this point, grandma and grandpa have not gifted anything to their grandkids. However, a total of $5,000 was invested by way of four annual premium payments of $1,250 into each of the thirty-two buckets (life insurance policies) insuring their grandchildren. The grandparents are enjoying tax-free growth on $160,000 of capital they transferred out of their bank CDs. They can access their money and the interest anytime they need on a tax-free basis. Even though there is no death benefit upon the grandparents' deaths, the ownership automatically changes to the insured or other named contingent at the time of their death. Then each grandchild has a tax-advantaged savings vehicle, along with life insurance, to use for college, the purchase of a first home, or to kick-start their own portfolio of buckets for retirement.

TAX-FREE ACCESS: THE SAD WAY

Let's now address the question, "How does a life insurance contract allow the owner to access cash values tax free?" Basically, there are three methods by which the owner of an insurance contract can access his money: 1) the sad way, 2) the dumb way, and 3) the smart way.

Of course, the sad way is by dying. If you establish an insurance contract that will accommodate premium payments up to $100,000 under TEFRA and DEFRA guidelines, the minimum death benefit may be $482,029 if you are age 45; $310,319 if you are age 55; and $210,773 if you are 65! Under TAMRA guidelines, if you paid close to the maximum allowed, approximately one-fifth of the guideline single premium or $20,000 per year, you are still insured for the full death benefit the minute the first minimum premium is paid. So, if the insured were to die the day after paying the initial $20,000, it would blossom immediately to whatever the face amount of the policy is, whether $200,000, $300,000, or $500,000. Not only that, but the death proceeds are transferred to the beneficiary and are tax free as provided under Section 101 of the Internal Revenue Code. That's a phenomenal rate of return, but it comes at a pretty dear price. Of course, I don't recommend accessing your money the sad way, but having that protection provides tremendous peace of mind regarding how beneficiaries would fare in the event of an untimely death.

I presently own seven universal life policies, my wife owns three, and my six children own two each. As you can imagine, the insurance that I have in force on my life is substantial. The first thing someone might ask is, "How can you afford that much life insurance?" I immediately reply, "It doesn't cost me anything!" I consider my life insurance free because of the way I have it structured. You see, the spigots (costs of the insurance) on my seven buckets are being paid for with otherwise payable income tax if I had my money invested elsewhere in taxable investments! In essence, Uncle Sam is paying for my life insurance!

I am often asked, "So, what do you do for a living?"

I answer, "I help people optimize their assets and enhance their net worth by repositioning their assets to make more money!"

That person might respond by asking, "Oh, what kind of investments do you use?"

I say, "Usually my clients choose life insurance."

Then the person might ask, "Oh, so you sell life insurance?"

To which I immediately respond, "No, I buy life insurance for my clients. By repositioning their assets, most of the time my clients end up with more life insurance than they thought they could afford. I help them pay for it with money they might have shelled out in unnecessary income tax! So, in some respects I bought it for them without increasing their outlay! What I actually sell is clarity, focus, balance, and confidence to families!"

In nearly thirty years as a financial planner, one thing has been very obvious. People do not object to insurance benefits, but sometimes object to paying for them! I have never had a widow turn down an insurance check, whether it was $10,000 or $1 million. If your employer came to you and said, "By the way, as your employer, we are now going to offer you some free life insurance. How much would you like?" My answer would be, "As much as I can get!" So it is when structuring an investment-grade insurance contract. Even when taking the minimum death benefit required under IRS guidelines, you may as well take as much as they give you, if it is not going to end up costing you anything.

Sometimes people can't catch this vision and say, "Well, I really do like the projected investment results of the insurance contract you are proposing; it appears it will out-perform the after-tax return on my CDs, money market accounts, and mutual funds. But, I really don't need any more life insurance." If I were to reply, "Well, that's okay—after the policy is issued, you can make me the beneficiary," they may rethink what they would be giving up. I remember hearing John Savage, tell his audience he would tease his wife by saying something like, "Honey, if I die, please try to look sad at my funeral!" This was because she knew about three weeks after his death she would be endowed with substantial cash from the insurance proceeds paid from his life insurance policies!

TAX-FREE ACCESS: THE DUMB AND SMART WAYS

The second and third ways to access your money are the dumb and smart ways. In order for you to understand the difference, let me explain the options and mechanics of accessing money from an insurance contract. Let's assume the following: You have an insurance policy that is large enough to accommodate up to $500,000 of aggregate premiums under TEFRA/DEFRA guidelines. You arrive at this size of bucket because you want to reposition $200,000 of net after-tax IRA and 401(k) funds over a five-year period—using a strategic conversion or roll-out from a qualified to a non-qualified status to alleviate up to 50 percent of ultimate tax. You plan to reposition $200,000 of home equity as you downsize by purchasing a new retirement home to increase its liquidity, safety and rate of return, and enjoy the tax benefits that help offset the taxes due on the IRAs and 401(k) roll-out. You also want to reposition $100,000 of CDs that are maturing at 4 percent interest, which is 2.68 percent after tax. Let's also assume you are a sixty-year-old male. The minimum death benefit under TEFRA/DEFRA guidelines might be $1,274,612 for a bucket that will allow a guideline single premium of $500,000. Through the use of side funds, you fully comply with TAMRA so your cash values accumulate tax free and so you can access your values tax free. Of course your death benefit is transferable tax free. Finally, let's assume you transfer $100,000 into the life insurance policy each year for five years by repositioning these above-mentioned assets. You would have to stop adding new money after five years. If by mistake you did try to send in more than $500,000, the insurance company would politely refund the overage back to you. You would have to start a new bucket if you wanted to continue to invest in this manner.

If you were to receive the equivalent average gross rate of 7.75 percent interest on your cash value, after deducting the mortality and expense charges (the spigot on the bucket), you may have approximately a cash value balance of $557,238 at the end of the fifth year (after you are finished filling your bucket to the brim with a basis of $500,000). You see, the bucket can overflow and grow far beyond the size of the guideline single premium allowed under TEFRA/DEFRA. After filling it to the brim with $500,000, if it went untouched for thirty-five years, at age 100 it might be worth $6,680,000, assuming a 7.75 interest crediting rate. That's okay with the IRS—the growth on the money inside the bucket can do so tax free and can far exceed the basis.

HOW THE SMARTS GET SMARTER

Let's say that, at age 65, after the policy has been fully funded, you just let it sit and grow for five more years to age 70. Then you decide to start pulling out some income to supplement your pension and Social Security. At that point, the bucket may have grown to $770,000. If the net rate of return after the spigot drains its portion (to cover the mortality and expense charges) is approximately 7 percent, you could theoretically withdraw about $50,000 a year and not deplete the corpus or principal. Now, the advantage of investment-grade insurance contracts over annuities is that when you withdraw money out of the policy it is treated with FIFO taxation, not LIFO taxation. Under FIFO tax treatment the First money Into the investment is considered by the IRS as the First money that you are pulling Out of the investment. So, if you as the policy owner choose to withdraw money from your insurance contract, it is tax free up to the basis. In this case, since you invested money into the insurance contract with after-tax dollars you do not need to pay tax on the first $500,000 you pull out. So at a withdrawal rate of $50,000 a year, income tax would be avoided during the first ten years (10 yrs. x $50,000/yr. = $500,000). Hence, in this example, for the first ten years your income would be tax free.

A term synonymous with withdrawal from an insurance policy is "partial surrender." If a policy owner wanted to cancel his insurance policy and surrender it to the insurance company, the insured and owner would relinquish all benefits and the insurance company would liquidate any cash values to the owner, less applicable surrender charges deducted from the cash accumulation value of the policy. Surrender charges usually apply during the early years of an insurance contract. If a person chooses to withdraw just some of his cash values rather than all of his cash values, the surrender may be deemed a partial surrender—only incurring limited surrender charges depending on the contract. In that case, only a portion of the contract and its benefits might be surrendered—the death benefit could be adjusted and reduced in direct proportion to the amount of the partial surrender (which wouldn't be a concern if the death benefit was originally intended as a secondary objective). If withdrawals were to be made in amounts equal to the net annual interest earnings, the insurance contract cash values would likely stay fairly consistent for several years. However, the death benefit would adjust and reduce because of the withdrawal.

A partial surrender permanently reduces the size of the insurance contract. So if the owner later wanted to replenish or reinvest more money back into the contract, he would not have the same latitude he originally had. Another problem is once the owner has withdrawn his entire basis (ten years worth, in this example) future withdrawals become taxable. That is because under FIFO taxation, all the basis comes out tax free first, and the remainder is deemed by the IRS as your gain. That gain would be subject to income tax as you begin to realize it. So, in this example, beginning the eleventh year, another $50,000 withdrawn from the bucket would be taxable. This would definitely be the dumb way to continue accessing money.

THE SMART WAY

That brings us to the smart way. The smart way is for the owner to change the "withdrawal" to a "loan." It's simply a change in nomenclature—remember, loan proceeds from any financial institution are not deemed earned, passive, or portfolio income, nor as a capital gain, by the IRS. Loan proceeds are simply tax free! Let's study the mechanics of how the tax-free loan provision works with a life insurance policy:

The owner in this example still has $770,000 of cash value remaining in the contract at the point in time at which he wants to begin taking out an annual $50,000 loan and continue with tax-free income under the loan provision of the contract. In essence, because he is no longer making $50,000 annual withdrawals from his basis in an amount equal to his interest earnings, his cash value balance will continue to grow and compound at the net rate of return (7 percent in this example). Instead of the cash value balance staying somewhat constant at $770,000 as it did when he was withdrawing $50,000 each year, the $770,000 increases to approximately $825,000.

If you had $770,000 in a certificate of deposit at a bank, wouldn't the bank be willing to loan you the equivalent of your annual interest? You bet they would, because of the collateral they have—your $770,000 deposit. Likewise, the insurance company is willing to loan you the equivalent of the interest you are earning and are no longer withdrawing. So at the end of the year the ledger for the insurance company may look like year 21 (age 81) of **figure 17.10**.

On one portion of the ledger you would have a beginning balance of $770,222, which grew by $55,637 to a year-end balance of $825,859 tax free. On the other side of the ledger, there is a loan balance of $50,000 from the loan you took out because you borrowed using your own money as collateral. The nice thing about loans on insurance contracts is the loan is technically not due and payable during the owner/insured's lifetime. In other words it is open until death. When the insured dies, the loan balance is deducted from the death benefit automatically. But the interest credited on the cash value side of the ledger can replenish some or all of the reduced death benefit.

As far as the insurance company is concerned, the owner still really owns only $774,094 in cash values. This is because the $825,859 year-end balance, less the loan balance of $51,765, plus interest equals almost the same $770,000 he would have had if he pulled the money out using the dumb way (withdrawals)! The smart way maintained the owner's income but was then qualified as tax free. The next year the cash values may grow to approximately $883,000. On the other hand, if he borrows another

Fig. 17.10 **TAX-FREE ACCESS VIA WITHDRAWALS AND LOANS**

Age	Yr	Annual Premium Outlay	Annual With-drawal	Annual Loan Amount (a)	Annual Loan Repayment (b)	Interest Charged To Loan (c)	Total Loan Balance (a) -(b)+(c)	Interest Earned on Loaned CV (d)	Net Loan Cost (c)-(d)	Accumulation Value	Surrender Value	Net Death Benefit
61	1	100,000	0	0	0	0	0	0	0	93,500	60,360	1,274,612
62	2	100,000	0	0	0	0	0	0	0	195,219	134,038	1,274,612
63	3	100,000	0	0	0	0	0	0	0	305,880	244,698	1,274,612
64	4	100,000	0	0	0	0	0	0	0	426,268	365,086	1,274,612
65	5	100,000	0	0	0	0	0	0	0	557,238	496,057	1,274,612
66	6	0	0	0	0	0	0	0	0	593,107	534,985	1,274,612
67	7	0	0	0	0	0	0	0	0	632,128	577,065	1,274,612
68	8	0	0	0	0	0	0	0	0	674,580	622,576	1,274,612
69	9	0	0	0	0	0	0	0	0	720,763	671,818	1,274,612
70	10	0	0	0	0	0	0	0	0	771,006	728,179	1,274,612
71	11	0	50,000	0	0	0	0	0	0	769,428	734,160	1,224,587
72	12	0	50,000	0	0	0	0	0	0	767,768	739,579	1,174,562
73	13	0	50,000	0	0	0	0	0	0	766,113	744,522	1,124,537
74	14	0	50,000	0	0	0	0	0	0	764,690	749,217	1,074,512
75	15	0	50,000	0	0	0	0	0	0	763,344	753,509	1,024,487
76	16	0	50,000	0	0	0	0	0	0	762,975	758,297	974,462
77	17	0	50,000	0	0	0	0	0	0	763,252	763,252	924,437
78	18	0	50,000	0	0	0	0	0	0	764,226	764,226	874,412
79	19	0	50,000	0	0	0	0	0	0	766,286	766,286	824,387
80	20	0	50,000	0	0	0	0	0	0	770,222	769,964	808,475
81	21	0	0	50,000	0	1,508	51,765	1,508	0	825,859	774,094	815,386
82	22	0	0	50,000	0	3,053	104,818	3,053	0	883,006	778,187	822,338
83	23	0	0	50,000	0	4,645	159,463	4,645	0	941,663	782,200	829,283
84	24	0	0	50,000	0	6,284	215,747	6,284	0	1,001,824	786,077	836,169
85	25	0	0	50,000	0	7,972	273,719	7,972	0	1,063,629	789,910	843,092
86	26	0	0	50,000	0	9,712	333,431	9,712	0	1,127,114	793,683	850,039
87	27	0	0	50,000	0	11,503	394,934	11,503	0	1,192,063	797,129	856,732
88	28	0	0	50,000	0	13,348	458,282	13,348	0	1,258,420	800,138	863,059
89	29	0	0	50,000	0	15,248	523,530	15,248	0	1,326,116	802,586	868,892
90	30	0	0	50,000	0	17,206	590,736	17,206	0	1,395,424	804,688	874,459
91	31	0	0	50,000	0	19,222	659,958	19,222	0	1,466,389	806,431	879,751
92	32	0	0	50,000	0	21,299	731,257	21,299	0	1,539,990	808,733	870,332
93	33	0	0	50,000	0	23,438	804,694	23,438	0	1,616,639	811,945	860,444
94	34	0	0	50,000	0	25,641	880,335	25,641	0	1,696,838	816,503	850,439
95	35	0	0	50,000	0	27,910	958,245	27,910	0	1,781,189	822,944	840,756
96	36	0	0	50,000	0	30,247	1,038,493	30,247	0	1,869,841	831,348	831,348
97	37	0	0	50,000	0	32,655	1,121,147	32,655	0	1,961,436	840,289	840,289
98	38	0	0	50,000	0	35,134	1,206,282	35,134	0	2,056,087	849,805	849,805
99	39	0	0	50,000	0	37,688	1,293,970	37,688	0	2,153,908	859,937	859,937
100	40	0	0	50,000	0	40,319	1,384,289	40,319	0	2,255,019	870,730	870,730

$50,000, his loan balance will accrue to $104,818, which still results in a net balance of $778,187. After ten years of using tax-free loans, this person has $1,395,424 in the cash value portion of the ledger and a loan balance of $590,736 (ten years of $50,000 plus interest) on the other side. The net balance is now $804,688, and he has enjoyed ten more years of retirement income totally tax free! He can continue this procedure until death occurs, as long as there is a death benefit sufficient to wash out the loan balance. Thus, a taxable event can permanently be avoided as long as the policy has at least enough cash value remaining in it at death to keep the life insurance in force by covering the mortality costs.

PREFERRED LOANS

There are a few features that make tax-free loans used for retirement income very attractive. In order for a loan to be construed as a true loan, and therefore not taxable, a reasonable interest rate needs to be charged to the loan by the insurance company. "Reasonable" interest can be 8 percent, 6 percent or even 4 percent interest. Let's say the insurance company charges 8 percent on the loan balance. That interest is not deductible, because the owner would be getting tax-free interest on the phantom excess that is on the cash value portion of the ledger. I call it "phantom" because in the final analysis all cash value over and above the corpus ($770,000 in this case) was really taken out of the policy. The policy owner is earning his regular interest on the corpus of $770,000. There is also an amount equal to the total loans taken out that is likewise earning interest. The insurance companies I recommend are contractually obligated to pay 6 percent interest on that money if the interest charged on the loan balance is 8 percent. In other words, there is a 2 percent net differential between the interest charged on the loan balance and the interest credited on the cash value portion that collateralized the loan—a pretty attractive rate.

The insurance companies I recommend have a special classification of loans they call "preferred loans." The preferred loans were created specifically with retirement income needs in mind. The insured, depending on his age, may qualify for preferred loans as early as the first year of the policy. This preferred loan is also known as a "zero wash loan." Usually when the insured is qualified to use the preferred loan provision, he is restricted to preferred loans of no more than 10 percent of the corpus annually. In the example we have been using, the owner could take zero wash loans of up to $77,000 annually. Then, the insurance company charges the same interest rate on the loan balance it credits with interest on the overage cash value used as collateral to secure the loan. This results in a net cost of zero percent. With the top companies I recommend, the preferred loan rate is 4 percent. That same interest rate of 4 percent is credited on the phantom cash value that collateralized the loan that would have been subject to tax if it was withdrawn the "dumb way." This has the tremendous long-term advantage of extending the tax-free income that can be generated because there is no depletion of cash values due to loan interest charges.

The next question to answer may be, "So, why even mess with pulling out money in the form of withdrawals or partial surrenders—why not start using zero wash loans from the moment you begin taking out your retirement income?" This is an excellent question. Perhaps the only thing that may prevent you from beginning preferred loans at the outset would be the waiting period required by the insurance company—or maybe a need to access more than 10 percent of your cash values in a particular year. Otherwise, it is definitely the smart way to access your money to avoid unnecessary income tax. I have clients who have enjoyed tax-free income of over $100,000 a year from their buckets, sometimes in the form of withdrawals up to their basis. Afterwards they continue to receive tax-free income using the zero wash loan provisions in their policies. Their policy ledgers may reflect several million dollars owing on a loan balance, but with proper management, the cash values (growing with interest) they pledged as collateral for the annual loans have exceeded the loan balance by a comfortable margin. They absolutely love having a cash flow that doesn't show up anywhere on their 1040 tax returns, in addition to full Social Security and Medicare benefits as a result!

There is one other reason why using zero wash loans for tax-free retirement income is the smart way to access your money from an insurance contract. Using the same figures as before, assume a couple took tax-free income in the amount of $50,000 a year for ten years using the zero wash loan provision. That would mean they would have a loan balance of $500,000 plus accrued interest. Now let's say they inherit some money or decide to downsize their home and take up to $500,000 in a capital gain tax free on their personal residence. They sell their home for $750,000 and use $250,000 for a low-maintenance condo or home in a retirement community or even a rest home. Now they have $500,000 in cash they don't know what to do with. In the meantime, maybe they have become uninsurable because of age or because they experienced a disqualifying, life-threatening medical episode that was successfully treated. Maybe Congressional revenuers got greedy and passed a new law—NMNTFBA (No More New Tax-Free Buckets Allowed), hurting themselves in the long run by taking away retiree incentives to provide for their own retirement. Maybe the couple simply needs to reposition assets that could be exposed to a liability lawsuit because they bumped into someone on the highway.

Under any of these circumstances this couple would have a grandfathered bucket they could still use. Whatever the reason, if the loan provision had been used instead of withdrawals, there is room to redeposit back into the life insurance contract as much as $500,000 in this example. This would be considered a loan repayment. Having replenished the contract with new money, they would then have the opportunity to use their insurance contract just like they always have for further tax-free accumulation and tax-free access!

Say this couple someday wants to access as much of the money as possible in one huge lump sum. Suppose it is the end of the fifteenth year and they have $1,074,264 of surrender value at that time because they have not been taking an annual income. They could totally surrender their insurance policy in order to access the cash, but that would be the dumb way to do it. This is because they would relinquish their death benefit and trigger a taxable event—let's say at an average tax rate of 35 percent—which would result in $200,992 in income taxes on the

$574,264 of earnings above their $500,000 basis (because it is taxed as ordinary income). So, after withdrawing $1,074,264 they would only net $873,272 and have no life insurance remaining.

Fortunately, there is a smart way to access a lump sum. The owner of an insurance contract can usually access up to 90 percent of cash surrender value without immediately relinquishing the death benefit. If they took out money the smart way, they could take out a loan of 90 percent of the $1,074,264—approximately $966,837—tax free. The remaining 10 percent, or $107,427 (which they would have lost to income tax had they taken it out the other way) may cover the cost of insurance benefits for several months or years before repayment would be required to keep the insurance benefit in force and to avoid a taxable event. Accessing their money in this way would at least postpone the triggering of a taxable event and would be even more advantageous if a death should occur in the interim. In this case, the death benefit, after deducting the 90 percent loan with interest, may still leave behind a substantial sum of cash to the beneficiaries—money that would have been lost by doing it the dumb way.

WHAT DO CONGRESSIONAL REVENUERS THINK ABOUT THIS?

Hopefully you now understand how money can be accessed tax free from an insurance contract and why it is deemed tax free. When people learn this, they sometimes comment, "Well, as soon as the IRS or Congress discovers this—they'll close up this loophole!" The fact is, this is not considered a loophole! The IRS and Congress are aware of these tax-favored vehicles and strategies that allow for tax-free accumulation of cash values and tax-free access. In fact, many Congressional leaders themselves own these types of policies. I doubt they would be short-sighted enough to change the law to hurt themselves or other prospective retirees trying to provide for their own retirement.

Nonetheless, I can't predict what Congress may do to alter the tax treatment on the inside build-up and access of life insurance contract cash values. But I would rather board my retirement ship as it comes in with a life preserver likely to keep me afloat while tested under current tax laws than board with an inner tube like IRAs and 401(k)s I know will lose air (by the payment of taxes) as soon as the valve stem is opened. My confidence also lies in one of the strongest lobbies in America—the insurance industry lobby. Hopefully, Congress would be smart enough to realize if it changed the rules regarding tax-free inside build-up and access of insurance contract cash values, it would be shooting itself in the foot. Probably all of the tax revenue it would hope to generate would be shelled out later in the form of additional Social Security and welfare benefits to the people from whom it took those benefits away! I am convinced that properly structured and properly used investment-grade life insurance contracts are the best retirement vehicles available for providing liquidity, safety, and tax-favored rates of return. And just in case Congressional tax revenuers do something stupid down the road, I am getting as many buckets as I can afford to fill up with cash, in hopes they will be grandfathered under the old laws. I believe it would behoove anyone to do likewise.

LEVEL DEATH BENEFITS VS. INCREASING DEATH BENEFITS

There is one additional option that I would like to explain regarding universal life. The insured can either choose to have a level death benefit or an increasing death benefit. Sometimes these two choices are referred to as Options A and B. Let's use the bucket analogy again to visualize the difference between these two options.

I recommend the level death benefit option if the primary objective of establishing an investment-grade insurance contract is to achieve the highest internal rate of return as soon as possible, (accumulating the most cash values in the shortest time period to use for living benefits), and the secondary objective is to obtain life insurance coverage that is paid for with a small portion of the interest earned that would otherwise go out the window in income tax. On the other hand, if the primary objective is to maximize what you leave behind when you die and the secondary objective is to accumulate cash to access, then I usually recommend the increasing death benefit option. What if your objectives change midway into the life of the policy? No problem! You can switch from one option to another with the stroke of a pen!

Under the level death benefit option the owner elects to have the death benefit stay level as the bucket grows. The bucket grows as a function of the new premium dollars paid into the bucket and the interest credited to the bucket. This represents the cash value of the policy. As the bucket grows with cash value, the cash value can actually qualify as part of the original death benefit required under TEFRA/DEFRA guidelines. The actual amount of insurance the insurance company is at risk to pay is the difference between your cash value and the original required death benefit. This means the spigot is draining a smaller amount of your interest because there is less insurance to pay for. Ultimately the differential between the cash value and the original level death benefit at the issuance of the policy can become so nominal that the net rate of return, is within one percent of the gross rate of return, retroactive back to the first day of the policy!

For example, if an insurance contract for a sixty-five-year-old male designed to accommodate a total of $200,000 of premiums ($40,000 a year for five years to comply with TAMRA), carried a minimum death benefit (required under TEFRA/DEFRA) of $422,741, and in its tenth year had $297,608 in cash value, then the true insurance risk paid by the company is the difference between $422,741 and the $297,608 cash value, or $125,133.

Even though the cost per $1,000 of life insurance goes up each month a person gets older, the amount of actual insurance the insured is paying for goes down! This phenomenon results in an enhanced rate of return—your money grows more effectively as the insurance cost gets smaller. In the fifteenth year the cash value might be $422,050, which, if subtracted from the original death benefit, would only leave $691 of insurance for which you are paying at that attained age. However, the IRS guidelines require the death benefit stay ahead of the cash values by a certain percentage (such as 5 percent up to age 90, then it can reduce 1 percent a year to age 95, at which point the death benefit may equal the cash value). So in actuality, the life insurance death benefit in the fifteenth year might increase from $422,741 to $443,152 (5 percent more). In the twentieth year the cash value may grow to $607,274, at which point the death benefit will have increased to $637,638 to stay in compliance with IRS guidelines. This would continue until at age 100, the cash value might be $1,805,795, which would equal the death benefit.

On the other hand, under the increasing death benefit option, the spigot will get bigger throughout the years as the cost per $1,000 of insurance goes up as the insured gets older. This is because the base insurance benefit stays at the original amount—$422,741 in this example. The advantage to the increasing death benefit option is that if death occurs, the beneficiaries get the cash value plus the death benefit added together. However, because of the cost associated with paying for the same amount of insurance as the insured gets older, the cash value will not be able to grow as quickly. The living benefits, such as the amount of tax-free retirement income, will not generate as much under the increasing death benefit option unless the death benefit is carved down.

Because of this difference, an insurance contract for a sixty-year-old male who pays maximum premiums totaling $200,000 ($40,000 a year) the first five years could have $1,279,609 of cash value and a death benefit of $1,343,589 at age 90 under the level death benefit option. In contrast he may only have $516,787 of cash value and a death benefit of $1,025,641 under the increasing death benefit option. As a general rule of thumb, unless you have some premonition you are going to die sooner than later (within approximately ten years) the level death benefit option will eventually generate greater cash values, as well as greater death benefits, based upon the same initial face amount of insurance and the same premiums paid into the contract. My advice under most circumstances is to start with the level death benefit option. Then if the owner's objectives change, the death benefit option can be changed later.

When do I recommend the increasing death benefit option? Let's assume a client had $1 million of life insurance with $500,000 of cash value that is growing approximately $30,000 per year with interest. She finds out that she has multiple myloma cancer, and the doctor gives her three to seven years to live. This would change the insured's original objective from maximizing a return on cash values to trying to maximize the death benefit left behind. If we left the policy alone, under the level death benefit option, the $30,000 per year of additional growth would be soaked into the $1 million original death benefit because the cash values have not grown yet to exceed the original required death benefit. To avoid this, I might advise the insured to switch to the increasing death benefit option at that point in time. That does not mean that the $500,000 cash value would be immediately added on top of the original $1 million. But at the point in time the option was changed, the actual life insurance would be reduced to the difference between the current cash value and the original death benefit—$500,000 in this case. If that person died the next day, the death benefit paid would still be a total of $1 million ($500,000 of cash value and $500,000 of life insurance). But if the doctor's prediction was correct, and death finally occurred five years later, the death benefit would have been enhanced by approximately $30,000 each year to $1,150,000. What incredible flexibility universal life insurance affords!

THE VARIOUS TYPES OF CASH-VALUE
LIFE INSURANCE CONTRACTS

Let me explain the basic difference between the major cash-value life insurance contracts available on the market today. Originally, the principal objective of cash-value life insurance was the same as that of term insurance—to create an immediate estate in the event of death to provide for the needs of heirs or to pay estate taxes. But in an expanded use of this kind of insurance contract, the cash value build-up inside a life insurance policy also provides a liquid fund that can be used for financial emergencies or investment opportunities. Additionally, cash-value life insurance can be used as a supplement to retirement income.

There are five generally recognized types of cash-value life insurance that have been on the market during the last decade or two: whole life, variable life, and three kinds of universal life—fixed, variable, and equity indexed.

WHOLE LIFE INSURANCE

As discussed earlier, whole life is typically referred to as permanent or traditional cash-value life insurance. Whole life insurance offers guaranteed death benefits, cash values, level premiums and possibly dividends. It can be an efficient method of purchasing insurance on a long-term basis. Remember that cash values are created by insurance company investment of excess premiums in a long-term portfolio with legal reserve requirements. The most basic form of this type of policy is referred to as "ordinary" or "straight" life. Newer whole life policies have lower costs due to upgraded mortality rates. Of course, there is tax-deferred growth of the cash value accumulation. The guaranteed cash values in the contract are supported by the company reserves. Whole life insurance features guaranteed premiums and contains flexibility with regard to single premium, potential-vanishing premiums and varying death benefits. A policyholder can access cash values via withdrawals or loans. The dividends of a whole life insurance policy are tax free. The projected return on a whole life policy is based upon a long-term portfolio of assets.

VARIABLE LIFE INSURANCE

Another interest-sensitive product that promotes the concept of flexible life insurance is variable life. Variable life, like universal life, has a death benefit created by term insurance with an equity investment side fund. Unlike fixed universal life, the insured may choose the investment vehicle to be used for cash accumulation. The cash accumulation values are dependent upon the return of the chosen investment vehicle. Variable life is similar to whole life with regard to premium payments. The premium payable is a specified annual amount based upon the insured's age and the face amount of the policy. Investment options may include:
- a money market fund
- guaranteed or fixed account
- government securities fund
- corporate bond fund

- total return fund
- a growth fund

As investors' objectives change, they may switch from one portfolio to another, just as they can within a family of funds.

UNIVERSAL LIFE INSURANCE

Universal life insurance was created with flexibility in mind. Both premium payments and insurance death benefits may be varied, within limits, to meet the needs of the client. As a policy owner pays premiums into a universal life contract, a portion is used to pay the pure term insurance rates. The balance is deposited into a side fund on which interest is paid. If the premium paid is not sufficient to cover the cost of the term insurance, the balance is taken from the side fund. The policy owner may elect to pay premiums higher or lower, subject to some limits, and may even elect to skip premium payments without losing coverage if there is adequate cash value in the savings portion of the contract. Universal life generally contains low mortality costs due to updated mortality rates. Of course, the same tax-advantaged growth of cash values is inherent in universal life as it is in whole life. Universal life typically credits a competitive interest rate to the cash values of the policy. Cash values can be accessed tax free via withdrawal or loan. The entire cash values and accumulated earnings can transfer to heirs free of income tax.

Fixed Universal Life Insurance

Fixed universal life is the most conservative approach. Of the three kinds of universal life, it is the least management intensive and incurs the smallest expense charges. The term "fixed" does not mean the interest that is credited on the policy owner's cash value is fixed at the same rate for the life of the contract. It more or less connotes the cash values are credited with interest that is earned by the relatively fixed portfolio of the insurance company. For example, a large life insurance company with strong ratings may have approximately 70 percent of its assets invested in high-grade bonds, 20 percent invested in mortgage-backed securities, and the remaining 10 percent of its assets represented by a combination of stocks, real estate, cash, and short-term investments or policy loans. So, if you owned a fixed universal life, the insurance company would credit you interest based on the amount it could afford as a result of the return it is getting on its invested assets. I know of some fixed universal life contracts that credited as high as 13.75 percent during the 1980s—although I did not recommend them because of the excessive amount of junk bonds rather than high-grade bonds they had. Most reputable companies credited between 9 to 11 percent during that high-interest rate era. Of course, the economy has changed since, and at the time of the publication of this book, the fixed universal life I primarily use for my clients is crediting interest in the 6 to 6.5 percent range while the federal discount rate is approximately 2 percent and the prime rate is at about 5 percent.

Depending on the company, a fixed universal life policy will generally have a guaranteed minimum interest rate, usually around 4 percent. I know of very few companies that have only credited the guaranteed interest rate. Whenever a universal life policy is purchased, the NAIC (National Association of Insurance Commissioners) requires the policy owner sign an illustration showing the projection of the policy benefits based upon the intended premium payments that will likely be made into the policy. The illustration can show projections based upon the interest rate credited by the company at the time the policy was taken out.

The illustration must also show the worst-case scenario. The worst-case scenario assumes only the minimum guaranteed interest rate is credited on the policy cash values from the inception of the policy. It also assumes that the maximum mortality charges allowed contractually by the company are assessed throughout the life of the policy. The worst-case scenario would be a highly unlikely event, but serves to show the owner of the life insurance contract what could happen under those circumstances. The fact of the matter is, the actual mortality charges assessed are usually considerably less than the maximum allowable, and policies will usually far outperform the minimum interest guarantee.

Insurance companies can usually afford to pay higher interest rates than banks and credit unions because their portfolio of investment assets doesn't turn over quickly. Fixed universal life insurance contracts tend to be more stable, responding slowly to market swings. **Figures 17.11** and **17.12** illustrate pie charts of two major life insurance companies with Comdex scores in excess of 90 according to VitalSigns. Note the five-year history of these companies' returns on invested assets. This is a good indication of the approximate interest rate investors might experience with those companies before subtracting the general and administrative expenses and the margin of profit companies must maintain to operate successfully.

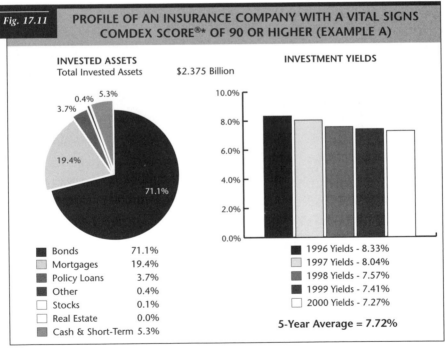

Fig. 17.11 — **PROFILE OF AN INSURANCE COMPANY WITH A VITAL SIGNS COMDEX SCORE®* OF 90 OR HIGHER (EXAMPLE A)**

INVESTED ASSETS
Total Invested Assets $2.375 Billion

INVESTMENT YIELDS

5.3%
0.4%
3.7%
19.4%
71.1%

Bonds	71.1%
Mortgages	19.4%
Policy Loans	3.7%
Other	0.4%
Stocks	0.1%
Real Estate	0.0%
Cash & Short-Term	5.3%

1996 Yields - 8.33%
1997 Yields - 8.04%
1998 Yields - 7.57%
1999 Yields - 7.41%
2000 Yields - 7.27%

5-Year Average = 7.72%

Comdex is a proprietary composite of carrier's ratings issued by LifeLink Corporation.
**Format and design created through the use of LifeLink Pro® software (www.lifelinkpro.com)*

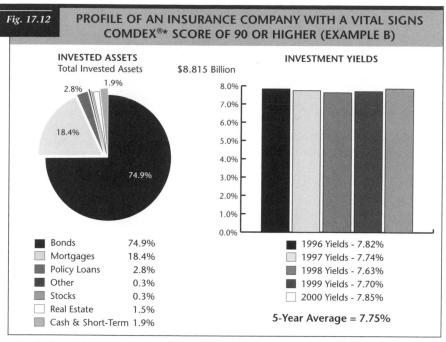

Fig. 17.12 PROFILE OF AN INSURANCE COMPANY WITH A VITAL SIGNS COMDEX®* SCORE OF 90 OR HIGHER (EXAMPLE B)

INVESTED ASSETS
Total Invested Assets $8.815 Billion

	Bonds	74.9%
	Mortgages	18.4%
	Policy Loans	2.8%
	Other	0.3%
	Stocks	0.3%
	Real Estate	1.5%
	Cash & Short-Term	1.9%

INVESTMENT YIELDS

1996 Yields - 7.82%
1997 Yields - 7.74%
1998 Yields - 7.63%
1999 Yields - 7.70%
2000 Yields - 7.85%

5-Year Average = 7.75%

*Comdex is a proprietary composite of carrier's ratings issued by LifeLink Corporation.
**Format and design created through the use of LifeLink Pro® software (www.lifelinkpro.com)

Variable Universal Life

The next type of universal life on the market is variable universal life. Variable universal life insurance was created to combine the premium flexibility of universal life with the investment flexibility of variable life. In addition to the ability to select from various investment funds like variable life, the policyholder may elect to vary the premiums higher or lower within limits determined by the insurance company and federal tax laws. As with universal life, the policyholder may even elect to skip premium payments without losing coverage if there are adequate accumulated values in the investment funds.

In essence, all of the cash values of the policy except the portion needed to cover the mortality and expense charges are removed from the umbrella of the insurance company. These cash values are usually invested in equity investments. These instruments can include money markets, fixed accounts, government securities funds, corporate bond funds, total return funds, or growth funds. As the policy owner's objectives change, she may switch from one portfolio to another as she could with a family of mutual funds. Therefore, with a variable universal life, there is no guaranteed minimum interest rate. In fact, if a loss is experienced during a certain time period and there is not sufficient value in the portfolio, the policy owner may have to pay additional premium payments to keep the mortality and expense charges covered, and continue doing so until the cash values of the policy have recovered.

So, just like a mutual fund, the variable universal life policy values fluctuate depending upon the market and the portfolio established. In some years, a handsome return may be realized on a variable universal life. But in other years, significant losses may also be experienced. It is critical to understand this when purchasing variable products of any type. It is unrealistic to expect the market to grow at 15 to 20 percent returns, year in and year out, without some periods of correction. Even so, in the last century, there was never a ten-year period in which the equities in America didn't outperform the inflation rate of the same period. During most ten-year periods, there were usually fluctuating periods of market loss and market gain. An investor should understand the ramifications of this volatility as it relates to her liquidity, safety, and rate of return objectives.

I believe an investor should choose such equity investments based on twenty-year averages. This is because most twenty-year periods will include a major cycle of a bullish era and a bearish era. A short five-year history is not a basis on which to make a choice of a long-term investment. Based on the last seventy to eighty years of market history on a well-managed portfolio, you could most likely expect a highest return of 20.9 percent for stocks, a lowest return of 5.4 percent and an average of 12.9 percent over a twenty-year period. In contrast, you could probably expect a highest return of 10.9 percent for bonds, a lowest return of 4.7 percent and an average of 7.8 percent over a twenty-year period.

Variable insurance contracts are vulnerable to market corrections, perhaps occurring at times when you may need liquidity the most. During the market crash that began in the spring of 2000, and was exacerbated by the September 11 World Trade Towers attack in 2001, many investors holding variable contracts suffered losses, having to liquidate some of their money in the down market. At the same time many fixed universal life contracts continued to credit a steady 6 to 7 percent interest.

When I do a comparison of internal rate of return on the actual premiums paid into a life insurance contract, typically a variable universal life must perform at about a 3 percent better gross rate of return to match a fixed universal life's internal rate of return. In other words, if I pay premiums into a fixed universal life in the amount of $500 per month for fifteen years and earn a gross interest rate of 8 percent (resulting in a net rate of return of 7.5 percent), I would have cash values of $166,590. During the same fifteen-year period with a variable universal life policy, I may have to earn a gross rate of as much as 10.5 percent to realize a net rate of return of 7.5 percent and end up with the same $166,590. This is because the administration fees are much greater on a variable universal life than a fixed universal life. If an investor chooses variable universal life, she should do so with the understanding that the gross return expected will hopefully be at least 3 percent higher than the return a fixed universal life will likely earn.

Variable universal life can be an attractive option for younger investors who have twenty to thirty years or more to experience possible growth. I discourage the use of variable universal life for elderly clients who are generally seeking more stability, which is inherent in fixed universal life products. Largely due to the upward spiral of the market during the 1990s, 1998 marked the first year the majority of life insurance premiums paid into policies in America went into variable contracts. Because of this trend, I believe investors need to be cautious about their approach to variable products so they are not disappointed if these products don't perform with the stability they needed to achieve.

Equity-Indexed Universal Life Insurance

The third type of universal life, which was recently introduced on the market, is equity-indexed universal life. Indexed universal life was designed to help investors who wanted to have a guaranteed floor on the minimum they would have credited on their insurance policy cash values, and yet have the potential to participate in the market when it is experiencing growth. What if you could receive additional interest on your life insurance contract based on a percentage of gains in the Standard and Poor 500 Index? (Let's assume the indexed universal life policy in this example is linked to the S&P 500 Index.)

With indexed universal life, you can get cash value protection combined with the potential from a rising S&P 500 Index. The S&P 500 Index is a commonly used broad indicator of performance and is considered a benchmark of U.S. stock market performance. It represents over 70 percent of the total domestic equity market value. The S&P 500 Index is a price index; therefore, it does not include dividends. Its broad diversification counterbalances the extreme highs and lows of any one stock.

Over the long term, the S&P 500 Index has outperformed government and corporate bonds, certificates of deposit, and the rate of inflation. Indexed universal life that is linked to the S&P 500 Index enables you to benefit from increases in the S&P 500 Index through an adjustable index factor. An additional feature is that your money is protected. If the S&P 500 drops or remains flat, your policy values are protected by a guaranteed interest rate—let's say 3 percent. For example, say the S&P 500 Index was at 1,000 when a premium was paid into the contract, and the smoothing period average close was 1,127. (Depending on the insurance company, the increase in the S&P 500 Index may be averaged. This may be referred to as a smoothing period, which could moderate the effect of any last minute downturn in the S&P 500. The six-month smoothing period method, for instance, has historically outperformed even a twelve-month average!) An index factor of, say, 60 percent would be applied to this increase of 127 points, or 12.7 percent, creating an adjustable index return of 7.62 percent. With 3 percent already guaranteed, the additional interest would be 4.62 percent, for a total of 7.62 percent.

The equity-indexed universal life I own and recommend determines the policy's additional interest by its index factor, which represents the percentage of the S&P 500 increases as provided under the terms of the policy. The index factor, which can be as high as 75 percent, is periodically set by the company, and though it is subject to change, in no event can it be less than 25 percent.

The nicest feature of equity-indexed universal life is the cash values of your insurance contract never leave the protective umbrella of the insurance company. The policy owner is allowed to participate in potential profits realized by virtue of having her interest linked to an index such as the S&P 500 Index, but it is not deemed an actual equity investment. So, in essence, the policyholder is saying to the insurance company, "Hey, if the market is bullish, let me participate anywhere from 25 percent up to 75 percent of whatever the S&P 500 Index achieves. As a trade-off for not allowing me to participate 100 percent in the index, when the S&P 500 loses money, don't let me lose—give me a floor of at least 3 percent interest!" Can you imagine how some owners of variable contracts would have felt if they could have avoided huge losses during the latter part of 2000 and throughout 2001?

An indexed universal life policy often carries slightly higher expense charges than a fixed universal life policy but substantially smaller charges than a variable universal life policy. In order to achieve the same internal rate of return that a fixed universal life may achieve with a gross interest rate of 8 percent (which may result in a net rate of return on premium dollars of approximately 7.5 percent), an indexed universal life may need to be credited with an average of 8.2 to 8.5 percent. As with variable universal life insurance, clients who choose indexed universal life need to be aware of this difference.

One thing is almost certain. In some years, a fixed universal life policy only crediting 6 percent will outperform an indexed universal life policy that may only credit 3 percent during the same period and a variable universal life policy that may have lost 15 percent during the same period. In other years, a fixed universal life policy may only credit 8 percent while an indexed universal life policy may earn 21 percent, all while a variable universal life policy is crediting 28 percent.

Thus, as relates risk and return, indexed universal life is positioned in the middle—between fixed universal life and variable universal life. I see three possible advantages to a person choosing equity-indexed universal life over the other two types of universal life. First, some clients may be more comfortable with their cash accumulation tied to an index rather than a portfolio rate of return. Second, an equity-indexed product allows for growth linked to an index such as the S&P 500 Index with lower loads and fees than most variable universal life contracts. Third, the S&P 500 Index has traditionally outperformed government and corporate bonds, CDs, and the rate of inflation (assuming the policy is linked to this index). In this example, the index factor is a percentage of the change in the S&P 500, which is recognized in computing the interest bonus that is paid in addition to the 3 percent guaranteed minimum. Also, in this example there is no cap on how much interest can be credited on an equity-indexed universal life depending on S&P 500 performance, no matter how high the S&P 500 may go.

Figure 17.13 is a comparison between fixed, variable, and indexed universal life in relation to their guaranteed returns, what their typical average returns would have been in the last twenty years, and some of the highest returns they have achieved. Pay particular attention to the rate of return that must be achieved in each of the three types of contracts in order to achieve the same bottom-line results over the long term.

Internal Revenue Code Compliance

One last item that must be addressed is the issue of Internal Revenue Code compliance when an insurance contract is structured to accommodate serious capital, such as equity funds coming from a mortgage

Fig. 17.13	EXAMPLES OF 3 TYPES OF UNIVERSAL LIFE INVESTMENT-GRADE INSURANCE CONTRACTS				
20-Year Historical Crediting Interest Rates					
	Guaranteed	Lowest	Average	Highest	Interest Rate Required to Achieve Same Accumulation Values
Fixed	4%	5.75%	7.5%	13.75%	7.44%
Variable	None	<30%>	10%	35%	10.52%
Equity Indexed	3%	3%	8.2%	21%	8.20%
(Linked to S&P 500)				(60%)*	

*participation rate

refinance. When using equity from a home sale as a person changes from one residence to another and a new mortgage is obtained on the new home, we don't have to worry about the deductibility of interest on the new mortgage. As discussed in chapter 12, qualified mortgage interest is deductible on the acquisition of a new residence for up to $1 million of indebtedness. We simply need to comply with TEFRA/DEFRA and TAMRA guidelines as we fund the insurance contract using our previous home's equity to avoid the insurance contract being classified as a MEC. If we choose to borrow equity from our existing or current residence and want to deduct the interest, we must comply with Section 163 of the Internal Revenue Code. Remember from chapter 12 that qualified residence interest, within the meaning of Section 163(h)(3), is allowable as a deduction *without regard* to the manner in which such interest expense is allocated. This section of the code should put a taxpayer at ease for deducting interest on home equity indebtedness (up to $100,000) when borrowing on a current residence and using the loan proceeds for any purpose, including investing them into an insurance contract.

In contrast, Section 264(a)(2)&(3) of the Internal Revenue Code stipulates no deduction shall be allowed for "(2) Any amount paid or accrued on indebtedness incurred or continued to purchase or carry a single premium life insurance, endowment, or annuity contract. (3) ...any amount paid or accrued on indebtedness incurred or continued to purchase or carry a life insurance, endowment, or annuity contract (other than a single premium contract or a contract treated as a single premium contract) pursuant to a plan of purchase which contemplates the systematic direct or indirect borrowing of part or all of the increases in the cash value of such contract (either from the insurer or otherwise)."

Section 264(b) states, "For the purposes of subsection (a)(2), a contract shall be treated as a single premium contract—(1) if substantially all the premiums on the contract are paid within a period of 4 years from the date on which the contract is purchased, or (2) if an amount is deposited after March 1, 1954, with the insurer for payment of a substantial number of future premiums on the contract."

It is unclear how Section 264 relates to a universal life contract versus a single premium life insurance contract. However, to be on the safe side, I recommend a taxpayer who desires to deduct interest expense from a cash-out refinance on an existing home where the loan proceeds are invested into an insurance contract (although Section 163 may allow deductibility) avoid having the life insurance classified or construed as a single premium insurance contract.

To assure we can enjoy full tax advantages, we should comply with the TAMRA rule and avoid the contract being construed as a single premium insurance contract by filling the bucket (funding the policy) at the prescribed premium schedule pace. Based on court cases, a life insurance policy is not deemed a single premium contract if it is not funded more than 72 percent by the fourth year. During the fourth year or thereafter, the remaining 28 percent could be paid into the policy or it could be funded safely from the beginning with five fairly equal annual installments (completed in as short as four years and one day). In doing so, we could avoid falling under the definition of a single premium life insurance contract and interest on borrowed funds on a current home should be deductible. Because a person's particular set of circumstances can be unique, I always recommend each person seek competent legal and accounting advice.

Section 264(b)(2) can be interpreted to mean any type of single premium immediate annuity or advance premium deposit fund with the same company acting as the insurer also falls under the general umbrella of a single premium life insurance policy. Once having removed equity from your current home using a mortgage or equity line of credit, those funds may need to be kept in a side fund not associated with the insurance company—while the premiums are paid over the five-year period. This assures and enables deduction of the interest on the mortgage, as well as enjoy tax-free access to the cash values in the insurance policy.

Because of this, I believe it is best a life insurance contract not be funded solely with the equity from a current home. I usually recommend that no more than 40 percent of the total premiums paid into an insurance contract should come from home equity obtained from an existing or current home as a result of that house's refinance or equity line of credit. The remaining 60 percent of premiums should come from other sources, such as repositioned IRA and 401(k) contributions or distributions, or perhaps from repositioned CDs, money markets, and mutual funds. This 60 percent differential could also include redirected annual planned savings meant for capital accumulation.

However, to re-emphasize, if a home is sold and a new one is purchased, the equity from the former home may be used capital gain tax free. In that case, the equity could be used solely to fund an insurance contract using a single premium immediate annuity or other side fund to comply with TAMRA. Interest on the new home mortgage would be deductible on up to $1 million of acquisition indebtedness as provided under Section 163. This strategy alone has motivated many couples (who were debating whether to sell their home and relocate) to sell their homes, take the tax-free capital gain, and use the equity to generate tax-free retirement income while using mortgage interest deductions on their new home to offset tax liability on their IRA and 401(k) distributions. So if you are looking for a good excuse to sell your home and purchase a new one, maximizing equity management may be the best reason not to hesitate.

Compliance with Sections 163 and 264 of the Internal Revenue Code can be a somewhat complex arrangement; however, a trained professional who understands these parameters and guidelines can structure and fund a life insurance policy to comply. I cannot overemphasize the importance of seeking advice from a competent tax advisor. With proper planning and counsel, modern cash-value life insurance can be designed to accumulate and store cash safely and provide tax-favored living benefits, as well as income tax-free death benefits, while maintaining liquidity, safety, and achieving an attractive rate of return.

17 WEALTH-ENHANCEMENT STRATEGY NUMBER SEVENTEEN

- *Life insurance is an excellent place to accumulate and store cash!*
- *Strongly consider managing some or all of your equity and repositioning some of your IRA and 401(k) contributions or distributions through properly structured investment grade life insurance contracts to maximize liquidity, safety, rate of return and tax benefits.*

CHAPTER 18

Choose Investments That Generate the Most

Choose financial instruments that generate or provide the most money at the time in life you will likely need the money most.

Wise investors choose investments that accumulate the most money.

When considering tax effects, greater growth investment vehicles may be inferior to other investments. Choose investments that generate the highest net spendable income.

Through nearly thirty years of assisting people with their financial planning, I have discovered many people have a tendency to choose investments they hope will grow to the highest sum based on the gross rate of return. Unfortunately, there are many investment vehicles that may result in great growth but are inferior to other investments after tax considerations. Some investments may grow to lower sums but generate higher net spendable income. This is generally true with regard to the tax-favored treatment some investments receive not only during the accumulation phase, but also during the distribution (withdrawal) phase of an investment.

TRYING TO AVOID THE TAX BITE

I have found that many people who invest in real estate enjoy the tax deductions they receive from writing off interest expense on the mortgage debt, as well as the depreciation on property. These combined deductions largely, if not totally, offset the rental income realized from investment property. However, if the property is held for an extended period of time, its cost basis may be substantially reduced. When the property is finally sold, a huge capital gains tax may be triggered on the difference between the reduced basis and the sales price of the property.

Most people think the only way to avoid the capital gain in this situation is to acquire another piece of like property through a 1031 exchange. Section 1031 of the Internal Revenue Code allows for the exchange of like property on a trade basis without triggering a taxable event on any of the gain realized. However, the gain is only postponed and the capital gains tax ultimately comes due. At that time, people often complain because of the huge tax bite out of their realized gain. Maybe they should be reminded of the deductions they had been taking for several years to offset all the income they had been receiving on the property!

Likewise, many people set aside money into investments such as IRAs, 401(k)s, and even annuities, all of which may accumulate money on a tax-deferred basis. When the money is withdrawn, the income or gain must be realized and taxes paid.

Let's assume a person were to set aside $15,000 per year for twenty years in a qualified retirement plan with pre-tax dollars at a 10.46 percent annual growth rate. At retirement he begins to withdraw the money based on a given formula. After twenty years he would have $1 million accumulated. For the sake of simplicity, let's say he then began earning an even 10 percent rate of return. If he were to withdraw $100,000 per year, in this example, he would need to report that as taxable income. Assuming a 34 percent tax rate, he would pay $34,000 in tax and net $66,000. On the other hand, if with the same variables, the individual who pays tax on the front end and only nets about $10,000 after tax on a $15,000 contribution (because of $5,100 in front-end taxes) will accumulate a smaller nest egg of $660,000 at the same interest rate of 10.46 percent. With the proper investment vehicle, such as a tax-advantaged insurance contract, withdrawing 10 percent may allow him to pull out $66,000 tax free.

Since, based on the same assumptions, the net spendable income is the same, you may be wondering how it makes a difference to set aside money before tax versus after taxes. The answer is, there may be no difference, but there are usually other variables that could make an investment that is tax free during the retirement years more attractive. For instance, the simple fact that Congress typically continues to increase taxes and decrease eligible deductions indicates it would likely be better to have tax-free income during your retirement rather than a larger taxable income. Using this logic, it makes better sense to pay the taxes at today's rates rather than postpone them to tomorrow's higher rates. Also, accumulating money and postponing the taxes until later may dramatically affect the amount of Social Security and Medicare benefits you may be entitled to receive.

QUALIFIED VS. NON-QUALIFIED RETIREMENT SAVINGS PLANS

Probably one of the greatest benefits savers and investors could hope for would be a lifting of the restrictions that dictate what percent of an income can be set aside in a retirement fund, so that during abundant years, larger contributions could be made. This is one distinct advantage of establishing a non-qualified private retirement planning strategy. Another benefit of non-qualified plans is that during emergencies, money can be accessed without penalty. It can later be replenished in lump sum payments. The flexibility of being able to contribute large sums without having to cover employees with similar benefits makes a non-qualified approach generally more attractive for business executives. I feel that non-qualified plans are also attractive for employees and would hope an employer would still consider matching benefits if an employee chose to contribute to such a plan. Company contributions to non-qualified plans can still be deductible to the business.

In choosing investments, you should determine which of them fall within your risk tolerance. Based on the risk-return model already introduced (figs. 17.2–17.5), investors have the choice of a number of different investments that meet the liquidity, safety, and rate of return tests. Let's review for a moment. Investment alternatives such as CDs and money market accounts perform at a lower rate of return. They are generally taxed as earned income unless they are IRA accounts. Mutual funds are generally for longer-term goals and may achieve a higher average rate of return. But these returns are generally accomplished through dividends and capital gains and are subject to market fluctuations. Mutual funds, whether IRAs or not, will usually be taxed at the time of withdrawal or taxed as earned. Annuities allow money to accumulate tax deferred, but they are taxable when the funds are withdrawn and incur a 10 percent penalty if withdrawn before the age of $59^1/2$. They are taxed LIFO rather than FIFO. IRAs and 401(k)s are likewise taxed upon distribution, with a 10 percent penalty if funds are accessed before age $59^1/2$, unless certain rules are met.

TAX-FREE VS. TAXABLE HARVESTS

Figure 18.1 helps analyze the impact of receiving money tax free during your harvest years and making an investment selection based on which investments provide or generate the most.

This example illustrates a sixty-year-old couple repositioning $300,000 of their home's equity as they sell it (possibly downsizing for retirement) and purchasing another home. Let's also assume they reposition $40,000, net after tax, each year for five years out of their IRAs and 401(k)s. Finally, they also reposition a total of $200,000 of CDs, non-qualified mutual funds and money market accounts. Thus, $700,000 of assets are strategically repositioned into an insurance contract during the final five years of their working careers. I am illustrating five equal annual installments of $140,000 into the main insurance contract to comply with TAMRA (chapter 17). Through the use of InsMark® software, we see the accumulation values in the insurance contract shown in column 6 have not had an opportunity to accumulate to a degree that compares much more favorably than the net after-tax results that might have been achieved in an alternative investment such as a CD, municipal bond fund, or even a mutual fund in just five short years, at age 65. In fact, a tax-deferred vehicle such as an annuity accumulated $794,191, about $14,000 more than the $780,243 accumulated in the insurance contract at that point. Not only that, but if the insurance contract were to be canceled at the end of five years, the net surrender value would only be $694,557.

Let's assume at retirement the couple stops making any further contributions. The maximum funding is completed in compliance with TAMRA. At that point in time (or any time from the inception of the policy up to that point) it is important to note if the person passed away suddenly in an accident, the insurance contract, because of the minimum death benefit required under TEFRA/DEFRA rules (chapter 17), would actually transfer a substantially greater tax-free net estate to the heirs than the money that had been contributed into any of the other investments. This death benefit of $1,785,117 is the minimum required under TEFRA/DEFRA guidelines to accommodate $700,000 of aggregate premiums for a sixty-year-old male; it is income-tax free; and it can also be structured to be estate-tax free. The life insurance benefit is shown in the far right-hand column 8. Let's assume these retirees are going to live to a normal life expectancy of about eighty-five years of age. We'll also

Fig. 18.1

AN INDEXED UNIVERSAL LIFE POLICY
VERSUS VARIOUS FINANCIAL ALTERNATIVES

		A Certificate of Deposit Yield 5.00%	A Municipal Bond Fund Yield 5.00%	An Annuity Yield 6.25%	Mutual Fund Yield 9.00%	An Indexed Universal Life Policy Interest Rate 7.75%		Tax Bracket 34.00%
Male Age 60	Initial Payment 140,000	AFTER-TAX VALUES				AN INDEXED UNIVERSAL LIFE POLICY		
		[1]	[2]	[3]	[4]	[5]	[6] Year End	[7] Year End	[8]
Clients Age	Year	Net Payment	A Certificate of Deposit	A Municipal Bond Fund	An Annuity	Mutual Fund	Accumulation Value*	Surrender Value*	Death Benefit
61	1	140,000	144,620	139,709	145,775	139,813	130,919	84,506	1,785,117
62	2	140,000	294,012	284,936	297,686	286,788	273,345	187,660	1,785,117
63	3	140,000	448,335	435,900	456,116	441,291	428,292	342,606	1,785,117
64	4	140,000	607,750	592,827	621,474	603,709	596,859	511,173	1,785,117
65	5	140,000	772,426	755,952	**794,191**	774,447	**780,243**	694,557	1,785,117
66	6	-50,000	746,266	733,837	775,828	761,557	774,095	694,975	1,735,092
67	7	-50,000	719,242	710,849	756,317	748,007	821,858	695,402	1,683,592
68	8	-50,000	691,327	686,952	735,587	733,762	871,292	695,955	1,630,547
69	9	-50,000	662,491	662,112	713,867	718,788	922,468	696,660	1,575,911
70	10	-50,000	632,704	636,290	691,252	703,047	975,463	701,707	1,519,635
71	11	-50,000	601,933	609,449	667,703	686,499	1,029,203	705,812	1,461,672
72	12	-50,000	570,147	581,547	643,183	669,103	1,083,670	708,905	1,401,969
73	13	-50,000	537,311	552,543	617,652	650,817	1,138,912	710,982	1,340,475
74	14	-50,000	503,393	522,394	591,068	631,594	1,195,189	712,248	1,277,137
75	15	-50,000	468,355	491,053	563,387	611,386	1,252,081	712,230	1,211,898
76	16	-50,000	432,160	458,475	534,564	590,143	1,311,018	712,299	1,144,702
77	17	-50,000	394,772	424,610	504,552	567,812	1,371,163	711,561	1,075,491
78	18	-50,000	356,149	389,407	473,303	544,337	1,432,751	701,861	1,004,202
79	19	-50,000	316,252	352,813	440,764	519,659	1,496,113	691,797	930,776
80	20	-50,000	275,038	314,774	406,883	493,718	1,561,726	681,780	855,146
81	21	-50,000	232,465	275,233	371,604	466,447	1,630,392	672,548	777,248
82	22	-50,000	188,486	234,130	334,871	437,779	1,703,044	664,965	750,117
83	23	-50,000	143,056	191,403	296,622	407,643	1,777,634	656,912	745,794
84	24	-50,000	96,127	146,988	256,795	375,964	1,853,356	647,513	740,181
85	25	-50,000	47,649	100,819	215,325	342,661	1,930,388	636,869	733,389
86	26	-50,000	**-2,429**	52,827	172,145	307,653	2,008,700	624,876	725,311
87	27	-50,000	-54,159	2,938	127,183	270,851	2,087,814	610,975	715,366
88	28	-50,000	-107,596	**-49,415**	80,367	232,164	2,167,542	594,898	703,275
89	29	-50,000	-162,797	-104,386	31,620	191,495	2,247,675	576,351	688,735
90	30	-50,000	-219,819	-162,105	**-19,529**	148,744	2,328,576	555,613	672,042
91	31	-50,000	-278,723	-222,710	-73,875	103,802	2,410,205	532,553	653,063
92	32	-50,000	-339,571	-286,346	-131,617	56,558	2,494,035	508,554	608,315
93	33	-50,000	-402,427	-353,163	-192,968	6,894	2,580,557	484,011	561,428
94	34	-50,000	-467,347	-423,321	-258,154	**-45,667**	2,670,361	459,418	512,825
95	35	-50,000	-534,430	-496,987	-327,413	-101,349	2,764,168	435,397	463,039
96	36	-50,000	-603,716	-574,336	-401,001	-160,340	2,861,947	411,813	411,813
97	37	-50,000	-675,288	-655,553	-479,189	-222,834	2,961,366	386,228	386,228
98	38	-50,000	-749,223	-740,831	-562,263	-289,040	3,062,374	358,482	358,482
99	39	-50,000	-825,597	-830,372	-650,530	-359,179	3,164,911	328,402	328,402
100	40	-50,000	-904,492	-924,391	-744,313	-433,484	3,268,907	**295,803**	295,803

Sales charge on payments to column [1]: MB = 4.00%, MF = 5.00%
Management fee reflected in columns [3] & [5]: MB = 1.00%, MF = 0.75%,
An annuity is assessed: • Tax on withdrawals before age 59 1/2: 10.00% • Tax on withdrawals in column [1].

*This illustration assumes that the nonguaranteed values shown continue in all years.
This is not likely, and actual results may be more or less favorable.
Format and design created through the use of InsMark® software.

Fig. 18.1 continued	AN INDEXED UNIVERSAL LIFE POLICY VERSUS VARIOUS FINANCIAL ALTERNATIVES		

Gross interest rate needed by various investments over 40 years to match an Indexed Universal Life Policy

Investment	Interest Rate	Indexed Universal Life Policy	
A Certificate of Deposit	11.77%	Accumulation Value	$3,268,907
A Certificate of Deposit	8.72%	Surrender Value	$295,803
A Certificate of Deposit	8.72%	Death Benefit	$295,803
A Municipal Bond Fund	9.08%	Accumulation Value	$3,268,907
A Municipal Bond Fund	7.10%	Surrender Value	$295,803
A Municipal Bond Fund	7.10%	Death Benefit	$295,803
An Annuity	10.19%	Accumulation Value	$3,268,907
An Annuity	8.49%	Surrender Value	$295,803
An Annuity	8.49%	Death Benefit	$295,803
Mutual Fund	13.49%	Accumulation Value	$3,268,907
Mutual Fund	10.50%	Surrender Value	$295,803
Mutual Fund	10.50%	Death Benefit	$295,803

Income Tax Considerations

1. A Certificate of Deposit - Interest is taxed as earned.
2. A Municipal Bond Fund - Interest is tax exempt.
3. An Annuity - Interest is tax deferred. (Values assume tax is assessed in year shown only.)
4. Mutual Fund - Interest is taxed as earned.
5. An Indexed Universal Life Policy:
    a. Death Benefit including cash value component is income tax free.
    b. Loans are income tax free as long as the policy is kept in force.
    c. Withdrawals and other non-loan policy cash flow up to cost basis
       (not in violations of IRC Section 7702) are income tax free as a return of premium.
    d. Cash values shown assume most favorable combination of b and/or c.

*This illustration assumes that the nonguaranteed values shown continue in all years.
This is not likely, and actual results may be more or less favorable.
Format and design created through the use of InsMark® software.

look at what happens if they live beyond that to age 100. Let's do an analysis to see which investment actually ends up providing the most.

As illustrated, we begin with a net spendable retirement income of $50,000. If that money was accessed under the tax-free provisions of the insurance contract, the amount withdrawn—the gross amount—is also the net amount because there is no tax on those distributions. If you withdraw $50,000, you get to keep and spend $50,000! With the alternative investments in the illustration, we have actually had to withdraw as much as $75,758 in order to net $50,000 after paying the tax at a 34 percent rate. If you have to withdraw $75,758 and pay tax of $25,758 to result in a net spendable income of $50,000, it stands to reason those accounts will deplete much faster than the one requiring only a $50,000 withdrawal.

As seen, the four alternative investments that were actually worth a little bit more money at age sixty-five begin to deplete quickly when compared to the insurance contract. When the other vehicles run out of money in the years shown, the insurance contract still has a substantial amount of money left because we only had to withdraw the net amount of $50,000 to have the same net spendable income. Please note the various values in year 26—when this couple has reached age 86. The CD is out of money, a municipal bond fund has been depleted down to $52,827, the annuity only has a balance remaining of $172,145, and the mutual fund is worth $307,653. In contrast, the insurance contract at that point has a surrender value of $624,876 with a death benefit of $725,311. Even the best alternative—mutual funds that yielded 9 percent average return—did not come close to performing as well as an insurance contract. So, if the couple were still living, the insurance contract allowed them to not outlive their money. Probably the greatest fear of many retirees is they will outlive their money. So, they feel forced to withdraw a lower amount of retirement income and perhaps not enjoy retirement to the fullest they desire. This would especially be true should they live beyond normal life expectancy, or should they have a catastrophic medical setback that would drain them of their financial resources.

In order to choose investments that will generate the most, you need to do a complete analysis of the tax treatment on the withdrawal and transfer phases rather than on just the contribution and accumulation phases of your retirement planning vehicles. The most important phases of a retirement account, or any long-term investment for strategic tax planning, should be the withdrawal (distribution) and transfer phases, not the contribution and accumulation phases.

MATCHING INVESTMENTS TO GOALS

I believe the biggest mistake investors make is often they will choose long-term investments for short-range goals or vice versa. They are doing just the opposite of what they need to do to accomplish what they are truly trying to achieve. If you are beginning an investment account for the purpose of retirement funding or college funding for young children, the goal is to have tax-favored access to those funds fifteen or twenty years down the road. A person needs to look at the potential for that investment return in the fifteenth or twentieth year, rather than look at what the surrender value of the investment is just one or two years into the investment. Too many people have given up the opportunity to have an investment that will truly blossom into the greatest net spendable income because they were too hung up on surrender charges, penalties for early withdrawal, or front-end loads and administration expense associated with some investments.

In the case of insurance contracts, IRS guidelines—such as TEFRA, DEFRA, and TAMRA—have to be met through the first few years. Sometimes, there are administration expenses or sales loads that must be met during the front end of an investment that will become very nominal by the time the investment has had the time to blossom into an amount that can generate the highest net spendable income during retirement.

As shown in the illustration, an insurance contract returning approximately 7.75 percent can outperform a mutual fund returning 9 percent, even up to 13 percent. It generates income, not only to a life expectancy of age 85, but continues to perform for fifteen additional years to age 100 with $295,803 of value remaining compared to the other investments that all ran out of money. At age 100, all of the alternative investments were dramatically in the red when the insurance contract finally was depleted to just under $300,000. If the investor had made the choice of which investment he wanted to go with the last five years of his working career (based on which investment might grow to the most at the end of five short years), he would have likely selected a mutual fund or a tax-deferred investment like an annuity. Had he done a complete analysis of which one generated the most benefits, he would have discovered that a properly structured insurance contract had the potential of generating an income about ten to fifteen years longer than a mutual fund or annuity. Another way to look at it is to consider when the other investments ran out of money between year 26 and year 34, the insurance contract still had values and death benefits in a net transferable amount to the heirs of any-where from $512,825 to $725,311, depending on the year.

If you look across the column in year 40 (at age 100), all the other investment alternatives are in substantially negative territory, meaning a retiree of that age would have long outlived his money. The insurance contract still has $295,803 at that point in time. The annuity would be $744,313 in the hole at that point. In other words, the insurance con-tract was effectively $1,040,116 ($295,803 plus $744,313) better than the annuity! The mutual fund would be $433,484 in the hole at age 100. Therefore the insurance contract was effectively $729,287 ($295,803 plus $433,484) better than the mutual fund!

As shown on the last page of **figure 18.1**, the other investments would have to achieve 10.50 to 13.49 percent return to match the same net tax-free results or income the insurance contract achieved by cred-iting an average gross interest rate of 7.75 percent. If this investor had chosen an investment that was grossing 9 to 12 percent over an invest-ment that performed tax free at 6 to 8 percent, he would likely have been severely disappointed, simply because he chose an investment that had a higher rate of return rather than one that would end up generat-ing the most at retirement! So for example, in the case of the fixed annuity, what appeared to be an investment that out-performed the insurance contract by $14,000 at age 65, was in fact inferior—possibly by as much as $1 million—by the time he reached age 100. That is a dramatic difference, the key to which is the tax treatment on the funds as they were distributed during the harvest years of their lives—the most important phase of a retirement plan.

Some people may argue, "Well I can achieve a higher return than what is being illustrated by these CDs, municipal bond funds, annuities, or mutual funds." That may be true, but likewise, a higher return can also be achieved with an insurance contract under similar market conditions. However, in an economic environment where an insurance contract might be crediting an average gross interest rate of 7.75 percent, the alternative investments shown would likely be performing at average yields as illustrated. If the alternative investments were to perform at

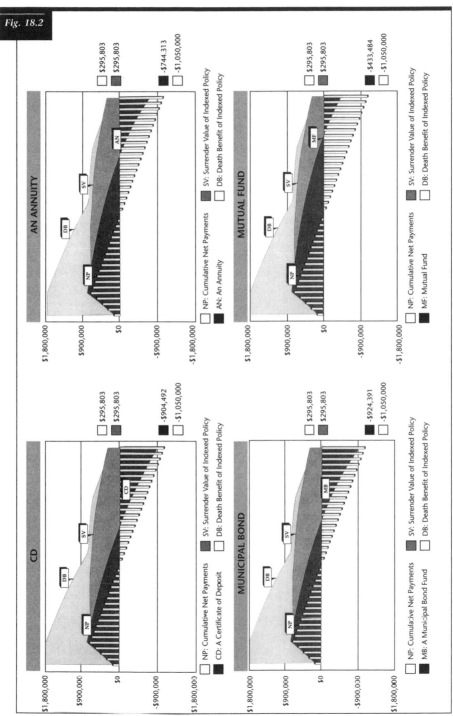

Fig. 18.2

Format and design created through the use of InsMark® software.

Fig. 18.3

AN INDEXED UNIVERSAL LIFE POLICY
VERSUS VARIOUS FINANCIAL ALTERNATIVES

		Initial	A Municipal Bond Fund Yield	An Annuity Yield	IRAs & 401(k)s Yield	Mutual Fund Yield	An Indexed Universal Life Policy Interest Rate	Tax Bracket
Male Age 30		Payment 6,000	5.00%	6.25%	7.75%	10.00%	7.75%	34.00%
			AFTER TAX VALUES				AN INDEXED UNIVERSAL LIFE POLICY	
		[1]	[2]	[3]	[4]	[5]	[6] Year End Accumulation Value*	[7] Year End Surrender Value*	[8]
Client's Age	Year	Net Payment	A Municipal Bond Fund	An Annuity	IRAs & 401(k)s	Mutual Fund			Death Benefit
31	1	6,000	5,988	6,033	6,054	6,029	5,331	2,155	635,176
32	2	6,000	12,212	12,242	12,344	12,407	11,064	4,712	635,176
33	3	6,000	18,681	18,636	18,888	19,152	17,230	10,879	635,176
34	4	6,000	25,407	25,225	25,703	26,287	23,859	17,507	635,176
35	5	6,000	32,398	32,018	32,808	33,835	31,012	24,660	635,176
36	6	6,000	39,665	39,028	40,223	41,818	38,731	32,697	635,176
37	7	6,000	47,219	46,263	47,969	50,262	47,062	41,345	635,176
38	8	6,000	55,072	53,738	56,069	59,194	56,051	50,652	635,176
39	9	6,000	63,235	61,462	64,549	68,641	65,751	60,670	635,176
40	10	6,000	71,720	69,451	73,434	78,635	76,219	71,773	635,176
41	11	6,000	80,541	77,717	82,753	89,205	87,977	84,166	635,176
42	12	6,000	89,710	86,276	92,535	100,386	100,611	97,435	635,176
43	13	6,000	99,241	95,141	102,813	112,212	114,182	111,641	635,176
44	14	6,000	109,148	104,329	113,622	124,722	128,764	126,858	635,176
45	15	6,000	119,447	113,856	124,997	137,953	144,440	143,170	635,176
46	16	6,000	130,153	123,741	136,979	151,949	161,284	160,649	635,176
47	17	6,000	141,281	134,002	149,609	166,754	179,375	179,375	635,176
48	18	6,000	152,850	144,658	162,933	182,413	198,819	198,819	635,176
49	19	6,000	164,875	155,730	176,998	198,976	219,718	219,718	635,176
50	20	6,000	177,375	167,240	191,857	216,496	242,183	242,183	635,176
51	21	6,000	190,369	179,209	207,563	235,028	266,336	266,336	635,176
52	22	6,000	203,876	191,662	224,177	254,630	292,330	292,330	635,176
53	23	6,000	217,916	204,625	241,761	275,364	320,316	320,316	635,176
54	24	6,000	232,511	218,123	260,382	297,296	350,457	350,457	635,176
55	25	6,000	247,683	232,184	280,113	320,494	382,943	382,943	635,176
56	26	6,000	263,454	246,838	301,030	345,032	417,972	417,972	635,176
57	27	6,000	279,848	262,115	323,216	370,986	455,771	455,771	665,426
58	28	6,000	296,890	278,047	346,758	398,440	496,454	496,454	704,964
59	29	6,000	314,604	294,669	371,752	427,479	540,207	540,207	745,486
60	30	6,000	333,019	312,017	398,297	458,195	587,275	587,275	786,949
61	31	6,000	352,160	355,864	469,449	490,685	637,924	637,924	829,301
62	32	6,000	372,058	377,083	503,711	525,051	692,351	692,351	886,209
63	33	6,000	392,742	399,296	540,209	561,402	750,842	750,842	946,061
64	34	6,000	414,243	422,556	579,100	599,852	813,709	813,709	1,008,999
65	35	6,000	436,593	446,917	620,548	640,523	881,289	881,289	1,075,173

Sales charge on payments to column [1]:
MB = 4.00%, AN = 4.00%, IRA = 5.00%, MF = 5.00%,

Management fee reflected in columns [2], [3], [4], & [5]:
MB = 1.00%, An = 1.00%, IRA = .75%, MF = .75%,

Tax deferred accounts are assessed: Income tax on withdrawals in column [1].
Additional income tax on withdrawals before age 59 1/2: 10.00%.

*This illustration assumes the nonguaranteed values shown continue in all years.
This is not likely, and actual results may be more or less favorable.
Format and design created through the use of InsMark® software.

Fig. 18.3 continued

AN INDEXED UNIVERSAL LIFE POLICY
VERSUS VARIOUS FINANCIAL ALTERNATIVES

Male Age 30	Initial Payment 6,000	A Municipal Bond Fund Yield 5.00%	An Annuity Yield 6.25%	IRAs & 401(k)s Yield 7.75%	Mutual Fund Yield 10.00%	An Indexed Universal Life Policy Interest Rate 7.75%		Tax Bracket 34.00%
			AFTER TAX VALUES			AN INDEXED UNIVERSAL LIFE POLICY		
		[1]	[2]	[3]	[4]	[5]	[6] Year End Accumulation Value*	[7] Year End Surrender Value*	[8]
Client's Age	Year	Net Payment	A Municipal Bond Fund	An Annuity	IRAs & 401(k)s	Mutual Fund			Death Benefit
66	36	-64,000	387,310	399,077	590,277	609,817	878,901	878,901	1,054,682
67	37	-64,000	336,081	348,755	557,800	577,338	942,069	876,149	1,055,143
68	38	-64,000	282,828	295,823	523,123	542,983	1,006,691	872,873	1,054,078
69	39	-64,000	227,472	240,145	486,038	506,645	1,072,768	869,016	1,051,387
70	40	-64,000	169,929	182,176	446,379	468,207	1,140,304	864,520	1,046,968
71	41	-64,000	110,114	122,222	403,967	427,550	1,209,302	859,324	1,040,720
72	42	-64,000	47,935	60,215	358,610	384,545	1,279,987	853,590	1,019,988
73	43	-64,000	**-16,868**	**-4,021**	310,105	339,057	1,352,454	847,345	996,115
74	44	-64,000	-84,912	-72,272	258,233	290,941	1,426,829	840,646	969,061
75	45	-64,000	-156,357	-144,790	203,132	240,047	1,503,263	833,575	938,804
76	46	-64,000	-231,375	-221,839	145,507	186,214	1,581,990	826,291	905,390
77	47	-64,000	-310,144	-303,704	85,241	129,272	1,662,319	818,029	901,145
78	48	-64,000	-392,851	-390,685	22,214	69,041	1,744,203	808,664	895,875
79	49	-64,000	-479,694	-483,103	**-45,024**	5,332	1,827,588	798,063	889,443
80	50	-64,000	-570,878	-581,297	-117,474	**-62,540**	1,912,400	**786,069**	881,689
81	51	-64,000	-666,622	-685,628	-195,538	-134,891	1,998,532	772,492	872,418
82	52	-64,000	-767,153	-796,480	-279,652	-212,018	2,085,878	757,136	861,430
83	53	-64,000	-872,711	-914,260	-370,285	-294,235	2,174,312	739,788	848,504
84	54	-64,000	-983,547	-1,038,401	-467,942	-381,879	2,263,691	720,212	833,396
85	55	-64,000	-1,099,924	-1,172,364	-573,168	-475,307	2,354,194	698,490	816,199
86	56	-64,000	-1,222,120	-1,313,636	-686,548	-574,901	2,445,742	674,447	796,734
87	57	-64,000	-1,350,426	-1,463,739	-808,716	-681,069	2,537,708	647,354	774,239
88	58	-64,000	-1,485,147	-1,623,222	-940,351	-794,243	2,629,816	616,831	748,322
89	59	-64,000	-1,626,605	-1,792,674	-1,082,188	-914,887	2,721,761	582,466	718,554
90	60	-64,000	-1,775,135	-1,972,716	-1,235,018	-1,043,494	2,813,929	544,536	685,232
91	61	-64,000	-1,931,092	-2,164,011	-1,399,692	-1,180,588	2,906,209	502,814	648,125
92	62	-64,000	-2,094,846	-2,367,261	-1,577,128	-1,326,731	3,000,312	458,896	578,908
93	63	-64,000	-2,266,789	-2,583,215	-1,768,315	-1,482,519	3,096,747	413,168	506,071
94	64	-64,000	-2,447,328	-2,812,666	-1,974,320	-1,648,590	3,196,133	366,126	430,049
95	65	-64,000	-2,636,894	-3,056,458	-2,196,289	-1,825,621	3,299,231	318,404	351,396
96	66	-64,000	-2,835,939	-3,315,486	-2,435,462	-2,014,335	3,405,890	269,719	269,719
97	67	-64,000	-3,044,936	-3,590,704	-2,693,170	-2,215,506	3,513,215	217,039	217,039
98	68	-64,000	-3,264,383	-3,883,123	-2,970,851	-2,429,953	3,621,030	160,049	160,049
99	69	-64,000	-3,494,802	-4,193,818	-3,270,052	-2,658,554	3,729,892	99,161	99,161
100	70	-64,000	-3,736,742	-4,523,932	-3,592,441	-2,902,242	3,844,000	**38,426**	38,426

Sales charge on payments to column [1]:
MB = 4.00%, AN = 4.00%, IRA = 5.00%, MF = 5.00%,

Management fee reflected in columns [2], [3], [4], & [5]:
MB = 1.00%, An = 1.00%, IRA = .75%, MF = .75%,

Tax deferred accounts are assessed: Income tax on withdrawals in column [1].
Additional income tax on withdrawals before age 59$^1/_2$: 10.00%.

* This illustration assumes the nonguaranteed values shown continue in all years.
This is not likely, and actual results may be more or less favorable.
Format and design created through the use of InsMark® software.

higher yields, the insurance contract should also be able to perform at higher yields over the long term. I have tried to be fairly conservative by comparing similar investments based on risk tolerance in order to do as close to an apples-to-apples comparison as possible.

GRAPHING THE DATA

Take a look at those same numbers applied to a graph format using InsMark® software (**fig. 18.2**). These graphs illustrate alternative investments being fairly equal to the insurance contract for the first five years to the age of sixty-five (shown at the peak), with the exception of the substantial death benefit that accompanies the insurance contract. Then, as retirement income and distributions are made, the CD, municipal bond fund, annuity, and mutual fund, as well as other types of similar investments taxable upon distribution, run out of steam and end up in the hole (below the $0 line). However, through age 85 (assumed life expectancy) and even to age 100, the insurance contract is continuing to generate a net spendable retirement income of $50,000 per year. The difference between the graph labeled SV (surrender value of the insurance contract) compared to the graphs labeled CD, MB, AN, or MF (alternative investments) are dramatic. This illustrates very powerfully the difference it can make to have investments that are tax advantaged during the harvest years (distribution and transfer phases of retirement).

STARTING YOUNG

For a moment, let's take a look at a thirty-year-old couple who hypothetically sets aside $6,000 a year in an insurance contract for thirty-five years, compared to alternative investments such as mutual funds, IRA/401(k)s, municipal bond funds, or annuities (**fig. 18.3**). Again, these instruments, even though they may be tax favored up until age 65, are not as attractive as the after-tax potential value of the insurance contract as shown in the right-hand column. So, in this example, alternative investments have not performed even as well as the insurance contract by age 65, as illustrated across the line in year 35. There is even a more dramatic difference as the retirement income commences after thirty-five years of accumulation. Notice how quickly a municipal bond fund and an annuity run out of steam, compared to the tax-free withdrawal or loan of $64,000 we can take out of the insurance contract to deplete the money gradually to age 100. (We have instructed the computer software to calculate the maximum average withdrawals and/or loans required to gradually deplete the insurance contract of cash value until age 100. Retirement income of $50,000 to $60,000, rather than $64,000, would prevent the depletion of the cash values and could even result in continued growth in spite of the withdrawals and loans taken.) The IRAs, 401(k)s, and mutual funds also run out of money long before an assumed life expectancy of age 85 as shown on the line in year 55 (age 85). They are, respectively, $573,168 in the hole at age 85, and $475,307 in the hole when the insurance contract is still generating a net spendable income of $64,000, with cash values remaining in the contract worth $698,490. The insurance contract crediting a gross interest rate of 7.75 percent provides $64,000 of retirement income for twenty-one years longer than a mutual fund yielding 10 percent. That equals $1,344,000 ($64,000/yr x 21 years) more in retirement resources!

Again, another way to look at it is to study the age 100 results (year 70). The mutual fund is negative $2,902,242. The IRAs and 401(k)s are negative $3,592,441 (based on the same interest crediting rate as the insurance contract) when the insurance contract is finally depleted. So, at age 65 (year 35), the insurance contract is valued at $881,289 versus the mutual fund with an after-tax value of $640,523, resulting in a difference of $240,766. But the significant difference is $2,902,242, which represents how much the insurance contract outperformed the mutual fund over a seventy-year period to age 100, based on a net spendable annual retirement income of $64,000! And don't forget to consider the tax-free transfer of the death benefit in the far right-hand column, should death occur any time during retirement, compared to the other investment alternatives.

Fig. 18.4

Male Age 30	Initial Payment 6,000	A Municipal Bond Fund Yield 5.00%	An Annuity Yield 6.25%	IRAs & 401(k)s Yield 7.75%	Mutual Fund Yield 10.00%	An Indexed Universal Life Policy Interest Rate 7.75%	Tax Bracket 34.00%

Gross interest rate needed by various investments over 40 years to match an Indexed Universal Life Policy

Investment	Interest Rate	Indexed Universal Life Policy	
A Municipal Bond Fund	9.08%	Accumulation Value	$3,844,000
A Municipal Bond Fund	8.22%	Surrender Value	$38,426
A Municipal Bond Fund	8.22%	Death Benefit	$38,426
An Annuity	10.19%	Accumulation Value	$3,844,000
An Annuity	9.49%	Surrender Value	$38,426
An Annuity	9.49%	Death Benefit	$38,426
IRA's / 401(k)s	9.94%	Accumulation Value	$3,844,000
IRA's / 401(k)s	9.24%	Surrender Value	$38,426
IRA's / 401(k)s	9.24%	Death Benefit	$38,426
Mutual Fund	13.43%	Accumulation Value	$3,844,000
Mutual Fund	12.13%	Surrender Value	$38,426
Mutual Fund	12.13%	Death Benefit	$38,426

Income Tax Considerations

1. A Certificate of Deposit - Interest is taxed as earned.
2. A Municipal Bond Fund - Interest is tax exempt.
3. An Annuity - Interest is tax deferred. (Values assume tax is assessed in year shown only.)
4. Mutual Fund - Interest is taxed as earned.
5. An Indexed Universal Life Policy:
   a. Death Benefit including cash value component is income tax free.
   b. Loans are income tax free as long as the policy is kept in force.
   c. Withdrawals and other non-loan policy cash flow up to cost basis
      (not in violations of IRC Section 7702) are income tax free as a return of premium.
   d. Cash values shown assume most favorable combination of b and/or c.

Format and design created through the use of InsMark® software.

Please note that on **figure 18.4** the various investment alternatives illustrated would have to be crediting interest rates between 8.22 percent up to 13.43 percent (depending on the investment vehicle) to match the same values achieved by the insurance contract crediting 7.75 percent. If the mutual fund in this example averaged a 12 percent yield, it would still be $234,428 in the hole at the end of seventy years, when the insurance contract crediting only 7.75 percent was finally depleted down to $38,426.

Keep in mind for these illustrations I have simply used a stable retirement income assumption. Most people would choose to have an inflation-indexed income coming out of their insurance contract, based on their needs and the increase in the cost of living. I also advise many clients to take out larger sums of income while they have the health to enjoy retirement and travel between the ages of 60 and 75. After age 75, I see many people begin to lose interest and physical capacity for doing as much extensive travel and activities. An insurance contract can really allow them to withdraw funds at whatever pace they need with no minimum distribution requirements. However, as with any investment, they want to avoid depleting their funds too quickly so the funds don't expire before they do! In almost every circumstance, based on the variables listed on the illustrations, the insurance contract can outperform other comparable, conservative investments at their normal, average rates of return if tax laws remain the same. A complete analysis should always be done regarding what happens to an investment through all four phases. Some investments may perform best during the contribution and accumulation phases. But more importantly, others may generate the most during the withdrawal phase, as well as the transfer phase, when death finally occurs.

USING INSURANCE CONTRACTS TO TRANSFER MONEY TAX FREE

One of the reasons why the insurance contract is probably the best alternative in most circumstances is because during the transfer phase, whatever remaining amount is left in the policy blossoms to a larger sum and is transferred income-tax free to the heirs. Other investments do not blossom upon transfer, but transfer at face value and may be subject to taxation—especially qualified accounts upon which the heirs ultimately have to pay income tax and possibly estate tax as well. Hence, many qualified accounts are double taxed, sometimes as high as 70 to 85 percent, and the children or other heirs may only realize about fifteen to thirty cents on the dollar. It behooves someone planning for retirement to choose investments that have a tax-favored umbrella during the accumulation, withdrawal, and transfer phases. Even if a person contributes money with after-tax dollars during the contribution phase, they can perhaps afford to contribute larger sums of money because they derive tax advantages indirectly on the front end through proper home equity management. Remember, managing home equity helps us to maximize the tax deductions through a mortgage rather than killing our best partner, Uncle Sam. Proper equity management also helps us maximize the rate of return on our dormant home equity.

Hopefully, through the illustrations provided thus far, you have begun to open your eyes to the fact that sometimes more conservative investments that are tax-advantaged, particularly during retirement years, may be far superior to higher performing investments where the tax has been compounded and postponed. Likewise it is important to understand if you choose investment grade insurance contracts for retirement income and equity management objectives, the more stable and conservative forms of insurance contracts may perform better in the long run.

MY PORTFOLIO

My own retirement planning portfolio is comprised of both fixed and indexed universal life. I diversify by having different types of universal life spread between a few different highly rated insurance companies insuring me, my wife, and each of my children. Smart diversification does not occur when a person chooses inferior performing investments in conjunction with superior performing investments. For instance, when it is very apparent, as illustrated in figures 18.1 to 18.4, that properly structured and funded insurance contracts can far outperform other types of comparable investments, why in the world would I choose to diversify by putting money into inferior investments?

Let me zero in on one type of insurance contract I own and why I deem it an excellent investment can generate the most in the long run for my retirement planning objectives. The indexed universal life I own is offered by ING Southland Life Insurance Company. It has several contractually guaranteed features you may want to consider when shopping for an insurance contract. It offers zero net interest loans after the tenth policy year (or sooner if you begin at an older age) that makes it attractive for retirement income. Even during the first ten years there is only a 2 percent net interest charge on tax-free loans. It has no cap on the interest credited to my cash values. It features an annual index reset as well as monthly linking to the S&P 500 Index. It uses the final six-month smoothing method and has a 3 percent guaranteed interest rate. Let me explain some of these features in more detail.

Since the first indexed universal life insurance policy was introduced late in 1996, many life insurance companies have designed and introduced their own versions of this exciting new type of life insurance product. Indexed universal life provides a life insurance policy in which the crediting rate can be substantially higher than the traditional (general account) portfolio earnings of the life insurance company by linking the crediting rate to the S&P 500 Index. At the same time, these products offer the safety of a guaranteed minimum interest rate.

On the surface, this immediately creates opportunities to benefit from tax-advantaged growth, without the market risk often associated with variable life insurance policies. Unfortunately, in the scramble for market share, much of the information used to market and promote indexed universal life insurance has been either misrepresented or misunderstood. Financial professionals who promote equity-related products for their upside cash value growth potential need to be informed.

TYPICAL INVESTOR CONCERNS

The first question most people ask when discussing indexed universal life is, "What is the participation rate?" The second question most frequently asked is, "Is it a point-to-point, or an averaging product?" or, "What is the linking method?" The most important questions should surround linking frequency. Participation rate and linking method are simply functions of dollars and cents in the overall market for call options, and can hardly be used to differentiate between a good and a bad product. Most financial services professionals have been led to believe the participation rate is the amount of the upward move in the S&P 500 Index that is actually credited to the policy cash values. In other words, if the S&P 500 Index goes up 100 percent and the participation rate is 50 percent, only 50 percent of the gain is credited to the cash value and the company keeps the remaining 50 percent. This is incorrect!

The participation (or index factor) is more correctly defined as the percent of the cash value actually linked to the performance of the S&P 500 Index. This linked percentage of the cash values is credited with 100 percent of the S&P 500 growth as measured by the linking strategy used by that particular product. It is important to make this distinction for a number of reasons. If the insurance company were keeping a percentage of the S&P 500 gains, it would be in the company's best interest to hold down the participation rate to increase profits. In addition, that would mean that each time the participation rate was lowered, the company would reap benefits. Under those circumstances, clients would have legitimate concerns about the likelihood of high participation rates in the future.

To better understand how equity-indexed universal life interest crediting works, it helps to contrast it with the crediting strategy for most traditional (general account) universal life products. In general, when you pay a premium on a fixed universal life product, the company takes out the cost of insurance, fees, and expense charges, after which the remainder of the premium is deposited in its general account portfolio. Let's assume the company earns 8 percent on its general account portfolio. The company will keep a "management spread" (in this example, let's say 2 percent), leaving 6 percent to be credited to the cash values of the policy owner. While simplistic, this is how crediting rates are determined on general account products. An important feature, then, of fixed universal life products is that cash values cannot be credited with a rate higher than the rate earned by the general account portfolio of the insurance company, minus the spread kept by the company.

The only major difference between fixed universal life and equity-indexed universal life is the method by which the interest crediting rate is determined. Instead of crediting the remaining 6 percent to the cash values of the client, the company credits only the guaranteed rate to the client. Assuming a 3 percent guaranteed rate, this would leave excess interest in the amount of 3 percent. Keep in mind these are not premium dollars, which are in the company general account. This is excess interest over and above the guaranteed rate credited to the policy owner. The company will then use this excess interest to purchase call options on the S&P 500 Index. In this example, assume the company could purchase a one-year call option on $1000 of S&P 500 Index shares for $50. Assuming a $10,000 account value in an equity-indexed universal life policy, the 3 percent excess interest—or $300—would be sufficient to purchase call options on $6,000 of S&P 500 Index shares. In other words, $6,000 out of the $10,000 account value is actually "participating" in the movement of the S&P 500 Index!

More important, any and all of the growth in the S&P 500 Index garnered on the $6,000 of participating cash value is credited to the policy owner. Where many people believe the company is only crediting the $10,000 account value with 60 percent of the growth, the reality is that the company is crediting 60 percent of the cash value with 100 percent of the growth! Thus, participation rates are a function of mathematics. The higher the general account rate of return, the more excess interest will be available to purchase call options. If the price of the call options were held constant, this would result in higher participation rates. If market volatility drives up the price of call options, lower participation will be the result. The strategies for determining crediting rates on equity-indexed universal life are generally applicable to all equity-indexed products on the market today. Currently, the participation rates (index factor) for the most popular equity-indexed universal life products on the market range from 36 percent to 80 percent.

THE EFFECT OF LINKING METHODS

Why is there such a wide variance from product to product and company to company? The answer lies in differing linking methods. If there were no differences in linking methods, you could legitimately assume the product with the highest participation rate would likewise have the highest interest-crediting rate potential. Unfortunately, this is one of the myths of equity-indexed universal life—nothing could be further from the truth! Different linking methods are used in different products. Linking methods may include: point-to-point linking, averaging, or six-month smoothing. The linking method affects the participation rate, but it is not an indicator of product performance potential, as you will see.

If you were to assume no individual life insurance company has a magic wand when it comes to its general account portfolio investment returns, then it is fair to assume that most large, highly rated, conservative carriers with a normal range of investment-grade assets earn approximately the same rate of return on their general account. (Differences may occur periodically from buying and selling assets or accounting methods.) In fact if any one company somehow had the know-how to outperform all the other carriers, its strategy could be duplicated by reviewing the company's filed "Financial Blue Book," which outlines a company's investment portfolio.

So, if the general account returns are generally similar, and the management spreads for profit are similar, and the guaranteed rates credited to cash values are similar, then why do participation rates vary so widely? The answer lies in the fact that call options vary widely in price. The higher the payout potential of a particular call option, the higher the cost. With a limited amount of excess interest available to purchase call options, the company that uses higher-priced call options will generally have a much lower participation rate than the company purchasing lower-priced call options.

Most financial services professionals would probably agree the appropriate client for an equity-indexed universal life is not particularly concerned about what happens in sluggish equity markets (bear years), since these products all contain minimum guaranteed interest rates. What is of interest to most people is the potential gain in an upward equity market (bull years). For the following examples, assume a person purchases a policy in January of any given year and the S&P 500 Index goes up 100 percent, reaching the highest point exactly one year later.

POINT-TO-POINT LINKING

Let's first look at the point-to-point linking method. One of the most popular point-to-point products on the market today has had a 36 percent participation rate. Point-to-point simply means the type of call options uses only two points to measure growth—the point at which the money is applied and the point reached exactly 365 days later. In this example, the growth is 100 percent, applied to the 36 percent of participation cash values, resulting in a 36 percent crediting rate to the policy owner. Or, a $10,000 starting account value, of which 36 percent is "participating" in 100 percent growth, results in a $3,600 credit to the cash values, or a 36 percent rate of return on the $10,000 account value. Thus, the point-to-point linking method with a 36 percent participation rate in this example would equal 36 percent credit to the client.

AVERAGING

An averaging product uses a different type of call option. This type uses the same starting point, but averages all of the closes of the S&P 500 Index on a daily or monthly basis (depending on the product), and uses that average to measure growth. In our example, the average close of the year would represent approximately 50 percent growth (**fig. 18.5**). Since averaging reduced the growth measurement from 100 percent to 50 percent, this type of call option is substantially less expensive, and the participation rate on an averaging product should be much higher than that of a point-to-point product.

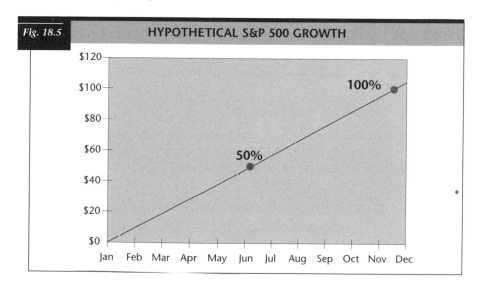

Fig. 18.5 HYPOTHETICAL S&P 500 GROWTH

A popular equity-indexed universal life product on the market that uses the averaging method advertises an 80 percent participation rate. Returning to our previous example, if 80 percent of the account value is participating in 50 percent S&P 500 growth as measured by the averaging method, the net crediting rate to the policy owner is 40 percent (80 percent multiplied by .50 equals 40 percent).

FINAL SIX-MONTH SMOOTHING

My policy with ING Southland Life uses a hybrid of the point-to-point and averaging methods, referred to as "final six-month smoothing." This simply means the type of call option purchased to support this product measures growth by comparing the starting point to the average daily close of the final six months of that premium year. In the same example, using a hybrid six-month smoothing method, that would represent approximately 75 percent growth. With an index factor (participation rate) of 60 percent, this results in 60 percent of the cash values receiving a credit of 75 percent growth (60 percent multiplied by .75 equals 45 percent). In other words, six-month smoothing with a 60 percent participation rate equals a 45 percent crediting rate in this example

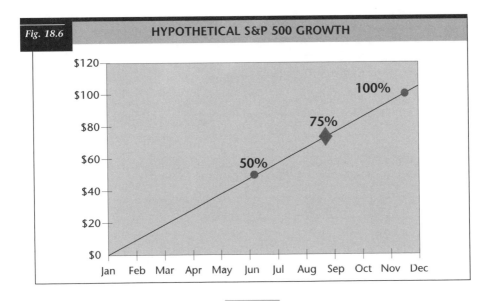

Fig. 18.6   **HYPOTHETICAL S&P 500 GROWTH**

(fig. 18.6). Remember, in these illustrations we have assumed a 100 percent S&P 500 Index growth for the sake of simplicity.

You can now see the participation rate is not a valid indicator of product performance. It should also be obvious that no one can predict which method will perform best in the future. To do so would require knowledge of what the S&P 500 Index will close at every single day for the life of the policy. That's impossible!

LINKING FREQUENCY

If I were to stop the analysis here, the only relevant conclusion would be that most, if not all, equity-indexed universal life products will perform similarly if held over the long term (to compensate for any short-term wins and losses based in a particular, unusual year). However, there is another factor that can make a difference—the linking frequency. There are two types of linking frequency available in equity-indexed universal life products currently on the market: monthly and annual linking. Let's take a look at how they affect policy performance.

In essence, monthly linking means there are twelve monthly buckets available in the equity-indexed universal life policy. If you pay a monthly premium in January, the cash values generated by that premium are linked to the S&P 500 Index in January, and the following January will realize any upside crediting potential. The February premium would land in the February bucket, and one year later would have upside crediting potential. March to March, April to April, and so on results in the same. If a person pays quarterly, he or she would be using four of the twelve buckets. Semi-annual payments would use two of the twelve buckets. But with monthly linking, no premiums, unscheduled deposits, or any other money applied to the policy from any source waits more than twelve months for upside potential.

In an annual link product, only the money in the policy on the annual link date has upside potential in twelve months, as there is only one bucket per policy. All subsequent premium payments sit in a fixed interest account at a discretionary rate declared by the company, until the next annual link date (up to eleven months), before they are linked, and must then wait twelve months for upside potential.

Because of monthly linking capability, a person paying monthly premiums on an equity-indexed product in 1997 could have been credited with all of the interest rates achieved ending a year later in 1998. As shown in **figure 18.7**, each rate applied to the corresponding monthly bucket.

Fig. 18.7	INDEXING POTENTIAL				

Actual Interest Crediting Rate: Using final six-month averaging, then current Index factors, 3% guaranteed interest rate, with an ending anniversary date of:

1/1/98	2/1/98	3/1/98	4/1/98	5/1/98	6/1/98
20.71%	15.26%	15.72%	22.39%	20.28%	17.26%

7/1/98	8/1/98	9/1/98	10/1/98	11/1/98	12/1/98
14.82%	12.04%	14.45%	11.14%	11.47%	8.81%

Past history is no guarantee of future performance.

The same person in an annual link product would have received a greater return on their January bucket, but the remaining eleven buckets would have received a fixed rate (4 percent to 6 percent) until the following annual link date, at which point they would finally be linked and have to wait an additional twelve months for an equity-related upside potential. For this reason, annual link product companies may try to convince you that people prefer to pay annually or should only pay annually. Many of these companies do not even provide monthly, quarterly, or semi-annual illustrations.

Now that you have a better understanding of how indexing works, let's see why it may perform best during a bull market and why it also competes best in a volatile market. Because of the sharp declines experienced after the unprecedented prosperity of the '90s, what was the mindset of the financial product consumer? Anxious investors had the dilemma of either staying in the market or locking in some profit. These investors asked themselves, "If I stay in the market and the market corrects, I lose; if I lock profits and the market goes higher, I miss out." Skeptical investors asked themselves, "Is this really the time to commit my funds to equities?"

TIMING THE MARKET

The general problem is that for most people, timing the market doesn't work, but investors continue to try! Historical results have shown that investor returns (the returns that individual investors in the market actually achieve by constantly trying to time when to buy and when to sell) do not equal investment returns (the returns achieved by buying and holding the same investment through the ups and downs)! The disparity between investment returns and investor returns sometimes has been dramatic. For example, during a six-year period ending December 31, 1994, an analysis of 199 growth funds showed an average of approximately 12 percent a year. In contrast, during the same six-year period, investor returns only averaged 2 percent a year according to *Morning Star.* Likewise, during the same basic period, bond investors also missed out. Out of 257 bond funds, the average over five years was 8 percent compared to investor returns of 1 percent!

Why was there such a dramatic difference? It was because the holding periods were too short. In other words, it is not so much which fund you own; it's how long you own it! According to *Dallbar Reports,* the average broker-sold equity fund is held only 3.1 years. The average direct-marketed equity fund is held only 2.9 years. People try to time the market and end up often buying and selling at the wrong times, instead of just buying and holding. For this reason, I usually advocate indexed products or even fixed products to minimize the impact of volatility and emotions.

HOW AN INDEXED INVESTMENT PERFORMS IN A VOLATILE MARKET

An equity-indexed insurance contract can help you stay in your emotional comfort zone without sacrificing the opportunity for competitive equity-linked performance. You can benefit from upside increases plus have downside protection without the need to "time the market."

Let's study a simple example of an index-linked approach versus a direct participation approach. If you were to have a direct participation investment portfolio that experienced an annual decline from $400,000 down to $300,000 (just as many actually did during the year 2001), you would have experienced a 25 percent loss. Then, let's say the market recovers and bounces back the next year, resulting in your portfolio regaining its previous value of $400,000. In order to regain its previous value of $400,000, the $300,000 portfolio that year had to experience a 33 percent gain! So, after a 25 percent loss, the portfolio requires a 33 percent gain to end up with a net gain of zero percent over the two-year period (**fig. 18.8**)! Many investors don't stop to comprehend this mathematical phenomenon! A 50 percent loss followed by a 50 percent gain results in a 25 percent overall loss! A 50 percent loss would have to be followed by 100 percent gain in order to break even with a net gain of 0 percent over a two-year period.

The beauty of an equity-indexed insurance contract that is linked to the S&P 500 Index is that a 3 percent interest rate is contractually guaranteed. So, using the same example, when the market dropped 25 percent the first year, the $400,000 portfolio would not have lost but would have gained the guaranteed rate of 3 percent! Then if the market rebounded with a 33 percent gain the next year, the equity-indexed universal life would gain approximately 20 percent, based on a 60 percent participation rate (**fig. 18.9**). Therefore, during the two-year example when a 25 percent loss year was followed by a 33 percent gain year, the direct participation product experienced a net gain of zero percent while the index-linked product experienced a gain of 23 percent!

Let's see how this plays out by comparing a variable insurance contract with an equity-indexed contract. As seen in **figure 18.10**, a variable insurance contract that started with $100,000 of cash values ended up breaking even after two years. On the other hand, the equity-indexed contract ended up increasing in value from $100,000 to $123,600. The next question in this two-year example might be, "How much and how fast does the variable insurance contract have to increase before it catches up with the equity-indexed insurance contract?"

Let's assume each policy begins with $100,000 account value. Next let's assume a 25 percent loss year is experienced, then the market (S&P 500) gains 16 percent each year thereafter. If we assume a 60 percent

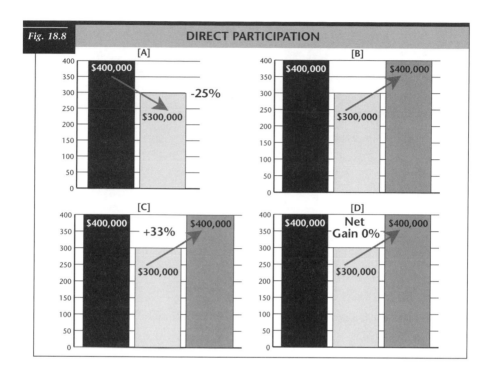

Fig. 18.8 — DIRECT PARTICIPATION

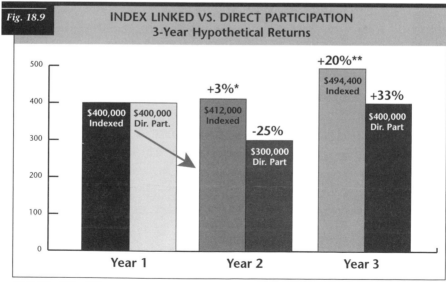

Fig. 18.9 — INDEX LINKED VS. DIRECT PARTICIPATION
3-Year Hypothetical Returns

** 33.3% x 60% = 20%
* 3% based on contractual guarantee

Fig. 18.10	INDEX-LINKED VS. DIRECT PARTICIPATION		
		VARIABLE	INDEXED
Beginning Cash Value		$100,000	$100,000
Year 1 Performance		-25%	3%*
Year 1 Ending Cash Value		$75,000	$103,000
Year 2 Performance		33.30%	20%**
Year 2 Ending Cash Value		$100,000	$123,600

* *Contractual guaranteed minimum percentage*
** *33.3% x 60% indexing factor = 20%*

participation rate for the indexed universal life, this would result in a net growth of 9.6 percent. It takes seven years for the variable universal life to catch up with the indexed universal life (**fig. 18.11**). Let's now assume that the market loses only 20 percent the first year and then gains 12 percent every year thereafter. As shown in **figure 18.12**, it still takes seven years for the variable universal life to catch up to the indexed universal life. It takes the same seven years for the variable universal life to catch up with the indexed universal life if only a 15 percent loss is experienced the first year, followed by 10 percent annual gains thereafter. If we have a repetitive cycle where a 25 percent loss is followed by seven consecutive years of 16 percent gains, again, after the second 25 percent loss was experienced in the seventh year, it takes until the fourteenth year before the variable universal life catches up (**fig. 18.13**).

Fig. 18.11	INDEX-LINKED VS. DIRECT PARTICIPATION	
	$100,000 Account Value Recovery after 25% Loss	
YEAR	DIRECT 16% NET GROWTH	INDEX-LINKED 9.6% NET GROWTH
1	$75,000	$103,000
2	$87,000	$112,888
3	$100,920	$123,725
4	$117,067	$135,603
5	$135,798	$148,621
6	$157,526	$162,888
7	$182,730	$178,526

Fig. 18.12

INDEX-LINKED VS. DIRECT PARTICIPATION

$100,000 Account Value Recovery after 20% Loss

YEAR	DIRECT 12% NET GROWTH	INDEX-LINKED 7.2 NET GROWTH
1	$80,000	$103,000
2	$89,600	$110,416
3	$100,352	$118,366
4	$112,394	$126,888
5	$125,882	$136,024
6	$140,987	$145,818
7	$157,906	$156,317

Fig. 18.13

INDEX-LINKED VS. DIRECT PARTICIPATION

Cyclical Account Value Recovery After 25% Loss

YEAR	DIRECT 16% NET GROWTH	INDEX-LINKED 9.6% NET GROWTH
1	$75,000	$103,000
2	$87,000	$112,888
3	$100,920	$123,725
4	$117,067	$135,603
5	$135,798	$148,621
6	$157,526	$162,888
7	$182,730	$178,526
	-25%	3%
8	$137,048	$183,884
9	$158,967	$201,537
10	$184,412	$220,884
11	$213,918	$242,089
12	$248,145	$265,330
13	$287,848	$290,802
14	$333,903	$318,718

Thus, the most important question to address is, "How many ten-year periods since 1925 has the stock market experienced no declines?" The answer is, only one (from 1991 to 2000), and even then, remember the nose dive it took and the subsequent slow recovery!

Remember, most people are not successful at timing the market. In early spring of 2000, the Dow Jones Industrial Stock Average hit 11,900 and the market experienced $50 billion in net inflows—people buying high. A little over two years later in the summer of 2002, the Dow bottomed out at 7,500 and the market experienced $50 billion in net outflows—people selling low.

Generally, during any given ten-year period, two to three years will likely experience a loss in the market versus the seven to eight years a gain is experienced. I believe that although an equity-indexed universal life can end up performing well during a bull market, it really competes best in a volatile market! If investors want to choose an investment that will likely generate not only the most net spendable income, but also the most stable income during a crucial time in life, an equity-indexed or fixed insurance contract should be a strong consideration.

18 EQUITY ENHANCEMENT STRATEGY NUMBER EIGHTEEN

- *Choose investments that provide/generate the most when you are likely to need the money and stability the most.*

CHAPTER 19

Increasing Your Net Spendable Retirement Income

Proper home equity management, coupled with your retirement planning, could significantly increase your net spendable retirement income.

COMMON MYTH-CONCEPTION

Home equity cannot safely be used to supplement retirement income.

REALITY

Through careful planning, home equity can be properly used and managed to increase net spendable retirement income by as much as 40 to 50 percent!

In this chapter I would like to marry two concepts I have presented in this book. I dedicated the first eleven chapters to helping you understand how to manage home equity in order to increase its liquidity, safety, rate of return, as well as the portability of that home equity. The remainder of the chapters have focused on concepts that help maximize return and minimize taxes. In this chapter I will take what was probably perceived as a negative in your budget prior to reading this book—a mortgage—and combine it with another perceived negative—the risk-management tool of life insurance—to create a huge positive that can dramatically enhance your net worth.

The common misconception among homeowners in America is that home equity cannot be safely used to supplement retirement income. As I will illustrate in this chapter, the reality is, through careful planning, home equity can be properly used and managed to increase net spendable retirement income by as much as 40 to 50 percent! As illustrated in the preceding chapters, an individual can develop a non-qualified private retirement planning strategy as a pension alternative by depositing money (making premium payments) into a properly structured investment-grade life insurance contract.

In review, an insurance contract can be established that enables money to accumulate tax free and also allows the money to be withdrawn or accessed tax free during the retirement years. The gain on those funds not only can avoid tax, but also can avoid tax on the transfer of the remaining funds on death to surviving heirs. So, a properly structured and maximum funded insurance contract can prove to be far more advantageous than a qualified retirement plan, such as an IRA or 401(k).

As shown in **figure 19.1**, a private retirement plan using an investment-grade insurance contract can provide tax-free accumulation, tax-free access, and tax-free transfer. This can outperform qualified plans, which may only give you tax advantages on the contribution and accumulation phases.

Fig. 19.1	FOUR PHASES OF RETIREMENT PLANNING			
	CONTRIBUTION	ACCUMULATION	WITHDRAWAL	TRANSFER
		IRA/401(k)		
	Tax Favored	Tax Favored	Taxed	Taxed
		Non-Qualified Alternative		
	After Tax	Tax Favored	Tax Favored	Tax Favored
		Home Equity Retirement Plan		
	Tax Favored	Tax Favored	Tax Favored	Tax Favored

HAVE YOUR CAKE AND EAT IT, TOO

Now, if you are like I am and want to have your cake and eat it too, then you prefer having a tax-favored umbrella on the contribution phase, but never at the expense of giving up the tax-free access during your harvest years. There is a way to indirectly achieve tax-favored benefits during the contribution phase on a retirement plan without giving up the tax-free accessibility and transferability later. This is called a home equity retirement plan.

For the sake of simplicity, let's first use an example of a thirty-year-old couple. In this example let's say between the husband and wife's contributions, this couple is contributing $6,000 a year to qualified plans. Their goal is to conservatively set aside $6,000 a year for thirty-five years, hoping to earn an average of 7.5 percent tax-deferred interest, which would allow their fund to grow to nearly $1 million ($994,922.86) thirty-five years down the road. This would allow them to then withdraw interest only in the amount of $74,619 per year at 7.5 percent, which equals approximately $6,200 per month. In other words, their goal is to set aside $6,000 *a year* for thirty-five years at 7.5 percent to accumulate about $1 million, which would generate $6,000 *a month* at 7.5 percent from age 65 on through the rest of their lives (**fig. 19.2**).

| Fig. 19.2 | WHY DIDN'T SOMEONE TELL ME "THE REST OF THE STORY"? |

Annual IRA/401(k) Contribution = $6,000 X 35 Years = $210,000 Total Contributions
Tax Bracket = 34%
Tax Savings = $6,000 X 34% = $2,040 X 35 Years = $71,400 Total Tax Savings

$6,000 Per Year at 7.5% for 35 Years = $994,923

$994,923	
X 7.5%	
$74,619	
X 34%	Tax Bracket
$25,370	**Annual Tax**
$74,619	Interest Income
- 25,370	Annual Tax
$49,249	**Net Income**

Remember, though, this couple is going to have to reckon with the IRS during the withdrawal and transfer phases of their retirement plan as explained in chapters 15 and 16. If they are fortunate enough to still be in only a 34 percent tax bracket by the time they reach age 65, the $74,619 of annual income would have an annual tax liability of $25,370, resulting in a net spendable income of just under $50,000. Also, they will need to begin withdrawals based on a minimum distribution formula beginning at age 70$1/2$ to avoid a 50 percent penalty on what they should have withdrawn if they don't.

Now let's assume this couple has a home valued at $200,000 with a mortgage balance owing of $80,000. The remaining $120,000 represents the equity in their property. Most mortgage lenders will loan at least 80 percent of the value of the home on a first mortgage basis with cash coming out to the homeowner. An 80 percent loan-to-value ratio would be $160,000. They could refinance their home or use a second-mortgage equity line of credit to obtain the remaining $80,000 of borrowable equity. If they refinance with a first mortgage in the amount of $160,000, they will be able to pay off the $80,000 existing mortgage and end up with an additional $80,000 of excess cash or equity separated from the property.

Remember the primary reasons for refinancing or taking a second mortgage are to increase liquidity, to increase safety, and to increase the rate of return on a home's equity. For the sake of simplicity, let's say the couple obtains the additional $80,000 of equity with an interest-only loan at 7.5 percent interest. If so, their annual interest expense would be $6,000.

If they took out an amortized loan, the additional $80,000 of equity on a thirty-year loan amortization would result in monthly payments of $559.37 at 7.5 percent interest. Twelve monthly payments of $559.37 would equal $6,712.44 per year, so about $60 per month would be allocated to the reduction of principal at the outset.

This couple would likely set aside a percent of their income for retirement objectives, which should increase each year over the thirty-five years. Also, most couples catch the vision of equity management and refinance their home every two to five years as it appreciates and more dormant equity can be separated and put to work. To avoid complexity in this illustration, let's just assume they were going to set aside no more than $6,000 a year, all the way to age 65. Let's also keep the original loan as an interest-only loan of $80,000 at 7.5 percent for the entire thirty-five years.

If this couple were incurring $6,000 of annual interest expense on an $80,000 loan, this would be equivalent to the amount they were paying in annual IRA or 401(k) contributions. A $6,000 interest expense deduction on an itemized tax return has the same impact as a $6,000 qualified plan contribution. They are simply reflected in different sections of the return. If this couple has an income of $60,000 with $6,000 of IRA/401(k) contributions, their taxable income is reduced to $54,000. In a 34 percent tax bracket they effectively save 34 percent on the $6,000 they didn't have to report as income. That is approximately $2,000 in taxes.

If you have a $6,000 interest deduction because of a mortgage, you will receive the same benefit on your taxes. Your income of $60,000 will be reduced to a taxable income of $54,000 by virtue of having the $6,000 deduction on Schedule A of your tax return. You in essence save $2,000 in taxes, and the mortgage really only costs you $4,000. A mortgage interest expense of $6,000 has the same effect on this couple's taxes as a $6,000 IRA or 401(k) retirement plan contribution. However, instead of a $6,000 contribution, what they did was take $80,000 of dormant equity from their home and used it to prefund a retirement account in one fell swoop, via a lump sum contribution of $80,000. Remember, depending on the investment vehicles used, this $80,000 may need to be spread out over a four- to five-year period to comply with laws that allow for tax-free accumulation and tax-free access to those funds, as well as tax deductibility of the mortgage interest (chapter 17). However, $80,000 at the same interest rate we borrowed at, which was 7.5 percent, will grow to $1,005,510 in thirty-five years to their retirement age of 65. Assuming you achieve an average internal rate of return of 7.5 percent through the use of an investment grade life insurance contract, what advantages do you have over an IRA or 401(k)? Based on the tax laws explained in chapter 17, you would be able to tap into these funds, if needed, at any time before age 59$^{1}/_{2}$ with no income tax penalty. You would also be able to leave the funds in the policy as long as you wanted to and not be forced to begin withdrawals at age 70$^{1}/_{2}$. There are no restrictions regarding the contribution percentage of your income you can put into the plan because it is a non-qualified retirement account. More important than any of these features is the ability to access income or cash flow on the back end during the harvest years of your retirement account—without incurring any taxes on those distributions. Money can be withdrawn tax free under Sections 72e and 7702 of the Internal Revenue Code, provided that all tax code and insurance company guidelines are met.

If you had a $1,005,510 retirement fund and then began to make the equivalent of interest-only withdrawals at 7.5 percent in the amount of $75,413 per year, you would be able to use the entire $75,413 for spending and consumption during your retirement if you wanted. It would not be reportable anywhere on your federal tax return as earned income, passive income, or portfolio income. Therefore, it would not be subject to any type of tax under current tax law—$75,413 is 50 percent greater than the $50,000 of net after-tax income the couple in this example would have realized on their IRA/401(k) account! The $75,413 of tax-free income would be the same as receiving $114,262 of gross taxable income and then having it be reduced by 34 percent due to taxes. And since the

$75,413 annual income is not deemed earned, passive, or portfolio income under current tax law, it would not affect or disqualify you from your fair share of Social Security or Medicare benefits and wouldn't affect the taxability of Social Security income. You would not only have increased spendable income by nature of your retirement planning vehicle, but you may also have an indirect benefit of possibly enhanced Social Security and Medicare benefits!

Now remember, most couples would have probably increased their annual retirement plan contributions as their income increased over a thirty-five-year period. They also would have likely refinanced their home or moved several times during this thirty-five-year period. At the retirement age of 65, they would likely downsize their home and the $80,000 interest-only mortgage used in this example could be paid off from the increased appreciation they would have realized in their home upon its sale. These factors would dramatically enhance their retirement planning outcome, but for simplicity, in this example I made the assumption all they ever did was separate $80,000 of equity from their home, one time, to prefund their retirement in a lump sum at age 30.

Assume this couple didn't downsize, and instead decided to continue residing in the same home. If so, they could withdraw $80,000 from their $1,005,510 to pay off the mortgage. Of course, if it were me, I would choose to continue to enjoy the tax deductibility of $6,000-per-year interest payments because the net cost in a 34 percent tax bracket would still be only about $4,000. Also, assuming I were still earning 7.5 percent interest on the $80,000, my annual earnings would be $6,000, resulting in a $2,000 annual profit. So if I deduct the true net cost of my annual interest expense in the amount of $4,000 from my annual retirement income of $75,413, I still net $71,413 in tax-free income, versus $50,000 if I had used an IRA or 401(k).

THE CHOICE IS SIMPLE

When presented with two options—$71,413 of tax-free income per year or $50,000 of net after-tax income per year—the choice is simple.

There is no question the majority of retirees would prefer to enjoy maximum retirement income using an investment vehicle that would also transfer the greatest amount to surviving heirs should death occur before the retirement asset is used up. Probably the most powerful comparison is to think that a taxable IRA/401(k) annual distribution would require a $108,202-per-year distribution to net, after tax, a $71,413 spendable income in a 34 percent tax bracket. An IRA/401(k) with an account value of $994,922 at age 65, earning an interest rate of 7.5 percent, would run totally dry within seventeen years, based on annual withdrawals of $108,202! In other words, if either spouse of this couple lived beyond age 82, he or she could be totally out of money if he or she had been trying to live on a net spendable income of $71,413 a year! On the other hand, if he or she had used the home equity retirement plan, at age 82, they could still have their $1,005,510 generating interest-only income in the amount of $71,413 into perpetuity!

So, in this example, the home equity retirement plan didn't provide just a 45 to 50 percent greater retirement income—it provided the income for as long as they lived, and still passed down the balance to their heirs tax free! Thus, at age 82, the home equity retirement plan would be $1 million better than an IRA/401(k)! If they lived to be ninety-two-years old, the home equity retirement plan would have generated the equivalent of $108,202 of annual income for ten more years without depleting the $1 million of corpus. So at age 92, the home equity retirement plan would be effectively $2 million better than the IRA/401(k)!

This superior retirement plan was accomplished by separating $80,000 of home equity at 7.5 percent and putting it to work at the same 7.5 percent rate. Can you imagine how this example could be enhanced if they had borrowed at 7 percent and then put the equity to work at 8 or 8.5 percent compounded over thirty-five years to age 65, and then during twenty to thirty more years of retirement? **Figure 19.3** shows what an 8 percent internal rate of return would generate from a one-time $80,000 investment.

By comparing the interest earned in each five-year period through the thirty-fifth year, we can see the extra half of a percent interest

Fig. 19.3	$80,000 GROWING AT VARIOUS INTEREST RATES OVER 35 YEARS			
End of Year	6.50% Compounding	7.50% Compounding	8.00% Compounding	8.50% Compounding
1	$85,200	$86,000	$86,400	$86,800
5	$109,607	$114,850	$117,546	$120,293
10	$150,171	$164,883	$172,714	$180,879
15	$205,747	$236,710	$253,774	$271,979
20	$281,892	$339,828	$372,877	$408,964
25	$386,216	$487,867	$547,878	$614,941
30	$529,149	$700,396	$805,013	$924,660
35	$724,980	$1,005,510	$1,182,828	$1,390,371

dramatically affects the outcome. At age 65 (year 35), the $80,000 would have grown to $1,182,828. If the couple continued to pay interest-only payments on the $80,000 loan at 7.5 percent after age 65, we would need to deduct $4,000 from 8 percent annual interest earnings on $1,182,828. This would result in a net income of approximately $90,626 per year, which is $19,213 greater annual retirement income by virtue of half-a-percent more interest. If they were able to earn an internal rate of return of 8.5 percent on the $80,000 of separated equity, it would grow to $1,390,371 by age 65. At 8.5 percent this would generate an interest-only income of $118,182. That would net $114,182 after servicing the annual interest on the $80,000 of separated equity. So by having a 1 percent differential between the gross borrowing rate of 7.5 percent and the net earning rate of 8.5 percent, this couple could end up with $114,182 of tax-free income!

In this example, if the couple only earned 6.5 percent interest on the $80,000 of separated equity, it would only grow to $724,980 by age 65, which would generate $47,000 of tax-free income. In that case, their net spendable difference would be about the same as the IRA and 401(k) earning 7.5 percent. Therefore, it would behoove this couple to employ their equity to earn at least greater than 1 percent less than the borrowing interest rate. But remember, it doesn't matter whether interest rates are in the 6 to 8 percent range, the 8 to 10 percent range or the 10 to 12 percent range. They are relative, and these arbitrage principles work the same. When borrowing rates are high, earning rates are also high. When borrowing rates are low, earning rates will also be low. That's okay. The concept of arbitrage works on just a 1 to 2 percent net differential between the net borrowing rate and the net earning rate.

WORKING WITH VERY LITTLE HOME EQUITY

It is important a person currently with little home equity not be intimidated by the example shown here. This same concept works whether you have a small amount of equity in your home or a large amount of equity in your home. Even if you have been paying only an extra $100 a month against the principal, the concepts and advantages still apply. If you redirect the $100 per month you may be sending to the mortgage banker, you can begin a retirement planning strategy that will give you tax deductions on the front end by using dormant equity—or money that would have been creating equity—and having it accumulate funds that will be sufficient to pay off your mortgage and enhance your retirement.

Again, the concept, is not to kill your partner, Uncle Sam, in helping you prepare for your retirement. Maximize all possible deductions on the front end by using idle dollars in your home to obtain deductibility indirectly on the contribution phase of your retirement plan—without giving up tax-free access to the funds during the withdrawal/distribution and transfer phases. This is a way for you to have your cake and eat it, too. So whether you already have a tremendous amount of equity in your home or simply are trying to develop equity by paying extra principal payments, a simple reallocation of your assets without increasing your outlay can make a significant difference. In just a few short years, you can dramatically enhance your net worth. Remember the indirect tax deductions you can receive may enhance the nest egg accumulating and maximize the net spendable income available down the road.

Hopefully, by now you can understand this strategy can be used for the accumulation of funds for retirement purposes, as well as any type of long-term goal where funds need to be accumulated and accessed possibly before the age of 59¹/₂,—without incurring any tax penalty. This positive lever can be a powerful tool, much like Archimedes' perception of the stick of wood. With this perspective, homeowners can experience the full potential growth and financial security of using home equity as a vehicle to increase liquidity, safety, and rate of return. As seen, home equity can also be used to increase net spendable retirement income by as much as 50 percent.

THE SMARTS—APPLYING THE CONCEPTS AND STRATEGIES

Let's now study another example of a husband and wife who want to implement these concepts and strategies. Let's assume they are both age 45. Their combined gross income is $100,000 annually, putting them in a 34 percent marginal federal and state combined tax bracket (**fig. 19.4**). Let's assume their home, purchased ten years earlier for $185,000, has appreciated at an average of 5 percent per year, bringing it to a current market value of $300,000. Let's also assume they paid about $50,000 down when they purchased it with equity from the sale of a previous home, and financed the balance on a thirty-year mortgage at 7 percent interest. Let's also assume after ten years their mortgage balance is $110,000 because they made extra principal payments, at times totaling $5,000 to $6,000, during the ten years of their mortgage. Their monthly mortgage payment is still $904.81 per month, based on the original $136,000 loan balance on a thirty-year amortization. Let's refer to this couple as Jim and Mary Smart.

Let's look at the Smarts' annual cash-flow allocation. The first category is their planned savings for their children—perhaps for college education, perhaps to help them with a down payment on a first home. The Smarts have allocated $150 per month for their two children, for a total of $1,800 per year, for future needs. Also, let's assume they are contributing $15,000 per year into their qualified plans. These qualified plans could consist primarily of 401(k) plans offered through an employer. Let's assume that Jim and Mary are matched on the first 6 percent of their

Fig. 19.4

PERSONAL FINANCIAL PROFILE
Prepared for: Jim and Mary Smart

Date of Birth: 01/02/1957   Age: 45   Sex: Male   Current Marginal Tax Bracket: 34%

Property Details
Fair Market Value of Property	$300,000.00
Original Purchase Price	$185,000.00
Verifiable Cost of Property Improvements	$0.00

Current Mortgage Details
Beginning Date:	04/01/1992
Term:	30 Years
Amount Financed:	$136,000.00
Interest Rate:	7.00%
Monthly Payment:	$904.81
Outstanding Balance:	$110,000.00

Annual Cash Flow Allocation
Planned Savings:	$1,800.00
Planned IRA/401(k) Contribution:	$9,000.00
Planned Premium on $500,000 of Life Insurance:	$800.00

Other Current Liabilities

	BALANCE	MONTHLY PAYMENTS	PAYMENTS REMAINING	INTEREST RATE
Credit Card	$ 3,350.00	$150.00	28	18.0%
Credit Card	$ 4,525.00	$150.00	41	18.0%
Auto Loan	$12,125.00	$565.00	24	8.0%
Home Equity Loan	$25,000.00	$500.00	62	8.0%
TOTAL	**$45,000.00**	**$1,365.00**		

Current Allocation of Liquid Assets
CDs	$20,000.00
Mutual Fund	$30,000.00

OBJECTIVES:
1. Successfully manage equity in their home to increase its liquidity, safety, and rate of return.
2. Utilize available tax strategies to their advantage.
3. Prepare financially for a comfortable retirement.
4. Increase overall yield on their savings and investments.
5. Complete proper estate planning utilizing trusts and wills.

contribution. Therefore, with their $100,000 combined gross income, they choose to contribute $6,000 to their 401(k)s to obtain 50 percent matching by their employers. However, they would like to reallocate the overage contribution they have been making into their qualified plan in the amount of $9,000 per year.

Jim and Mary Smart are also paying an annual premium of $800 for $500,000 of twenty-year term life insurance. Besides the first mortgage on their home, other current liabilities include two credit card balances, an automobile loan, and an equity line of credit they just took out in order to remodel their home. One credit card has a balance of $3,350 with a monthly payment of $150. The second credit card has a $4,525 balance, also with a monthly payment of $150. They also have an automobile loan with a balance owing of $12,125, which has a monthly payment of $565, with twenty-four payments remaining at 8 percent interest. Their $25,000 home equity line of credit seemed attractive because they could pay off this loan over a five-year period with payments of $500 per month at 8 percent interest; it did not cost them any fees in closing costs; and the interest is deductible on their taxes. The equity line of credit could be referred to as preferred debt because of its deductibility, but the credit cards and automobile loan would be referred to as non-preferred (i.e., non-deductible) debt. Also, please note that the Smarts have $20,000 on deposit in CDs currently earning 5 percent taxable interest. They also have $30,000 accumulated in mutual funds that have experienced volatile growth but which they hope will conservatively achieve an 8 percent compounded interest equivalent return.

The Smarts' objectives are to:
1) Successfully manage equity in their home to increase its liquidity, safety, and rate of return
2) Use available tax strategies to their advantage
3) Prepare financially for a comfortable retirement
4) Increase the overall yield on their savings and investments
5) Complete proper estate planning using trusts and wills

Please refer to **figure 19.5** showing the plan summary and proposed asset allocation. Assuming a fair market value of their home in the amount of $300,000 the Smarts could take out a new 80 percent loan-to-value cash-out refinance mortgage in the amount of $240,000. With the $240,000 loan proceeds, they would pay off the current mortgage balance in the amount of $110,000. They would also pay off the equity line of credit in the amount of $25,000. Other liabilities could also be paid off including the two credit card balances and the automobile loan, which together total $20,000. Let's also assume the closing costs incurred for

Fig. 19.5	**PLAN SUMMARY** Prepared for: Jim and Mary Smart April 21, 2002	

PROPOSED ASSET ALLOCATION

Fair Market Value of Property:		$300,000.00
Amount of Proposed Mortgage:		$240,000.00
LESS:		
Current Mortgage Payoffs	$110,000.00	
Other Liabilities	$45,000.00	
Closing Costs	$5,000.00	
Balance of Mortgage Proceeds:		$80,000.00
PLUS:		
Repositioned Assets		
Annual Amounts:		
Excess Annual IRA/401(k) Contribution	$9,000.00	
Annual Insurance Premium ($500,000 Face)	$800.00	
Planned Annual Savings	$1,800.00	
Lump Sum Amounts:		
CDs	$20,000.00	
Mutual Fund	$30,000.00	
TOTAL	$61,600.00	$61,600.00
Liquid Assets Available:		$141,600.00

refinancing a $240,000 mortgage would be approximately $5,000. After deducting the first mortgage payoff, the equity line of credit, the other liabilities, and closing costs, they have a balance of $80,000 of net equity that can be transferred.

It is also recommended the Smarts reallocate the $9,000 per year of unmatched overage contribution they have been making into their 401(k). In addition, we can use the $800 per year they are spending toward term life insurance if they use an investment grade life insurance contract for the reallocation of their funds. Also, it would behoove the Smarts to reallocate the $1,800 per year they are saving for long-term goals for their children. Let's also assume the Smarts would like to reposition the $20,000 in CDs when they mature one year from the plan implementation, and that they would like to reposition the mutual fund balance during the second year—if the market timing is prudent—to earn a more stable, tax-advantaged return.

Let's now study their current mortgage versus the proposed mortgage to see how the Smarts can afford the newer house payment and also be able to set aside $9,000 per year in a non-qualified retirement plan because of the same tax benefits they would have been receiving if they continued to deposit that money into their 401(k)s. Please refer to **figure 19.6** showing the Smarts' current first mortgage analysis illustration.

Figure 19.6 shows a thirty-year mortgage that began ten years earlier in the amount of $136,000 at 7 percent interest. The principal and

Fig. 19.6		CURRENT MORTGAGE ANALYSIS				
	Principal $136,000			*Rate* 7.00%		
	Balance $110,000			*Type* Amortized		
	Payment $904.81			*Years* 30		
END OF YEAR	[1] LOAN BALANCE	[2] PRINCIPAL PAYMENT	[3] INTEREST PAYMENT	[4] TOTAL PAYMENT	[5] TAX SAVINGS	[6] NET PAYMENT AFTER TAX
1	$106,739	$3,261	**$7,597**	**$10,858**	**$2,583**	**$8,275**
2	103,242	3,497	7,361	10,858	2,503	8,355
3	99,493	3,750	7,108	10,858	2,417	8,441
4	95,472	4,021	6,837	10,858	2,325	8,533
5	91,161	4,311	6,546	10,858	2,226	8,632
6	86,538	4,623	6,235	10,858	2,120	8,738
7	81,581	4,957	5,901	10,858	2,006	8,852
8	76,265	5,315	5,542	10,858	1,884	8,973
9	70,566	5,700	5,158	10,858	1,754	9,104
10	64,454	6,112	4,746	10,858	1,614	9,244
11	57,900	6,554	4,304	10,858	1,463	9,394
12	50,873	7,027	3,830	10,858	1,302	9,555
13	43,338	7,535	3,322	10,858	1,130	9,728
14	35,258	8,080	2,778	10,858	944	9,913
15	26,593	8,664	2,194	10,858	746	10,112
16	17,303	9,290	1,567	10,858	533	10,325
17	7,341	9,962	896	10,858	305	10,553
18	0	7,341	228	7,569	78	7,491
19	0	0	0	0	0	0
20	0	0	0	0	0	0
TOTAL		$110,000	$82,150	$192,150	$27,931	$164,219

Notes:
a. *Tax Savings [5] assumes a state and federal marginal tax bracket of 34.00% multiplied by the Interest Payment [3].*
b. *Mortgage interest is generally tax deductible; however, certain limitations are applicable. Please review with your tax advisor.*
c. *Net Payment After Tax [6] equals Total Payment [4] less Tax Savings [5].*

interest payment is $904.81 per month; however, because the Smarts have made $5,000 to $6,000 of extra principal payments during the first ten years of their mortgage, the current balance owing is $110,000. As you can see, during the next year the interest payment would be $7,597, as shown in column number 3, out of the total annual mortgage payment of $10,858 shown in column number 4. In a 34 percent tax bracket, they would be realizing tax savings in the amount of $2,583 that year (34 percent of the $7,597 of interest paid that year). This would result in a net after-tax, annual house payment of $8,275 as shown in column 6. If you were to divide $8,275 by twelve months, this would tell us the monthly out-of-pocket payment is approximately $690 per month.

Now let's study **figure 19.7**, which shows the proposed mortgage analysis for Jim and Mary Smart. This shows a refinance in the amount $240,000, which is 80 percent loan-to-value based on a $300,000 fair market of their home. At the same 7 percent interest rate, their monthly principal and interest payment would be $1,596.73 per month. At first this may seem alarming. We are proposing that Jim and Mary Smart increase their house payment by $692 per month! However, please remember that the Smarts do not personally have to end up paying the entire $1,596.73 per month with the help they will get from Uncle Sam.

Notice that twelve months of $1,596.73 payments equals a total annual house payment of $19,161 as shown in column number 4. Of that $19,161, the first-year interest portion equals $16,723 as shown in column 3. Therefore, the Smarts would be able to deduct the $16,723 of interest off Schedule A of their tax return the next year, rather than deduct the $7,597 of interest expense from their previous mortgage. They would be allowed to deduct the entire amount of interest because they borrowed a total of $130,000 over and above their acquisition indebtedness, which was reduced down to $110,000. However, because they incurred $5,000 in closing costs, which are deductible, and spent $25,000 in home improvements, these expenses added to the basis of their home.

The remaining $100,000 of separated equity that was used to pay off the credit card balances and an automobile loan, leaving $80,000 to invest, qualifies for deductible interest. Therefore, the entire $16,723 in

Fig. 19.7

PROPOSED MORTGAGE ANALYSIS

Principal	$240,000		*Rate*	7.00%	
Balance	$240,000		*Type*	Amortized	
Payment	$1,596.73		*Years*	30	

END OF YEAR	[1] LOAN BALANCE	[2] PRINCIPAL PAYMENT	[3] INTEREST PAYMENT	[4] TOTAL PAYMENT	[5] TAX SAVINGS	[6] NET PAYMENT AFTER TAX
1	$237,562	**$2,438**	**$16,723**	**$19,161**	**$5,686**	**$13,475**
2	234,948	2,614	16,547	19,161	5,626	13,535
3	232,145	2,803	16,358	19,161	5,562	13,599
4	229,139	3,006	16,155	19,161	5,493	13,668
5	225,916	3,223	15,938	19,161	5,419	13,742
6	222,459	3,456	15,705	19,161	5,340	13,821
7	218,753	3,706	15,455	19,161	5,255	13,906
8	214,779	3,974	15,187	19,161	5,164	13,997
9	210,518	4,261	14,900	19,161	5,066	14,095
10	205,949	4,569	14,592	19,161	4,961	14,200
11	201,049	4,900	14,261	19,161	4,849	14,312
12	195,796	5,254	13,907	19,161	4,728	14,432
13	190,162	5,634	13,527	19,161	4,599	14,562
14	184,121	6,041	13,120	19,161	4,461	14,700
15	177,644	6,477	12,683	19,161	4,312	14,848
16	170,698	6,946	12,215	19,161	4,153	15,008
17	163,250	7,448	11,713	19,161	3,982	15,178
18	155,264	7,986	11,175	19,161	3,799	15,361
19	146,701	8,564	10,597	19,161	3,603	15,558
20	137,518	9,183	9,978	19,161	3,393	15,768
21	127,672	9,846	9,314	19,161	3,167	15,994
22	117,113	10,558	8,603	19,161	2,925	16,236
23	105,792	11,321	7,839	19,161	2,665	16,495
24	93,652	12,140	7,021	19,161	2,387	16,774
25	80,635	13,018	6,143	19,161	2,089	17,072
26	66,676	13,959	5,202	19,161	1,769	17,392
27	51,708	14,968	4,193	19,161	1,426	17,735
28	35,659	16,050	3,111	19,161	1058	18,103
29	18,449	17,210	1,951	19,161	663	18,497
30	0	18,449	707	19,156	240	18,915
TOTAL		**$240,000**	**$334,818**	**$574,818**	**$113,838**	**$460,980**

Notes:

a. *Tax Savings [5] assumes a state and federal marginal tax bracket of 34.00% multiplied by the Interest Payment [3].*

b. *Mortgage interest is generally tax deductible; however, certain limitations are applicable. Please review with your tax advisor.*

c. *Net Payment After Tax [6] equals Total Payment [4] less Tax Savings [5].*

the first year is deductible on their tax return. That amount is $9,126 more dollars of deductions than they would have had if they had kept their previous mortgage. This means the $9,126 of interest deduction would offset the $9,000 of reallocated 401(k) contribution that is now going to be deposited with after-tax dollars. Since the $9,000 of 401(k) reallocation is being put into a non-qualified retirement account, it must be regarded as an after-tax contribution. With the increased mortgage interest offset, the Smarts are receiving the same effective tax treatment they previously had with a 401(k) contribution.

Another way to look at the situation is to realize with $16,723 of interest deduction in a 34 percent tax bracket, the Smarts would realize a tax savings of $5,686, versus the $2,583 they would have experienced keeping their current mortgage. If the $5,686 of tax savings is deducted from the total new annual house payment of $19,161 shown in column 4, this results in a new net payment after tax of $13,475, as shown in column 6. If we divide $13,475 by 12, we arrive at a net after-tax monthly payment of $1,122.92. If we subtract the net after-tax current mortgage payment of $689.58 from the proposed mortgage net after-tax payment of $1,122.92, we arrive at a net increase in house payment of $433.34.

The fact of the matter is the Smarts would be freeing up two monthly credit card payments in the amount of $150 each, totaling $300. They would also be freeing up a $565 monthly automobile payment. And they would be freeing up a $500 monthly equity line of credit for their home improvements. The total of those liabilities equals $1,365 per month. On the surface, therefore, we have exchanged $1,365 in monthly payments for an increased house payment of $692. This leaves net positive monthly savings of $673 per month that can be allocated toward short-term goals such as the purchase of their next automobile. In just three short years the Smarts could have over $30,000 accumulated to pay cash for their next automobile rather than finance it.

Besides freeing up monthly cash flow that can be allocated for savings, where interest is working for you (rather than debt, where interest is working against you), the deductible interest portion of the proposed mortgage is the most significant factor of this retirement plan.

Remember the Smarts will be able to offset the $9,000 of non-qualified retirement plan, after-tax contribution, which in effect gives them the same tax benefit as a pre-tax contribution into a qualified plan.

Let's now study where these assets are reallocated to maximize the growth and net spendable income potential. Let's assume Jim and Mary Smart select an equity-indexed universal life insurance contract in which to reposition these assets. As explained in chapter 17, we need to calculate the size of the bucket. Therefore, we need to add up the sum total of all of the assets that will be reallocated and repositioned during the first eleven years (**figs. 19.8** and **19.9**).

Fig. 19.8	DETERMINING THE SIZE OF THE BUCKET		
Cash-out Refinance		source 1:	$80,000
Net Proceeds			
Fair Market Value	$300,000		
Loan Amount	$240,000		
Mortgage Payoff	$110,000		
Other Liabilities	$ 45,000		
Closing Costs	$ 5,000		
Net Proceeds	**$80,000**		
Repositioning Annual Savings		source 2:	$19,800
for the children ($150 p/m for 11 years)			
Repositioning IRA/401(k)		source 3:	$99,000
contribution at $9,000 per year for 11 years			
Repositioning Annual Insurance		source 4:	$8,800
Premium for $500,000 Death Benefit			
Repositioning CDs		source 5:	$20,000
Repositioning Mutual Fund		source 6:	$30,000
Net Proceeds from sale of		source 7:	$74,000
Home in the 6th year			
Net Proceeds			
Sale Price	$383,000		
Mortgage Payoff	$226,000		
20% Down Payment on New Home	$76,600		
Closing Costs	$6,400		
Net Proceeds	**$74,000**		
TOTAL			**$331,600.00**

Fig. 19.9	A TAX-ADVANTAGED LIFE INSURANCE AND RETIREMENT FUND
	Illustration of Values of An Indexed Universal Life Policy

[1] AGE	[2] YEAR	[3] NET PAYMENT	[4] ACCUMULATION VALUE	[5] SURRENDER VALUE	[6] NET DEATH BENEFIT
46	1	$82,600	$ 82,023	$ 65,944	$1,607,861
47	2	70,600	157,971	125,814	1,607,861
48	3	11,600	177,566	145,409	1,607,861
49	4	11,600	198,747	166,590	1,607,861
50	5	11,600	221,642	189,485	1,607,861
51	6	85,600	324,778	294,228	1,607,861
52	7	11,600	357,871	328,929	1,607,861
53	8	11,600	393,642	366,308	1,607,861
54	9	11,600	432,308	406,582	1,607,861
55	10	11,600	474,102	451,592	1,607,861
56	11	11,600	519,818	500,523	1,607,861
57	12	11,600	568,766	552,687	1,607,861
58	13	11,600	621,133	608,271	1,607,861
59	14	11,600	677,231	667,584	1,607,861
60	15	11,600	737,404	730,973	1,607,861
61	16	11,600	802,219	799,003	1,607,861
62	17	11,600	871,840	871,840	1,607,861
63	18	11,600	946,707	946,707	1,607,861
64	19	11,600	1,027,307	1,027,307	1,607,861
65	20	11,600	1,114,212	1,114,212	1,607,861
66	21	0	1,195,710	1,195,710	1,607,861
67	22	0	1,284,162	1,284,162	1,607,861
68	23	0	1,380,070	1,380,070	1,628,482
69	24	0	1,483,938	1,483,938	1,736,207
70	25	0	1,595,493	1,595,493	1,850,772
71	26	0	1,715,304	1,715,304	1,972,599
72	27	0	1,844,302	1,844,302	2,084,061
73	28	0	1,983,295	1,983,295	2,201,458
74	29	0	2,133,200	2,133,200	2,325,188
75	30	0	2,295,043	2,295,043	2,455,696
76	31	0	2,470,051	2,470,051	2,593,554
77	32	0	2,658,101	2,658,101	2,791,006
78	33	0	2,860,102	2,860,102	3,003,107
79	34	0	3,077,026	3,077,026	3,230,877
80	35	0	3,309,893	3,309,893	3,475,387
81	36	0	3,559,750	3,559,750	3,737,737
82	37	0	3,827,726	3,827,726	4,019,113
83	38	0	4,115,018	4,115,018	4,320,769
84	39	0	4,422,879	4,422,879	4,644,023
85	40	0	4,753,308	4,753,308	4,990,973
86	41	0	5,107,956	5,107,956	5,363,354
87	42	0	5,487,459	5,487,459	5,761,831
88	43	0	5,893,254	5,893,254	6,187,917
89	44	0	6,326,838	6,326,838	6,643,180
90	45	0	6,791,460	6,791,460	7,131,033
91	46	0	7,289,477	7,289,477	7,653,950
92	47	0	7,828,087	7,828,087	8,141,210
93	48	0	8,412,107	8,412,107	8,664,470
94	49	0	9,047,140	9,047,140	9,228,083
95	50	0	9,739,774	9,739,774	9,837,172
96	51	0	10,494,546	10,494,546	10,494,546
97	52	0	11,307,809	11,307,809	11,307,809
98	53	0	12,184,101	12,184,101	12,184,101
99	54	0	13,128,307	13,128,307	13,128,307
100	55	0	14,145,688	14,145,688	14,145,688

* This illustration assumes the nonguaranteed values shown continue in all years.
  This is not likely, and actual results may be more or less favorable.

In this example, the Smarts would reposition $9,000 each year from their overage 401(k) contribution. They would also reposition the $800 per year they were paying in term insurance premiums. In addition, $1,800 per year in planned savings for the children would be repositioned. Also, to the annual reallocation of savings, they would have some lump sum deposits. In the first year, they transfer $80,000 of net equity out of their home. In the second year, the Smarts plan to reposition $20,000 of matured CDs and $30,000 from mutual fund accounts.

To make this example both interesting and realistic, let's assume their home continues to appreciate in value by approximately 5 percent each year. At the end of five years their home would have increased in value from $300,000 to $383,000. Because Jim and Mary Smart are catching the vision of equity management, let's assume at the end of the fifth year the Smarts sell their home and purchase a new one valued the same. They take out an 80 percent loan-to-value mortgage on their new home. This means they would take out a new mortgage of $306,400 (80 percent of $383,000). This would allow them to use an additional $80,400 of equity. In other words, after five years they sell their home for $383,000 and pay off the mortgage on their previous home in the amount of $226,000, leaving a balance of equity coming from their previous home of $157,000. They then take $76,600 from the $157,000 and pay a 20 percent down payment on the new $380,000 home, leaving a balance of $80,400. This exercise allows the Smarts to establish a new acquisition indebtedness to deduct the interest on the new mortgage. Assuming $6,400 in closing costs, the Smarts could end up with a net equity transfer in the fifth year for an additional $74,000.

The grand total of the 401(k) overage reallocation, the insurance premium, the planned savings for the children, the equity transfer from a refinance of their home in the first year, the equity from the home sale at the end of the fifth year, and the $50,000 in CDs and mutual funds equals a total amount of $331,600 during the first eleven years.

A bucket (insurance policy) that will accommodate a guideline single premium of $331,600 would require a minimum death benefit in the amount of $1,607,861 for a forty-five-year-old, non-smoking male. This would be the minimum death benefit under the TEFRA/DEFRA guidelines, as explained in chapter 17. To stay in compliance with the TAMRA regulation, the Smarts should not deposit more than a cumulative $84,097 per year during the first five years.

The Internal Revenue Code allows a policyholder to overfund an insurance contract in excess of the TAMRA premium and then "perfect" the contract within sixty days of the end of the first policy anniversary. A policy owner could violate the TAMRA premium limit, request a refund of the overage that was paid into the contract and then redeposit it during the first sixty days of the second year. My clients have used this strategy several times in order to perfect a contract and avoid a modified endowment contract. This preserves the tax-free accessibility of cash values, as explained in chapter 17. When someone overfunds a contract in violation of TAMRA, the insurance company should still credit interest during the time they have the funds. However, when a refund is made during the sixty-day window after the first policy anniversary, the excess interest earned over and above the TAMRA premium may be subject to tax. After realizing the refund, the second-year premium that is fully allowable under TAMRA could be immediately paid and the contract would then be in full compliance provided no more than the total of two annual TAMRA premiums have been paid into the contract.

In this illustration let's assume the Smarts deposit only $82,600 during the first year into their insurance contract. The $82,600 came from $80,000 of net home equity transfer and repositioning the $1,800 per year of planned savings for long-term goals, and the $800 per year they were paying for $500,000 of term insurance. Let's assume they are accumulating their repositioned 401(k) overage contribution on a monthly basis during the first year in a side fund. Then during the second year, the Smarts contribute $9,000 that has accumulated in the side fund from their first-year retirement plan contributions, in addition to the second-year contribution of $9,000. Also, they continue to allocate the $800 of annual insurance premium and $1,800 of annual planned savings. In addition, the Smarts are repositioning $20,000 of CDs and

$30,000 of mutual fund values during the second year for a grand total of $70,600 in premium payments. For the remainder of the years until age 65, the Smarts will continue to deposit only $11,600 into the insurance contract with the exception of year 6. Remember at the end of year five we are assuming the Smarts decide to sell their home and employ a net of an additional $74,000 of home equity. Therefore, in the sixth year please note there is a total premium payment of $85,600.

Based on an interest rate assumption of 7.75 percent using an equity-indexed universal life insurance contract, the accumulation values would result in the numbers shown in column 4. Based on these assumptions, the Smarts, could accumulate $1,114,212 at the end of the twentieth year at age 65. Please keep in mind that should Jim Smart pass away, Mary would receive $1,607,861 of tax-free life insurance proceeds (column 6). This is over three times the amount of life insurance they were paying for with term insurance.

Remember from chapter 17 that this $1,607,861 of life insurance is more or less coming along for the ride and being paid for with a portion of the interest they are earning on their premium payments. They could choose to allocate $1 million of the life insurance to Jim and $600,000 to Mary—or any other ratio they desire—if both Jim and Mary are insurable. The portion of interest that covers or compensates for the mortality charges on a $1,607,861 death benefit is likely money that would have been going to Uncle Sam in income tax had they chosen other investment alternatives. Please note if the Smarts do not need this resource for retirement at age 65, they could let the money continue to accumulate for another ten years. Based on the same assumptions of a 7.75 percent interest rate, the $1,114,212 at age 65 would grow to $2,295,043 at age 75 in the thirtieth year. This would be achieved without requiring any additional premium payments into the contract. In other words, based on the Rule of 72, assuming a net rate of return of approximately 7 percent after the cost of insurance, the account values will double approximately every ten years!

In actuality, in this example, from the twentieth year until the thirtieth year, the cash value growth equals a 7.5 percent net compounded annual return even though the gross return was 7.75 percent. This means that during that time period, the insurance mortality costs (the spigot on the bucket) only drained out .25 of 7.75 percent. That's pretty inexpensive life insurance—a small price to pay to have tax-free retirement funds of over $2 million!

Fig. 19.10	PLAN NET WORTH ILLUSTRATION						
END OF YEAR	[1] PROPERTY VALUE	[2] YEAR-END ACCUMULATION VALUE	[3] PLAN ASSET VALUE [1] + [2]	[4] DEATH BENEFIT	[5] TOTAL MORTGAGE BALANCE	[6] PLAN NET WORTH [3] - [5]	[7] PLAN ESTATE VALUE [1] + [4] - [5]
1	$315,000	$ 82,023	$397,023	$1,607,861	$237,562	$159,461	$1,685,299
2	330,750	157,971	488,721	1,607,861	234,948	253,773	1,703,663
3	347,288	177,566	524,854	1,607,861	232,145	292,709	1,723,004
4	364,652	198,747	563,399	1,607,861	229,139	334,260	1,743,374
5	382,884	221,642	604,526	1,607,861	225,916	378,610	1,764,829
6	402,150	324,778	726,928	1,607,861	303,288	423,640	1,706,723
7	422,258	357,871	780,129	1,607,861	299,950	480,179	1,730,169
8	443,370	393,642	837,012	1,607,861	296,371	540,641	1,754,860
9	465,539	432,308	897,847	1,607,861	292,534	605,313	1,780,866
10	488,816	474,102	962,918	1,607,861	288,419	674,499	1,808,258
11	513,257	519,818	1,033,075	1,607,861	284,007	749,068	1,837,111
12	538,919	568,766	1,107,685	1,607,861	279,275	828,410	1,867,505
13	565,865	621,133	1,186,998	1,607,861	274,202	912,796	1,899,524
14	594,159	677,231	1,271,390	1,607,861	268,762	1,002,628	1,933,258
15	623,867	737,404	1,361,271	1,607,861	262,929	1,098,342	1,968,799
16	655,060	802,219	1,457,279	1,607,861	256,674	1,200,605	2,006,247
17	687,813	871,840	1,559,653	1,607,861	249,966	1,309,687	2,045,708
18	722,204	949,707	1,671,911	1,607,861	242,774	1,429,137	2,087,291
19	758,314	1,027,307	1,785,621	1,607,861	235,062	1,550,559	2,131,113
20	796,230	1,114,212	1,910,442	1,607,861	226,793	1,683,649	2,177,298
21	836,041	1,195,710	2,031,751	1,607,861	217,926	1,813,825	2,225,976
22	877,843	1,284,162	2,162,005	1,607,861	208,417	1,953,588	2,277,287
23	921,735	1,380,070	2,301,805	1,628,482	198,222	2,103,583	2,351,995
24	967,822	1,483,938	2,451,760	1,736,207	187,289	2,264,471	2,516,740
25	1,016,213	1,595,493	2,611,706	1,850,772	175,566	2,436,140	2,691,419
26	1,067,024	1,715,304	2,782,328	1,972,599	162,995	2,619,333	2,876,628
27	1,120,375	1,844,302	2,964,677	2,084,061	149,516	2,815,161	3,054,920
28	1,176,394	1,983,295	3,159,689	2,201,458	135,063	3,024,626	3,242,789
29	1,235,213	2,133,200	3,368,413	2,325,188	119,564	3,248,849	3,440,837
30	1,296,974	2,295,043	3,592,017	2,455,696	102,945	3,489,072	3,649,725

ILLUSTRATING THE PLAN NET WORTH AND ESTATE VALUE

Let's import these various numbers into a plan net worth and estate value illustration (**fig. 19.10**). Column 1 shows the value of their property appreciating at an average of 5 percent annually. Please keep in mind their home will increase in value regardless of whether it is free and clear or fully mortgaged. Column 2 shows the year-end accumulation value from the equity-indexed universal life insurance contract, based on the premium payment schedule shown in **figure 19.9**. Column 3 shows the plan asset value, which is the sum total of the value of the home in column 1 plus the accumulation value of the insurance contract, in column 2. Therefore, column 1 plus column 2 equals column 3.

Column 4 represents the insurance death benefit that comes with the insurance contract. Column 5 shows the mortgage balance of the initial mortgage for five years, as well as the mortgage on the new home purchased at the end of year 5. As seen, their home, by appreciating at 5 percent, would be valued at approximately $383,000 at the end of the fifth year and their mortgage balance owing would be $225,916. If we subtract the mortgage balance shown in column 5 from the plan asset value in column 3, we arrive with the plan net worth, as shown in column 6. The Smarts' net worth will grow substantially greater, as shown in column 6, as a function of having a portion of the equity from their property value in column 1 separated and growing in column 2. As column 6 illustrates, the plan net worth equals $378,610 in the fifth year. And in the twentieth year, at age 65, the plan net worth equals $1,683,649! Column 7 shows the plan estate value, which is the value of their property plus the death benefit, less the total mortgage balance in column 5. Column 7 is what would be left behind to the heirs at any point in time should death occur.

If the Smarts were to sell their home in the fifth year and purchase a new one valued at $383,000, thus taking out a new mortgage at 80 percent loan-to-value, the $306,400 mortgage at 7 percent interest on a thirty-year amortization would result in a monthly payment of $2,038.49. However, their interest deduction would increase from approximately $16,000 per year up to $21,000 per year, saving them another $1,700

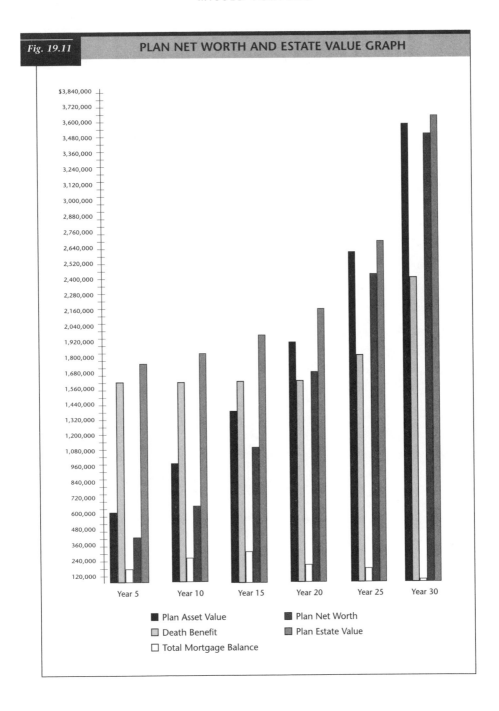

Fig. 19.11 — PLAN NET WORTH AND ESTATE VALUE GRAPH

Legend:
- Plan Asset Value
- Death Benefit
- Total Mortgage Balance
- Plan Net Worth
- Plan Estate Value

per year in taxes. At that point in time, if the Smarts could not afford to set aside a net after-tax increase of $310 per month for a new mortgage payment on their home equity retirement plan, they could opt to reposition money they had been contributing into their 401(k) and get the same tax benefit. It may be wise to do this even if they relinquished the 50 percent matching they might be receiving from their employer. Of course, they could always access money from their insurance contract (which has an accumulation value of $221,642 at the end of year 5 in this example) at any time to meet a house payment.

Figure 19.11 takes the plan net worth and estate value ledger and shows graphically what the plan asset value, death benefit, total mortgage balance, plan net worth, and plan estate value would be. Note even though a mortgage balance is shown in each five-year period, the net worth bar is substantially greater. In other words, the plan net worth and the plan estate value is more than sufficient to compensate and wash out the mortgage at any point in time if required.

Figure 19.12 shows because of the premium payment contributions to the indexed universal life insurance contract, there would be enough accumulation value in the insurance contract in the sixth year to totally compensate for the new, higher mortgage balance. Of course, at any time should Jim pass away, the $1,607,861 of income-tax-free life insurance proceeds would be more than sufficient to pay off the mortgage balance and leave a substantial amount for Mary to live on the rest of her life.

For sake of illustration, let's assume Jim and Mary both live well into their life expectancy. As shown in figure 19.10, the mortgage that began at $240,000 and increased to $306,400 becomes relatively small in comparison to the growth of the assets included in the separated equity. By the time the Smarts are age 75, the plan net worth would equal $3,489,072, after deducting the mortgage balance remaining of only $102,945. At any point in time, the insurance contract could be liquidated and the mortgage could be paid off, leaving a substantial overage for the Smarts to use for retirement income purposes. However, I believe it would be wiser for the Smarts to continue to enjoy mortgage interest deductions and to allow the funds in the insurance contract to accumu-

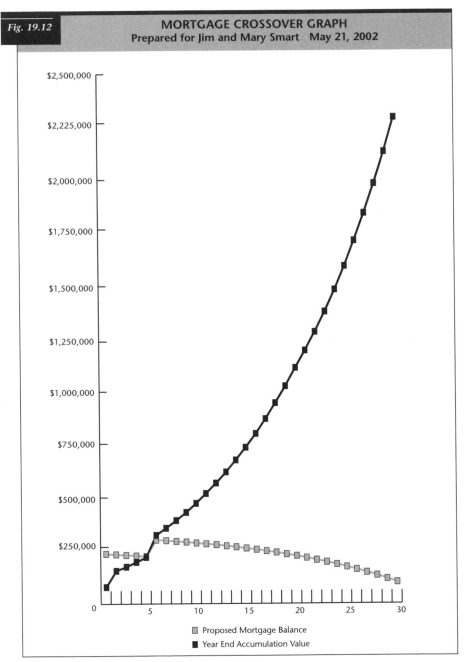

Fig. 19.12

MORTGAGE CROSSOVER GRAPH
Prepared for Jim and Mary Smart   May 21, 2002

☐ Proposed Mortgage Balance
■ Year End Accumulation Value

Notes:
a. This Mortgage Crossover Graph illustrates the year that the insurance Year End
   Surrender Value exceeds the Mortgage Balance.
b. Indexed Universal Life values are based on the current interest rate of 7.75%.

late. Then if the Smarts wanted to make a mortgage payment with some of the money they withdrew from the insurance contract, they would in effect be taking money or interest out of their insurance contract they do not have to report as taxable income, and they would continue to get tax deductions for what they did with the money! In other words, tax-free insurance contract distributions are making house payments that maintain tax-deductible interest.

Figure 19.13 is one of my favorite and most powerful reports: the internal rate of return analysis. Remember in chapter 18, I indicated people should choose investments based on which ones generate the most at the time in life when they will be using the money the most? Because we have to fill up the insurance contract in increments that comply with TEFRA/DEFRA and TAMRA Internal Revenue Code guidelines, the internal rate of return may not look attractive during the initial years. In other words, when we have the insurance contract only funded at about 25 percent or even 50 percent during the first or second year, the insurance that is required now to give us the tax advantages we will enjoy later temporarily affects our internal rate of return.

Note in column 3 the internal rate of return during the first year is -0.69 percent. In year 2 it only improves to 2.00 percent retroactive back to the first day the first premium dollar was paid into the contract. But as you'll notice, the internal rate of return gets better each year of the contract. This is a result of the premium payments made into the contract as the bucket is filled up to the brim, as well as the compounded interest that adds to the insurance contract and the amount of insurance we are having to pay for decreases. By year 20, when Jim and Mary Smart are age 65, the internal rate of return in this illustration would be 6.49 percent. If the Smarts stopped making premium payments and let their money sit for an additional ten years, it would more than double (earning a net rate of return that ten-year period of 7.5 percent) during that ten-year period to $2,295,043.

In year 30 of column 3, the internal rate of return is 6.88 percent. This does not mean the internal rate of return was only 6.88 percent for the previous year, but instead it means a person would have to realize a

Fig. 19.13			INTERNAL RATE OF RETURN ANALYSIS					
		ACCUMULATION VALUES				DEATH BENEFIT		
[1]	[2]	[3]	[4]	[5]	[6]	[7]	[8]
End of Year	Net Payment	Policy Accumulation Value	Internal Rate of Return	Pre-Tax Equivalent Return	Death Benefit	Internal Rate of Return	Pre-Tax Equivalent Return
1	$82,600	$ 82,022	-0.69%	-0.69%	$1,607,861	1846.56%	2797.82%
2	70,600	157,970	2.00%	3.03%	1,607,861	300.52%	455.33%
3	11,600	177,566	3.10%	4.70%	1,607,861	141.76%	214.79%
4	11,600	198,746	3.69%	5.59%	1,607,861	89.45%	135.53%
5	11,600	221,641	4.10%	6.21%	1,607,861	64.35%	97.50%
6	85,600	324,777	4.50%	6.82%	1,607,861	47.87%	72.53%
7	11,600	357,870	4.88%	7.39%	1,607,861	38.34%	58.09%
8	11,600	393,641	5.17%	7.83%	1,607,861	31.73%	48.08%
9	11,600	432,307	5.40%	8.18%	1,607,861	26.91%	40.77%
10	11,600	474,102	5.59%	8.47%	1,607,861	23.25%	35.23%
11	11,600	519,817	5.76%	8.73%	1,607,861	20.38%	30.88%
12	11,600	568,765	5.90%	8.94%	1,607,861	18.09%	27.41%
13	11,600	621,133	6.01%	9.11%	1,607,861	16.21%	24.56%
14	11,600	677,230	6.10%	9.24%	1,607,861	14.64%	22.18%
15	11,600	737,404	6.19%	9.38%	1,607,861	13.32%	20.18%
16	11,600	802,219	6.26%	9.48%	1,607,861	12.19%	18.47%
17	11,600	871,839	6.32%	9.58%	1,607,861	11.22%	17.00%
18	11,600	946,706	6.38%	9.67%	1,607,861	10.37%	15.71%
19	11,600	1,027,307	6.44%	9.76%	1,607,861	9.62%	14.58%
20	11,600	1,114,212	6.49%	9.83%	1,607,861	8.95%	13.56%
21	0	1,195,710	6.54%	9.91%	1,607,861	8.41%	12.74%
22	0	1,284,162	6.58%	9.97%	1,607,861	7.93%	12.02%
23	0	1,380,070	6.63%	10.05%	1,628,482	7.57%	11.47%
24	0	1,483,938	6.68%	10.12%	1,736,207	7.52%	11.39%
25	0	1,595,493	6.72%	10.18%	1,850,772	7.48%	11.33%
26	0	1,715,304	6.75%	10.23%	1,972,599	7.44%	11.27%
27	0	1,844,302	6.79%	10.29%	2,084,061	7.36%	11.15%
28	0	1,983,295	6.82%	10.33%	2,201,458	7.28%	11.03%
29	0	2,133,200	6.85%	10.38%	2,325,188	7.22%	10.94%
30	0	2,295,043	6.88%	10.42%	2,455,696	7.15%	10.83%

Notes:
a. Internal Rate of Return [3] and [6] illustrates the net rate of return within the policy, after deductions
   for mortality, administrative fees, premium fees, and any other applicable internal charges.
b. Pre-Tax Equivalent [4] and [7] assumes a 34% tax bracket.
c. Indexed Universal Life Values are based on a 7.75% interest rate.

6.88 percent annual cash-on-cash rate of return on the premium payments made years 1 through 20 to end up with $2,295,043 at the end of
the thirtieth year! The $2,295,043 is tax free by virtue of using the insur-
ance contract. In order to achieve the same net after-tax accumulation,
column 4 shows us that 10.42 percent taxable interest would have to be

earned in order to have a net after-tax 6.88 percent return. In other words, when I illustrate the internal rate of return shown in column 3, this represents a cash-on-cash return based on the premium dollars paid into the contract shown in column 1. This means the death benefit shown in column 5 is essentially along for the ride absolutely free!

Of course, we know life insurance is not really free. Actually, the interest rate being credited on the contract is 7.75 percent, as shown in the footnotes to **figure 19.13**. However, if we refer to the thirtieth year, we realize the difference between the 7.75 percent gross rate of return and the 6.88 percent internal rate of return results in .87 percent difference. This .87 percent difference is what pays for the insurance. Would it be worth giving up .87 of interest rate during that thirty-year period to accumulate $2.3 million tax free? It would be worth it to me! Otherwise, I would have to earn 10.42 percent in a taxable investment to net 6.88 percent (3.54 percent would go to taxes), and I wouldn't even have a life insurance benefit along for the ride. I would have to buy my life insurance rather than letting otherwise payable income taxes pay for it!

Let's now take a look at where Jim and Mary Smart would end up at age 65 with regard to their retirement income. If Jim and Mary were like most typical Americans, they would have likely continued to have outstanding credit card balances, possibly until their retirement at age 65. They also would have likely financed their automobiles, thus having some type of automobile payment throughout their earning years. Therefore it is highly likely if Jim and Mary Smart had not repositioned their assets as we have illustrated, they would have only continued to set aside the money in their 401(k)s and also the $1,800 per year they were saving for their children and other long-term goals. The Smarts would have also continued to pay approximately $800 per year for $500,000 of term life insurance until age 65. However, at that time, if they decided to continue with $500,000 of insurance, the premiums would have gone up dramatically.

Under these assumptions, the $9,000 per year they repositioned and the $1,800 per year they were saving for their children's long-term goals would equal an annual savings in the amount of $10,800 over a twenty-year period. If the Smarts had set that much aside in a tax-deferred investment earning 8 percent, it would have grown to $533,767.55 by age 65. At 9 percent interest it would have grown to $602,256.93. If they would have achieved a 10 percent return, their balance would have been $680,426.99. In addition, had the Smarts not repositioned their CDs and their mutual fund accounts, the $50,000 they had at age 45 would have been worth $233,047.86, assuming both earned an average of 8 percent interest. At a 9 percent compounded interest rate their balance would have grown from $50,000 to $280,220.54. And at 10 percent interest they would have accumulated $336,375.

So let's look at the possible income that the Smarts could realize from the annual savings of $10,800 a year from age 45 to age 65, plus the $50,000 in CDs and mutual funds as it grew over the same twenty-year period. Assuming an 8 percent average return, the total of these accounts would equal $766,815.41. If the Smarts were to withdraw only interest beginning at age 65, they would be able to withdraw $61,345.23 each year, which would in turn be subject to tax. Assuming a 34 percent marginal tax bracket, they would have to pay $20,857.38 in taxes, which would only leave them a net of $40,487.85 in spendable income. If the Smarts had earned the equivalent of 9 percent interest, their total account balances would equal $882,477.47. This could generate an interest-only income of $79,422.97, resulting in an annual tax liability of $27,003.81 and leaving a net spendable income of $52,419.16. And, assuming a 10 percent annual interest equivalent, the Smarts would have accumulated $1,016,802. This would allow them, at a 10 percent interest-only withdrawal, to have $101,680.20 in taxable income. The annual tax liability would be $34,571.27, leaving a net of $67,108.93 to spend and use.

Let's now compare those results with the possible income the Smarts could realize from their equity-indexed investment-grade insurance contract. Remember in this illustration the Smarts accumulated $1,114,212 by disciplining themselves to set aside the same amount of money, plus the savings they achieved through using the insurance contract and repositioning their assets. Keep in mind we have only used a gross interest rate of 7.75 percent. The Smarts realized a 6.49 percent internal rate of return on their premium dollars paid into the contract during that twenty-year period. Based on these assumptions, we usually mathematically calculate how much the Smarts could take via withdrawals and tax-free loans from their insurance contract on an annual basis without depleting their account until age 100 (**fig. 19.14**).

Figure 19.14 illustrates how the Smarts could take $80,000 per year in tax-free retirement income, under the provisions explained in chapter 17. This annual tax-free retirement income would not be deemed earned, passive, or portfolio income, as explained earlier. With no tax liability, they would be able to use the entire $80,000 for their needs. At this cash flow rate, the Smarts would gradually deplete their account, as illustrated from the twenty-first year at age 65, through to the fifty-fifth year, ending at age 100. Please note their account value would gently reduce from $1,114,212 at age 65 and stay at over $1 million through age 80, and then slowly deplete to approximately $500,000 at age 94. We purposely had it deplete to $131,785 at age 100; however, it is not necessary to deplete the account. If, instead of withdrawing $80,000 per year, the Smarts withdrew $75,000 per year tax free, their net cash surrender value would never dip below $1 million! But to illustrate the power of what a tax-advantaged insurance contract can do compared to alternative investments, we like to illustrate withdrawing enough money to gradually deplete the account until age 100. Keep in mind that the Smarts would have to be realizing a $121,212 taxable retirement income to net $80,000 of spendable income in a 34 percent tax bracket!

Of course, some people may say, "But the Smarts still have a mortgage payment!" That's true. However, the Smarts could opt to pay off the mortgage by using some of the $1,114,212 of accumulation values in their insurance contract. Or, as I usually advise, they could continue to make the mortgage payment and manage their equity throughout their retirement years. At age 65 they could still be realizing $21,448 a year in interest deductions, thereby saving $7,292 in taxes had they taken out an interest-only mortgage or refinanced their amortized mortgage periodically. Why not continue to use the tax advantages of equity management throughout your entire lifetime? Their home might be worth $796,230

| Fig. 19.14 | **A TAX-ADVANTAGED LIFE INSURANCE AND RETIREMENT FUND** |
| | Tax-Advantaged Cash Flow Using An Indexed Universal Policy |

AGE	YEAR	NET PAYMENT	RETIREMENT INCOME TAX-FREE CASH FLOW	ACCUMULATION VALUE	SURRENDER VALUE	NET DEATH BENEFIT
46	1	$82,600	0	$ 82,023	$ 65,944	$1,607,861
47	2	70,600	0	157,971	125,814	1,607,861
48	3	11,600	0	177,566	145,409	1,607,861
49	4	11,600	0	198,747	166,590	1,607,861
50	5	11,600	0	221,642	189,485	1,607,861
51	6	85,600	0	324,778	294,228	1,607,861
52	7	11,600	0	357,871	328,929	1,607,861
53	8	11,600	0	393,642	366,308	1,607,861
54	9	11,600	0	432,308	406,582	1,607,861
55	10	11,600	0	474,102	451,592	1,607,861
56	11	11,600	0	519,818	500,523	1,607,861
57	12	11,600	0	568,766	552,687	1,607,861
58	13	11,600	0	621,133	608,271	1,607,861
59	14	11,600	0	677,231	667,584	1,607,861
60	15	11,600	0	737,404	730,973	1,607,861
61	16	11,600	0	802,219	799,003	1,607,861
62	17	11,600	0	871,840	871,840	1,607,861
63	18	11,600	0	946,707	946,707	1,607,861
64	19	11,600	0	1,027,307	1,027,307	1,607,861
65	20	11,600	0	1,114,212	1,114,212	1,607,861
66	21	0	80,000	1,109,470	1,109,470	1,527,836
67	22	0	80,000	1,187,233	1,104,833	1,445,436
68	23	0	80,000	1,267,440	1,100,168	1,360,564
69	24	0	80,000	1,350,341	1,095,651	1,325,209
70	25	0	80,000	1,435,484	1,090,753	1,320,430
71	26	0	80,000	1,522,507	1,085,034	1,313,410
72	27	0	80,000	1,611,697	1,078,700	1,288,221
73	28	0	80,000	1,703,180	1,071,793	1,259,143
74	29	0	80,000	1,797,118	1,064,389	1,226,130
75	30	0	80,000	1,893,708	1,056,597	1,189,157
76	31	0	80,000	1,993,247	1,048,624	1,148,286
77	32	0	80,000	2,094,874	1,039,512	1,144,255
78	33	0	80,000	2,198,537	1,029,113	1,139,040
79	34	0	80,000	2,304,170	1,017,264	1,132,473
80	35	0	80,000	2,411,691	1,003,777	1,124,362
81	36	0	80,000	2,520,972	988,421	1,114,470
82	37	0	80,000	2,631,886	970,959	1,102,553
83	38	0	80,000	2,744,287	951,132	1,088,346
84	39	0	80,000	2,858,003	928,653	1,071,553
85	40	0	80,000	2,973,268	**903,638**	**1,052,301**
86	41	0	80,000	3,089,997	875,878	1,030,377
87	42	0	80,000	3,207,408	844,465	1,004,835
88	43	0	80,000	3,325,165	808,935	975,193
89	44	0	80,000	3,442,900	768,782	940,927
90	45	0	80,000	3,561,114	724,372	902,428
91	46	0	80,000	3,679,686	975,442	859,426
92	47	0	80,000	3,800,798	624,027	776,059
93	48	0	80,000	3,925,118	570,644	688,398
94	49	0	80,000	4,053,456	515,948	597,017
95	50	0	80,000	4,186,808	460,774	502,642
96	51	0	80,000	4,325,012	404,798	404,798
97	52	0	80,000	4,464,428	344,207	344,207
98	53	0	80,000	4,604,863	278,635	278,635
99	54	0	80,000	4,746,103	207,688	207,688
100	55	0	80,000	4,888,752	131,785	131,785

* This illustration assumes the nonguaranteed values shown continue in all years.
This is not likely, and actual results may be more or less favorable.

at age 65—think of the additional retirement income they could generate by managing the difference between a mortgage balance of $306,400 and a house worth $796,230!

Assuming they kept an interest-only mortgage of just $306,400 on their home during their retirement years at a 7 percent rate, their true net (after-tax) annual mortgage payment would be $14,156. If this were deducted from the $80,000 of tax-free cash flow they would still net $65,844 of tax-free income. This would be the equivalent of having almost a $100,000 taxable income. Please keep in mind all of this can be achieved assuming only a 7.75 percent gross interest rate on their universal life insurance contract, incurring approximately 1 percent insurance expense, thereby producing an internal rate of return of only approximately 6.75 percent! As you study **figure 19.14**, note the insurance contract allowed the Smarts to realize an income of $80,000 per year tax free for a grand total of thirty-five years to age 100. Assuming they pass away at a normal life expectancy of age 85, they would have still left behind a net death benefit of $1,052,301 income-tax free to their heirs. Or if Mary outlived Jim, Jim would have left behind $1 million dollars for Mary's benefit. Of course the original $1.6 million of death benefit could be divided between both Jim and Mary. Jim could have an insurance contract insuring him for $1 million and Mary could have had an insurance contract insuring her for $600,000. At any point in time, should death occur, the income-tax-free insurance proceeds would likely leave behind a greater resource for the survivors than money set aside in a qualified plan, assuming the same interest rates.

Please study **figure 19.15**. This illustrates four snapshots in time. In the tenth year the Smarts would have set aside $320,000 in cumulative net payments. They would only be age 55 and would not have withdrawn any money. The surrender value of their insurance contracts at that point in time would be $451,592. The death benefit still remains at $1,607,861 if they should die.

In the next quadrant please notice the twentieth-year summary. Cumulative net payments total $436,000. They still have not withdrawn any money at that point. Their surrender value would be $1,114,212.

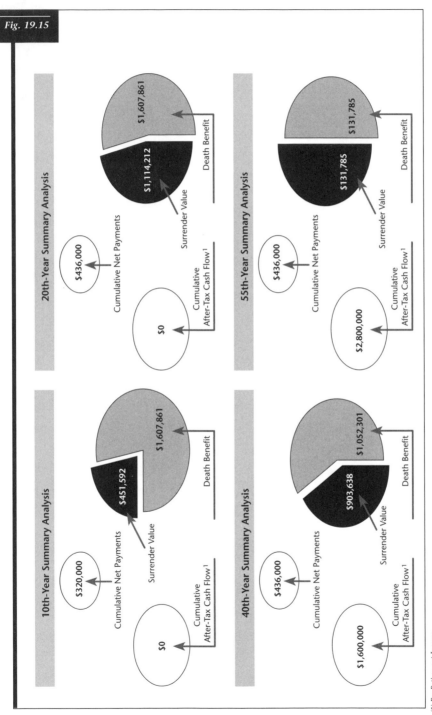

Fig. 19.15

10th-Year Summary Analysis

Cumulative Net Payments — $320,000

Surrender Value — $451,592

Death Benefit — $1,607,861

Cumulative After-Tax Cash Flow[1] — $0

20th-Year Summary Analysis

Cumulative Net Payments — $436,000

Surrender Value — $1,114,212

Death Benefit — $1,607,861

Cumulative After-Tax Cash Flow[1] — $0

40th-Year Summary Analysis

Cumulative Net Payments — $436,000

Surrender Value — $903,638

Death Benefit — $1,052,301

Cumulative After-Tax Cash Flow[1] — $1,600,000

55th-Year Summary Analysis

Cumulative Net Payments — $436,000

Surrender Value — $131,785

Death Benefit — $131,785

Cumulative After-Tax Cash Flow[1] — $2,800,000

(1) For Retirement Income
Format and design created through the use of InsMark® software.

Their death benefit would still be at $1,607,861. As explained in chapter 17, in reality the only insurance the Smarts are paying for at age 65 is the difference between the $1,607,861 death benefit and the $1,114,212 of cash value. This would be a total of $493,649 of actual exposure the insurance company has. This is one of the reasons the insurance contract performs with a better net internal rate of return through the years as cash values are included in the death benefit under the level death benefit option A (as explained in chapter 17).

Please refer to the fortieth-year summary analysis shown in the southwest quadrant. This is assuming the Smarts live to age 85. Remember their cumulative net payments were only $436,000. At that point in time they have enjoyed a total of $1.6 million of tax-free income ($80,000/year x 20 years). Their surrender value is still $903,638, and, if they should die at age 85, they would leave behind $1,052,301 tax free.

The fifty-fifth-year summary is shown in the southeast quadrant. Here the Smarts would have realized tax-free income totaling $2.8 million during the thirty-five years of their retirement to age 100. If they passed away at that point, they would have gradually depleted their resources, only leaving behind $131,785 at age 100. **Figure 19.16** shows the fifty-five-year graphic analysis with the surrender value (SV) in medium shade, the net cumulative payments (NP) shown in the white bars, the death benefit (DB) shown in light shade, and the tax-free cash flow (CF) shown in the dark shade. The Smarts would have realized $2.8 million in tax-free retirement income versus the $436,000 of basis invested over twenty years into the contract.

Let's now compare how the same investment would have performed using alternative vehicles. Please study **figure 19.17**. This assumes that the Smarts would have set aside the same schedule of annual investments from age 45 to age 65 in CDs, annuities, IRAs, and 401(k)s, or mutual funds. Keep in mind that investments such as IRAs and 401(k)s would not have allowed the Smarts to set aside the amount of lump sums that would be allowed by using a non-qualified alternative. Let's assume the equity-indexed universal life insurance contract credits a gross rate of return of 7.75 percent, resulting in a twenty-year net rate of return of just under 6.5 percent, and compare it to these other investments at their probable rates

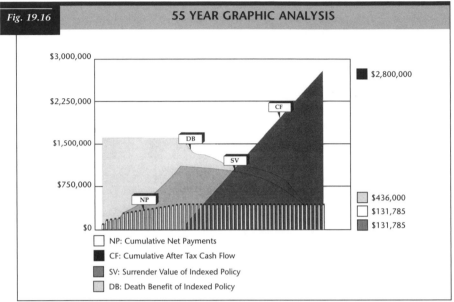

| Fig. 19.16 | 55 YEAR GRAPHIC ANALYSIS |

Format and design created through the use of InsMark® software

of return. Let's assume that CDs yield an average of 5 percent, fixed annuities yield an average of 6.25 percent, an IRA and 401(k) portfolio yields an average of 7.75 percent, and mutual funds yield an average of 10 percent. Immediately some critics may say, "But I would expect to achieve a greater rate of return in my IRAs, 401(k)s, and mutual funds!" They may do so, but if mutual funds, IRAs, and annuities were to achieve higher rates, then an equity-indexed universal life insurance contract should also realize a higher rate of return than I am illustrating!

Probably the greatest difference between indexed universal life shown in columns 6 to 8 compared to the CD, annuity, IRAs/401(k)s, and mutual funds illustrated in columns 2 to 5 is the death benefit that comes along for the ride with the universal life. Keep in mind if at any time Jim and/or Mary Smart should pass away, they would leave behind $1.6 million income tax free to their beneficiaries rather than just the cash that had accumulated in their investment! But for purposes of comparison, let's ignore the death benefit and look at the cash-on-cash return comparison between these five different investment alternatives.

Fig. 19.17

AN INDEXED UNIVERSAL LIFE POLICY VS. VARIOUS FINANCIAL ALTERNATIVES

	Male Age 45	Initial Payment 82,600	A Certificate of Deposit Yield 5.00%	An Annuity Yield 6.25%	IRAs & 401(k)s Yield 7.75%	Mutual Fund Yield 10.00%	An Indexed Universal Life Policy Interest Rate 7.75%		Tax Bracket 34.00%
			AFTER TAX VALUES				AN INDEXED UNIVERSAL LIFE POLICY		
		[1]	[2]	[3]	[4]	[5]	[6] Year End Accumulation Value*	[7] Year End Surrender Value*	[8]
Clients Age	Year	Net Payment	A Certificate of Deposit	An Annuity	IRAs & 401(k)s	Mutual Fund			Death Benefit
46	1	$82,600	$ 85,326	$ 83,053	$ 83,338	$ 83,002	$ 82,023	$ 65,944	$1,607,861
47	2	70,600	161,071	156,464	157,830	158,738	157,971	125,814	1,607,861
48	3	11,600	178,370	172,747	175,811	179,562	177,566	145,409	1,607,861
49	4	11,600	196,239	189,611	194,686	201,588	198,747	166,590	1,607,861
50	5	11,600	214,697	207,084	214,516	224,886	221,642	189,485	1,607,861
51	6	85,600	310,207	299,605	310,030	323,889	324,778	294,228	1,607,861
52	7	11,600	332,427	320,566	334,898	354,250	357,871	328,929	1,607,861
53	8	11,600	355,379	342,349	361,139	386,365	393,642	366,308	1,607,861
54	9	11,600	379,090	364,998	388,847	420,334	432,308	406,582	1,607,861
55	10	11,600	403,583	388,556	418,124	456,264	474,102	451,592	1,607,861
56	11	11,600	428,884	413,073	449,079	494,270	519,818	500,523	1,607,861
57	12	11,600	455,020	438,596	481,828	534,471	568,766	552,687	1,607,861
58	13	11,600	482,018	465,178	516,497	576,993	621,133	608,271	1,607,861
59	14	11,600	509,907	492,874	553,218	621,970	677,231	667,584	1,607,861
60	15	11,600	538,717	521,743	592,134	669,546	737,404	730,973	1,607,861
61	16	11,600	568,478	580,816	676,932	719,868	802,219	799,003	1,607,861
62	17	11,600	599,220	615,749	726,450	773,097	871,840	871,840	1,607,861
63	18	11,600	630,977	652,290	779,133	829,400	946,707	946,707	1,607,861
64	19	11,600	663,782	690,522	835,198	888,954	1,027,307	1,027,307	1,607,861
65	20	11,600	697,670	730,532	894,882	951,948	1,114,212	1,114,212	1,607,861
66	21	-80,000	638,053	676,589	861,159	922,303	1,109,470	1,109,470	1,527,836
67	22	-80,000	576,469	619,847	825,096	890,946	1,187,233	1,104,833	1,445,436
68	23	-80,000	512,852	560,162	786,528	857,778	1,267,440	1,100,168	1,360,564
69	24	-80,000	447,136	497,380	745,284	822,694	1,350,341	1,095,651	1,325,209
70	25	-80,000	379,252	431,670	701,177	785,585	1,435,484	1,090,753	1,320,430
71	26	-80,000	309,127	363,710	654,007	746,333	1,522,507	1,085,034	1,313,410
72	27	-80,000	236,688	293,424	603,564	704,813	1,611,697	1,078,700	1,288,221
73	28	-80,000	161,859	220,731	549,618	660,896	1,703,180	1,071,793	1,259,143
74	29	-80,000	84,560	145,549	491,928	614,443	1,797,118	1,064,389	1,226,130
75	30	-80,000	4,711	67,794	430,801	565,307	1,893,708	1,056,597	1,189,157
76	31	-80,000	-77,774	-12,969	366,873	513,334	1,993,247	**1,048,624**	1,148,286
77	32	-80,000	-162,980	-98,780	300,017	458,359	2,094,874	1,039,512	1,144,255
78	33	-80,000	-250,999	-189,954	230,097	400,209	2,198,537	1,029,113	1,139,040
79	34	-80,000	-341,921	-286,826	156,974	338,701	2,304,170	1,017,264	1,132,473
80	35	-80,000	-435,845	-389,752	80,501	273,641	2,411,691	1,003,777	1,124,362

*This illustration assumes the nonguaranteed values shown continue in all years.
This is not likely, and actual results may be more or less favorable.
Format and design created through the use of InsMark® software.*

Fig. 19.17 continued		AN INDEXED UNIVERSAL LIFE POLICY VS. VARIOUS FINANCIAL ALTERNATIVES							
	Male Age 45	Initial Payment 82,600	A Certificate of Deposit Yield 5.00%	An Annuity Yield 6.25%	IRAs & 401(k)s Yield 7.75%	Mutual Fund Yield 10.00%	An Indexed Universal Life Policy Interest Rate 7.75%		Tax Bracket 34.00%
			AFTER TAX VALUES				AN INDEXED UNIVERSAL LIFE POLICY		
		[1]	[2]	[3]	[4]	[5]	[6] Year End Accumulation Value*	[7] Year End Surrender Value*	[8]
Clients Age	Year	Net Payment	A Certificate of Deposit	An Annuity	IRAs & 401(k)s	Mutual Fund			Death Benefit
81	36	$-80,000	$ -532,868	$ -499,112	$ 524	$204,824	$2,520,972	$988,421	$1,114,470
82	37	-80,000	-633,092	-615,306	**-85,636**	132,032	2,631,886	970,959	1,102,553
83	38	-80,000	-736,624	-738,763	-178,473	55,037	2,744,287	951,132	1,088,346
84	39	-80,000	-843,573	-869,936	-278,504	**-26,611**	2,858,003	**928,653**	1,071,553
85	40	-80,000	-954,051	-1,009,307	-386,288	-113,647	2,973,268	903,638	1,052,301
86	41	-80,000	-1,068,175	-1,157,388	-502,426	-206,428	3,089,997	875,878	1,030,377
87	42	-80,000	-1,186,064	-1,314,725	-627,564	-305,332	3,207,408	844,465	1,004,835
88	43	-80,000	-1,307,845	-1,481,895	-762,400	-410,764	3,325,165	808,935	975,193
89	44	-80,000	-1,433,643	-1,659,514	-907,686	-523,154	3,442,900	768,782	940,927
90	45	-80,000	-1,563,594	-1,848,234	-1,064,231	-642,962	3,561,114	724,372	902,428
91	46	-80,000	-1,697,832	-2,048,748	-1,232,909	-770,678	3,679,686	675,442	859,426
92	47	-80,000	-1,836,501	-2,261,795	-1,414,660	-906,823	3,800,798	624,027	776,059
93	48	-80,000	-1,979,745	-2,488,157	-1,610,496	-1,051,953	3,925,118	570,644	688,398
94	49	-80,000	-2,127,717	-2,728,667	-1,821,509	-1,206,662	4,053,456	515,948	597,017
95	50	-80,000	-2,280,571	-2,984,209	-2,048,876	-1,371,581	4,186,808	460,774	502,642
96	51	-80,000	-2,438,470	-3,255,722	-2,293,864	-1,547,386	4,325,012	404,798	404,798
97	52	-80,000	-2,601,580	-3,544,204	-2,557,839	-1,734,793	4,464,428	344,207	344,207
98	53	-80,000	-2,770,072	-3,850,717	-2,842,271	-1,934,570	4,604,863	278,635	278,635
99	54	-80,000	-2,944,124	-4,176,387	-3,148,747	-2,147,531	4,746,103	207,688	207,688
100	55	-80,000	-3,123,920	-4,522,411	-3,478,975	-2,374,548	4,888,752	131,785	131,785

Sales charge on payments to column [1]:
MB = 4.00%, AN = 4.00%, IRA = 5.00%, MF = 5.00%,

Management fee reflected in columns [2], [3], [4], & [5]:
MB = 1.00%, AN = 1.00%, IRA = .75%, MF = .75%,

Tax deferred accounts are assessed: Income tax on withdrawals in column [1].
Additional income tax on withdrawals before age 59 1/2: 10.00%.

* This illustration assumes the nonguaranteed values shown continue in all years.
This is not likely, and actual results may be more or less favorable.
Format and design created through the use of InsMark® software.

LOOKING DOWN THE ROAD

At year 5, the CD would have an after-tax value of $214,697, the annuity would be worth $207,084, the IRAs/401(k)s would be worth approximately $214,516, and the mutual fund would be worth approximately $224,886. The accumulation value of the universal life would be $221,642; however, the surrender value would only be $189,485 by nature of it being an insurance policy. Keep in mind if the intent were only to keep the account for five years, the insurance contract should be structured differently, rather than designed to accommodate eleven to twenty years of deposits. Then the surrender value would be much closer to the accumulation value. However, remember from chapter 18 we don't choose investments based on which ones grow to the most, we choose investments based on which ones generate the most when we are going to use the money the most! So let's move down to the twentieth year at age 65.

At year 20, note that the CD has an after-tax value of $697,670, versus the annuity with $730,532, the IRAs/401(k)s at $894,882, and the mutual funds at $951,948. Although not true in this case, sometimes a mutual fund that is taxed as earned is worth less than tax-deferred vehicles even though it had a higher yield (because IRAs and 401(k)s have tax advantages during the accumulation phase and different fees may be assessed on different types of investments as shown in the footnotes). However, please note the insurance contract has an accumulation value, which also equals the surrender value in the amount of $1,114,212. Therefore, the non-qualified investment-grade life insurance contract had approximately $219,330 more dollars accumulated at age 65 than the IRA and 401(k) would have accumulated net after tax given the same interest rate. Also, the insurance contract would transfer $1.6 million on death, whereas the IRAs and 401(k)s would only transfer $894,882 on death at age 65.

As we begin our retirement income out of the five different investment alternatives, keep in mind that to net $80,000 of spendable income, some investments will require as much as $121,212 of gross income to be taken to net $80,000 after tax at a 34 percent tax rate. The after-tax values reveal the CDs and fixed annuities would be out of money in year 31 (age 76), based on these assumptions. The IRA/401(k) accounts crediting the same interest rate as the insurance contract (7.75 percent) would be totally depleted by year 37 (age 82), and mutual funds crediting the equivalent of 10 percent would be empty of cash by year 39 (age 84). When all of the other investment alternatives to the insurance contract are totally depleted of value, the net surrender value of the insurance contract is still between $928,653 (year 39) to $1,048,624 (year 31).

In that respect, the insurance contract is not just $384,000 better than an annuity, or $220,000 better than an IRA or 401(k), or $163,000 better than a mutual fund as shown in comparison at age 65. Rather, analyzing the comparison based on what each investment generated in terms of net spendable retirement income out to a life expectancy of age 85, the insurance contract is about $1 million better than any of the other alternatives! And that's not even the end of the story. What if Jim or Mary lives beyond life expectancy, even to age 100? Based on these assumptions, in year 55 (age 100), CDs would be -$3,123,920, annuities would be -$4,522,411, IRAs and 401(k)s would be -$3,478,975, and mutual funds would be -$2,374,548! In other words, the alternative investments would be all substantially in the hole if they had been required to generate $80,000 of income, all while the insurance contract kept generating tax-free income of $80,000 through age 100—and still left behind $131,785 of positive death benefit if death occurred at that time! When analyzed this way, the insurance contract could prove to be effectively $2.3 to $4.5 million better than the other alternative investments over the long run—at the time in life when the money is needed the most!

As illustrated in **figure 19.18**, a CD would have to credit 10.19 to 11.91 percent interest to match the benefits of the insurance contract crediting 7.75 percent. A fixed annuity would have to credit 9.63 to 10.53 percent interest to match the insurance contract. IRAs and 401(k)s would have to credit 9.40 to 10.29 percent interest to match the insurance contract. And mutual funds would have to credit 11.77 to 13.46 percent to match such an insurance contract.

By transforming the numbers of each of these four alternative investments into a graph over a fifty-five-year period compared to the insurance contract, you can visually see why it is advantageous to have tax advantages on the back end or harvest years (withdrawal and transfer phases) of an investment, rather than on the front end (contribution phase). In **figure 19.19**, in all four graphs shown, you can see the alternative investment illustrated in the dark gray accumulates fairly comparably to the insurance contract illustrated in the medium gray during the initial years—even out to year 20 (age 65) for some investments. The major dif-

Fig. 19.18	AN INDEXED UNIVERSAL LIFE POLICY VS. VARIOUS FINANCIAL ALTERNATIVES						
Male Age 45	Initial Payment 82,600	A Certificate of Deposit Yield 5.00%	An Annuity Yield 6.25%	IRAs & 401(k)s Yield 7.75%	Mutual Fund Yield 10.00%	An Indexed Universal Life Policy Interest Rate 7.75%	Tax Bracket 34.00%

Gross interest rate needed by various investments over 40 years to match an Indexed Universal Life Policy

Investment	Interest Rate	Indexed Universal Life Policy	
A Certificate of Deposit	11.91%	Accumulation Value	$4,888,752
A Certificate of Deposit	10.19%	Surrender Value	$131,785
A Certificate of Deposit	10.19%	Death Benefit	$131,785
A Municipal Bond Fund	10.53%	Accumulation Value	$4,888,752
A Municipal Bond Fund	9.63%	Surrender Value	$131,785
A Municipal Bond Fund	9.63%	Death Benefit	$131,785
An Annuity	10.29%	Accumulation Value	$4,888,752
An Annuity	9.40%	Surrender Value	$131,785
An Annuity	9.40%	Death Benefit	$131,785
Mutual Fund	13.46%	Accumulation Value	$4,888,752
Mutual Fund	11.77%	Surrender Value	$131,785
Mutual Fund	11.77%	Death Benefit	$131,785

Income Tax Considerations

1. A Certificate of Deposit - Interest is taxed as earned.
2. An Annuity - Interest is tax deferred. (Values assume tax is assessed in year shown only)
3. IRAs / 401(k)s - Interest is tax deferred. (Values assume tax is assessed in year shown only)
4. Mutual Fund - Interest is taxed as earned.
5. An Indexed Universal Life Policy:
   a. Death Benefit including cash value component is income tax free.
   b. Loans are income-tax free as long as the policy is kept in force.
   c. Withdrawals and other non-loan policy cash flow up to cost basis
      (not in violations of IRC Section 7702) are income tax free as a return of premium.
   d. Cash values shown assume most favorable combination of b and/or c.

*This illustration assumes the nonguaranteed values shown continue in all years.
This is not likely, and actual results may be more or less favorable.
Format and design created through the use of InsMark® software.

ference during the twenty-year accumulation phase is in the event of premature death, the insurance contract provides a death benefit of $1,607,861, as illustrated in the light gray, that is substantially greater than what the other investments would leave behind at death. But the most dramatic difference is reflected in years 20 through 55. Notice how quickly the other investments run out of capital (dark gray) in relation to the insurance contract (medium gray). When every one of the alternatives has crossed below the $0 line into negative territory, the insurance contract is still about $1 million above. Also notice how far in the hole the other investments have dropped below the $0 line after year 30 or 40, continuing to year 55 (age 100), in comparison to the insurance contract.

Sometimes, a person will say, "Well, I don't think my wife and I are going to live beyond age 85, and we don't care to leave anything behind

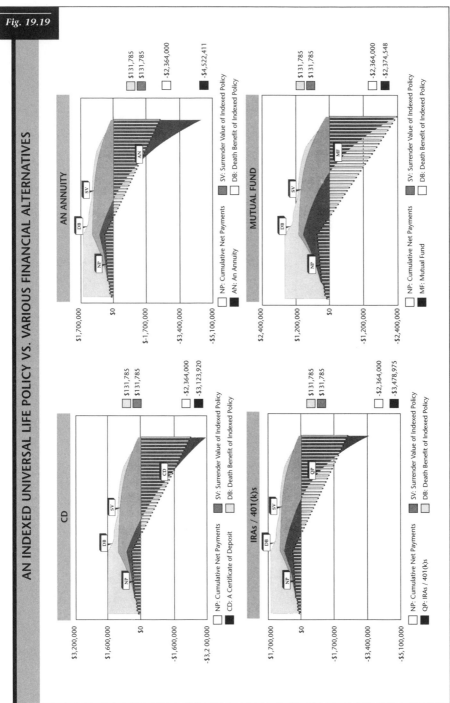

Fig. 19.19

AN INDEXED UNIVERSAL LIFE POLICY VS. VARIOUS FINANCIAL ALTERNATIVES

AN ANNUITY

$131,785
$131,785
-$2,364,000
-$4,522,411

NP: Cumulative Net Payments
AN: An Annuity
SV: Surrender Value of Indexed Policy
DB: Death Benefit of Indexed Policy

$1,700,000
$0
-$1,700,000
-$3,400,000
-$5,100,000

MUTUAL FUND

$131,785
$131,785
-$2,364,000
-$2,374,548

NP: Cumulative Net Payments
MF: Mutual Fund
SV: Surrender Value of Indexed Policy
DB: Death Benefit of Indexed Policy

$2,400,000
$1,200,000
$0
-$1,200,000
-$2,400,000

CD

$131,785
$131,785
-$2,364,000
-$3,123,920

NP: Cumulative Net Payments
CD: A Certificate of Deposit
SV: Surrender Value of Indexed Policy
DB: Death Benefit of Indexed Policy

$3,200,000
$1,600,000
$0
-$1,600,000
-$3,200,000

IRAs / 401(k)s

$131,785
$131,785
-$2,364,000
-$3,478,975

NP: Cumulative Net Payments
QP: IRAs / 401(k)s
SV: Surrender Value of Indexed Policy
DB: Death Benefit of Indexed Policy

$1,700,000
$0
-$1,700,000
-$3,400,000
-$5,100,000

Format and design created through the use of InsMark® software

to our heirs or a charity, so our IRAs and mutual funds will probably last until we die." That may be true, but if I solve for the insurance contract depleting to age 85 instead of age 100, the Smarts may be able to take $110,000 of annual tax-free income instead of $80,000. Based on that income, the other investment alternatives would deplete several years prior to age 85. It doesn't matter when you think you're going to die or whether you care to leave anything behind. Why not have the option of enjoying a greater net spendable income if you can? Why not enjoy retirement with less fear of the possibility of outliving your money? Why not leave behind an extra $100,000 or even $1 million to your spouse, family, or a charity, if it doesn't end up costing you anything out of your retirement benefits?

Sometimes older couples come to me who are about to retire and say, "Oh, we're too old now to do anything; we missed the boat for using equity management strategies to enhance our retirement. We're just going to have to do our best with what we've accumulated, and we'll refer our children to you so they don't make the same mistakes we have!"

It's never too late to maximize your income and benefits while minimizing taxes. It's never too late to seize any opportunity. If a person puts off doing something that will increase their capacities simply because of age, I always ask, "How old will you be in five or ten years if you don't learn to play the piano, get a college degree, or establish an estate plan?" You know, whether that person does those things or not, it's always the same answer. I will illustrate in chapter 22 how people who are between the ages of seventy-five to ninety can dramatically enhance their cash flow and their net transferable estate with little or no out-of-pocket cash!

Actually, some of my greatest satisfaction comes from serving new clients who are more mature. Even though they are predominantly in cure mode rather than prevention mode with regard to their financial challenges and strategies, mature couples have been "around the block." They are generally more disciplined and can readily see the benefits of a sophisticated financial plan. Occasionally older clients who are still financially immature ("financial jelly fish," as I like to say) establish an equity management retirement planning strategy; but in most cases, financial jellyfish seem to be the younger people who have not yet been challenged by the windstorms of life. Unfortunately, I have discovered it is better to let them float about aimlessly, rather than begin something they can't follow through with.

The strategies contained in this book are not for financial jellyfish. Flexibility is an inherent part of every plan I prepare for my clients. I also make contingency plans to accommodate for many unforeseen, uncontrollable financial setbacks. Only when someone dramatically alters his or her original commitment are major adjustments necessary that may incur surrender charges or penalties. But this is true with almost any worthwhile long-term investment. If a person can stay somewhat committed and disciplined, an equity-management retirement planning strategy can prove extremely beneficial during the retirement years, and for those whom the retiree leaves behind at death.

THE WISES—APPLYING RETIREMENT PLANNING STRATEGIES

Let me share one final, typical example with you: a sixty-year-old couple soon to retire. We'll name this couple Bob and Martha Wise. Let's assume that Bob and Martha are both age 60, and plan on retiring at age 65. They have a home that is paid off—and has a fair market value of $700,000. Bob and Martha paid $200,000 for the home twenty-five years earlier, and it has appreciated about 5 percent per year. Let's say that Bob has an income of $80,000 per year and works for a company that provides no defined benefit pension; however, he has participated in a company-sponsored 401(k) and has established other retirement savings. Martha has an annual income of $60,000 as a school teacher/administrator and has a defined benefit pension from the state in which they live. They have $500,000 in qualified plans such as IRAs and 401(k)s earning an average return of 7.75 percent, $100,000 of which is in Roth IRAs.

Additionally, the Wises have $220,000 of non-qualified funds comprised of $100,000 in mutual funds they hope will earn an average return of 12 percent, $60,000 in deferred annuities earning 6.5 percent, and

$60,000 in CDs, money market accounts, and cash management accounts deposited with their bank, credit union, and brokerage firm earning 5 percent. For the sake of simplicity, let's assume with the exception of the deferred annuity, the non-qualified accounts are all newly acquired from using taxed assets or have been taxed as earned so that all taxes are paid and current on any gains up to this point. They have done well for themselves and want to enjoy retirement beginning at age 65 with a minimum of $5,000 per month net spendable income to go on a couple of cruises a year, golf a bit, and feel no financial restrictions from traveling and visiting their children and grandchildren a few times each year. They feel they have more house than they need but feel trapped in their current home, not knowing what will happen tax-wise if they sell it. They would prefer a smaller home that requires less maintenance so they can feel free to travel. Ideally, they would like to have a winter home in a warm climate and a summer home in a cool climate.

We meet with Bob and Martha Wise for a consultation and they learn they can sell their home and realize the entire $500,000 gain tax free. They excitedly begin shopping for a summer condo and a winter condo each at a price of $250,000. Their first inclination is to purchase the condos outright with the cash proceeds from the sale of their home, avoiding any mortgages. Before doing so, we prepare an equity transfer plan for them to review. In conjunction with the equity transfer plan, we analyze where they are headed financially in preparation for retirement. Please refer to **figure 19.20.** Their mutual funds valued at $100,000 are projected to be worth $145,577 after tax at the end of five years at an average gross return of 12 percent, which equals a net annual return of 7.8 percent at a 35 percent tax rate. Their fixed annuities valued at $60,000 are projected to be worth $82,205 at the end of five years at an average return of 6.5 percent. The $60,000 on deposit in their bank, credit union, and brokerage cash management account is projected to be worth only $70,405 after tax at the end of five years at an average gross return of 5 percent, which equals a net of 3.25 percent (5.00 less 35 percent). Keep in mind their home equity of $700,000 will be earning a return of 0 percent during that time period even though the value of the

| Fig. 19.20 | FINANCIAL PROFILE FOR BOB AND MARTHA WISE |
| | Retirement Asset Values |

VALUE OF ACCOUNTS AT AGE 60	INVESTMENT DESCRIPTION	VALUE OF ACCOUNTS AT AGE 65	GROSS ANNUAL INCOME (INTEREST ONLY)
NON-QUALIFIED:			
$100,000	Mutual Fund Portfolio (taxed as earned), Projected to Yield 12% (7.8% after tax).	$145,577	$17,469
$60,000	Fixed Deferred Annuities - Yield 6.5%.	$82,205	$5,343
$60,000	Various CDs, Money Market & Cash Management Accounts - Average Yield 5% (3.25% after tax).	$70,405	$3,520
		$298,187	
QUALIFIED:			
$400,000	IRAs & 401(k)s, Projected to Yield 7.75%.	$580,960	
$2,500 p/m	New Monthly Contributions to 401(k) at 7.75% Yield	$183,678 $764,638	$59,259
	TOTAL VALUE	**$1,062,825**	
	Total Annual Retirement Income (Interest Only) Subject to Tax:		$85,591
	LESS: Federal & State Income Tax at 32%		$-27,389
	Net Spendable Retirement Income from These Resources:		**$58,202**

OTHER ASSETS AVAILABLE TO MEET RETIREMENT OBJECTIVES:

$36,000 p/yr.	Martha's defined benefit pension.
$40,000 p/yr.	Combined Social Security income beginning at age 65.
$145,240	Roth IRA projected to yield 7.75%.
$700,000	Home free & clear of any mortgages.

property may increase. Likewise, if they paid $500,000 cash for their new summer and winter condos, that equity would also not be earning a return. Thus, the total after-tax value of non-qualified funds will equal $298,187 at the end of five years. The $400,000 of qualified funds in traditional IRAs and 401(k)s is projected to be worth $580,960 at the end of five years at an average return of 7.75 percent. Their Roth IRAs valued today at $100,000 are projected to be worth $145,240 at the end of five years. The Wises have some other assets that can also be converted into income.

We advise them to keep their Roth IRAs but not add new money to them. They are anxious for an analysis to see if they can improve the results from their other retirement resources. Excluding the Roth IRAs, the total of the qualified accounts and non-qualified accounts at the end of five years is projected to be $1,062,825 (fig. 19.20). If the Wises were to live on just the interest they are earning and continued to average 7.75 percent, they could take an annual income of $85,591 from these resources without depleting the principal. If they took an income that would gradually deplete the principal to zero by age 100 (35 years from age 65), they could take $88,889 per year. Either way, the income would be taxable. They would only net about $55,635 ($85,591 less 35 percent) and maybe as good as $60,445 ($88,889 less 32 percent). This is because the Wises would likely have to pay between 32 to 35 percent tax, assuming a federal rate of 25 to 28 percent (after the years 2006 to 2010) and a state tax rate of 7 percent. Why would they be in that bracket?

Remember, both Bob and Martha worked throughout their careers, contributing to and qualifying for Social Security. If a person's income were $60,000 in the year 2001 and she were age 60, the estimate of monthly Social Security benefits she'd be eligible for would equal $1,578. If a person's income were $80,000 in the year 2001 and she were age 60, the estimate of monthly Social Security benefits she'd be eligible for would equal $1,741. If this were the case, Bob and Martha together would receive Social Security benefits of $3,319 per month or about $40,000 per year.

In addition to Social Security, Martha will receive a defined benefit pension from her state retirement fund. Assuming she was employed for thirty years, let's say she is entitled to receive 2 percent of the average of the best three years of her last five years' salary for every year of service (this is a typical formula for computing school teacher/administrator retirement). Assuming a $60,000 average salary, she could receive 60 percent of that, which is $36,000 per year, with a 2 to 3 percent cost of living increase each year as a retirement income benefit.

As Martha is preparing to retire, she meets with the state retirement benefits office and they give her a few options. She can take the 100 percent no-survivor benefit, or she can select a reduced income that provides a survivor benefit. Under the no-survivor benefit, she will receive $36,000 per year, which equals $3,000 per month. However, if she were to die any time after six months following her retirement starting date, the income would cease. In order to generate an income for someone who has a remaining life expectancy of twenty to twenty-five years (age 65 to age 85 or 90) under an interest-only solution, an investment worth $450,000 would have to earn an average of 8 percent to generate an annual income of $36,000 ($36,000 divided by 8 percent). Under a principal and interest solution, where the resource gradually depletes over twenty-five years, an investment of $415,000 would have to earn an average of 8 percent to generate an annual income of $36,000.

Martha is asked by her retirement office, "Don't you want to share this $450,000 asset with your husband?" A person's answer will usually be, "Of course I do!" In order to share this asset with a surviving spouse, a reduction in income benefits will be required depending on the option chosen. There are usually three to five options from which to choose. The most popular are the 100 percent survivor benefit and the 50 percent survivor benefit options. For the sake of brevity, let's study only the 100 percent benefit option.

Under the 100 percent survivor option, Martha will get about 54 percent of her last working average salary of $60,000 rather than 60 percent. This means she would receive $32,400 per year ($2,700 per month) instead of $36,000 per year ($3,000 per month). Martha would be giving up $300 per month the rest of her life in order to assure that Bob continues to receive $2,700 per month of income the rest of his life should she die first. In essence, Martha would be paying a life insurance premium of $300 per month to protect her husband in the event of her death. What Martha doesn't realize is this will likely be the most expensive life insurance premium she will ever pay, and it only contains limited benefits!

Martha will not likely pass away first. In fact, if they are the same age, Martha is expected to outlive her husband by about seven years. However, if she should die first, Bob would only receive the $2,700 of income the rest of his life; then it stops. The $450,000 asset is not left behind to the family. Only the income that it was generating is provided to the survivor, which is discontinued upon the second death. Not only that, but if they both die in a common disaster, the benefit ceases— there is nothing left behind to their children. The $450,000 asset has vanished, or rather, it has been confiscated by the state retirement fund. What's more, if Bob should die first, Martha cannot rename a new beneficiary even if she remarries. Of course, this is all calculated on actuarial tables, so the retirement benefits are what they are because she is willing to accept this risk. Would you knowingly purchase a life insurance policy with those restrictions? There is usually a better way.

Generally, if a person with a defined benefit pension that contains such options can carefully plan in advance, she can self-insure with far better provisions than outlined in this example. In other words, if Martha were to own a private life insurance policy in the amount of $405,000 ($32,400 divided by 8 percent) or more, on her demise, Bob could have the same $32,400 of annual income at an 8 percent interest rate earned on $405,000—and still leave behind $405,000 to their children on his death. Not only that, but the benefit is not relinquished if Bob should die first. The children could be named as contingent beneficiaries, or Martha could rename a new spouse as primary beneficiary. But how does Martha afford to pay for $405,000 of private life insurance?

As I have taught throughout this book, I try to pay for life insurance benefits with otherwise payable income taxes. So let's see if we can kill two, maybe three birds with one stone as we reposition some of Bob and Martha's assets to enhance their retirement.

As explained earlier, if Bob and Martha keep heading down the traditional path, the projected $1,062,825 of retirement assets, comprised of their traditional IRAs, 401(k)s, and non-qualified funds, could generate an annual income of $85,591 if they were to withdraw interest only. We are assuming they continue to earn an average of 12 percent on their mutual funds, 6.5 percent on their annuities, 5.0 percent on their CDs and money markets, and 7.75 percent on their IRAs and 401(k)s. Because of their Social Security income and Martha's defined benefit pension income of $32,400, the additional $85,591 of income would put them into a 35 percent tax bracket on some of that income. Again, this is because the Wises will have $32,400 in annual taxable income from Martha's defined benefit pension, and 85 percent of Social Security income will be taxable. So they, like millions of other retired Americans, get caught in the trap of thinking they will save tax by postponing taking their income out of their IRAs and 401(k)s. Remember that realizing income does not mean you have to consume it. If Bob and Martha take the $85,591 of income at an average 32 percent tax rate, they will pay $27,389 in taxes annually and only net $58,202 to use however they want. Let's explore what they could do better.

First, let's sell the Wises' home for $700,000 and take the entire capital gain tax free as allowed on the sale of a personal residence. But instead of paying cash for the summer and winter condos, let's use an equity management plan. So instead of paying cash for the new residences, the Wises pay 20 percent down, or $50,000 (for a total of $100,000), on each of two condos valued at $250,000. They take out a combined mortgage of $400,000 on $500,000 of real estate that is regarded as a primary and secondary residence. This leaves us with $600,000 of equity out of their previous home. This strategy also establishes an acquisition indebtedness on the new properties that allows deductibility of interest on the full $400,000 of mortgages. For the sake of simplicity, let's assume the Wises are able to obtain interest-only mortgages at an interest rate of 7.5 percent. Their annual mortgage payment, which is deductible, equals $30,000 ($400,000 times 7.5 percent). They can easily afford this with the interest they will be earning on the $400,000 of invested equity. They could also cover the mortgage payments from the other income-producing assets they don't need in order to draw retirement income of $5,000 per month. What does equity management do for them?

By doing a strategic roll-out (not roll-over) from their qualified accounts valued at $400,000 at age 60, assuming a 7.75 percent return while we are rolling the funds out, we can transfer $92,365 each year for five years from their IRA and 401(k) portfolios and get the taxes over and done with. The Wises may say, "But what about the income tax we will have to pay if this $92,365 of income is added on top of Bob's $80,000 a year income and Martha's $60,000 a year of income?" But I say, "You're already headed for the same income tax bracket on that money in five years; let's not delay the inevitable by postponing the tax liability, thus compounding the problem. Let's get you positioned for substantial tax-free income starting after age 65 to enhance the benefits you and your children can receive."

First of all, $30,000 of the $92,365 annual roll-out is in essence tax free because of the mortgage-interest deduction offset we created. That alone saves the Wises $10,500 per year in tax ($30,000 times 35 percent). Over just a five-year period while the Wises are repositioning their IRAs and 401(k)s, they can save $52,500 in tax. Let's say that the Wises' combined gross income of $140,000 was already reduced to a taxable income of $110,000 on their Form 1040 tax return without the mortgage interest deduction. This is because they have a total of $30,000 in deductions and exemptions, such as $10,000 in property and other tax deductions, $14,000 in charitable contributions, and $6,000 in exemptions. If we add $92,365 of IRA/401(k) roll-out income to the previous taxable income of $110,000 each of five years, the new total would equal $202,365. However, now the Wises would have an additional $30,000 of interest deduction, so their taxable income would really be $172,365, which keeps them below the next income tax threshold—above which an additional 5.5 percent is payable in tax. Even if we go over the threshold by $1,000, the Wises only have to pay an extra 5.5 percent on the $1,000 ($55) they went over.

Let's assume they have to pay income tax at a 35 percent rate on the difference between the former $110,000 of taxable income and the new $172,365 of taxable income. The tax due would be 35 percent of $62,365, which is $21,828. When we divide $21,828 by $92,365, we find that we, in effect, paid only 23.63 percent in tax versus 35 percent by virtue of the mortgage interest offset. We realize we can effectively transfer $461,825 ($92,365 for five years) out of the Wises' IRAs and 401(k)s at a lower effective tax rate (23.63 percent) than they will probably ever experience otherwise. Sometimes we are able to totally offset all income tax due on a strategic transfer, depending on the ratio of annual qualified roll-out to mortgage interest.

If we subtract the income tax liability of $21,828 from the gross amount of the annual transfer of $92,365, we net $70,537 that we can reposition into an insurance contract. By doing so, upon the first death of Bob or Martha, the death benefit can blossom and more than replenish the tax we had to pay, so the surviving beneficiary has a rejuvenated resource to live on the rest of his or her life. If Bob and Martha had paid the annual tax of $27,389 at a 32 percent rate on their IRA and 401(k) income as previously calculated, over a period of twenty years they would have paid $547,780 in taxes. In this example, using equity management, the Wises were able to get their tax liability over with in five short years by paying only $109,140 in tax ($21,828 per year for five years). As painful as it may seem in the short run, it is usually far to their advantage to do this in the long run.

Let's now structure a portfolio of life insurance contracts, in which we will reposition the Wises' retirement resources, to comply with TEFRA/DEFRA and TAMRA guidelines. We want to diversify their assets perhaps into several buckets (policies) that may be comprised of a mixture of fixed and index policies using different companies and, if possible, using both Bob and Martha as insureds. However, for simplicity in this example, let's refer to them collectively as one bucket or policy. Remember from chapter 17 we have to determine the size of the bucket (policy) in order to accommodate the ultimate amount of aggregate premiums they may want to pay into the policy. The Wises have $600,000 of net equity from the sale of their home as they purchase two new condos (**fig. 19.21**). In addition, they will have about $70,500 net after tax from the roll-out of their qualified accounts for five years which totals $352,500. Let's plan on repositioning the CDs, money market accounts, and cash management accounts valued at $60,000 at some strategic point to increase the yield. Let's also plan on repositioning the $60,000 in annuities at an appropriate time for the same reason. Finally, let's plan on liquidating the mutual funds valued at $100,000 at a strategic time to convert them to an investment that receives a more stable, tax-free return.

Fig. 19.21

A STRATEGIC COORDINATION OF AN IRA/401(k) STRATEGIC ROLL-OUT AND
A Properly Structured Investment-Grade Life Insurance Contract in Harmony with an Equity Management Retirement Plan

	TAX BRACKET 35%	GROSS ANNUAL ROLL-OUT FOR 5 YEARS $92,365		VALUE OF ASSETS AT THE BEGINNING $400,000	IRA/401(K) INTERIM YIELD 7.75%
YEAR	GROSS ROLL-OUT	MORTGAGE INTEREST OFFSET	NET TAXABLE	INCOME TAX	NET TRANSFER TO LIFE INSURANCE POLICY
1	$92,365	$30,000	$62,365	$21,828	$70,537
2	$92,365	$30,000	$62,365	$21,828	$70,537
3	$92,365	$30,000	$62,365	$21,828	$70,537
4	$92,365	$30,000	$62,365	$21,828	$70,537
5	$92,365	$30,000	$62,365	$21,828	$70,537
TOTAL	$461,825	$150,000	$311,825	$109,140	$352,685

$109,140 is 23.63% of $461,825

	TAXABLE INCOME WITHOUT ROLL-OUT	TAXABLE INCOME WITH ROLL-OUT
Bob's Income:	$80,000	$80,000
Martha's Income:	$60,000	$60,000
Deductions:	[24,000]	[54,000]
Exemptions:	[6,000]	[6,000]
Roll-Out:	$0	$92,365
Taxable:	$110,000	$172,365

$62,365 Difference

SUMMARY OF BENEFITS

Qualified Plan Assets are all repositioned & taxes complete at a cost of $109,140

OTHERWISE

Taxes on Qualified Retirement Income of $59,259 per year (see **fig.** 19.18 would have been over $20,000 per year for as long as the asset existed.

(20 years x $20,000 = $400,000 in taxes)

A STRATEGIC COORDINATION OF EQUITY TRANSFERRED FROM THE SALE OF A HOME IN CONJUNCTION WITH REPOSITIONING CERTAIN MUTUAL FUNDS, ANNUITIES, CDS, & MONEY MARKET ACCOUNTS AND
A Properly Structured Investment-Grade Life Insurance Contract in Harmony with an Equity Management Retirement Plan

	TAX BRACKET 35%	GROSS ANNUAL TRANSFER ALLOWED UNDER TAMRA GUIDELINES $200,000		VALUE OF ASSETS AT THE BEGINNING* $820,000	INTERIM YIELD 7.75%
YEAR	TRANSFER INTO INSURANCE POLICY	BALANCE IN SIDE FUND	ANNUAL INTEREST EARNED	TAX DUE ON INTEREST	NET BALANCE
1	$200,000	$620,000	$48,050	$16,818	$641,232
2	$200,000	$451,232	$34,970	$12,240	$473,962
3	$200,000	$273,962	$21,232	$7,431	$287,763
4	$200,000	$87,763	$6,802	$2,381	$92,184
5	$92,184	$0	$0	$0	$0
TOTAL	$892,184		$111,054	$38,870	

* Assets at the beginning are comprised of:
1) $600,000 of Net Equity realized from the sale of a $700,000 home and purchasing two retirement condos with a combined value of $500,000 and paying only $100,000 in the form of a down payment.
2) $100,000 of Mutual Fund assets.
3) $60,000 of Annuity assets.
4) $60,000 of CDs, Money Market and Cash Management assets.

The total of the net transferable equity ($600,000) and the non-qualified funds ($220,000) equals $820,000. However, to comply with TAMRA guidelines so the insurance contract is not considered a Modified Endowment Contract, preventing a potentially tax-free retirement income stream—we need to pay particular care to how quickly we fill up the bucket (pay premiums into the policy). I am going to assume we roll-out the Wises' qualified funds on an annual basis in the amount of $92,365, paying the reduced tax of $21,828, and paying a net of $70,500 as a premium into the policy. On the remaining $820,000 of assets, we will assume while we are strategically transferring them into the policy using any one or a combination of the methods described, we will earn an average of 7.75 percent taxable interest during the process.

As seen by studying **figure 19.21**, we will transfer $200,000 into the life insurance policy each year in addition to the strategic qualified plan annual net roll-out of $70,500. Thus the annual maximum premium we will pay into the insurance contract will be $270,500 for the first four years. In the meantime, the Wises will be earning 7.75 percent and will be required temporarily to pay tax on that interest each year. Through careful planning, we will assume here the amount and timing of the transfer of funds in accordance with the tax thresholds that increase yearly will keep the Wises in a 35 percent average tax bracket. As seen in figures 19.21 and 19.22, after four years of transferring $200,000 each year into the insurance contract, the Wises still have about $92,000 left to transfer in addition to the last qualified plan after-tax transfer of $70,500. So in the beginning of year 5 (as soon as four years and one day after the policy inception), the remaining $162,500 ($92,000 plus $70,500) is paid into the contract. The grand total of all the premiums paid into the insurance contract over the five-year period equals $1,244,500. If the five annual premiums were paid in equal installments, the policy could be funded at the rate of $248,900 per year. When we solve for the minimum face amount of life insurance for a sixty-year-old male who might be rated preferred, TEFRA/DEFRA guidelines dictate that the death benefit must be at least $3,175,000. Now let's see how this life insurance, (which is required to receive tax-free growth and a tax-free income stream) can be paid for with otherwise payable income taxes.

Please study **figure 19.22**. I am going to assume Bob and Martha's insurance contracts credit 7.75 percent interest over the life of the policy. I am using an example of an equity-indexed universal life so as to illustrate a realistic, but conservative, average that might be achieved with a portfolio of fixed, indexed, and variable insurance contracts. Keep in mind the illustration shows a life insurance death benefit of $3,175,000, all on Bob's life. In reality, I would recommend that Martha's life be insured for at least 12.75 percent of $3,175,000 ($405,000) in order to allow her to choose the no-survivor benefit on her defined benefit pension. That would provide the Wises with $300 per month of additional income without jeopardizing Bob's financial situation in the event of Martha's death. If Martha lives to age 90, this strategy alone would create $90,000 of additional income they didn't have to give up if they had chosen the 100 percent survivor option. The time value of that $300 per month equates to $275,754 over twenty-five years! Of course, the Wises can opt for half or even all of the $3,175,000 of life insurance to be placed on Martha, provided she qualifies from a medical and financial underwriting standpoint. However, I usually want to insure the husband for more in order to provide security for the wife, because she will likely live longer.

There are a few issues that hinder us from making this equity management retirement planning strategy really shine. First, we have to comply with TEFRA/DEFRA and TAMRA guidelines by spreading out the funding of the insurance contract over five years. Second, the Wises will be starting a retirement income stream immediately after filling the bucket to the brim (funding the insurance contract to the maximum allowed). Therefore, the Wises' internal rate of return will not be as handsome as it otherwise could be had we some time to let the cash values grow and compound as with younger clients. Perhaps if they didn't need the income or could get by on a reduced income during the initial years of their retirement by using other resources such as their Roth IRAs, the internal rate of return would be enhanced. Nonetheless, let me illustrate how even an internal rate of return of 5.88 percent that is tax free can

Fig. 19.22	A TAX-ADVANTAGED LIFE INSURANCE AND RETIREMENT FUND

After-Tax Cash Flow Using An Indexed Universal LIfe Policy

Age	Year	Net After-Tax Payment	Retirement Income Tax-Advantaged Cash Flow	Accumulation Value	Net Surrender Value	Death Benefit
61	1	$270,500	$ 0	$ 255,819	$ 173,269	$3,175,000
62	2	270,500	0	534,125	381,725	3,175,000
63	3	270,500	0	836,895	684,495	3,175,000
64	4	270,500	0	1,166,279	1,013,879	3,175,000
65	5	162,500	0	1,409,474	1,257,074	3,175,000
66	6	0	96,000	1,496,086	1,252,426	3,076,120
67	7	0	96,000	1,585,461	1,247,575	2,974,274
68	8	0	96,000	1,677,695	1,242,527	2,869,372
69	9	0	96,000	1,772,889	1,237,292	2,761,323
70	10	0	96,000	1,871,150	1,239,502	2,650,033
71	11	0	96,000	1,970,611	1,239,575	2,535,404
72	12	0	96,000	2,071,238	1,237,374	2,417,336
73	13	0	96,000	2,173,111	1,232,877	2,295,726
74	14	0	96,000	2,276,669	1,226,416	2,170,468
75	15	0	96,000	2,381,222	1,217,193	2,041,452
76	16	0	96,000	2,489,150	1,207,475	1,908,565
77	17	0	96,000	2,599,094	1,195,786	1,771,692
78	18	0	96,000	2,711,492	1,167,205	1,630,713
79	19	0	96,000	2,826,962	1,137,466	1,485,504
80	20	0	96,000	2,946,396	1,107,336	1,335,939
81	21	0	96,000	3,071,212	1,078,099	1,231,660
82	22	0	96,000	3,200,256	1,048,470	1,208,483
83	23	0	96,000	3,330,545	1,015,326	1,181,853
84	24	0	96,000	3,461,825	978,269	1,151,360
85	25	0	96,000	3,594,334	937,392	1,117,108
86	26	0	96,000	3,727,917	892,386	1,078,781
87	27	0	96,000	3,861,573	842,096	1,035,174
88	28	0	96,000	3,994,843	785,902	985,644
89	29	0	96,000	4,127,219	723,130	929,491
90	30	0	96,000	4,259,239	654,147	867,108
91	31	0	96,000	4,390,680	578,555	798,089
92	32	0	96,000	4,524,065	498,696	679,659
93	33	0	96,000	4,660,085	415,075	554,877
94	34	0	96,000	4,799,584	328,343	424,335
95	35	0	96,000	4,943,611	239,353	288,789
96	36	0	96,000	5,091,879	147,614	147,614
97	37	0	96,000	5,247,563	56,090	56,090
98	38	0	96,000	0	0	0

* This illustration assumes the nonguaranteed values shown continue in all years.
This is not likely, and actual results may be more or less favorable.
Format and design created through the use of InsMark® software.

Fig. 19.22 continued	Gross Interest Rate Required on a Hypothetical Taxable Investment to Match an Indexed Universal Life Policy Values Over 38 Years

		Hypothetical Taxable Alternative
To match Accumulation Value of:	$5,247,563	12.31%
To match Surrender Value of:	$56,090	8.63%
To match Death Benefit of:	$56,090	8.63%

INCOME TAX CONSIDERATIONS

1. A hypothetical taxable investment: Interest is taxed as earned.

2. An Indexed Universal Life Policy
   a. Death Benefit including cash value component is income tax free.
   b. Loans are income-tax free as long as the policy is kept in force.
   c. Withdrawals and other non-loan policy cash flow up to cost basis (not in violation of IRC Section 7702) are income-tax free as a return of premium.
   d. Cash values shown assume most favorable combination of b and/or c.

37-YEAR GRAPHIC ANALYSIS

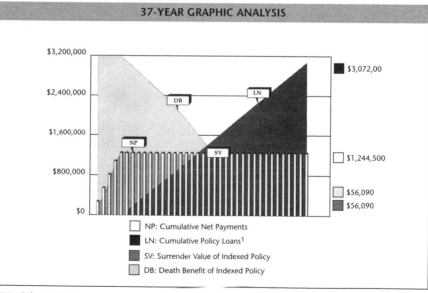

- NP: Cumulative Net Payments
- LN: Cumulative Policy Loans[1]
- SV: Surrender Value of Indexed Policy
- DB: Death Benefit of Indexed Policy

(1) For Retirement Income.
Format and design created through the use of InsMark® software.

create a much superior retirement benefit than where Bob and Martha Wise were headed using the traditional approach.

Let's say that Bob and Martha would like to take the maximum income they can from their insurance contract without depleting it until between ages 98 and 100. However, Bob and Martha would still like to leave behind over $1 million tax free to the surviving spouse, their children, or a charity if either one of them died at life expectancy of age 85. As shown in **figure 19.22**, the Wises could take an income stream of $96,000 per year and still leave behind over $1 million if death occurred at age 85 (year 25). They could both live to age 98, still taking an annual income of $96,000 tax free, before they would run out of funds. This is where careful and strategic planning must come into play.

Based on the interest rate credited, the mortality charges, and the cash values accessed, particular care needs to be taken to ensure there are sufficient cash values remaining in the policy to keep the insurance death benefit in force until the time death finally occurs. Why? A life insurance policy that lapses or is surrendered can trigger a taxable event on the gain realized from accessing cash values in excess of the basis (premiums paid) in the contract.

Fortunately, it is easy to monitor this to ensure cash values are not depleted to the degree that would put the policy in jeopardy prior to death. If a policy were neglected or there were a desperate need for liquid funds that depleted the cash values of a policy—putting it in jeopardy of lapsing—several things can remedy the situation if planned in advance. In the unlikely event the Wises neglected advice, both lived to over age 98, and totally depleted the policy of cash values, it would behoove them or their heirs to beg or to borrow resources to keep the policy in force until death by paying a minimum premium back into the contract to avoid triggering a tax.

In this example, if the Wises indeed took an income of $96,000 a year for thirty-three years, it would total $3,168,000. Their basis in the insurance contract would have been $1,244,500, resulting in a gain of $1,923,500, which would be taxed as ordinary income. Although this has never even come close to happening with any of my clients, I've often wondered how the IRS would proceed to collect tax on $1,923,500 from a ninety-eight-year-old couple who perhaps had used up all their resources for medical or other reasons. In any case, the insurance agent and insurance company's job is to do everything in their power to ensure something like that will not happen. As explained earlier, based on these assumptions, just taking about 6.25 percent less income (in this case about $90,000 instead of $96,000) would have prevented the insurance contract from ever getting into jeopardy.

What we have provided for the Wises is a potential retirement income stream of $96,000 per year totally free of income tax if they access the money under the methods explained in chapter 17. If they don't need the income, they don't have to start pulling it out at age 70^1/$_2$ to avoid a penalty. If they happen to die, the amount remaining in the account blossoms and transfers tax free, usually to the degree that it replenishes or reimburses not only the tax that was paid on the front end during the funding process, but also any depletion of the account that may have occurred.

Remember that Martha was able to take an extra $3,600 a year of income from her pension without leaving Bob out of the picture financially. So, between the $96,000 of possible tax-free retirement income and $3,600 of additional pension income, the Wises could have almost $100,000 a year ($96,000 of which would be tax free) in income compared to the $85,591 of taxable income that nets them around $58,200. So what's missing from the equation? Oh yeah, the mortgage!

After the first five years, Bob and Martha Wise would have several options regarding the mortgage, by which they could offset $50,500 of taxes on their 401(k) and IRA roll-out. At that point, they could have planned to simply pay off the $400,000 mortgage on their two retirement condos. However, even at an internal rate of return of only 5.88 percent, they would be earning interest greater than the net cost of the mortgage, which would be 4.88 percent in a 35 percent tax bracket. That one percent differential is enough arbitrage to make a handsome profit during their retirement years. The net after-tax cost of $30,000 a year of deductible interest at a 35 percent tax rate is $19,500. So if we deduct $19,500 from the $100,000 income stream to service the mortgage, the

Wises still have a net of over $80,000 per year, compared to $58,200 if they had maintained the status quo. That is still a difference of $21,800 per year. Over a twenty-five-year period, if Bob or Martha lives to age 90, that equates to $545,000 of extra retirement income. The time value of $21,800 per year at 7.75 percent equals $1,655,773.

If they had sold their home, paid cash for the two condos, and invested the remaining $200,000 of home equity at the same 7.75 percent we have used in this illustration, that investment would have only generated $15,500 a year of taxable income. This nets them only $10,075 ($15,500 less 35 percent) per year on top of their $58,200 after-tax income.

If these kinds of results can be achieved with a conservative internal rate of return of 5.88 percent, can you imagine what the difference could be if we could achieve 7, 8, or 9 percent? You dream with me.

Finally, let's take a quick look at what the actual tax computation may look like for the Wises (**fig. 19.23**). First of all, under either scenario, the income taken from the Roth IRA would be the same and would not affect their income tax computation. If the Wises maintained the status quo as shown in column A, their annual gross income would be comprised of $85,591 from their IRAs, 401(k)s, mutual funds, annuities, and bank accounts as explained earlier. In addition, Martha's defined benefit pension would be $32,400 because she took the 100 percent survivor option. On top of that, let's assume they receive combined Social Security income of $40,000 per year. Under current tax law, 85 percent of their Social Security ($34,000) would be subject to tax. The total of these three categories equals $151,991. Let's continue to assume the Wises have $10,000 in tax deductions, $14,000 in charitable contributions, and $6,000 in exemptions for a total of $30,000. We also will ignore the slight difference that would be reflected in the reduction of exemptions and itemized deductions for high-income taxpayers since they are being phased out with the 2001 Act. Let's use the tax year 2002 thresholds as an example and assume a 7 percent flat state income tax rate. However, let's use the reduced tax rates projected for the tax years 2006 and beyond for the third and fourth brackets, according to the 2001 Act. So the taxable income in this scenario would be $121,991.

Fig. 19.23

COMPARISON OF ANNUAL TAX LIABILITY*
ON RETIREMENT INCOME
for Bob and Martha Wise

A Maintaining their Current Plan of Qualified and Non-Qualified Assets		B Converting to a Home Equity Retirement Plan Utilizing a Life Insurance Contract
$85,591	Gross Annual Income from IRA/401(k) & other assets.	$96,000
$32,400	Martha's Defined Benefit Pension	$36,000
$40,000	Social Security	$40,000
$157,991	TOTAL	$172,000
$151,991	Net Portion Subject to Tax LESS Deductions:	$70,000
$10,000	Taxes	$10,000
$14,000	Charitable Contributions	$14,000
$6,000	Personal Exemptions	$6,000
$0	Mortgage Interest	$30,000
$121,991	TOTAL TAXABLE INCOME	$10,000
	Tax Rates:	
$2,020	On first $12,000 = 17%	$1,700
$7,634	On next $34,700 = 22%	$0
$21,168	On next $66,150 = 32%	$0
$3,199	On next $9,141 = 35%	$0
$34,021	TOTAL ANNUAL TAX	$1,700

Which Annual Tax Bill Would You Prefer?

** Based upon 2002 Federal Income Tax Thresholds and a 7% flat State Income Tax Rate.
However, the tax rates used for the third and fourth brackets are the projected reduced rates
according to the 2001 Act.*

On the first $12,000 of taxable income, $2,020 (17 percent) would be owed. On the next $34,700 of income up to $46,700, $7,634 (22 percent) would be owed. On the next $66,150 of income up to $112,850, $21,168 (32 percent) would be owed. And on the last $9,141, $3,199 (35 percent) would be owed. The total effective tax that would be paid would equal $34,021. Subtracting the tax from the gross income of $157,991 (that number includes the $6,000 of Social Security that was not subject to tax), the Wises would net $123,970.

In column B, please study the tax consequence of the recommended plan. The Wises would have $96,000 of tax-free income. In addition, they would have a taxable income of $36,000 from Martha's defined benefit pension (no-survivor benefit option). Lastly, they would also have the same $40,000 of Social Security, of which only $34,000 is subject to tax. (Although they may qualify for some of their Social Security to be only 50 percent subject to tax, for simplicity, let's just assume that a full 85 percent is subject to tax.) The only income that would show up on the Wises' tax return would be $70,000. If we subtract the same $30,000 of deductions and exemptions they already had, plus the additional $30,000 of mortgage interest deduction, their taxable income is a mere $10,000. This puts the Wises in the absolute lowest bracket a taxpayer can be in. At 17 percent, they would have an annual tax liability of $1,700 versus $34,021, which is what they would have owed if they had retained the status quo! It would take twenty years of paying $1,700 in tax to equal one year of paying $34,000 in tax. Twenty years of $34,041 of tax payments equals $680,420 given up in taxes at the time in life when Bob and Martha may need the money the most. Should the IRS and their state tax commission be upset? They shouldn't be! Even though Bob and Martha paid them a reduced tax up front of $21,828 for five years on the strategic roll-out, as well as $38,870 in tax on the side fund while complying with TEFRA/DEFRA and TAMRA, if the revenuers were prudent investors and good stewards of the taxes we pay them, they could realize $680,420 by just earning a 7.3 percent return over that same period instead of spending it!

Through the same basic strategy used hypothetically with the Wises, I have been successful with many clients in substantially reducing or eliminating unnecessary tax, maximizing net spendable income, and creating a sizable estate for transfer to heirs or charity.

TRUE-LIFE CLIENTS

I distinctly remember the first time two of my favorite clients came in for an initial consultation after attending a seminar. They were sixty-two years old and intrigued with equity management concepts, but hesitated at the idea of mortgaging their free and clear properties. They both had defined benefit pensions we maximized through bringing life insurance along for the ride, as we strategically repositioned their supplemental IRAs and 401(k)s. They chose no-survivor benefit options, thus creating an additional $500 per month of income they didn't think they would get. To make a long story short, they were likely going to pay a minimum of $160,000 in tax on their IRAs and 401(k)s if they strung out the withdrawals based on minimum distributions. But by accelerating the process and doing a strategic roll-out over a five-year period, we successfully reduced their tax liability to $60,000. They were thrilled with that.

Then, out of curiosity, this ultra-conservative couple asked me to just prepare a simple illustration of what benefit they might receive if they separated the equity in their home by taking out a mortgage. We found by doing so they would reduce the tax liability further to $20,000. They asked what would happen if they also refinanced their cabin. We reduced the tax liability even further to just $9,000. They moved ahead and mortgaged both properties.

These two clients have made an excellent return above the net cost of the mortgages. I remember about two years after beginning their roll-out plan, they came in for an annual review and wanted to withdraw enough to pay off both mortgages. They had forgotten the benefits and why we did what we did. I told them that was easy to do and began to prepare the form to liquidate enough from their insurance contracts to pay off their mortgages. Before signing the form, they asked if the withdrawal would be taxed. I explained to them that it wouldn't be, but they would pay $10,200 per year for the ensuing three years in additional tax by not having the mortgage interest deduction. They changed their minds and have continued their mortgages ever since. This has generated an additional positive cash flow of several hundred dollars per month in profit over the cost of employing their equity. In addition, the tax deduction keeps helping to offset taxes on their defined benefit pension income.

I have another set of clients who have been extremely successful with this strategy. This is primarily because they have remained committed to their plan. For the first five years of their strategic conversion from their qualified accounts to a non-qualified status, I had them come to my office to resell them on the wisdom of enduring the tax pain on the front end. At a minimum, they were headed toward paying over $1.2 million in tax by stringing out the distributions from age 70$1/2$ for the rest of their lives. By completing a roll-out in five years, they paid over $500,000 in taxes, some of which were at a high 38.2 percent rate. Every year I felt like Sam I Am in Dr. Seuss's, *Green Eggs and Ham*. I kept promising my clients, "You will like this, you will see!" Well, after the five years of pain were completed and several years of considerable tax-free earnings and income have followed with no tax liability on their tax return, they do like the green that provides them plenty of eggs and ham! They've never spent even half of what they earn each year, but it's okay because Uncle Sam is not forcing them at their current age of seventy-five to pull out any money they don't want to!

19 WEALTH ENHANCEMENT STRATEGY NUMBER NINETEEN

- *Maximize tax-favored benefits on the contribution, accumulation, distribution, and transfer phases of retirement planning.*
- *Trade traditional retirement savings and accumulation vehicles for a strategic plan that repositions retirement plan contributions or distributions in harmony with home equity management principles.*

CHAPTER 20

Repositioning Assets and Attitude

Determine which assets to reposition to enhance your net worth.

Only lucky people with lots of money or discretionary dollars, taking high risks and achieving high rates of return, get wealthy.

REALITY

You can often reposition current expenditures or investments in order to gain positive leverage. Returns of just 6 to 8 percent interest can create tremendous wealth. Your attitude will be the most important factor in determining the altitude of your wealth.

Unfortunately, many people think wealth is only for the lucky few—those with lots of money or discretionary dollars who take high risks and achieve high rates of return. Hopefully, this book helps you realize wealth is attainable—and perhaps it's merely the view from where you sit that makes you fear defeat in achieving financial independence. Contrary to what many people believe, the essential common denominator among self-made millionaires is not luck, nor the level of their education, but rather their positive attitudes. They look for and find the good in every situation.

A closed mind has proven to be the reason more people don't attain the heights they could have achieved in life. It's truly sad when a person goes to the grave with so much potential trapped within. By changing our perspective, we can often enhance our potential for achieving greater net worth, dramatically enhancing our retirement.

FOCUS ON THE POSITIVE

Let's pinpoint some financial areas traditionally viewed from main floor seating and raise a loftier perspective. You can often reposition current expenditures or investments to leverage the equity in your home. Remember returns of 6 to 8 percent can create tremendous wealth! You now should have the understanding to leverage money safely when purchasing property by putting little or nothing down. If a piece of property is acquired with little or nothing down and it has an appreciation rate of 5 percent, you achieve a 5 percent rate of return—not just on your invested capital, but on the entire investment.

For example, if you bought a new home worth $100,000 and only had to pay 10 percent down, $10,000 is the amount of personal money you have invested in the property. Let's say this new home is income property in a good area, and the rental income basically pays the mortgage payments. Maybe it even has a small negative cash flow—in other words, the rental income on the property doesn't quite service the mortgage payment and maintenance expenses. If the property is located in an area where real estate is appreciating, it would be possible to achieve an average appreciation rate of about 5 percent per year. If it appraises for $105,000 at the end of the first year, then you have actually achieved a $5,000 gain on the $10,000 you personally tied up in the property—a 50 percent increase!

If you had a negative cash flow of $100 per month, that would mean $1,200 of your money was invested, in addition to the $10,000 down payment. You would have had an $11,200 investment in a piece of property on which you made an additional $3,800. If you sold the property, you could not only receive back the $10,000 initial investment, but also the extra $5,000 realized in appreciation. If you calculate the return on your net profit of $3,800, you still achieved a 34 percent increase. The next year, if the negative cash flow continued to total $1,200 for the year, but the property appreciated another 5 percent ($5,250), the investment in the property would be $10,000, plus two years of negative cash flow ($2,400). This totals $12,400, compared to the equity of $20,250. The second year $5,250 of appreciation, less the negative cash flow of $1,200, results in a net gain of $4,050. Although real estate with negative cash flow is not usually viewed as desirable, if the property eventually appreciates, the returns can be attractive (if the investor has the ability to cover the negative cash flow). The key is not to view this as a losing proposition, but as an investment into an eventual winning proposition, if and when the conditions are right to realize the gain.

Of course, other factors would need to be considered, such as the cost of possible realtor's fees when the property is sold. Property can often be leveraged safely by putting little or nothing down and by keeping yourself highly liquid in case of down markets or occasional vacancies. By only tying up small amounts of capital, you may achieve the appreciation rate on the entire value of the asset, rather than just the amount you had invested in the property.

THE "I CAN FIND A WAY" ATTITUDE

When someone tells me he can't do something he has not yet tried, he's defeated before he's even started! It has been said, "Whether you think you can or can't, you're probably right!" A young reporter once asked Thomas Edison how he felt about failing in over 10,000 attempts to invent the incandescent light bulb. He replied, "Young man, since you are just getting started in life, I will give you a thought that should benefit you in the future. I have not failed anything 10,000 times. I have successfully found 10,000 ways that will not work." In fact, it took over 14,000 experiments by Mr. Edison to perfect the incandescent light bulb! Henry Ford was the same way when inventing the V-8 engine. He wasn't an engineer, but he had the right attitude for success. Even though his engineers repeatedly told him the V-8 engine was economically unfeasible and an engineering impossibility, he insisted they persist until they succeeded. His engineers, then with the proper change of attitude, succeeded in inventing the V-8 engine, and the rest is history.

Often people will want to manage the equity in their property as I explained in chapter 19. They want to place that equity into a safe environment earning a conservative rate of return on a tax-favored basis. As explained, returns of only 6 to 8 percent are all we generally need in order to create tremendous wealth. Always remember that a return of 8 percent in a tax-free environment can be the same as achieving a 12 to 14 percent return in many taxable environments. All we really need to achieve is a rate of return equal to or greater than the net cost of the invested funds.

Most investments compound, whereas the servicing of the debt on a mortgage is based on a simple-interest declining balance. Once these concepts are understood, some people get excited and yet frustrated because they feel they cannot come up with the money necessary to make the net higher mortgage payment. In doing this analysis with these people, I calculate the real difference in higher house payments. Often I am able to consolidate someone's first mortgage and second mortgage. Or I change a fifteen-year amortization over to a thirty-year amortization and separate equity without increasing outgo.

For example, a $100,000 mortgage at 7.25 percent under a fifteen-year amortization has a monthly payment of $912.86. For the same monthly payment of $912.86, you could have a $130,555, thirty-year mortgage at 7.5 percent. So if your home appraised for $162,500 ($130,555 divided by 80 percent), you could take out an 80 percent loan-to-value cash-out refinance and separate $30,000 of equity without increasing your monthly outlay even one dollar. The net after-tax annual house payment would in fact decrease with the tax deductible mortgage interest. During the first year of a $100,000, fifteen-year mortgage, the net after-tax annual payment would be $8,532. ($912.86 multiplied by 12 equals $10,954, less 34 percent of the tax-deductible interest of $7,124, which would be $2,422). Compare this to a thirty-year mortgage of $130,555 with an identical payment of $912.86 at 7.5 percent. The net after-tax annual house payment is only $7,639 ($912.86 times 12 equals $10,954, less 34 percent of the tax-deductible interest of $9,751, which would be $3,315 the first year). So you could really have a gross house payment of $1,020, which would be a mortgage of $146,000 and would result in the same net out-of-pocket annual house payment of $8,532. Thus, $46,000 of equity could be separated if the house appraised for at least $182,500 ($146,000 divided by 80 percent). So, on the surface your house payment may be more, but with the tax advantages you will achieve on the higher mortgage, your net after-tax payment actually decreases or can stay the same!

Let me give you an actual example. A couple came to my office one day. Their home had a fair market value of about $300,000. They were considering refinancing a fifteen-year first mortgage in the amount of $95,000 at 7.25 percent and an equity line of credit with a $50,000 balance at 8 percent, which had total payments of $1,473.86, as shown in **figure 20.1**. By refinancing their first and second mortgages and using a new thirty-year amortization, we were able to draw out $95,000 of equity to begin their side fund for equity management. Their new mortgage was for $240,000 at 7.5 percent. Even though their payments increased $204 on the surface, their house payments did not go up at all; they actually went down about $2 per month! This is because of the increased tax deduction they got after refinancing, which allowed them to realize that extra money in tax savings. Often a person does not need to increase outgo; he simply needs to reposition assets to be able to manage equity to afford what is perceived as a higher house payment.

Fig. 20.1	SEPARATING EQUITY WITHOUT INCREASING OUTGO		
	MORTGAGE BALANCE	GROSS PAYMENT	NET AFTER TAX PAYMENT
Current First Mortgage:	$95,000	$867.22	$675.42
Equity Line of Credit:	$50,000	$606.64	$496.75
Current Totals:	$145,000	$1,473.86	$1,172.17
PROPOSED REFINANCE	$240,000	$1,678.11	$1,170.25
NET DIFFERENCE			
Equity Removed		$95,000.00	
Increased Surface payment		$204.25	
Actual Net After-Tax Payment		[$1.92]	

MY HOUSE PAYMENT IS MY RETIREMENT CONTRIBUTION

Often people look at my personal house payment and exclaim, "How can you afford that?" I do not view my house payment as a regular house payment at all. I perceive it as my retirement- and investment-funding mechanism. It is a method of forced savings. When I put aside the monthly house payment, this is money I would have otherwise been paying into an IRA, 401(k), or other retirement fund. Instead of getting tax deductions using these retirement vehicles, I am able to get a similar tax deduction on the front end by using the mortgage. I prefund my retirement account with several hundred thousand dollars of my home equity. My fund is extremely liquid in the event I need to access it for emergencies. Additionally, my retirement fund has the potential to grow to a much larger sum of money that will generate a greater net spendable income than if I were plodding along making monthly or annual contributions toward a retirement nest egg. Houses were made to house families, not cash!

REPOSITIONING CURRENT CASH FLOW TO FIND MONEY TO INVEST

A comprehensive analysis can be completed by a professional advisor who is knowledgeable in these concepts to determine a client's current cash flow patterns. Then, recommendations can be made on how to reposition that cash flow to afford the higher house payment, managing the dormant equity separated from his property. This can be accomplished through possibly repositioning several different assets. The first and most obvious place to reposition funds might be to eliminate non-preferred or non-deductible debt and exchange it for preferred debt.

Remember from chapter 7 that exchanging non-preferred debt for preferred debt is almost always a wise move (fig. 7.2). Say a couple has an automobile loan that is not deductible, and they have credit cards in addition to the automobile loan. This is all non-preferred or non-deductible debt. The total payments might be $550 for an automobile loan of $27,000 at 8.2 percent for sixty months and $300 for monthly payments on credit cards. The interest on this non-preferred debt will simply be servicing that debt, without receiving the benefit of a tax deduction. We can eliminate the automobile loan and the credit card balances by exchanging them for preferred debt, provided the couple can stay disciplined and not incur new credit card debt. To pay off that debt, we use some of the equity from the home. However, we need to be careful not to consume that equity but to use it wisely, first to reposition the money we were paying toward retiring non-preferred debt, then to conserve and compound it.

By paying off the automobile and the two credit cards, we can reposition that $850 each month to make the higher house payment and to set the excess aside in an investment side fund. By getting into this habit, we can enjoy having money work for us instead of against us. Soon we will have accumulated a nest egg that can be dipped into, should the need arise, when buying a new automobile a few years later. So as explained earlier, at least you would have the capital accumulated to pay cash for a depreciating asset such as most automobiles, rather than borrow.

Of course, when the automobile market is soft, like it was shortly after the World Trade Center attacks, automobile manufacturers may give tremendous incentives to buy, such as 0 percent or 1.9 percent financing. If I can't get the equivalent result through a cash discount, I will use their money at 0 percent interest instead of my own money (which may be earning 6 to 8 percent tax free), to use the same principles of arbitrage I do with deductible mortgage interest!

Again, you can have interest working for you instead of against you in that the interest that you are paying—based upon the consolidation of that debt through the mortgage—is now deductible. A person paying 18 percent on credit card debt that is not deductible can exchange it for deductible debt at just 7 or 8 percent, which is really only a net, after-tax cost of about 5 percent! By doing that he can effectively achieve a 12 percent return on his money as shown. Thus he frees up a monthly amount he was using to service non-preferred debt and reallocates it for use in the accumulation of wealth through systematic investments.

Occasionally people can also reposition money they had to spend to assist their children for college funding. Sometimes the College Scholarship Service has turned down applications for PELL grants, GSL, and SEOG loans not because people have too much income, but because they have substantial home equity available to them. There have been times when they prefer these people use their home equity to help fund their children's college rather than justify a grant or loan. Requirements may change from one time to another.

I know of an individual who was spending nearly $16,000 a year to support two children in college. Even though he applied for various college grants and loans, he was turned down because he had discretionary dollars available to him in the form of equity in his home. He was able to reposition that equity by borrowing on his home, and was able to afford the higher house payment through the repositioning of funds he was spending on term life insurance. Through a cash-out refinance on his home, his monthly outlay did not increase. However, he was able to transfer a large portion of his home equity into an investment-grade life insurance contract. At that time, cash values of an insurance contract were not deemed discretionary dollars by the College Scholarship Service. Thus, he was able to qualify for nearly $36,000 of federal aid over a three-year period because he changed the status of this asset from discretionary to non-discretionary. This freed up money that he was having to shell out under a tight $40,000 budget and allowed him to save, invest, and afford the higher house payment.

ANALYZING YOUR FINANCIAL PROFILE

Usually when new clients seek a comprehensive equity management plan, we spend two hours filling out what I call a "confidential personal financial profile." This is where we determine where they are now and where they want to go. That allows me to prepare two or three different sixty- to seventy-page hypothetical plans showing different alternatives they may consider. Often, I recommend not just one solution, but several, showing what assets could be repositioned and which monthly income resources they could reallocate in order to dramatically enhance their liquidity, safety of principal, and rate of return, as well as maximize tax deductions. They can thereby enhance their net worth and achieve their goals to help them realize a much higher net spendable retirement income.

When we complete a financial profile, we take into consideration:

- income;
- tax bracket;
- how many years remaining until retirement; or,
- if already retired, how many years might be remaining in their lifetimes based on life expectancy tables.

We then do a careful analysis of all real estate holdings, paying particular attention to a client's residence. Many only have one real estate holding—their primary residence. We look at the mortgages, if any, that exist on that home (as well as other real estate, if applicable), and determine whether it is wise to refinance to separate equity. Maybe a refinance makes sense just to improve the interest rate to earn a better rate of return on a client's equity. It may behoove that person to sell his property and enjoy up to $500,000 of capital gains tax free, move into a new home, and re-establish a high amount of acquisition indebtedness, as illustrated in the examples in chapter 19.

We also analyze other investment holdings. We look at the husband and the wife's pension or profit-sharing plans, their IRAs, and 401(k)s to determine whether it is wise to reposition a portion or all of those contributions into vehicles that will achieve a higher net spendable retirement income. We then determine whether to do a strategic conversion at that time, or to do a strategic conversion with a roll-out plan, starting as early as age 59^1/$_2$. Sometimes we decide to wait until retirement to begin the roll-out.

We then look at planned savings. I have found many people have $20,000 or $30,000 in a credit union or a bank savings account only earning 2 to 4 percent interest. Sometimes I find people who have $300,000 or more in CDs, money markets, savings, and checking accounts. Not only that, but they've been in that position for years! When I ask them why they keep that much in low—or no—interest bearing accounts, they sometimes reply, "Oh for a possible emergency," or "That's our little slush fund," or "We were thinking about going on a trip." I usually retort with, "Where, to the space station on the shuttle?" Most of the time, it is only necessary to have emergency funds on hand in the amount of a few thousand dollars. This, of course, is dependent upon the nature of the emergency and the type of income a person is accustomed to having.

Often, money positioned in other investments, such as insurance contracts, can be almost as liquid as a bank account, even though they are not located down the street with a drive-up window. Those funds can usually be accessed within a few days. Most emergencies can wait at least a few days while funds are liquidated. Even if it took a week to obtain funds from investment accounts that pay higher returns in a tax-favored environment, that would be the better place to park excess funds than in a low-interest bearing account. If the truth were known, many "put and keep" accounts would probably pass the liquidity test as well or better than "put and take" bank and credit union accounts. By having money in an investment such as an insurance contract, it may also be wise for a person to have an equity line of credit or a credit card that allows him to access $5,000 or $10,000 immediately in the event of an urgent emergency. I have many clients who maintain in excess of $50,000 or even $100,000 of immediate credit available through various lines of credit. I personally maintain about $150,000 of credit on various credit cards and a line of credit I can tap into immediately. This then becomes my source of immediate liquid funds rather than dipping into my investment side funds until it is wise.

We next analyze a client's other investments—money market accounts, CDs, annuities, stocks, bonds, or any others. We determine whether those vehicles are for long-range goals or for short-range goals. If for long-range goals, we analyze the net rate of return, after tax, that is being achieved on all of those investments. If the money in a CD is likely not going to be used for a five- to ten-year period, it would behoove that individual to reposition that money into something that would achieve a higher net rate of return—in the 6 or 7 percent range on a tax-free basis—rather than leave it in a CD only earning 5 or 6 percent (or less) interest that is taxable. We would also likely create a greater position of safety by doing so. Money market accounts are also assets that can be repositioned to achieve higher rates of return. Most times I recommend money markets and CDs only be used for short-range goals, probably under two years long, such as, saving for a baby or impending events, such as an automobile purchase or a planned vacation.

Often people have been lured into purchasing annuities because they were sold as a safe investment earning a good rate of return on a tax-deferred basis. All of these features are true. However, as explained earlier, often, a properly structured investment-grade life insurance policy, when funded to a maximum, will outperform an annuity. Remember, when withdrawing funds from an insurance contract, money can be accessed on a tax-free basis rather than a tax-deferred basis. Likewise, people want to reposition money they are investing in mutual funds or stocks and bonds when they realize the average rates of return may only be 10 to 12 percent. After tax, they are actually not achieving as high a return as they could from tax-favored investments, especially during the withdrawal years.

After an analysis of all investments and assets is completed, recommendations can be made for repositioning some of those funds either in a lump sum or in strategic transfers to comply with IRS guidelines. Any new contributions made in those particular investments can also be reallocated. By doing that, money often is freed up that will help cover the higher house payment that might be created when transferring a large amount of equity out of property.

So, by having these various assets available to reposition, most of the time, my clients' outlay doesn't increase at all. They simply reposition where they are currently allocating funds. Then, charts and graphs can be created to illustrate how much their net worth will be enhanced over a ten, twenty, or thirty-year period.

Another category people may want to analyze is life insurance premiums. As I explained before, life insurance has been described by some as a necessary evil. People may feel they only need term insurance for the critical years when they are raising their families. Then they later discover they want life insurance—maybe to make sure a spouse is taken care of, or perhaps to pay off estate taxes with discounted dollars. While obtaining adequate life insurance later in life is wise, it can prove cost prohibitive. It would behoove an individual to begin obtaining permanent life insurance in the early years if he can structure it so the premiums are more or less paid for with money that would have otherwise gone to taxes.

I often discover people are shelling out money that goes down the drain in term insurance. They are more or less renting their insurance. This may not be bad for certain purposes. But, if they are paying $50 to $200 per month for term insurance, by repositioning home equity, they could establish a properly structured permanent life insurance policy and load it full of cash. Then perhaps the minimum death benefit that comes along for the ride under TEFRA/DEFRA guidelines may end up providing all, or greater than, the amount of life insurance they had to pay for in term insurance premiums.

I have also found instances where people are concerned they may not be able to keep their permanent insurance in force because they only can afford the minimum premium. Restructuring those policies could allow them to be funded at maximum IRS guidelines. Or, if the policy has not historically been performing well, it may behoove them to replace that policy with another permanent life insurance policy that has a better history of performance—then fund that policy at maximum guideline levels so a small portion of the interest or dividends realized will pay for the cost of the insurance. In this way, the nominal, tax-free portion paying for the insurance is money reallocated that would have otherwise been shelled out in taxes.

Remember a careful analysis must be done to determine whether it is wise to replace any insurance. Adjustments can often be made to a person's current insurance portfolio to maximize the returns achievable in those policies and minimize the effect of the mortality costs and expense charges associated with an insurance policy. Don't overlook existing life insurance as a source to free up cash flow to meet the higher mortgage payment that may result from separating equity in an equity management plan.

A comprehensive analysis, performed by a properly trained professional, should include consideration of all these areas:

- life insurance premiums;
- planned savings;
- IRAs;
- 401(k)s;
- 403(b), or tax-sheltered annuities;
- and lump-sum transfers of capital from investments such as CDs, money markets, and mutual funds.

Also, money from monthly investments into those types of vehicles can be reallocated. Such an analysis, can help determine if greater net spendable income and return can be achieved by repositioning those assets.

THE ADVANTAGES OF SUCCESSFULLY MANAGING EQUITY

Let's now summarize and review the nine primary advantages that can be realized from successfully managing your home equity. These advantages can also help provide the resources to help implement strategies for managing that home equity. With proper equity management a homeowner can effectively:

1. Increase liquidity
2. Increase safety
3. Earn a rate of return by employing dormant equity
4. Realize tax savings through higher tax deductions
5. Eliminate non-preferred debt
6. Create opportunities for grants, loans, or investments

7. Create greater property portability (sales options)
8. Create an emergency fund
9. Establish a private retirement planning strategy perhaps superior to qualified plans

Let's now see how the six components of sound financial planning fit in with equity management (**fig. 20.2**). The six components include: 1) cash flow management, 2) credit management, 3) asset management, 4) risk management, 5) tax planning, and 6) estate planning.

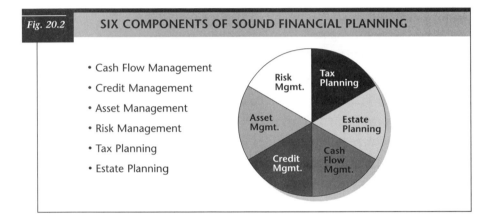

Fig. 20.2 — **SIX COMPONENTS OF SOUND FINANCIAL PLANNING**

- Cash Flow Management
- Credit Management
- Asset Management
- Risk Management
- Tax Planning
- Estate Planning

Successfully managing equity allows a homeowner to employ a large sum of cash on an installment basis in a manner that can fit into his budget. The additional monthly interest expense, if any, can be offset by repositioning cash flow. Most people take their house payments seriously. By having the house payment become your investment or your retirement fund contribution, you are in effect disciplining yourself for good installment investing. Otherwise, if you had to make the choice to invest each month, you may not be as faithful in setting aside money for future goals. It provides a method of systematic savings that can enhance the long-term results without increasing outgo (**fig. 20.3**).

Successfully managing equity allows the opportunity for good credit management. By having cash in a position of liquidity, you do not have to worry about getting behind on your mortgage—you can dip into your liquid cushion if the need arises. I would rather have a slightly higher

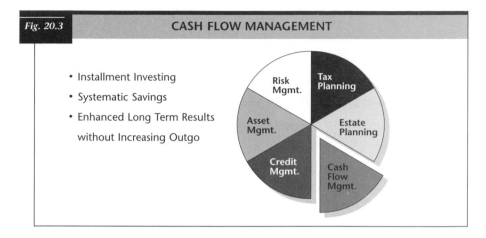

Fig. 20.3 — CASH FLOW MANAGEMENT

- Installment Investing
- Systematic Savings
- Enhanced Long Term Results without Increasing Outgo

house payment with a liquid side fund than a slightly lower house pay-ment with no liquidity—especially if I get into a pickle and need to maintain my credit rating by making timely payments. So you can pro-tect your credit rating and use the equity earning a rate of return as a source of payment if the need arose (**fig. 20.4**).

Controlling your home equity is good asset management. In this book I have outlined the primary reasons for this: increased liquidity, increased safety, and increased rate of return. A secondary reason is you gain total control of your cash. You can establish an emergency fund and also use the strategy as a hedge against inflation. It also allows for the establishment of a pre-funded retirement strategy (**fig. 20.5**).

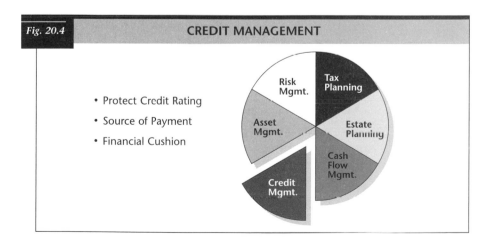

Fig. 20.4 — CREDIT MANAGEMENT

- Protect Credit Rating
- Source of Payment
- Financial Cushion

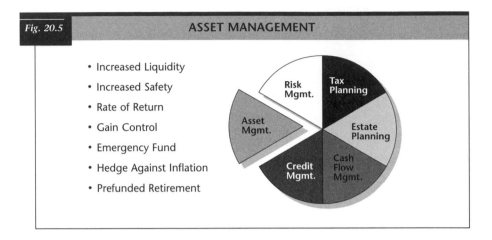

Fig. 20.5 — **ASSET MANAGEMENT**

- Increased Liquidity
- Increased Safety
- Rate of Return
- Gain Control
- Emergency Fund
- Hedge Against Inflation
- Prefunded Retirement

Managing your home equity properly is also good risk management. You are maintaining the greatest position of safety for your equity. The initial risk accepted by the mortgage company can remain at the same ratio rather than gradually transferring to you. Also, you can transfer the risk to an insurance company (a specialist in managing risks) if you employ your equity in an insurance contract. The insurance contract can replace your income and your equity asset as a tax-favored living benefit. It can also replace the asset at death while also allowing liquid access to funds, and it can be structured to supplement your income should you become disabled (**fig.20.6**).

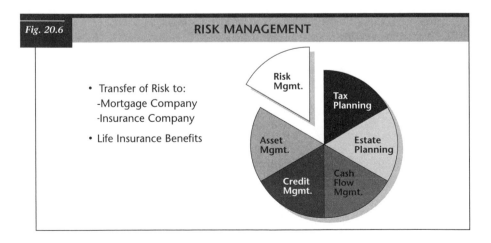

Fig. 20.6 — **RISK MANAGEMENT**

- Transfer of Risk to:
  -Mortgage Company
  -Insurance Company
- Life Insurance Benefits

Successfully managing equity is great for tax planning by potentially providing an interest deduction. Remember to always consult your own tax advisor, because tax planning relates to your personal situation. In doing so, a plan can usually be created that allows tax deductibility in compliance with the rules of the Internal Revenue Code, as explained earlier. Tax-deferred earnings and tax-free access is another feature you can implement through the use of properly structured life insurance contracts. If the side fund uses a life insurance policy, you have the benefit of allowing your cash to grow on a tax-favored basis. You also have tax-advantaged proceeds should you die because the death benefit will pass to the beneficiary income-tax free. Through the use of mortgage interest offsets, unnecessary tax can be avoided on a strategic roll-out of qualified funds (**fig. 20.7**).

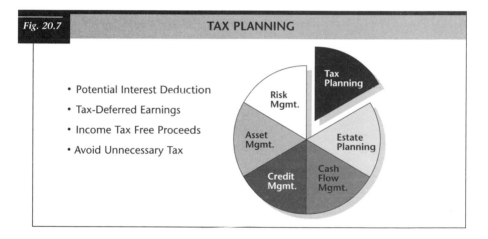

Fig. 20.7 **TAX PLANNING**

• Potential Interest Deduction

• Tax-Deferred Earnings

• Income Tax Free Proceeds

• Avoid Unnecessary Tax

Risk Mgmt.
Tax Planning
Asset Mgmt.
Estate Planning
Credit Mgmt.
Cash Flow Mgmt.

Successfully managing your equity is an excellent estate-planning tool because it multiplies the estate while avoiding probate (**fig. 20.8**). Let's use an example. One of our associates had a client who came to an equity management seminar without his wife. This is fairly common because in most marriages, one spouse is a detail person, and the other is not. One likes to use day planners; the other does not. One enjoys technical seminars; the other would rather stay home and get a report on it later.

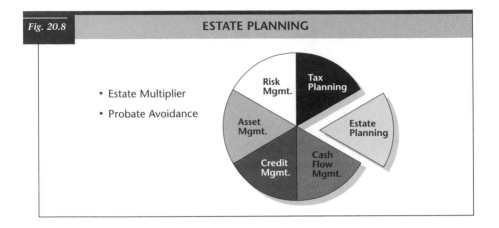

Fig. 20.8 — ESTATE PLANNING

- Estate Multiplier
- Probate Avoidance

(Risk Mgmt., Tax Planning, Estate Planning, Asset Mgmt., Credit Mgmt., Cash Flow Mgmt.)

Well, this man went home from the seminar, burst through the door, and told his wife they were going to sell their home, get a mortgage on a new home, and buy a life insurance policy! What do you think her response was? She said, "You're out of your mind! I want a new home, but there's no way you're going to get a new mortgage!" Well, you can appreciate her concern was natural. The man was in business for himself and had business debt to the degree that his assets barely exceeded his liabilities. If he happened to die, she knew the business would be sold to liquidate all the liabilities. She wanted to make sure their home was free and clear so she would not have to worry about making mortgage payments if her husband died. She had not worked for thirty years and didn't feel she could to get a job and make mortgage payments.

Even though this planner shared the same concerns, all parties realized the risk of doing nothing was greater than the risk of mortgaging a home. If her husband died, she may have a home that was paid for, but without the ability to pay property taxes or utilities, she wouldn't be able to keep it. With no income for thirty years, it would be next to impossible, or, at the least, very expensive, for her to qualify for a mortgage. The qualifying income would die if her husband died.

By transferring a substantial amount of home equity (they sold their home and purchased a new one) into an insurance contract, they created liquidity. They simply moved their asset from pocket to another; they didn't spend anything. Using home equity in this manner, they were able to maximum fund an insurance contract that covered the husband for $2.5 million of life insurance! Now if he dies, his wife will get $2.5 million income tax-free. She could use $500,000 of that to pay off the mortgage if she chose, and she would still have $2 million left over to live on! "I can relate to $2 million of cash," she said. This is why equity management can be a tremendous estate multiplier. It can turn $500,000 of idle equity dollars into $2.5 million of benefits! Not only that, but life insurance proceeds are not subject to probate, even without the use of a trust.

The concept of successfully managing equity is a dynamic strategy. However, it is not for everyone. It is only for disciplined homeowners who have accumulated equity, have good credit, and have the earning power sufficient to put their equity to work. To take advantage of these opportunities, it is wise to establish home ownership and begin exercising equity management strategies. In my practice, we have developed four modules, depending what phase clients are in.

EQUITY DEVELOPMENT

The first module is Equity Development. This is for homeowners who want to accumulate equity the fastest and smartest way possible. If someone wants to pay off his home as quickly as possible (whether that means literally paying off the home or having it paid for on paper by having sufficient liquid assets on his balance sheet to wash the liability of a mortgage), we lay out a plan to do this by using the strategies contained in this book. We can start with the same concept as a bi-weekly mortgage plan and improve it with a mortgage acceleration plan. If an insurance contract is used to accumulate the money required to pay off the mortgage, a death benefit will accompany it that is usually more than adequate to cancel the mortgage should you die.

EQUITY MANAGEMENT

The second module is Equity Management. This is for homeowners who might have a home worth $300,000, with a $120,000 first mortgage, a $30,000 second mortgage, $20,000 auto loan, two children headed for college, four credit cards, traditional IRAs and 401(k)s. There are a lot of people in this category.

EQUITY TRANSFER

The third module is Equity Transfer. This is for homeowners who may have a property worth $300,000 to $1 million with little or no debt. Our goal with Equity Transfer is to simply increase liquidity, safety, rate of return, and to enhance retirement income. This module is often used to strategically coordinate qualified plan roll-outs (i.e. IRAs and 401(k)s) to offset unnecessary tax.

EQUITY CONVERSION

The fourth module is Equity Conversion. This is for homeowners over the age of 62 and may qualify for a reverse mortgage as explained in chapter 14. They are, in essence, house rich and cash poor. Through this strategy, retirees can receive a lifetime interest in the home and tax-free income until both the husband and wife move out of the home or die. By using a portion of the tax-free income to purchase a life insurance policy, the life insurance can cancel the reverse mortgage upon death.

As you can see, using insurance contracts to manage home equity helps to minimize the risks under any phase of equity management.

"CONSERVE, DON'T CONSUME"

If you are excited about employing your home equity for all of the advantages I have outlined, let me issue a warning. It is important you proceed with a detailed and organized plan to get you successfully to your desired destination. If you were to take a road trip from New York

City to Los Angeles, you would increase your chances of a safe and time-ly arrival with the use of road signs and maps. Likewise, your journey to arrive at financial independence and a secure retirement should involve the use of a detailed road map so you do not get lost. Occasionally I have learned of people who attended one of our seminars and, rather than establishing a conservative, detailed plan to accumulate wealth, they ran out, borrowed their home equity, and either spent it or put it at unnec-essary risk in speculative investments. They forgot the most important concept regarding managing equity successfully—to conserve rather than to consume it. Always remember we want to enhance liquidity, safety, and rate of return!

THE MERITS OF ADEQUATE LIFE INSURANCE PROTECTION

Let me change hats for a moment from an equity management, asset optimization, and retirement specialist to a life insurance advisor. I want to share a simple story, then relate personal examples of the merits of having adequate life insurance.

The story is told of a wise Indian guide leading a group of people on horseback through an enchanted forest at night. As they came to a river crossing, they could see small stones glistening in the riverbed under the dim moonlight. The guide stopped his horse midstream and told the men and women if they would like, they could gather some of the stones and put them in their pockets. He explained their feet would get wet and the stones may add a bit of uncomfortablity, but if they took them along for the rest of the journey, by morning, they would be both happy and sad. Some heeded the guide's advice and filled their pockets with the stones. Others took only a few, while others didn't want to bother. During the remainder of the ride, some who filled their pockets gradu-ally discarded some of the stones as the journey grew tiring, or as they wanted to make room for other treasures along the way. When they finally arrived at their destination, dawn was breaking. As the sun rose, it revealed the true identity of the stones—they were glistening dia-monds! Yes, many were happy they had gathered and kept some, and yet they were sad they had not carried more. Others were dismayed they hadn't bothered to pick up any. Thus it is with life insurance.

I had a close business relationship with a gentleman who was a mentor to me during the infant stages of my financial and estate-planning career. At one point he had a substantial amount of life insurance in force on his life to provide for his wife and children should something happen to him. Due to circumstances beyond his control, there was a period of time wherein he had to relinquish those benefits. He intended to reinstate new life insurance coverage as soon as the opportunity presented itself. He knew the importance and sensed the urgency. Unfortunately, when he was preparing to apply for new coverage, he suffered a heart attack and the opportunity to secure new life insurance was put on hold until his health stabilized. In the interim, he passed away with a second cardiac arrest at the young age of forty-five with only about 15 percent of the coverage (in the form of group life insurance provided by his employer) he previously had. Even though his wonderful wife and family have been successful with the most important categories of True Wealth (see chapter 23), the financial category could have been less of a concern had more life insurance been in place. As I have taught earlier, it is much better to have and not need than need and not have.

Just recently I witnessed a couple who felt the need to eliminate some of the life insurance they had because they wanted to reallocate some of their planned savings and premium dollars into expanding their hobby of collecting antique cars. Less than a year after reducing their life insurance, the husband experienced a 90 percent blockage in his circulatory system and underwent surgery for six heart bypasses. They immediately put some of their antique cars up for sale and wanted to purchase more life insurance. There was little, if any, opportunity to recover what they gave up.

I have a client and dear friend who lost her husband due to an unfortunate accident. At the time of his passing, they were enjoying their wonderful family of six children, all under the age of nineteen. The family has always possessed strong values and ethics. Their children continue to be a strength and blessing to their mother as she likewise respects and helps provide for their needs. At the time of his death, her husband had a 401(k) through his employment with a $63,000 balance. In addition, he carried a $1 million life insurance contract that had $40,000 of cash values. Both plans were designed to accumulate capital for living retirement income benefits. The 401(k) left behind a net value of $40,950 after the income-tax liability. On the other hand, the $40,000 of cash values in the insurance contract blossomed into $1 million that transferred to the beneficiary income-tax free and estate-tax free.

Most of her family and friends advised her to pay off her mortgage. Instead, I advised her not only to keep her mortgage, but to refinance it to a higher amount—separating additional equity for management purposes. She needed to continue to establish and maintain her own credit rating as a single parent. Using the concepts taught in this book, she has been able to supplement her income by earning a return several thousand dollars a year greater than the net employment cost of the interest on the mortgage. We kept her tax deductions sufficient to help offset taxable income. We also took tax-free insurance proceeds and kept them tax free by establishing new buckets (life insurance policies) on her and her six children. If you were to ask her which retirement planning vehicle she appreciated the most—her husband's 401(k) or the life insurance contract—what do you think her answer would be?

I had another client who came to me in his retirement for a consultation and analysis to see if we could improve his net spendable income and minimize unnecessary taxes. As we completed a strategic repositioning of his assets, he established two insurance policies to accommodate about $200,000 of assets. The minimum death benefits under TEFRA/DEFRA guidelines totaled $500,000. About halfway through the funding process ($2^{1}/_{2}$ years after establishing the insurance contracts) under TAMRA guidelines, it was discovered he had terminal cancer. We immediately adjusted his plan because of the flexibility it afforded. Rather than continue to maximum fund his contracts, we minimum funded them, and for the last three years of his life he was able to build priceless memories without financial worry for him and his sweet wife. Just hours prior to him passing away (three years after his cancer diagnosis) I sat by his bedside, and we reminisced. He was at peace. He told me that he was not afraid to die and thanked me one last time for taking care of his wife financially through the incredible benefit of life insurance he knew would shortly blossom to care for her.

The last, most personal example is that of my brother and his family. One evening at about 11:45 P.M., I had just dozed off when the telephone rang. My sister-in-law, sobbing on the other end of the line, told to me that her husband—my only brother—had been killed in a horrible automobile accident while on a business trip. The police had just arrived at their home to break the news. My wife and I immediately called my sisters and our children as we prepared to travel to my brother's home to help give and receive comfort and advice for the difficult hours and days ahead. My first stop, however, was at my office. I wanted to make absolutely sure the life insurance contract my brother had established a few years before was current and I had a copy of the summary of benefits.

From a financial standpoint, my brother was not by any means rich when compared to a typical American household. When compared to the wealth of the average individual in the world, he enjoyed the many comforts of life that put most Americans among the top one percent of the world's wealth. From a human asset standpoint, the family, friends, relationships, virtues, and values my brother possessed places him among one of the richest men I've ever known. He took the opportunity to make every person he encountered feel better about him- or herself.

As my wife drove the car the lonely, long forty-two miles to my brother's home, I reviewed his file. My memory flashed back to that day in his office when I was filling out the life insurance application. My brother had told me he wanted to establish a life insurance contract for retirement purposes. When I calculated the minimum death benefit to accommodate the amount of monthly premium he could afford to set aside for retirement, he initially felt the amount of life insurance coming along for the ride would be adequate. I distinctly remember stopping for a moment and calculating what I felt he should have to protect his family. I admonished him to increase the life insurance amount by 67 percent through the temporary use of a term rider until he could afford to establish another bucket (policy). He agreed. Little did I know what was designed to be a living retirement benefit would in a few short years turn into a tax-free death benefit allowing my dear sister-in-law to continue to accomplish the family's dreams. What tremendous peace of mind for my sister-in-law during that crucial moment in her life because one of the most important facets of my brother's financial life was in order!

FOUR CONSIDERATIONS

Before moving ahead with an application for life insurance, I like my clients to think about it long enough to not feel rushed into the proposed plan—but not so long that valuable time is lost. The underwriting process can take three to six weeks before an approval is obtained for life insurance coverage. During that time, the proposed insured(s) can analyze the plan, and make adjustments when the policy is hopefully approved. Otherwise, after implementation, there is a free-look provision allowing the client usually ten to twenty days (depending on the state and company) to study the contract with the option to cancel it and receive a full refund of premiums paid. Of course, life insurance is usually flexible enough that changes can be made at any time after the policy is put in force, but care should be taken to alleviate any unnecessary fees or surrender charges, or to make a material change to a contract that changes its tax-advantaged status.

Before repositioning assets into a properly structured life insurance contract, I urge clients to consider the following four issues:

1) How large do you feel the bucket should be? In other words, what is the total of the assets you will likely reposition over the time frame of the plan funding? This approximate number allows us to determine the minimum death benefit required to meet TEFRA/DEFRA guidelines to accommodate the ultimate aggregate amount of premiums that may eventually be paid into the policy or policies.

2) What type or types of insurance contracts would you like to use and at what ratios? For example, would you like to use whole life,

fixed universal life, or indexed universal life? A combination of any can be structured depending upon goals and objectives.

3) Do you want to use one insurance company or would you prefer to diversify among two or more companies? Some companies may offer more competitive types of products than others. For example, I own equity indexed policies with one company and fixed universal life policies with three different companies.

4) If married, do you want to spread the life insurance coverage over both the husband and wife and if so, at what ratio? As explained before, I generally feel the majority of life insurance death benefit should be placed on the one in a marital relationship who would create the greatest economic loss at death. Other considerations would include the family history of longevity. Who in the relationship will likely pass away first from a health and age standpoint? Sometimes, one spouse or both may not even qualify for insurance. In that case, an appropriate surrogate insured (children or grandchildren) could be used.

OVERCOMING MISCONCEPTIONS

I hope the reader will take away some fundamental concepts related to interest rates and investment returns. When interest rates are high, they are high not only for borrowing, but also for saving and investing. There are two sides to the coin. When interest rates are low, they are low for borrowing as well as for saving and investing. To have the potential of achieving the best results in both environments, new financial products are available that can help us achieve our goals, as explained in chapters 17 to 19.

I feel one of the most important concepts is that long-term investments should be used for long-range goals. In the long run (generally at least a fifteen- to twenty-year period), the interest rate of fixed and indexed products can perform favorably in comparison with variable products. Retirees, in particular, should keep this principle in mind as they make decisions on which products to use based upon stability versus volatility. I constantly remind people not to get hung up on interest rates and rates of return on conservative long-term investments, because in the long run, all will probably come out equivalent.

In recent years, the life insurance industry has occasionally suffered from the bad reputation of trying to disguise life insurance as a savings and investment vehicle. Agents have been accused of selling life insurance as a "retirement plan." If a planner fails to disclose the risks with any investments, or if he uses illustrations that project unrealistic interest or dividend accumulations history cannot substantiate, then he ought to be reprimanded. I have my clients sign my company's authorized illustrations whenever applying for a life insurance contract. I also use a Life Insurance Contract Acknowledgement of Full Disclosure and Understanding. I require a client to read and sign this acknowledgement form after we have spent several hours explaining all the details and parameters of an insurance contract.

What if a properly structured investment-grade life insurance contract is used for strategic retirement planning objectives and it outperforms alternatives such as IRAs or 401(k)s by generating a greater net spendable retirement income? Can this strategy by referred to as a retirement plan?

There has been litigation that resulted in fines levied against certain life insurance companies for selling improper life insurance policies as retirement plans to people who claimed they didn't know they purchased life insurance, even though most had physical exams to qualify for the coverage. The insurance industry has had to walk on eggshells when structuring insurance contracts intended for use as a superior retirement funding vehicle. It is a sad day when one of the best retirement funding vehicles available on the market today cannot be referred to a retirement plan without fear of litigation.

ATTITUDE MAKES A WORLD OF DIFFERENCE

I would like to reemphasize a concept covered earlier in this book. I have noticed sometimes the investing public gets confused with the way the American economy operates. As an illustration, I like the story of a successful hot dog stand owner. For years this man experienced tremendous success selling what were touted as the best hot dogs in the state. When people stopped at his stand, the most important thing they liked about the experience was his positive attitude. Customers wanted to be around him because his countenance was bright and his charismatic personality upbeat. The relish, onions, mustard, ketchup, and the sauerkraut that dressed his "special dogs," were excellent but not unique. His attitude was the unique difference.

As his business grew, he expanded his services, perks, and advertising. He put up signs, placed new advertisements, and added menu items his customers gladly paid for because of the unique experience they were having! In time, his eldest son graduated from high school. The son had been a great asset to the business, working side by side with his father. But this good father wanted something better for his son—he wanted his son to have a college education. So the father bade his son farewell as he left home to pursue a bachelor's degree in business and a master of business administration.

Five years passed, and the father welcomed his son home from college. As the son visited the father's expanded and flourishing hot dog stand, in alarm, the son asked his father, "Dad, what have you been doing? Don't you know the country is experiencing a severe recession? The economy is depressed! You can't afford to advertise like this and offer all these unique perks for your customers. You better brace yourself for the hard times we're in by cutting costs to stay profitable!"

So, at the advice of his educated son, this devoted father and business man cut back on advertising. He took down some of the signs and discontinued using the flyers. He switched to parchment paper wraps and then to napkins in place of foil lined hot dog wraps. He even began to water down the relish, mustard, and ketchup to make it go further. He put in fewer chips with the hot dogs and reduced the drinks from sixteen-ounce to twelve-ounce servings.

Sure enough, his son was right and business began to slack off. The father's attitude started to show signs of negativism. His business diminished, and at the advice of his son, the father cut costs further by eliminating advertising and cutting all the things that had created the unique experience his customers once enjoyed—including his positive attitude! Finally the day arrived when the once-successful hot dog stand was forced to close permanently due to the lack of sales. As the father sat down that evening with his son, he exclaimed, "Thanks son, for warning me about the economy! If I had not cut my costs, I don't know where I would be today!"

So it is when we take the attitude that always cutting costs will result in greater profits. Our attitude often ends up turning to our demise.

Appropriately enough, after the World Trade Center attacks of September 11, 2001, President George W. Bush and New York City Mayor Rudy Giuliani told Americans and New Yorkers the best way to fight terrorism is to keep traveling, keep growing, keep patronizing business, and keep investing in America!

I have discovered that some of the best answers to staying positive are found in three booklets with accompanying audio recordings: *Laws of Lifetime Growth, Learning How to Avoid The Gap,* and *The Gratitude Principle,* all by Dan Sullivan. You can learn more about these inspirational and informative materials by visiting Mr. Sullivan's website at www.strategiccoach.com.

20 WEALTH ENHANCEMENT STRATEGY NUMBER TWENTY

- *Determine where you are now and where you want to go financially.*
- *Carefully study your financial profile to analyze the current expenditures, investments, and savings you could reposition to create greater liquidity, greater safety of principal, and higher rates of return, while maximizing tax benefits to the highest degree.*
- *Most important, be a possibility thinker and let your positive attitude enable you to achieve the highest altitude of wealth you desire.*

Using Dynamic Strategies to

Enhance, Preserve, and

Perpetuate Wealth

CHAPTER 21

Charitable Remainder Trusts

Learn to sell highly appreciated assets and avoid the long-term capital gains tax.

COMMON MYTH-CONCEPTION

There is no way to avoid long-term capital gains tax on the sale and final liquidation of highly appreciated assets.

REALITY

There is a legitimate method to avoid the payment of capital gains tax on the liquidation of properties, maximize retirement income from the proceeds, and still pass the value of the properties down to your heirs income-tax free.

Through the wise implementation of wealth enhancement strategies, you can be on the road to the accumulation of tremendous financial wealth. Time will be on your side in accomplishing financial independence. Perhaps you may already have attained a substantial financial net worth. If so, congratulations!

When you have arrived at the station of financial independence, several dynamic strategies can help you preserve, enhance, and perpetuate your wealth through future generations in your family. I will not attempt to outline all of these strategies in this brief section. They alone would justify another entire book!

Instead, I have chosen only three concepts I feel especially excited about. The first concept is the power of using a Charitable Remainder Unit Trust. The second concept is called the Ultimate Arbitrage. The third concept is optimizing the human, intellectual, and financial assets comprising "True Wealth," called Empowered Wealth®.

AVOIDING THE LONG-TERM CAPITAL GAINS TAX

When people come to me for financial planning assistance, especially as they approach retirement, many feel trapped in a highly appreciated home because of the perception of heavy capital gain tax incurred upon its sale. Remember, as a result of the Taxpayer Relief Act of 1997, a married couple filing a joint tax return may realize up to $500,000 of capital gains on the sale of a primary residence every two years without a capital gain tax liability. But what if they have substantial equity trapped inside other highly appreciated real estate properties they want to liquidate and convert to retirement income?

Let's suppose a woman is retiring at age 65 and has been reluctant to sell a building comprised of four townhouse condominiums she purchased thirty years earlier for $200,000. During the thirty years she owned the property, the positive cash flow rental income covered the mortgage payments, maintenance, and other expenses related to the property. But to help offset the positive cash flow rental-income tax liability, the property was depreciated during the thirty years from the original basis of $200,000, down to a basis of zero. Yet during those same thirty years, let's say the four townhouses collectively appreciated an average of about 5 percent a year. So, based upon the Rule of 72, the townhomes would have doubled in value about every fifteen years (72 divided by 5 equals 14.4). So, they might be worth approximately $800,000 after thirty years—an attractive investment!

But now this woman is tired of being a landlord and does not want to pay a property management company to manage it. The real estate market is strong, and she has the opportunity of selling the four townhouse complex for $800,000. She realizes that acquiring a similar piece of property through a 1031 exchange for other real estate doesn't accomplish the goal. It only postpones the tax until a stepped-up basis can possibly be realized at death as it transfers to her heirs. (Remember the step-up in basis provision may be taken away by the year 2010, according to the Economic Growth and Tax Relief Reconciliation Act of 2001.)

Under an outright sell, the $800,000 sales price would be subject to a capital gains tax. In this example, in which the income property was depreciated to a basis of zero, $600,000 would be subject to a 20 percent capital gains tax rate (which by the way, is better than the former 28 percent tax rate). In addition, the "unrecaptured Section 1250 gain" of $200,000 would be taxed at a special rate of 25 percent. Therefore, the total tax liability due upon sale of the townhomes in this example would be $170,000 ($600,000 x 20 percent = $120,000 added to $200,000 x 25 percent = $50,000).

If she then took the net after-capital gain tax sales proceeds of $630,000 and invested them earning 8 percent interest, they should generate $50,400 in annual interest income. However, the $50,400 would likely be taxable. So, in a 34 percent tax bracket, the annual tax liability on $50,400 would be $17,136. This results in a net spendable income of $33,264, which is only 4.16 percent annual return on the original $800,000 asset! No wonder people in this situation are reluctant to sell even though the property may feel like an albatross around their necks during retirement!

A person in these circumstances could benefit greatly from a tax-exempt unitrust. Why? Because she could totally avoid the $170,000 of capital gains tax! She could also avoid having the sale of the asset subject to estate tax. She could increase her income immediately, pass more money to her heirs, and immediately save some income tax. She could also benefit her favorite charity in the process and use it as a retirement trust.

How is this accomplished?

- Prior to selling the property, a charitable remainder unitrust is established.
- The owner of the property becomes the donor and transfers the asset to the unitrust.
- The donor receives an immediate charitable tax deduction.
- The unitrust now sells the property for $800,000 tax free because it received a stepped-up basis from $0 to $800,000 when it was transferred to the trust.
- The unitrust invests the $800,000 of sales proceeds and makes income payments to the donor, as its beneficiary, for the rest of her life at a pay-out rate of, say 8 percent, which is $64,000 annually.
- The donor uses part of the income (probably less than the portion that would have gone to Uncle Sam in taxes had the property been sold outright) to fund an Asset Replacement Trust through the use of a second-to-die life insurance policy. For example, a second-to-die life insurance policy with a death benefit of $800,000 for a husband age 65 and a wife age 63 both rated preferred could have an annual premium of about $6,336. In this example, the difference in annual income of $12,800 ($64,000 versus $51,200) by using a tax-exempt unitrust more than covers the cost of the insurance policy. Otherwise, a single premium of approximately $100,000 (perhaps derived from the capital gain tax savings of $170,000) could likely keep an $800,000 second-to-die life insurance policy in force until they both passed away.
- At the end of the income payments, the heirs receive tax-free insurance proceeds (usually equal to at least the $800,000 asset they were replacing).

- At the end of the income payments, the donor's selected charity receives the remainder of the money in the unitrust.

So what are the specific characteristics of a tax-exempt unitrust? A unitrust is defined as a legal fiction—essentially an artificial person. Unitrusts, which are legally binding contracts, are sanctioned and approved by the Internal Revenue Service as prescribed in Section 664 of the Internal Revenue Code. Unitrusts have assets and a trustee, who can be the donor. They can have an income beneficiary, who can also be the donor. The remainder of assets that reside in the trust at the death of both the husband and wife donors transfers to a charity of choice. As they are tax exempt, unitrusts are also called tax-exempt trusts.

There can be several distinct advantages in the use of a Charitable Remainder Unit Trust, sometimes referred to as a CRUT or a CRT.

CRUTS:

- can increase the income from the asset transferred into the trust;
- can provide a guaranteed income from the sales proceeds of the asset;
- can increase the time a person has to enjoy retirement without having to deal with a management intensive property;
- decrease the capital gain tax liability on the sale of the asset;
- decrease income-tax liability for the donor(s);
- decrease estate-tax liability for the donor(s);
- benefit a non-profit charity of the donor's choosing;
- can provide public recognition for the donor, if desired;
- and protect the asset from creditor or liability exposure.

So, if you own assets that have appreciated in value, that's good! But if you are thinking about selling them, appreciation may not be so good, unless you take advantage of a tax-exempt unitrust that will enable you to avoid capital gain tax and receive the other valuable benefits listed above.

Let's study another example of how a tax-exempt unitrust can provide tremendous advantages over selling highly appreciated property outright. Please refer to **figure 21.1**. I feel that capital gain tax laws are like a penalty for selling an asset at a profit. Let's assume that a couple, Jim and Mary Smith, both age 60, bought or started a business thirty years earlier

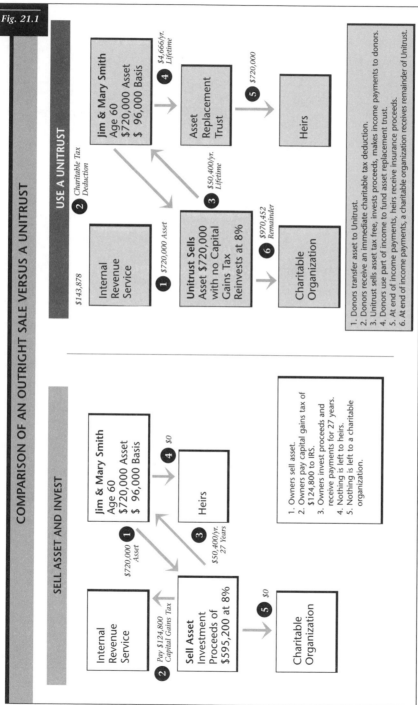

Fig. 21.1

COMPARISON OF AN OUTRIGHT SALE VERSUS A UNITRUST

SELL ASSET AND INVEST

Jim & Mary Smith
Age 60
$720,000 Asset
$ 96,000 Basis

Internal Revenue Service

Heirs

Sell Asset Investment Proceeds of $595,200 at 8%

Charitable Organization

1 $720,000 Asset
2 Pay $124,800 Capital Gains Tax
3 $50,400/yr. 27 Years
4 $0
5 $0

1. Owners sell asset.
2. Owners pay capital gains tax of $124,800 to IRS.
3. Owners invest proceeds and receive payments for 27 years.
4. Nothing is left to heirs.
5. Nothing is left to a charitable organization.

USE A UNITRUST

Jim & Mary Smith
Age 60
$720,000 Asset
$ 96,000 Basis

Internal Revenue Service

Asset Replacement Trust

Heirs

Unitrust Sells Asset $720,000 with no Capital Gains Tax Reinvests at 8%

Charitable Organization

$143,878

1 $720,000 Asset
2 Charitable Tax Deduction
3 $50,400/yr. Lifetime
4 $4,666/yr. Lifetime
5 $720,000
6 $970,452 Remainder

1. Donors transfer asset to Unitrust.
2. Donors receive an immediate charitable tax deduction.
3. Unitrust sells asset tax free, invests proceeds, makes income payments to donors.
4. Donors use part of income to fund asset replacement trust.
5. At end of income payments, heirs receive insurance proceeds.
6. At end of income payments, a charitable organization receives remainder of Unitrust.

Format and design created by Alden B. Tueller.

with $96,000 of capital. They worked hard in their family business, but now are ready to retire. None of their children have expressed interest in running the business, so the Smiths decide it is time to sell the business and ride off into the sunset of life in a retirement community.

When the business is appraised, the Smiths discover it has a fair market value of $720,000. They are excited to have this valuable asset as a resource in addition to other retirement savings—until they visit with their accountant who discloses the potential capital gains tax. If they sell the business for $720,000 they will realize a gain of $624,000 (because they only paid $96,000 for the business, which was their basis). So at a 20 percent capital gain tax rate, the tax due and payable when they sell the business will be $124,800! Fortunately, the accountant explains there is an alternative route which may avoid the capital gain tax.

After understanding how a tax-exempt unitrust works, the Smiths forget about selling the business outright. They transfer it into a trust with themselves as trustees. This enables them to sell the business free of capital gains tax, thereby saving $124,800 of unnecessary tax, allowing them to earn income on the full $720,000. They then receive an income for the rest of their lives (after the death of the first spouse, the survivor will continue to receive the income). They can set the pay-out rate, but it must be a minimum of 5 percent. They decide on a pay-out rate of 7 percent, which would generate an annual income of $50,400 on a principal of $720,000.

The Smiths also receive an immediate charitable deduction for the portion of the trust assets that will eventually pass to a charity of their choice. (IRS mortality tables and discount rates are used to make this calculation.) The lower the pay-out rate, the greater the deduction. In this example, assuming a 7 percent pay-out rate, the deduction will amount to $148,878. If they exceed the charitable deduction limit on their tax return in a single year, they can carry it over for up to five additional years. The Smiths also avoid, or at least reduce, their estate-tax liability, because when the business is transferred into the trust, it is removed from the Smiths' estate. Moreover, the asset will avoid probate proceedings.

The Smiths can now enjoy a stable income of $50,400 per year and be relieved from paying expenses associated with owning the business (taxes and insurance). This income will last throughout both their lifetimes, whereas if they took the same income under the outright sale, the $595,200 (net after-tax asset) would be totally depleted in twenty-seven years under the same assumptions. Using the Charitable Remainder Trust, the Smiths are able to experience relief from the management responsibilities of running the business. The Smiths are also excited they will be making a substantial gift to their favorite charity to be used in accordance with their wishes.

Through competent legal counsel, the Smiths not only establish a CRUT, but also an asset replacement trust (ART) so their children's inheritance is not reduced. Through the use of a second-to-die life insurance policy, after both Jim and Mary have passed away, their children can receive $720,000 in tax-free insurance proceeds. The premiums for the insurance can be funded in most cases with the contribution deduction savings, plus the increased cash flow achieved as a result of avoiding capital gains tax. In this way, the Smiths' children can eventually receive as much as or more than they would have received had the trust not been used. Take a moment and study **figure 21.2**, which is a line-by-line comparison of an outright sale versus a tax-exempt unitrust for this case study of Jim and Mary Smith. This example could also relate to the sale of any highly appreciated asset such as stock.

Fig. 21.2	OUTRIGHT SALE VERSUS A UNITRUST	
	SALE	UNITRUST
Asset Sale	$720,000	$720,000
Capital Gains Tax	$124,800	$0
Net to Invest	$595,200	$720,000
Charitable Deduction	$0	$143,878
Annual Payments	$50,400	$50,400
Duration of Payments	27 years	Lifetime
Expected Total Payments	$1,360,800	$1,663,200
Net to Heirs	$0	$720,000
To Charitable Organization	$0	$970,452
Total Expected Family Benefit	$1,360,800	$2,382,766*

*Total payments plus insurance proceeds plus tax savings less before tax insurance cost

It is imperative that competent professional legal advice be obtained when establishing a Charitable Remainder Unit Trust because these trusts are very complex.[1]

I quote the following from chapter 12 in Alden Tueller's *Practical Guide to Planned Giving* in order to stress the importance of obtaining expert professional advice in preparing these trusts:

> The Internal Revenue Code requires strictly that all the vehicles include government instrument language to get the tax benefits. Also, all of these trusts must comply with the private foundation rules. Donors, non profits, and their advisors who make mistakes drafting these trusts can create the worst of all possible tax worlds, a non-tax-exempt, irrevocable trust, subject to all private foundation excise taxes and penalties, but offering no tax deductions for contributions. Often, these cases end up in court, either to amend the documents—often in vain—or to recover damages from those who made the mistakes. Donors and non-profits must have expert professional advice in preparing these trusts.
>
> A Charitable Remainder Unitrust, sometimes referred to as a CRUT, must meet strict requirements of the Internal Revenue Code in order to be tax exempt and receive a charitable deduction. It must, among other things, be an irrevocable trust that, once set up, cannot be taken back or changed in any way by its donor or beneficiaries. One exception allows these trusts to be changed, under very limited conditions, but only so that they will qualify. A separate section of the Internal Revenue Code, Section 664, sets out the requirements for these trusts.
>
> A Charitable Remainder Unitrust must make annual payments, equal to a fixed percentage—at least 5 percent—of the trust's value each year, to one or more beneficiaries. The beneficiaries of the payments usually are the donors of the trust, or family members

---

[1] When I have clients who may benefit from the use of a CRUT, I usually refer them to Alden B. Tueller, a specialist in tax-exempt unit trusts. Mr. Tueller advises other attorneys, accountants, financial professionals, donors, and non-profit organizations nationwide, assisting them, their respective clients, staffs, volunteers, and friends with tax-exempt planning and with financial and estate planning. Mr Tueller took his law degree at the University of California at Berkley in 1967, then practiced estate, trust, and tax law in New York City for eight years before moving to Utah, where for another eight years he was counsel to the LDS Foundation of The Church of Jesus Christ of Latter-day Saints. He is the author of five books about tax-exempt planning, four published by the Taft Group of Rockville, Maryland. Mr. Tueller also conceived and prepares material for a monthly Taft Newsletter about tax-exempt planning. He is a founder and chairman of Premier Administration, a charitable trust administration and compliance company. He is a member of the bar in New York, Connecticut, California, and Utah. The law firm of Jones, Waldo, Holbrook, and McDonough retains him as of counsel. (They have offices in Salt Lake City, Utah and Washington, D.C.) An excellent, concise, and informative chapter, entitled "Irrevocable Planned Giving Trusts," is contained in Mr. Tueller's book, *Practical Guide to Planned Giving*.

(particularly spouses), or both. These beneficiaries are sometimes called recipients or income beneficiaries.

To qualify legally, Charitable Remainder Unitrusts must last for as long as the beneficiaries live, for a set period of time, or for the longer or shorter of someone's life or a set period. If the trust is to be measured by someone's life, that person must be alive when the trust is created. If there is a set period, it cannot be more than twenty years.

In the remainder of chapter 12, Mr. Tueller explains how a Charitable Remainder Unitrust may take one of three forms. He outlines fourteen distinct advantages for donors and three tremendous advantages for non-profit charitable organizations. He also identifies possible disadvantages to both the donor and the charity. Finally, Mr. Tueller addresses the tax aspects of the gift in a Charitable Remainder Unitrust.

To summarize, following is a list of some of the features that make a Charitable Remainder Unitrust flexible:

- The donor can be the trustee.
- The donor can change trustees.
- The donor can change investment advisors.
- Payments can be for one or more lives, for a fixed term, or both.
- The donor can choose the pay-out rate.
- Payments may be from income and principal.
- Payments may be from income only with make up.
- Payments may be deferred.
- The donor may use the trust as a retirement plan.
- The donor may later add more assets to the trust.
- The donor can name one or more charities or none.
- The donor can name charities at the time of the trust's establishment or later.
- The donor can include early termination conditions.

So what is the profile of a possible candidate for a Charitable Remainder Unitrust? A person is a possible candidate if he or she:

- has highly appreciated assets;
- is avoiding sale due to capital gains tax;
- is considering a lifestyle change;
- doesn't need the principal for his or herself;
- could use a current tax deduction;
- has estate-tax problems;
- wants higher income from his or her assets;
- wants a built-in inflation hedge;
- or wants to defer income.

21 WEALTH ENHANCEMENT STRATEGY
NUMBER TWENTY-ONE

- *If applicable, use a tax-exempt unitrust to avoid capital gains tax, provide a higher tax-advantaged retirement income, and benefit your favorite charity.*
- *Then couple it with an insurance-funded asset replacement trust to pass the value of your properties to your heirs tax free.*

CHAPTER 22

The Ultimate Arbitrage

How to leave behind an extra $2 to $4 million for your family or favorite charity without spending a dime of your own money.

COMMON MYTH-CONCEPTION

You can't create positive cash flow income while living without working or using some of your own money, neither can you create an immediate estate or endowment at death without expending some of your own money.

REALITY

Through the use of arbitrage, affluent, high net-worth individuals can create additional positive cash flow income while living, possibly without spending any money from their own pockets. They also can leave behind substantial endowments upon death to their families, businesses, or favorite charities.

Throughout this book, I have illustrated how a homeowner can potentially make hundreds of thousands of dollars by borrowing funds with a net after-tax cost of approximately 4 to 5 percent (assuming a gross interest rate of 6 to 8 percent) and investing the loan proceeds in tax-advantaged instruments, compounding conservatively at 6 to 8 percent interest.

You should now understand arbitrage occurs when borrowing money at a lower interest rate, then investing it to earn a higher interest rate. As explained, depending on the market, banks and credit unions are willing to pay depositors 2 to 4 percent interest on savings accounts, money market accounts, and certificates of deposit. Why? Because they are confident they can invest the money or loan it back out, earn a higher rate of return than the cost of the funds, and turn a profit. If savers and investors do not deposit enough money into banks and credit unions, thereby lending them money, these institutions then borrow from the Federal Reserve Bank at discount rates of 2 to 4 percent in order to meet demand.

There are basically five different tiers of borrowing rates in the market:

- The first is the rate which banks charge individuals like you and me, which is prime plus 1 or 2 percent, or more.
- The second is the rate at which banks loan money to their large corporate clients. This is referred to as the prime rate.
- The third is the broker call rate, which is what brokerage firms charge their preferred clients (like Ford Foundation or a large pension fund) on debit balances in their accounts.
- The fourth is the discount rate the Federal Reserve Bank charges member banks, as set by the Federal Open Market Committee.
- The fifth is the rate that banks charge each other.

Banks and smart entrepreneurs have used the concept of arbitrage to amass fortunes. So, now when you hear people quip, "There are two kinds of people in the world: those who earn interest and those who pay it," you can smile because you know better! You should now understand there is really a third kind of person in the world—those independently wealthy individuals who have learned when and how to pay interest using OPM (Other People's Money) to earn even more interest!

Remember figure 7.1, in chapter 7, which depicts a beaver, a caveman, and Archimedes all looking at the same stick of wood but perceiving it differently? The beaver may perceive that stick of wood as breakfast, wanting to consume it for nourishment. The caveman may perceive the same stick as firewood, wanting to consume it for warmth. But a man of vision may view that stick of wood as a lever for moving the world! In much the same way, many independently wealthy people are men and women of vision who have learned to perceive their financial lives in a unique way.

The opportunity now exists to use the Ultimate Arbitrage Plan® to generate a tremendous amount of extra money, possibly without spending a dime from your own pocket! Seem too good to be true? Just take a moment to study an example using the following steps that are generating millions of extra dollars for families, businesses, and charities.

Let's use a hypothetical example of a non-smoking female, age 80, who is healthy enough to be insurable (several top-rated insurance companies will insure people up through age 90). Let's assume this female has a net worth greater than $10 million. Please refer to the flowchart in **figure 22.1** while studying the following steps:

1) A life insurance trust is created in order to keep life insurance proceeds from being included in the owner or insured's estate.

2) The trust borrows $8 million from a lender. The lenders we have typically used have been loaning such amounts at 1.5 percent over the London Inter-Bank Offered Rate (LIBOR)[1] as published in the Wall Street Journal. Let's say the LIBOR rate is 3.5 percent, which is slightly higher than what it has been during the time this book was published. So the total would be approximately 5 percent interest. The loan is non-recourse and is open until death

---

[1] LIBOR is the rate of interest at which banks borrow funds from other banks, in marketable size, on the London Interbank Market. It is the most widely used benchmark or reference rate for short-term interest rates. The British Banker's Association determines this rate, so LIBOR is often called BBA LIBOR. The BBA compiles LIBOR as a free service and releases it to the market at about 11:00 A.M. Greenwich Mean Time each day.

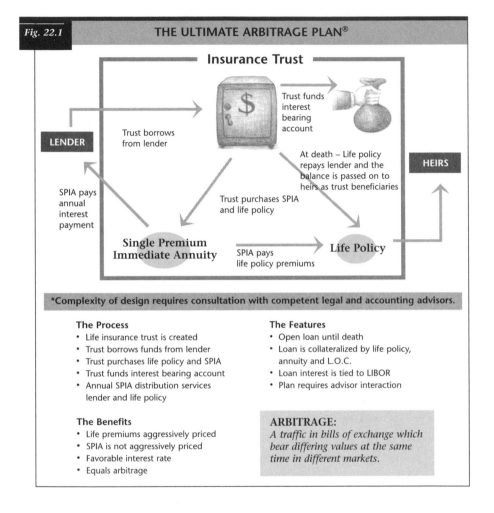

Fig. 22.1 — THE ULTIMATE ARBITRAGE PLAN®

Insurance Trust

Trust funds interest bearing account

LENDER

Trust borrows from lender

At death – Life policy repays lender and the balance is passed on to heirs as trust beneficiaries

HEIRS

SPIA pays annual interest payment

Trust purchases SPIA and life policy

Single Premium Immediate Annuity

SPIA pays life policy premiums

Life Policy

*Complexity of design requires consultation with competent legal and accounting advisors.

The Process
- Life insurance trust is created
- Trust borrows funds from lender
- Trust purchases life policy and SPIA
- Trust funds interest bearing account
- Annual SPIA distribution services lender and life policy

The Features
- Open loan until death
- Loan is collateralized by life policy, annuity and L.O.C.
- Loan interest is tied to LIBOR
- Plan requires advisor interaction

The Benefits
- Life premiums aggressively priced
- SPIA is not aggressively priced
- Favorable interest rate
- Equals arbitrage

ARBITRAGE:
A traffic in bills of exchange which bear differing values at the same time in different markets.

with interest-only payments required. The loan is collateralized by a life insurance policy and an annuity (steps 3 and 4). In addition, a letter of credit may be required by some lenders, depending on circumstances and objectives of the client.

3) The trust purchases a $10 million life insurance policy using $600,000 of the loan proceeds to pay for the initial premium payment.

4) Using the remaining loan proceeds ($7.4 million), the trust purchases a single-premium immediate annuity that generates a guaranteed lifetime annual income of $1,036,000. (In this example,

the insured/annuitant is a female age 80 and the offered pay-out rate is 14 percent based upon a life-expectancy of ten years.)

5) The annual annuity distribution services the lender ($400,000 per year assuming a 5 percent interest rate) and the life insurance policy (with annual premiums of $380,000).

6) The difference between the $1,036,000 annual annuity distributions and the sum of the annual interest payment and the life insurance premium ($400,000 plus $380,000), results in a positive cash flow annual income in the amount of $256,000.

7) The taxable amount of the annuity after exclusion would be $227,920 each year, resulting in an annual tax liability of approximately $91,168 (at 40 percent) during the first ten years of the annuity pay-out.

8) If this annual tax liability were paid from the positive cash flow of $256,000, a net of $164,832 in annual income could come to the family, business, or charity without requiring any personal cash investment or outlay by the client. It could also accrue in an interest-bearing account.

9) At the time of the client's death, the annuity distributions stop and the $10 million insurance policy pays off the $8 million loan, thus leaving behind an extra $2 million to the family, business, or charity of choice.

KEY ELEMENTS

The key elements allowing the Ultimate Arbitrage to work are: 1) the life insurance premiums need to be aggressively priced, 2) the single-premium immediate annuity needs to not be aggressively priced (in other words, age-rated), and 3) a favorable borrowing interest rate must be obtained. Thus, the concept works best with affluent, high net-worth individuals between the ages of 75 to 90. The combination of these elements results in arbitrage!

Let me briefly expound on these components. In order for an insurance company to underwrite a life insurance policy in the amount of $10 million, the insured should have a substantial net worth that justifies the need for that amount of insurance. That substantial net worth also helps the lender to feel comfortable financially justifying an $8 million loan. The life insurance company that is offering the $10 million life insurance policy also needs to favorably rate the life expectancy of the insured. This satisfies the need for the premiums to be aggressively priced. It is essential the life insurance policy and annuity be approved and placed on an elderly family member. Generally, it works best if the insured/annuitant is between the ages of 75 and 90. This person must be insurable with no serious health risks that would dramatically reduce their mortality or life expectancy. (Past life-threatening health problems or episodes that have been successfully treated or alleviated are often not a problem with underwriters. In order to obtain the best rate, several companies may be shopped.)

On the other hand, the insurance company offering the single-premium immediate annuity (SPIA) needs to *not* be aggressively priced. This means it is guaranteeing a lifetime-only annual pay-out based on the assumption the annuitant has a shorter life expectancy than the insurance company issuing the life insurance predicts life expectancy to be. Therefore, it is referred to as an age-rated SPIA. Often, the annuity guarantees an age-based pay-out rate of 14 to 19 percent on elderly annuitants because the income ceases at death.

To understand how an annuity-issuing insurance company can guarantee a 14 percent pay-out, consider the following analogy. If someone borrowed $1 million from you and the loan agreement stipulated that the interest borrowing rate was 6.5 percent and the loan needed to be paid according to a ten year amortization, the annual principal and interest payment would be $140,000. $140,000 represents 14 percent of the $1 million loan. With an annuity, the insurance company is guaranteeing an annual payment of 14 percent of the principal, based upon the premise they will likely only be paying that amount ten years (the life expectancy of the 80-year-old annuitant in this example). If the annuitant should die before ten years, the insurance company comes out ahead. If the annuitant should live beyond ten years, the insurance company is obligated to pay the annual income for the duration of her life.

The last key element is a favorable borrowing rate needs to be obtained.

In this example, a 6 percent borrowing rate would still make sense. Even if the borrowing rate were variable and started out at 4.5 percent and increased .5 percent each year, the positive cash flow in the early years (if set aside in an interest-bearing account) can cover higher interest rates in the later years. Some lenders will loan at higher rates, such as 7 percent, which stay fixed during the life of the loan. However, these lenders may only require annual interest payments equal to 2 percent over the LIBOR rate at the time the loan was originated. The interest differential between the loan servicing rate and the fixed rate in such a contract can accrue and be paid from the life insurance proceeds at death. Such an arrangement could be non-recourse, meaning that the lender cannot look to the individual for repayment; it can only look to the insurance policy and SPIA.

If the objective is to maximize what is left behind at the death of the insured to her family, business, or favorite charity, a non-recourse, variable-interest loan may be the best solution. This would mean the loan is only collateralized by the insurance policy and the annuity. However, any positive cash flow from the annuity—after paying the annual interest payment and the insurance premium—must accrue in an interest-bearing account as a cushion against interest rate increases. Such loans are usually made at 1.5 percent over the yearly, or even the five-year LIBOR rate. The interest rates would have to climb substantially to require the lender to tap into the accrued cash account cushion. This would only affect the amount of additional money left behind on top of the net death proceeds from the life insurance policy.

On the other hand, if your objective is to use the positive cash flow generated by the arbitrage, a letter of credit may be required by the lender in case the interest rate increases to the degree the annuity pay-out is not sufficient to pay both the annual interest on the loan and the premium for the life insurance policy that secures the lender. Remember the loan is open until death, so only the annual interest payment needs to be made and the insurance policy kept in force to keep the lender happy. The lender secures the loan with a collateral assignment of the life insurance and the annuity to assure they receive interest payments during the term of the loan and the loan being paid off at death.

All Ultimate Arbitrage Plans® are handled on a case-by-case basis and are structured as attractively as possible depending on the client's objectives, along with factors such as age, health, net worth, gender, the interest rate obtained, and options selected. Sometimes it works better to use about half of the loan proceeds to pay a single premium into the insurance contract, leaving the rest to go into the SPIA. Also, different lenders will have different availability of currencies. The two currencies currently seeing the greatest usage are the U.S. dollar and the Japanese yen. Sometimes it would be attractive to borrow funds in a foreign currency because the loan is based on that currency's LIBOR. So, sometimes we lock in a lower five-year borrowing rate using the Japanese yen at 2.5 percent with an option to convert to U.S. dollar rates after five years if advantageous. Depending on the circumstances, sometimes additional collateral is only required in the amount of about 20 percent of the loan amount, which amount may decrease within four or five years—even to where that collateral is no longer necessary because the insurance cash values, annuity, and interest-bearing accounts are sufficient.

Let's take a moment and study a few hypothetical ledgers of this example. In **figure 22.2** you will see that $600,000 of the loan money was applied to the life insurance policy the first year, as shown in column 5. The remaining $7.4 million of loan proceeds were applied to the annuity that generates a lifetime income of $1,036,000, as shown in column 1. This illustration shows the insured living to age 104, or twenty-five more years. Because the normal life expectancy for an eighty-year-old is approximately ten years, not all of the $1,036,000 of annual annuity income is subject to income tax. In other words, a large portion of the income would be deemed as a return of the basis or principal put into the annuity. The taxable portion of the annuity after this exclusion would be $227,920 during the first ten years, as shown in column 2. Thereafter, if the person continued to live, there would be a greater tax liability on up to 100 percent of the annuity distribution beginning the twelfth year.

If this eighty-year-old female were in a 40-percent tax bracket, the income tax liability on $227,920 of annual interest from the annuity the first ten years would be $91,168 as shown in column 3. After the first ten

Fig. 22.2

Ultimate Arbitrage®

COMPREHENSIVE ANALYSIS
LOAN + S.P.I.A. + Retained Capital + Life Insurance Policy

Loan to I.L.I.Trust - $8,000,000

Income tax credits are NOT reflected in these numbers.

Loan money applied to policies - $600,000   Loan money applied to S.P.I.A. - $7,400,000

Age	Year	Annuity Income	Taxable after Exclusion	Income Tax on column (2) at 40.00%	Loan Interest 5.00%	Total Premiums	Net Cash Flows: column (1) minus: (3)+(4)+(5)	Cash Flows column (6) at 5.00% at End of Year	$10,000,000 Death Benefit Net of Loan (+) column (7)
		1	2	3	4	5	6	7	8
80	1	$1,036,000	$227,920	$91,168	$400,000	$600,000	0		$2,000,000
81	2	1,036,000	227,920	91,168	400,000	380,000	$164,832	$173,074	2,173,074
82	3	1,036,000	227,920	91,168	400,000	380,000	164,832	354,801	2,354,801
83	4	1,036,000	227,920	91,168	400,000	380,000	164,832	545,615	2,545,615
84	5	1,036,000	227,920	91,168	400,000	380,000	164,832	745,969	2,745,969
85	5	1,036,000	227,920	91,168	400,000	380,000	164,832	956,341	2,956,341
86	7	1,036,000	227,920	91,168	400,000	380,000	164,832	1,177,232	3,177,232
87	8	1,036,000	227,920	91,168	400,000	380,000	164,832	1,409,167	3,409,167
88	9	1,036,000	227,920	91,168	400,000	380,000	164,832	1,652,699	3,652,699
89	10	1,036,000	227,920	91,168	400,000	380,000	164,832	1,908,407	3,908,407
90	11	1,036,000	936,722	374,689	400,000	380,000	-118,689	1,879,204	3,879,204
91	12	1,036,000	1,036,000	414,400	400,000	380,000	-158,400	1,806,845	3,806,845
92	13	1,036,000	1,036,000	414,400	400,000	380,000	-158,400	1,730,867	3,730,867
93	14	1,036,000	1,036,000	414,400	400,000	380,000	-158,400	1,651,090	3,651,090
94	15	1,036,000	1,036,000	414,400	400,000	380,000	-158,400	1,567,325	3,567,325
95	16	1,036,000	1,036,000	414,400	400,000	380,000	-158,400	1,479,371	3,479,371
96	17	1,036,000	1,036,000	414,400	400,000	380,000	-158,400	1,387,020	3,387,020
97	18	1,036,000	1,036,000	414,400	400,000	380,000	-158,400	1,290,051	3,290,051
98	19	1,036,000	1,036,000	414,400	400,000	380,000	-158,400	1,188,233	3,188,233
99	20	1,036,000	1,036,000	414,400	400,000	380,000	-158,400	1,081,325	3,081,325
100	21	1,036,000	1,036,000	414,400	400,000	0	221,600	1,368,071	3,368,071
101	22	1,036,000	1,036,000	414,400	400,000	0	221,600	1,669,155	3,669,155
102	23	1,036,000	1,036,000	414,400	400,000	0	221,600	1,985,292	3,985,292
103	24	1,036,000	1,036,000	414,400	400,000	0	221,600	2,317,237	4,317,237
104	**25**	**1,036,000**	**1,036,000**	**414,400**	**400,000**	**0**	**221,600**	**2,665,779**	**4,665,779**
		Guaranteed Lifetime Income (Single Premium Immediate Annuity)	Portion of S.P.I.A. Income subject to tax	Actual Income Tax Effect of column (2)	Interest Payment on Loan at 5.00% E.O.Y.	Schedule of Premiums: $100,000,000	Column (1) minus columns (3)+(4)+(5)	Column (6) at 5.00%	Net Value in Trust

years, the income tax liability could equal $414,400, assuming the same tax bracket. Assuming the LIBOR rate is 3.5 percent, the loan interest rate in this example would be 5 percent. Column 4 shows the annual loan interest in the amount of $400,000 being paid from the annuity proceeds. Column 5 shows $380,000 of annual premium being paid to the life insurance policy from the second year on. This would be the minimum premium required to keep the life insurance death benefit in force under the assumptions used here. Therefore, column 6 shows the net result of the $1,036,000 of annuity income, less the $91,168 of tax liability, the $400,000 of annual loan interest, and the $380,000 life-insurance premium. After these three amounts are deducted from the annuity distribution, there is $164,832 of positive cash flow remaining!

Column 7 shows what would accumulate if the insured set aside the $164,832 annual positive cash flow in an investment earning 5 percent interest after tax. Of course, this person's family could use the $164,832 of annual cash flow if they did not want it to accrue as a cushion for possible increases in the interest rate or increased tax liability after the tenth year. Column 8 shows the $10 million gross death benefit less the $8 million collateral assignment to the lender to pay off the loan. Hence, if death occurred in the first year, the $10 million life insurance proceeds would pay off the $8 million loan, leaving behind a net of $2 million tax free to the heirs. If column 7, which is the positive cash flow accruing with interest, were added to the net death benefit of $2 million the result would be larger proceeds transferred to the heirs each year. If death occurred in year 10, the heirs could possibly receive a $2 million, net death benefit plus $1,908,407 in cash accumulation during that ten-year period, leaving behind a grand total of $3,908,407!

Please note when the income-tax liability increases beginning in the eleventh year (see column 3), this results in the beginning of a negative cash flow as shown in column 6. However, because of the nearly $2 million cushion accumulated, as shown in the tenth year of column 7, the negative cash flow is easily compensated from the accumulated values of column 7.

Let's study the same example based on an alternative assumption (**figure 22.3**).

Fig. 22.3

COMPREHENSIVE ANALYSIS
LOAN + S.P.I.A. + Retained Capital + Life Insurance Policy
Ultimate Arbitrage®

Income tax credits are NOT reflected in these numbers. Income taxes are paid by Grantor from Estate.

Loan to I.L.I.Trust - $8,000,000   Loan money applied to policies - $600,000   Loan money applied to S.P.I.A. - $7,400,000

Age	Year	Annuity Income (1)	Taxable after Exclusion (2)	Income Tax on column (2) at 40.00% (3)	Loan Interest 5.00% (4)	Total Premiums (5)	Net Cash Flows: column (1) minus: (4)+(5) (6)	Cash Flows column (6) at 5.00% at End of Year (7)	$10,000,000 Death Benefit Net of Loan (+) column (7) (8)
80	1	$1,036,000	227,920	$91,168	$400,000	$600,000	0		$2,000,000
81	2	1,036,000	227,920	91,168	400,000	380,000	$256,000	$ 268,800	2,268,800
82	3	1,036,000	227,920	91,168	400,000	380,000	256,000	551,040	2,551,040
83	4	1,036,000	227,920	91,168	400,000	380,000	256,000	847,392	2,847,392
84	5	1,036,000	227,920	91,168	400,000	380,000	256,000	1,158,562	3,158,562
85	6	1,036,000	227,920	91,168	400,000	380,000	256,000	1,485,290	3,485,290
86	7	1,036,000	227,920	91,168	400,000	380,000	256,000	1,828,354	3,828,354
87	8	1,036,000	227,920	91,168	400,000	380,000	256,000	2,188,572	4,188,572
88	9	1,036,000	227,920	91,168	400,000	380,000	256,000	2,566,800	4,566,800
89	10	1,036,000	227,920	91,168	400,000	380,000	256,000	2,963,940	4,963,940
90	11	1,036,000	936,722	374,689	400,000	380,000	256,000	3,380,938	5,380,938
91	12	1,036,000	1,036,000	414,400	400,000	380,000	256,000	3,818,784	5,818,784
92	13	1,036,000	1,036,000	414,400	400,000	380,000	256,000	4,278,524	6,278,524
93	14	1,036,000	1,036,000	414,400	400,000	380,000	256,000	4,761,250	6,761,250
94	15	1,036,000	1,036,000	414,400	400,000	380,000	256,000	5,268,112	7,268,112
95	16	1,036,000	1,036,000	414,400	400,000	380,000	256,000	5,800,318	7,800,318
96	17	1,036,000	1,036,000	414,400	400,000	380,000	256,000	6,359,134	8,359,134
97	18	1,036,000	1,036,000	414,400	400,000	380,000	256,000	6,945,890	8,945,890
98	19	1,036,000	1,036,000	414,400	400,000	380,000	256,000	7,561,985	9,561,985
99	20	1,036,000	1,036,000	414,400	400,000	380,000	256,000	8,208,884	10,208,884
100	21	1,036,000	1,036,000	414,400	400,000	0	636,000	9,287,128	11,287,128
101	22	1,036,000	1,036,000	414,400	400,000	0	636,000	10,419,285	12,419,285
102	23	1,036,000	1,036,000	414,400	400,000	0	636,000	11,608,049	13,608,049
103	24	1,036,000	1,036,000	414,400	400,000	0	636,000	12,856,252	14,856,252
104	**25**	**1,036,000**	**1,036,000**	**414,400**	**400,000**	**0**	**636,000**	**14,166,864**	**16,166,864**
		Guaranteed Lifetime Income (Single Premium Immediate Annuity)	Portion of S.P.I.A. Income subject to income tax	Actual Income Tax Effect of column (2)	Interest Payment on Loan at 5.00% E.O.Y.	Schedule of Premiums: $10,000,000	Column (1) minus columns (4)+(5)	Column (6) at 5.00%	Net Value in Trust

All of the assumptions remain the same in this figure, with the exception of income taxes, which are paid by the grantor from the estate. If the grantor of the trust were willing to pay the income tax shown in column 3, then the full $256,000 of positive cash flow would be available to the family, business, or charity. If $256,000 of annual positive cash flow were to accrue at 5 percent interest as shown in column 7, we could accumulate nearly $3 million by the tenth year, thereby leaving behind a net of nearly $5 million if death occurred at normal life expectancy. A grantor may be willing to cover the income-tax liability as shown because this would be a nominal outlay for the amount of tax-free transfer generated as a result!

Sometimes people ask, "Why don't we use the positive cash flow generated to maximize the net death benefit that can be left behind?" This is an excellent question. **Figure 22.4** uses the same assumptions as figure 22.3. However, not only are the income taxes paid by the grantor from the estate in this figure, but the positive cash flow is used to purchase additional insurance. In this example, the $256,000 of additional positive cash flow was added to the $380,000 minimum premium on the $10 million life insurance policy. By paying a $636,000 life insurance premium each year, a $17 million life insurance policy can be afforded in this hypothetical example. As shown in column 8, if a $17 million life insurance policy were in force at the time of the insured's death, the $8 million loan would still be paid from proceeds, leaving behind a net of $9 million to the heirs! Hence, an insurance policy can be structured to maximize the death benefit based on the positive cash flow experienced through the arbitrage.

The next question that may be asked is, "What if we could structure the loan so the annual interest paid on the loan could be deductible?" Through the use of competent accounting advice, it may be possible to structure the loan so the annual interest payment is deductible. If that could be accomplished, **figure 22.5** shows the result.

If the $400,000 of annual loan interest shown in column 5 were deductible, it would wash out the income tax liability during the first ten years in the amount of $91,168. Not only would $400,000 of deductible

Fig. 22.4

COMPREHENSIVE ANALYSIS
LOAN + S.P.I.A. + Retained Capital + Life Insurance Policy

Ultimate Arbitrage®

Income tax credits are NOT reflected in these numbers.   Income taxes are paid by Grantor from Estate.

Loan to I.L.I.Trust - $8,000,000   Loan money applied to policies - $600,000   Loan money applied to S.P.I.A. - $7,400,000

Age	Year	Annuity Income	Taxable after Exclusion	Income Tax on column (2) at 40.00%	Loan Interest 5.00%	Total Premiums	Net Cash Flows: column (1) minus: (4)÷(5)	Cash Flows column (6) at 5.00% at End of Year	$17,000,000 Death Benefit Net of Loan (+) column (7)
		1	2	3	4	5	6	7	8
80	1	$1,036,000	$227,920	$91,168	$400,000	$600,000	0	0	$9,000,000
81	2	1,036,000	227,920	91,168	400,000	636,000	0	0	9,000,000
82	3	1,036,000	227,920	91,168	400,000	636,000	0	0	9,000,000
83	4	1,036,000	227,920	91,168	400,000	636,000	0	0	9,000,000
84	5	1,036,000	227,920	91,168	400,000	636,000	0	0	9,000,000
85	6	1,036,000	227,920	91,168	400,000	636,000	0	0	9,000,000
86	7	1,036,000	227,920	91,168	400,000	636,000	0	0	9,000,000
87	8	1,036,000	227,920	91,168	400,000	636,000	0	0	9,000,000
88	9	1,036,000	227,920	91,168	400,000	636,000	0	0	9,000,000
89	10	1,036,000	227,920	91,168	400,000	636,000	0	0	9,000,000
90	11	1,036,000	936,722	374,689	400,000	636,000	0	0	9,000,000
91	12	1,036,000	1,036,000	414,400	400,000	636,000	0	0	9,000,000
92	13	1,036,000	1,036,000	414,400	400,000	636,000	0	0	9,000,000
93	14	1,036,000	1,036,000	414,400	400,000	636,000	0	0	9,000,000
94	15	1,036,000	1,036,000	414,400	400,000	636,000	0	0	9,000,000
95	16	1,036,000	1,036,000	414,400	400,000	636,000	0	0	9,000,000
96	17	1,036,000	1,036,000	414,400	400,000	636,000	0	0	9,000,000
97	18	1,036,000	1,036,000	414,400	400,000	636,000	0	0	9,000,000
98	19	1,036,000	1,036,000	414,400	400,000	636,000	0	0	9,000,000
99	20	1,036,000	1,036,000	414,400	400,000	636,000	0	0	9,000,000
100	21	1,036,000	1,036,000	414,400	400,000	0	636,000	667,800	9,667,800
101	22	1,036,000	1,036,000	414,400	400,000	0	636,000	1,368,990	10,368,990
102	23	1,036,000	1,036,000	414,400	400,000	0	636,000	2,105,240	11,105,240
103	24	1,036,000	1,036,000	414,400	400,000	0	636,000	2,878,301	11,878,301
104	**25**	**1,036,000**	**1,036,000**	**414,400**	**400,000**	**0**	**636,000**	**3,690,017**	**12,690,017**
		Guaranteed Lifetime Income (Single Premium Immediate Annuity)	Portion of S.P.I.A. Income subject to income tax	Actual Income Tax Effect of column (2)	Interest Payment on Loan at 5.00% E.O.Y.	Schedule of Premiums: $17,000,000	Column (1) minus columns (4)÷(5)	Column (6) at 5.00%	Net Value in Trust

Fig. 22.5

COMPREHENSIVE ANALYSIS

Ultimate Arbitrage®

LOAN + S.P.I.A. + Retained Capital + Life Insurance Policy

Loan to I.I.I.Trust - $8,000,000   Loan money applied to policies - $600,000   Loan money applied to S.P.I.A. - $7,400,000

Age	Year	Annuity Income (1)	Taxable after Exclusion (2)	Income Tax on column (2) after deduction (-40%) (3)	Income Tax Savings column (5) from column (2) (4)	Loan Interest at 5.00% (5)	Total Premiums (6)	Net Cash Flows column (1) + (4) minus (3) + (5) + (6) (7)	$2MM Net DB PLUS Estate Tax Savings PLUS column (7) @ 5% (8)
80	1	$1,036,000	$227,920			$400,000	$600,000	$324,832	$6,400,000
81	2	1,036,000	227,920		$68,832	400,000	380,000	324,832	6,741,074
82	3	1,036,000	227,920		68,832	400,000	380,000	324,832	7,099,201
83	4	1,036,000	227,920		68,832	400,000	380,000	324,832	7,475,235
84	5	1,036,000	227,920		68,832	400,000	380,000	324,832	7,870,070
85	6	1,036,000	227,920		68,832	400,000	380,000	324,832	8,284,647
86	7	1,036,000	227,920		68,832	400,000	380,000	324,832	8,719,953
87	8	1,036,000	227,920		68,832	400,000	380,000	324,832	9,177,024
88	9	1,036,000	227,920		68,832	400,000	380,000	324,832	9,656,949
89	10	1,036,000	227,920		68,832	400,000	380,000	324,832	10,160,870
90	11	1,036,000	936,722	$214,689		400,000	380,000	41,311	10,392,290
91	12	1,036,000	1,036,000	254,400		400,000	380,000	1,600	10,593,585
92	13	1,036,000	1,036,000	254,400		400,000	380,000	1,600	10,804,944
93	14	1,036,000	1,036,000	254,400		400,000	380,000	1,600	11,026,871
94	15	1,036,000	1,036,000	254,400		400,000	380,000	1,600	11,259,895
95	16	1,036,000	1,036,000	254,400		400,000	380,000	1,600	11,504,570
96	17	1,036,000	1,036,000	254,400		400,000	380,000	1,600	11,761,478
97	18	1,036,000	1,036,000	254,400		400,000	380,000	1,600	12,031,232
98	19	1,036,000	1,036,000	254,400		400,000	380,000	1,600	12,314,474
99	20	1,036,000	1,036,000	254,400		400,000	380,000	1,600	12,611,877
100	21	1,036,000	1,036,000	254,400		400,000	0	381,600	13,323,151
101	22	1,036,000	1,036,000	254,400		400,000	0	381,600	14,069,989
102	23	1,036,000	1,036,000	254,400		400,000	0	381,600	14,854,168
103	24	1,036,000	1,036,000	254,400		400,000	0	381,600	15,677,557
104	25	1,036,000	1,036,000	254,400		400,000	0	381,600	16,542,115
		Guaranteed Lifetime Income (Single Premium Immediate Annuity) E.O.Y.	Portion of S.P.I.A. Income subject to income tax	Actual Income Tax Effect of column (5) deducted from column (2)	Effect of Interest deduction on excess of column (5) from column (2)	Interest Payment on Loan at 5.00% End of Year	Schedule of Premiums: $10,000,000	Column (1) + column (4) minus columns (3) + (5) + (6)	Net Value of Plan

loan interest eliminate the tax liability of the annuity during the first ten years, but also there would be the difference between a $400,000 deduction and the taxable portion of the annuity ($227,920) that would carry over in the form of tax savings offsetting other taxable income. Column 4 shows during the first ten years this could possibly result in $68,832 ($400,000 – $227,920 = $172,080 x 40 percent) of income tax savings, besides eliminating the $91,168 tax liability!

Note that beginning the eleventh year, the entire annuity pay-out is subject to tax, therefore the $400,000 of deductible interest would still leave a net tax liability of $254,400 beginning the twelfth year and thereafter. However, if all other variables remain constant, column 7 shows that there would be a net result of $324,832 of positive cash flow the first nine years in this example. This would result in a net death benefit of $2 million plus estate tax savings plus column 7 accumulating at 5 percent, which could leave behind as much as $10,160,870 if death occurred in the tenth year!

ULTIMATE ARBITRAGE—IN SIMPLE FORM

Let's summarize this concept with two examples. Elderly retirees often approach me seeking to reposition assets from unstable, volatile investments to stable, guaranteed investments.

Let's assume a female, age 80, with a life expectancy of ten years implements this strategy using $1 million of her own money. If she were to secure a single premium immediate annuity with a pay-out of 14 percent, she would receive a guaranteed lifetime income with that annuity of $140,000 annually. With the 78 percent exclusion she would be allowed, she would only need to pay taxes on 22 percent of the annual income (to her life expectancy) which would be $30,800. Assuming a 37 percent tax bracket, her annual tax liability would be $11,396. Her after-tax income the first ten years would be $128,604. She would likely want to replace the $1million when she passes away (because it would be relinquished to the annuity-issuing company) to leave behind to her heirs or favorite charity. Assuming the asset replacement life insurance with a death benefit of $1 million had an annual premium of $38,000 per year, she would still enjoy a net annual income of $90,604. That is over 9 percent net return!

Let's now apply the principle of arbitrage. If she borrowed $1million at 5 percent interest with a loan open until death, repaid by life insurance proceeds and serviced with annual interest payments from the annuity, it would require an annual loan payment of $50,000. This loan payment can be easily paid from the $90,604 of net annual cash flow generated from the annuity. Then the annual income to her family or a charity would be $40,604 per year—without requiring any cash outlay on her part!

I have used this strategy with clients who had health histories enabling them to receive higher age-rated pay-outs on the annuity and yet receive favorable ratings from life insurance issuers. For example, a 77-year old male with cancer, artery blockage and diabetes history (that were all successfully treated), was able to receive a 17.6 percent pay-out on his annuity (due to an age-rating of 85). Per $1 million deposited into the annuity, he receives a guaranteed annual income of $176,000 for the remainder of his life. His exclusion ratio is 51 percent, so 49 percent of the $176,000 is subject to tax. At a 34 percent tax rate, his net after-tax annual income is $147,000. We were able to secure $1 million of life insurance with an annual premium cost of $57,000. After deducting the premium for the asset replacement life insurance, his annual income is $90,000, or a 9 percent return. Subsequently, be borrowed money to add to his own and was able to greatly enhance his annual income, and the amount he will leave behind upon his demise.

The principle of arbitrage can be used with these situations, provided that the spread is sufficient to cover the annual loan payment. Care should be taken to ensure that the loan interest will be covered by the spread between the net after-tax annuity pay-out and the asset replacement life insurance. Otherwise, additional collateral may need to be secured.

In these two final examples, the objective was to maximize the internal rate of return to generate income. By using that income to leverage a higher life insurance death benefit than required (to replace the asset or repay the loan), a large endowment may be left behind at death as illustrated previously.

The Ultimate Arbitrage Plan® is a patented and proprietary process that has been successfully implemented for numerous clients across the country. It should be obvious the complexity of design for an Ultimate Arbitrage Plan® requires consultation with competent legal and accounting advisors. Of course, the Ultimate Arbitrage can be structured larger or smaller than the examples given, with varying results based on individual circumstances. Ideally, such a plan could be implemented for both a husband and wife, potentially leaving behind twice as much to the family, business, or designated charity. Why not leave behind an extra $2 to $4 million if it doesn't cost you anything?[2]

---

[2] For more information on the Ultimate Arbitrage Plan® you may contact Douglas Andrew at Wealth Enhancement Strategies and Creative Opportunities (WESCO) via email (info@pfs-inc.org) or call toll-free at 1-888-987-5665 or visit www.missedfortune.com.

Potomac Group West, Inc. a partner in WESCO holds a patent and trademark for the Ultimate Arbitrage Plan®.

22 WEALTH ENHANCEMENT STRATEGY NUMBER TWENTY-TWO

- *Provided your net worth is sufficient (usually $10 million or more) and you or a family member is age 75 to 90 with adequate health to be insurable, consider exploring an Ultimate Arbitrage Plan® to maximize what is left behind to your family, business, or favorite charity—possibly without using any of your own money.*

CHAPTER 23

Empowering True Wealth

Optimize the human, intellectual, financial, and civic
assets comprising true wealth.

COMMON MYTH-CONCEPTION

The estate-planning industry has created intellectual
strategies and products designed to win the game of the
U.S. taxpayer's right to earn and keep wealth, versus the
government's right to confiscate and redistribute wealth.

REALITY

*With or without estate and inheritance taxes, with or without
"traditional" estate planning, family wealth rarely survives three
generations!*
                    —LEE BROWER

This book has focused primarily on unique strategies for the creation of financial wealth. It is my sincere hope the reader will not experience the misfortune of a missed fortune due to money myth-conceptions!

I wish to now draw your attention to the creation, preservation, and perpetuation of the human, intellectual, financial, and civic assets that comprise "True Wealth." I admire disciplined savers and investors. However, when the passion for money becomes all consuming, especially at the expense of more important things in life, after forty years of working, saving, and investing, we may ask ourselves, "What was all that for?"

The story is told of one rich man who thought he had figured out how to take his gold, silver, money and stocks with him after he died. On his deathbed he instructed his wife to take all his earthly possessions and stack them together in the attic of their home. Then on the way through he would take them with him to heaven! She did as she was told and on the night he passed away she hurried upstairs to see if he had succeeded. She beheld everything stacked there just as she had left it. She then exclaimed in frustration, "Oh, I knew I should have arranged all of his stuff in the basement!"

I believe what we take with us into eternity are the memories we create, the relationships we develop, and the knowledge and wisdom we gain while here on earth. These are the true riches of life.

GETTING LIFE'S PRIORITIES STRAIGHT

You may remember the words to the song, "Cat's in the Cradle" by Harry Chapin (lyrics by Sandra Chapin). The words are significant. They are as follows:

> *My child arrived just the other day,*
> *He came to the world in the usual way.*
> *But there were planes to catch, and bills to pay.*
> *He learned to walk while I was away.*

And he was talking 'fore I knew it, and as he grew,
He'd say, "I'm gonna be like you, dad.
You know I'm gonna be like you."

CHORUS
And the cat's in the cradle and the silver spoon,
Little boy blue and the man in the moon.
"When you coming home, dad? I don't know when,
But we'll get together then."
You know we'll have a good time then.
My son turned ten just the other day.
He said, "Thanks for the ball, dad, come on let's play.
Can you teach me to throw?" I said, "Not today,
I got a lot to do." He said, "That's ok."
And he walked away, but his smile never dimmed,
Said, "I'm gonna be like him, yeah.
You know I'm gonna be like him."

CHORUS

Well, he came from college just the other day,
So much like a man I just had to say,
"Son, I'm proud of you. Can you sit for a while?"
He shook his head, and he said with a smile,
"What I'd really like, dad, is to borrow the car keys.
See you later. Can I have them please?"

CHORUS

I've long since retired and my son's moved away.
I called him up just the other day.
I said, "I'd like to see you if you don't mind."
He said, "I'd love to, dad, if I could find the time.
You see, my new job's a hassle, and the kid's got the flu,
But it's sure nice talking to you, dad.
It's been sure nice talking to you."
And as I hung up the phone, it occurred to me,
He'd grown up just like me.
My boy was just like me.

CHORUS

A MISER'S LIFE—A CHEAP FUTURE

We all know there is a significant difference between saving prudently while keeping priorities straight, and becoming obsessed with the accumulation of financial wealth and possessions. The contrasts between the two value systems are amazing! I think of one couple in particular where both the husband and wife worked hard each to age 70 before they retired. They were so frugal—they scrimped and saved everything they could. They got by with a two-bedroom, 900-square-foot home, raising four children who were a great blessing to them. They were good parents. But almost every time the opportunity came to take a vacation, go on an outing, or even take a trip to Disneyland with their kids, the reply from Mom and Dad was, "Oh, we'd better not, we can't afford it!" They worked, worked, worked with very little play and sacrificed tremendously to prepare for "the future."

When they became my clients at age 70, they had accumulated about $1.5 million. We strategically repositioned the $1.5 million and saved them several hundred thousand dollars in unnecessary income tax, in addition to the estate tax they will save as their assets continue to grow. They have earned over $100,000 a year in interest on their nest egg. Yet they still have never spent more than $30,000 a year in their lifetimes! They just can't get themselves to do it! They will leave behind a tremendous estate to their children and charities. However, just like the father in "Cat's in the Cradle," they now call their children and invite them to bring the grandkids and come and visit with them. They even offer to pay their family's airfare and compensate their time away from work. Their children reply, "Oh, Mom and Dad, we love you, but you taught us well; we are so busy working, we just can't afford to get away!"

I believe the saddest part of this couple's story is not the lack of memories and relationships with their children. As husband and wife, they failed to cultivate the most important relationship of all—between themselves! When they retired at age 70 they were strangers to each other and had very few common interests. At first, being together in retirement was a chore rather than a cherished delight. For the first few years of retirement, they simply co-existed and tolerated one another under the same secure roof they had built fifty years before!

AN INVESTED LIFE—A RICH LEGACY

On the other hand, ten years ago I attended the funeral of the wife of one of my most cherished clients. This couple learned to grow closer together through their married years and constantly catered to one another's needs. They methodically saved 10 percent of their modest income. They didn't accumulate a giant nest egg, but they had sufficient for their needs and wants as they approached retirement. I could have asked the husband on any day during the fifteen years I knew him prior to retirement, "How many days until you retire?" He could tell me precisely the years, months, and days until he retired. He looked forward with a passion to being full-time with his wife!

We always assumed they would retire and spend a good twenty years or more together, as they both appeared to be in good health. Statistics tell us the man usually passes away first. She worked as a secretary of a high school. He was a master electrician. Three months after they both retired, she suddenly had a massive heart attack and passed away. I was on the East Coast that day on business. I immediately flew home. Because things were well under control financially, the family could focus full attention on other things. The three children who spoke at their mother's funeral, as well as other friends, left a lasting impression on me. Their family life was filled to the brim with wonderful memories. Sure, they missed their mother, but there were no regrets. Instead, there was comfort and an abundance of gratitude for the countless gatherings and outings they had enjoyed together with family and friends! In fact, their mother's favorite phrase had been, "Hey, let's go create another memory!" I have never forgotten that. Since that time, I strive to create a significant memory at least every month with my wife, with my children, and with my friends.

Keep balance with your financial pursuits. Don't gamble or lose relationships with your loved ones in the process of trying to provide for them financially.

WHAT DOES THE FUTURE HOLD?

To ensure the future is rich in all facets of life, each of us must assess and plan for a life of meaningful balance. I urge everyone to identify the method or program that best meets individual needs. As a reference point, I'll forward principles here recommended by **Empowered Wealth, LC** ("Empowered Wealth") a professional firm with which I am a national advisory board member.

| Fig. 23.1 | THE EMPOWERED WEALTH QUADRANTS™ |

Assets

FINANCIAL (Things)
- House
- Cash
- Stocks
- Bonds
- Insurance
- Real Estate

Your financial and material possessions

©Copyright 2001-2003, Empowered Wealth, LLC

QUADRANTS OF TRUE WEALTH

Empowered Wealth organizes life's "True Wealth" assets into four quadrants. When most people think of the word "asset," what immediately comes to mind? Most people first think of money, houses, or other real estate, stocks and bonds, business enterprises, etc. These *things* comprise a person's financial and material possessions. So let's categorize them as financial assets. In a simple diagram comprised of the Empowered Wealth Quadrants™, we put financial assets in the southwest quadrant (**fig. 23.1**).

When you think about it, though, are financial assets really a person's most important assets? There are actually other categories of assets that are more important than financial assets. Human assets, for instance, enhance the individual health, happiness, and well-being of each family member. They include such intangibles as family, health, habits, values, virtues, unique abilities, environment, relationships, attitude, ethics, morals, character, and heritage. We put these assets in the northwest quadrant, with the understanding that they involve *people*, rather than *things* (**fig. 23.2**).

Fig. 23.2 | **THE EMPOWERED WEALTH QUADRANTS™**

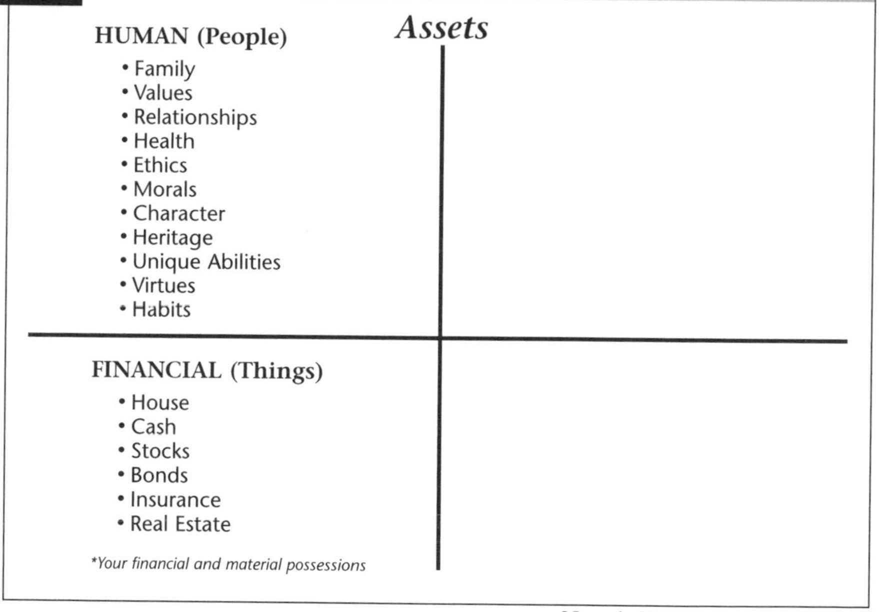

HUMAN (People)   *Assets*
- Family
- Values
- Relationships
- Health
- Ethics
- Morals
- Character
- Heritage
- Unique Abilities
- Virtues
- Habits

FINANCIAL (Things)
- House
- Cash
- Stocks
- Bonds
- Insurance
- Real Estate

Your financial and material possessions

There is a third category of assets that forms the northeast quadrant comprised of intellectual assets which includes the wisdom we gain which is a product of knowledge times experience. Intellectual assets, when captured, are available for the benefit of each family member. They include knowledge, education, experiences, reputation, skills, alliances, ideas, traditions, talents, and systems (**fig. 23.3**).

Fig. 23.3	THE EMPOWERED WEALTH QUADRANTS™

Assets

HUMAN (People)
- Family
- Values
- Relationships
- Health
- Ethics
- Morals
- Character
- Heritage
- Unique Abilities
- Virtues
- Habits

INTELLECTUAL (Wisdom)
- Knowledge
- Education - formal
- Experiences - good & bad
- Reputation
- Systems
- Methods
- Alliances
- Skills
- Talents
- Ideas
- Traditions

FINANCIAL (Things)
- House
- Cash
- Stocks
- Bonds
- Insurance
- Real Estate

Your financial and material possessions

©Copyright 2001-2003, Empowered Wealth, LLC

So the family balance sheet hierarchy is comprised of first, human assets (people), then intellectual assets (wisdom), and, lastly, financial assets (things). The sum of these three equals True Wealth.

Most families would want to make sure all three of these asset categories are successfully transferred into future generations. In other words, we would want to transfer our values, systems for health and well-being, family traditions, the wisdom gained from experiences—both good and bad—to future generations, along with the financial assets we accumulate.

Now, if a family had no choice but to leave one of these categories behind, which category would it be? Most say they would choose to bankrupt the financial assets category. Why? Because they could rebuild that category of assets using their human and intellectual assets! Why then, do most estate plans focus on the least important of the three categories?

Where the focus on financial assets preempts the focus on human and intellectual assets, there is a good chance that financial assets will be misused and eventually dissipate. It is more important that values are understood before assets are valued.

CHOICE AND CONTROL

There is an element of financial assets that is as important, if not more important, than the actual return on those assets. That element is *choice* and *control*. There are certain financial assets over which we give up, for all practical purposes, choice and control. These assets are our civic, or social, assets. When people think of civic assets, they usually think of taxes. Most governmental systems require that people give back to society in the form of taxes. Most people think of taxes as a liability, but taxes are actually an asset. The government has given us avenues to take control over this asset. However, when we don't take control, they do! The way a person can regain choice and control over civic assets is to be involved in charitable activities controlled through their own personal foundations. True involvement includes not only financial assets but human and intellectual assets, as well. These are identified in the southeast quadrant (**fig. 23.4**).

In the simplest form, the Empowered Wealth Quadrants are described clockwise as **live, learn, give,** and **earn.**

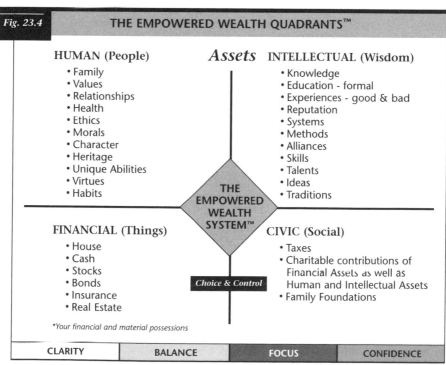

Fig. 23.4   THE EMPOWERED WEALTH QUADRANTS™

HUMAN (People)
- Family
- Values
- Relationships
- Health
- Ethics
- Morals
- Character
- Heritage
- Unique Abilities
- Virtues
- Habits

Assets   **INTELLECTUAL (Wisdom)**
- Knowledge
- Education - formal
- Experiences - good & bad
- Reputation
- Systems
- Methods
- Alliances
- Skills
- Talents
- Ideas
- Traditions

THE EMPOWERED WEALTH SYSTEM™

FINANCIAL (Things)
- House
- Cash
- Stocks
- Bonds
- Insurance
- Real Estate

Your financial and material possessions

Choice & Control

CIVIC (Social)
- Taxes
- Charitable contributions of Financial Assets as well as Human and Intellectual Assets
- Family Foundations

CLARITY   BALANCE   FOCUS   CONFIDENCE

PERPETUATING TRUE WEALTH

The key to perpetuating True Wealth is to capitalize assets. When an asset is capitalized, it develops a life of its own and consequently has the opportunity to thrive. A reactive *versus* proactive approach to capitalizing assets in each of the four Empowered Wealth Quadrants™ would be illustrated as follows:

- **Human Assets**
  - *Reactive Approach* – Spending your health to obtain wealth—only to spend your wealth to regain your health.
  - *Proactive Approach* – Following a regular program of exercise to maintain health and well-being.

  Human assets must be capitalized through proactive encouragement and awareness—such as developing a written Family True Wealth Philosophy Statement and conducting regular family retreats with a purpose.

- **Intellectual Assets**
  - *Reactive Approach* – Waiting until your deathbed to share your wisdom and experiences.
  - *Proactive Approach* – Developing a system that will capture and make life's experiences and wisdom come alive.

  Certain intellectual assets are of no value to anyone until you give them away—such as your experiences, knowledge or wisdom. Other intellectual assets must be transferred with respect, responsibility and accountability— such as your relationships or alliances.

- **Civic Assets**
  - *Reactive Approach* – Waiting until your accountant tells you how much you owe in taxes.
  - *Proactive Approach* – Designing a proactive plan that allows the redirection of taxes to causes you support—including your family.

Civic assets must be managed, planned for and shared with family members. Involve children and give them a sense of ownership; your passion and purpose will live on.

- **Financial Assets**
  - ○ *Reactive Approach* – Advisors working reactively and not in sync with your vision nor coordinated with other key advisors.
  - ○ *Proactive Approach* – Identifying a proactive lead-advisor who coordinates all advisors with your vision and objectives.

  Financial assets are tools that can contribute to the individual health, happiness, and well-being of family members. Money does not create happiness nor misery—but your relationship with money can.

MANAGING TRUE WEALTH

So, how can a person best manage and control all four categories of assets? While Empowered Wealth has developed a proprietary system to help individuals maximize True Wealth, its principles are universal.

First, we must focus on those activities that are most important—human assets—the individual health, happiness, and well-being of each family member, values and good habits. Through this we obtain *clarity* with respect to those activities that matter most.

With that clarity, individuals are able to harness the power of all of their assets to work in harmony with each other to exponentially increase results. The whole is greater than the sum of the parts! This provides *balance.*

With increased clarity and balance, you are able to *focus* on those activities that take advantage of your unique abilities. Consequently, your achievements will soar to ever-increasing heights of accomplishment.

Finally, with clarity, balance, and focus, you and your family will have increased *confidence* in every relationship you have within your family, community, and business. After all, isn't confidence the greatest asset we can bring to any relationship?

Albert Szent-Gyorgyi, a brilliant scientist who won the Nobel Prize twice in his lifetime, once said, "Discovery consists of seeing what everybody has seen and thinking what nobody has thought." Rather than taking the traditional financial approach to estate planning, perhaps we should primarily focus on the perpetuation of a family's human and intellectual assets. In his book, *Finding The Better Way*, multi-billionaire James LeVoy Sorenson said, "My family and good health are what make me truly rich … . True wealth only comes through health and family and friends."

A family's empowerment begins with its understanding of its responsibility and stewardship to True Wealth. Two books I strongly recommend that everyone must read are *The Ultimate Gift* by Jim Stovall, and *Empowered Wealth* by Lee Brower. Through powerful stories, they teach about why human and intellectual assets are the most important on the family balance sheet and what really comprises True Wealth.

George Bernard Shaw said, "There are two sources of unhappiness in life. One is *not* getting what you want; the other is getting it!" According to the Family Firm Institute of Brooklyn, Massachusetts, "nearly 70 percent of all family firms fail before reaching the second generation and 88 percent fail before the third generation; only a little more than 3 percent of all family enterprises survive to the fourth generation and beyond." The third generation seems to be the volatile generation. Hence, the saying, "Shirt sleeves to shirt sleeves in three generations!" William K. Vanderbilt, grandson of Cornelius Vanderbilt, (for whom Vanderbilt University was named after) said, "It has left me with nothing to hope for, with nothing definite to seek or strive for. Inherited wealth is a real handicap to happiness."

The Rothschilds were one of the few families who perpetuated their family wealth for several generations. Basically, the Rothschilds followed a three-part philosophy:

1) They loaned their heirs money, which their heirs had to repay.
2) The knowledge and experiences those heirs gained had to be shared with other family members.
3) The family gathered at least once a year to reaffirm its virtues and intentions.

Nathan Rothschild said, "It requires a great deal of boldness and a great deal of caution to make a great fortune; and when you have got it, it requires ten times as much wit to keep it."

THE FEDERAL ESTATE TAX

Let's look briefly at the history of the Federal Estate Tax, which ultimately initiated the game of traditional estate planning. The Federal Estate Tax was first imposed from 1797 to 1802 through the Death Stamp Tax for the purpose of naval build up. It was reimposed from 1862 to 1870 to generate revenue for the Civil War. It was again reimposed from 1898 to 1902 to help finance the Spanish-American War. And finally, in 1916, it was again reimposed, this time to stay, although initially it was intended to help finance World War I. Because of the over twenty revisions of the Estate Tax since 1916, an industry emerged to promote the game. What is the game? It is the U.S. taxpayer's right to earn and keep wealth versus the government's right to confiscate and redistribute that wealth. Ironically, traditional estate planning has done more to destroy American families than the Federal Estate Tax could ever do! All too often traditional estate planning eventually takes the family from "We" to "Me."

There are four reasons why typical estate planning usually fails:

1) The game becomes paramount—it isn't important what happens to the money as long as you have enough and the government gets less.

2) The estate-planning industry has created intellectual strategies and products designed to make you believe you are winning.

3) Regardless of its complexity, traditional estate planning has become a process of four Ds: **Divide** up the estate, **Defer** the distribution, **Dump** the financial assets on ill-prepared heirs, and eventually it **Dissipates**. In other words, wealth is transferred without responsibility or accountability.

4) The division of assets (gifting) not only diminishes the assets but actually encourages extraordinary consumption and discourages savings. United they stand, divided they fall!

Hence, with or without estate and inheritance taxes, with or without traditional estate planning, family wealth dissipates and rarely survives three generations. We ought to focus on the four **Ps**: **Preserve** the assets, **Protect** true wealth, **Perpetuate** it to future generations, and Em**Power** family members with stewardship and accountability of more than just financial assets.

Abraham Lincoln once said, "The worst thing you can do for those you love is the things they could do for themselves." And Robert Frost said, "Every affluent father wishes he knew how to give his sons the hardships that made him rich."

Families do well to manage the private and social sides of their assets. Under the proper system, the private side can be perpetual, offer loans and grants to family members, enter into joint ventures with family members, and protect assets from estate taxes. The social side also can be perpetual, create family significance and social significance, not be subject to inheritance tax, and can make loans to family members and others.

Families should work to optimize their human assets with health and wellness programs, family retreats with a purpose, philanthropic awareness and participation, identification and sharing of unique abilities and talents, accountability and responsibility, and a sense of purpose and balance.

Families should likewise maximize intellectual assets with the capture of life's experiences, the deposit of intellectual assets for the benefit of other family members, the enhancement of strategic relationships, the use of formal education, the recording of family events and accomplishments, and the recognition and use of skills.

Finally, families should optimize financial assets with proprietary wealth optimization strategies, income and estate tax reduction/elimination, asset protection, creative philanthropic strategies, financial wealth accountability, and responsible financial management.

It would behoove any family to develop and use some type of system designed to enhance the individual health, happiness, and well-being of each of the family members; to support and encourage family leadership; to capture family virtues, memories, and wisdom; and to protect, optimize, and empower the family's intellectual and financial capital. Such a system would provide tremendous clarity, balance, focus, and confidence for the family.

Victor Hugo once said, "There is something that is more powerful than all the armies in the world, and that is an idea whose time has come!" I believe The Empowered Wealth System® for the development, preservation, and perpetuation of True Wealth is one of those ideas.[1]

| 23 | WEALTH ENHANCEMENT STRATEGY NUMBER TWENTY-THREE |

- *Develop and implement some type of system designed:*
  - *to enhance the individual health, happiness, and well being of each of your family members;*
  - *to support and encourage family leadership;*
  - *to capture family virtues, memories, and wisdom;*
  - *and to protect, optimize, and empower your family's intellectual and financial assets.*
- *Such a system would provide tremendous clarity, balance, focus and confidence for your family.*

---

[1] For more information on how to optimize your human, intellectual, and financial assets, visit www.empoweredwealth.com. You may also contact Douglas Andrew via email, info@pfs-inc.org, or call toll free, 1-888-987-5665.

Glossary

Amortization: The process of repayment of mortgage debt through regular periodic installment payments.

Amortization Schedule: A chart that outlines the periodic installment payments, portion of principal and interest paid and unpaid principal balance of amortized loan.

Annual Cap: The maximum amount the interest rate of an adjustable rate loan can increase annually.

Annual Percentage Rate: The effective annual rate of interest charged on a loan as required by the Truth in Lending Law.

Annuity: (1) Cash payment over a given period. (2) A fixed amount given or left by will, paid periodically.

Appraisal: An expert's (appraiser's) valuation or estimate of a specific property's value.

Appraiser: The person qualified to conduct an appraisal.

ARM: See adjustable-rate mortgage.

Assessed Value: Value placed on a parcel by a public tax assessor for the purpose of taxation. This value does not necessarily correlate to the property's market value.

Assignment: The transferring of rights in a contract or mortgage from one party to another.

Assumable Loan: A mortgage loan that allows a purchaser to take over the obligation of the seller. This transfer may or may not cause a change in the mortgage terms.

Assumption: An agreement whereby the purchaser assumes the mortgage obligations of the seller. The seller may or may not be released from financial liability upon transfer, dependent upon lender and loan type.

Balloon Payment: A large principal payment due at a specified time. The balloon is typically the final payment required in a balloon mortgage and may include both principal and accumulated interest.

Basis: The figure on which profit from the sale of real estate is based for income tax purposes. The cost of acquiring the property is the original basis. The adjusted basis is the basis at some point in the future after the cost of improvements is added to the original basis.

Bear Market: A term used to describe the stock market when prices have been declining in value.

Bid: An amount offered to purchase a property.

Bi-weekly Mortgage: A mortgage that calls for payments of one-half the normal monthly amount every two weeks, 26 payments annually. The Bi-weekly mortgage allows for full amortization of the loan in considerably less time than when normal monthly payments are made.

Bond: Basically an IOU or promissory note of a corporation, usually issued in multiples of $1,000. A bond is evidence of a debt on which the issuing company usually promises to pay the bondholders a specified amount of interest for a specified length of time, and to repay the loan on the expiration date. In every case, a bond represents debt – its holder is a creditor of the corporation and not a part owner, as is the shareholder.

Bridge Loan: A temporary mortgage loan intended for short-term needs. Bridge loans may be used for the purchase of a new home prior to selling an existing home or for construction of a new home until permanent financing is secured.

Buy-Down: A sum of money paid to the lender at closing, in exchange for a reduction in the interest rate of the mortgage loan. The reduction may be permanent or temporary.

Cap: The limitation of adjustment increases for an adjustable rate loan. The cap can be for the life of the loan (life cap) or for a specified period (monthly, annually, etc.) Also known as a ceiling cap or payment cap.

Capital Gain or Capital Loss: Profit or loss from the sale of a capital asset. A capital gain, under current federal income tax laws, may be either short-term (12 months or less) or long-term (more than 12 months). A short-term capital gain is taxed at the reporting individual's full income tax rate.

Certificate of Eligibility: A certificate granted by the Veterans Administration to those who qualify (based on length and time of service) for a VA loan.

Closing Statement: The summary of all expenses, adjustments and perorations of a transaction.

Collateral: Securities or other property pledged by a borrower to secure repayment of a loan.

Commercial Bank: An institution offering checking accounts, loans, savings accounts, and other services usually not found through savings and loan associations. Banks are more likely to offer installment loans on vehicles and boats and construction financing, rather than long-term real estate financing. See also Institutional Lenders.

Common Stock: Securities that represent an ownership interest in a corporation. If the company has also issued preferred stock, both common and preferred have ownership rights. Claims of both common and preferred stockholders are junior to claims of bondholders or other creditors of the company. Common stockholders assume greater risk, but generally exercise greater control and may gain greater reward in the form of dividends and capital appreciation.

Compound Interest: Interest paid on the original principal and on interest accrued.

Compounded Taxes: Tax liability that is deferred on an asset that is growing at a compounded rate resulting in greater future tax liability.

Constructive Receipt: A doctrine of the Internal Revenue Service that requires the reporting of income (including capital gains) in a year in which it could have been received had the taxpayer so wished. Thus, dividends of a mutual fund automatically reinvested are taxable in the year which reinvested on the basis that the taxpayer could have received them in cash at his or her option.

Contingency: An event that must occur before a contract becomes binding.

Conventional Loans: Loans that are not insured, guaranteed nor backed by the Federal Government.

Conversion Option: A mortgage loan feature that allows the loan to be changed from a Variable Rate to a Fixed Rate by the payment of a service fee.

Convertible ARM: Adjustable-rate mortgage which can convert to a fixed-rate mortgage.

Creative Financing: Financing other than government or conventional loans.

Deed: The legal document that transfers interest in real estate.

Deed of Trust: A document that grants a property's title to a third party (as security) until the secured debt is paid in full.

Deferred Taxes: Tax liability that is deferred or put off to a future triggering event.

Discount Points: See Points

Diversification: Spreading investments among different companies in different fields. Another type of diversification is offered by the securities of many individual companies because of the wide range of their activities.

Dividend: The payment designated by the board of directors to be distributed prorata among the shares outstanding. Preferred shares generally pay a fixed dividend, while common shares pay a dividend that varies with the earnings of the company and the amount of cash on hand. Dividends may be omitted if business is poor or the directors withhold earnings to invest in plant and equipment. Sometimes a company will pay a dividend out of past earnings even if it is not currently operating at a profit.

Dollar-Cost-Averaging: A system of buying securities at regular intervals with a fixed dollar amount. Under this system the investor buys by the dollars' worth rather than by the number of shares. If each investment is the same number of dollars, payments buy more shares when the price is low and less when it increases. Temporary downswings in price thus benefit the investor if he continues to make periodic purchases in both good and bad, and the price at which the shares are sold is more than their average cost.

Dow-Jones Average: Widely quoted stock averages computed regularly. They include an industrial stock average, a rail average, a utility average, and a combination of the three.

Due on Sale: A mortgage clause that requires any outstanding loan balance to be paid when title to a property is transferred.

Estate Tax: The tax imposed on the value of an estate when it is passed down to, or inherited by, non-spousal heirs at the death of the owner of the estate.

Equity: The value of a property that remains after all liens and other charges against the property are paid. This also includes the ownership interest of common and preferred stockholders in a company. It also refers to excess of value securities over the debit balance in a margin account. Property owner's equity generally consists of his or her monetary interest in the property in excess of the mortgage indebtedness. In the case of long-term mortgage, the owner's equity builds up quite gradually during the first several years because the bulk of each monthly payment is applied not to the principal amount of the loan, but to the interest.

Equity Conversion: The annuitization of accumulated home equity to provide income during periods of financial difficulty or to increase disposable income during retirement.

Equity Conservation: The protection and conservation to accumulated equity through a self-directed financial plan to transfer risk and control capital.

Equity Development: A financial strategy established to specifically pay off a mortgage in advance of its standard amortized period.

Equity Exchange: The consolidation of non-deductible consumer debt from loan proceeds of a home equity loan or cash-out refinance of an existing mortgage and/or consumer loans.

Equity Transfer: Redeployment of dormant, non-liquid home equity into an investment program.

Execute: To sign a contract for the purpose of legally binding the parties involved.

Fair Credit Reporting Act: A federal law granting consumers the right to examine and correct credit information collected and used by credit reporting bureaus.

Fair Market Value: The price a ready, willing, able and informed buyer would pay for a property with the seller's consent.

Fannie Mae: A nickname for the Federal National Mortgage Association.

Farmers Home Administration (FmHA): An agency under the U.S. Department of Agriculture which administrates assistance programs to farmers for the purchase of homes and farms in rural areas.

Federal Deposit Insurance Corporation (FDIC): The federal corporation that insures bank depositors against loss up to a specified amount currently at $100,000.

Federal Home Loan Banks: Regulated by the Federal Home Loan Bank Board. These are regional branches where banks, savings and loans, insurance companies, or similar institutions may join the system and borrow for the purpose of making available home-financing money. Its purpose is to make a permanent supply of financing available for home loans.

Federal Home Loan Mortgage Corporation (FHLMC): An organization created to purchase mortgages. FHLMC more commonly purchases mortgages from savings and loans.

Federal National Mortgage Association (FNMA): A private organization (originally chartered by the Federal Government) which purchases mortgages, predominantly from mortgage bankers.

FHA: Federal Housing Administration.

FHA Mortgage Loan: A loan insured by the Federal Housing Administration.

FIFO: An acronym representing First In First Out. For tax purposes, FIFO taxation means the first money you invested (your basis) is the first money that comes out. If your basis was funded with after-tax dollars, there is no tax with FIFO taxation until the basis is withdrawn.

Finance Charge: Fees charged to a credit customer. May include interest and related expenses.

First Mortgage: A mortgage or lien that has been recorded in public records prior to any other mortgage or lien. Also known as a *Senior Mortgage*.

Fixed Mortgage: A real estate loan in which the interest rate remains constant. Also known as a *Fixed Rate Mortgage*.

Foreclosure: The elimination of a mortgage borrower's right in and to a property for the purpose of satisfying a mortgage debt. Foreclosure may also eliminate other interested party's rights.

Freddie Mac: A nickname for Federal Home Loan Mortgage Corporation.

Fulcrum: The support about which a lever turns; it supplies capability for action.

Ginnie Mae: A nickname for the Government National Mortgage Association.

Government Bonds: Obligations of the U.S. Government, regarded as the highest grade issues in existence.

Growth Fund: A fund comprised of companies whose rate of growth over a period of time is considerably greater than that of business generally.

Growth Stock: Stock of a company with a record of relatively rapid earnings growth.

Government National Mortgage Association (GNMA): A government program that assists in financing of homes by purchasing mortgages from primary lenders. GNMA's purchase of these loans provides primary lenders additional money to lend for other home purchases.

Grace Period: The amount of time in which a borrower can be late on a payment without being considered in default.

Graduated Payment Mortgage (GPM): A mortgage that provides for lower payments in the initial years, then higher payments in the later years.

Grantor: The person giving title to real property.

Hazard Insurance: Insurance that protects the policyholder from loss caused by dangers such as fire, theft or storm.

Homeowners Association: A group of homeowners in a subdivision who manage common area and/or enforce deed restrictions.

Income Fund: A mutual fund with a primary objective of current income.

Index: A statistic which serves as an indicator of the current financial state of the economy. Used primarily in real estate to make adjustments in mortgage interest rates.

Inflation: The increase in an economy over its true or natural growth. Usually identified with rapidly increasing prices.

Institutional Lenders: Banks, savings and loans, or other businesses that make loans to the public during their ordinary course of business, as opposed to individuals who fund loans.

Interest: The fee charged for the use of money.

Investment: The laying out of the money in the purchase of some form of property intending to earn a profit.

Investment Company: A company or trust that uses its capital to invest in other companies. There are two principal types: the closed-end and the open-end mutual fund. Shares in closed-end investment companies are readily transferable in the open market and are bought and sold like other shares. Capitalization of these companies remains the same unless action is taken to change. Open-end funds sell their own shares to investors, stand ready to buy back their old shares, and are not listed. Open-end funds are so named because their capitalization is not fixed; they may issue more shares as needed to satisfy the demand of investors.

Investor: An individual whose principal concerns in the purchase of a security are regular dividend income and/or capital appreciation without unnecessary risk.

Junior Mortgage: A mortgage or lien which is filed in public records after the first mortgage (Senior Mortgage) on a specific property.

Leverage: The use of a small amount of cash to control a much greater value of assets.

LIFO: An acronym representing Last In First Out. For tax purposes, LIFO taxation means the last money you're earning (the interest) is the first money that comes out to be taxed.

Loan-to-Value: The ratio between the amount of mortgage liens on a property and the value of a property.

Lock-In: Lender commitment to allow the borrower a certain interest rate, subject to loan approval. Lock-in rates typically last forty-five to sixty days.

Long-term Debt: For the sake of mortgage qualification, any debt that will not be paid in six months; e.g. Mary's car will be paid for within four months, therefore it will not be considered long-term debt.

Margin: A percentage spread between an "index" and the charged rate. Used in calculating the revised interest rate on adjustable rate loans.

Market Value: The price a property would be expected to bring on the open market.

M.I.P.: Mortgage Insurance Premium. *See Mortgage Insurance.*

Mortgage: A legal document that creates a lien against property. Also called Deed of Trust.

Mortgage Acceleration: The prepayment of future principal payments.

Mortgage Broker: A person who receives a fee for placing loans. The mortgage broker seldom services these loans.

Mortgage Endowment: The accumulation of principal and interest in an investment that is specifically established to pay off a mortgage once the investment balance equals the mortgage balance.

Mortgage Guaranty Insurance Corporation (MGIC): Private corporation that insures mortgage loans.

Mortgage Insurance: Coverage, purchased by the borrower, that protects a lender against default by the borrower. Known as *Private Mortgage Insurance (PMI)* for conventional loans, *Mortgage Insurance Premium (MIP)* for FHA loans, and *Funding Fee* for VA loans.

Municipal Bond: A bond issued by a state or a political subdivision such as a county, city, town, or village. The term also designates bonds issued by state agencies and authorities. Generally, interest paid on municipal bonds is exempt from federal income taxes and from state and local income taxes within the state of issue.

Mutual Fund: An open-end investment company that continuously offers new shares to the public in addition to redeeming shares on demand as required by law. While in common use, the term mutual fund has no meaning in law.

Negative Amortization: The process of adding unpaid interest to the principal balance of a loan.

Net Worth: Total assets less liabilities of an individual, corporation, or business.

Origination Fees: Charges assessed by the lender for issuing a mortgage loan.

P.M.I.: Private Mortgage Insurance: *See Mortgage Insurance.*

Proration: To divide, distribute or assess proportionately, to make a pro-rata distribution.

Points: A finance charge or inducement for the lender the make a loan. A point is equal to 1% of the loan amount. Also called *Discount Points.*

Preferred Interest: Interest expense that is tax-deductible as opposed to interest that is non-deductible.

Preferred Stock: A class stock with a claim on the company's earnings before payment may be made on the common stock and usually entitled to priority over common stock if the company liquidates. Usually entitled to dividends at a specified rate, when declared by the board of directors and before payment of a dividend on the common stock, depending upon the term of the issue.

Pre-qualification: An assessment to determine the approximate loan amount a bank will lend a potential borrower.

Primary Lender: Lenders who provide mortgage money to the public.

Principal: The amount borrowed.

Promissory Note: The document setting forth a borrower's promise to repay a debt.

Prospectus: The document that offers a new issue of securities to the public. It is required under the Securities Act of 1933.

Recording: The act of recording documents or instruments into public record (usually at the county recorder's office) to notify others of liens, transfers, security interest, etc.

Refinance: The exchange of one mortgage for another on the same property location. Typically considered when interest rates are lower or when cash out is desired.

Return: The dividends or interest paid by a company expressed as a percentage of the current price. A stock with a current market value of $20 a share that has paid $1 in dividends in the preceding twelve months is said to return 5 % ($1.00/$20.00). The current return on a bond is figured the same way. Another term for yield.

Reverse Mortgage: A mortgage in which the borrower is paid an annuity (income) drawn against the equity of the home or a lump sum.

Sale-Leaseback: A sale of a subsequent lease from the buyer back to the seller.

Secondary Lenders: Those companies or organizations which buy mortgages from primary lenders.

Semi-monthly Mortgage: A mortgage that calls for two half-payments each month (twenty-four payments annually). The semi-monthly mortgage is virtually identical to a thirty-year mortgage, except it requires semi-monthly payments versus one monthly payment.

Senior Mortgage: The first mortgage recorded in public records.

Spread: The difference between the net after-tax cost of borrowing and the net rate of return earned on investing those borrowed funds. For example, the net cost of borrowing money at 6 percent interest tax-deductible in a 33.3 percent tax bracket equals 4 percent. If the after-tax rate of return realized from investing borrowed funds were 6 percent, the spread would be 2 percent.

Stock: Ownership shares of a corporation.

Stock Exchange: An organization registered under the Securities Exchange Act of 1934 with physical facilities for the buying and selling of securities in a two-way auction.

Term: The period over which a debt will be repaid.

Title: The evidence of ownership through a legal document.

Title Insurance: Insurance that protects from losses which may occur as a result of legal defects in title, such as forged deeds, overlooked judgments, or liens. There are two types of coverage: *mortgagee's coverage* insures the lender, and *owner's coverage* insures the homeowner.

Trade-Down: The sale of a larger, more expensive home for a smaller, less expensive one. Usually considered when a family retires and does not want excess living area and higher maintenance.

Trust Account: An account secured for the sole purpose of holding other's funds. Also known as an *escrow account.*

Underlying Mortgage: Refers to mortgages "in front of" (senior to) other mortgages when wrap-around mortgage is used.

Variable Rate Loan (VRM): *See Adjustable Rate Loan.*

V.A. Loan: Veterans Administration Loan. A mortgage loan which is guaranteed by the V.A.

Yield: Also known as *return.* The dividends or interest paid by a security expressed as a percentage of the current price. A stock with a current market value of $20 a share that is currently paying dividends at the rate of $1 a year is said to return five percent ($1,00/$20.00). The current return on a bond is figured the same way.

Warranty Deed: A deed that conveys warranties by the seller as to the validity of the property's title, and that the title is good and can be transferred with no liens, judgments or encumbrances.

Wrap-Around Mortgage: A financing arrangement where old and new financing are combined, or wrapped, together.

Select Bibliography

Black, Henry L. *Black's Law Dictionary, Revised Fourth Edition.*
West Group

Bruss, Robert. "Large Equity in Your Home Can Be a Big
Disadvantage." *Chicago Tribune.* 20 February 1988: page 1

Chapin, Harry. "Cat's in the Cradle." rec. 1974 *Verities and
Balderdash,* Elektra, 1974

Frost, Robert. 1847-1963

Harding, MariJo. "Home Equity on Tap." *Senior Market Advisor*
September 2001

Harvey, Paul. ABC Radio Networks. 2002 <www.paulharvey.com>

Hugo, Victor. 1802-1885

Department of Treasury, *Internal Revenue Code.* Section
264(a)(2)(3)&(b)

Knudsen, Max. "Reverse Mortgages." *Deseret News* 9 September 2001

Lincoln, Abraham. 1809-1865

Merriam-Webster. *Merriam Webster's Collegiate Dictionary, Tenth
Edition.* Merriam 1 Dec 1995

Reverse Mortgage Calculator Page. Freedom Financial. 2002
<financialfreedom.com>

Rogers, Will. 1879-1935

Rothschild, Nathan. 1777-1836

Schembari, James. "A Study Dares to Question the 401(k)." *New York
Times* 27 May 2001: late ed. Section 3, page 11, column 1

Shaw, George Bernard. 1856-1950

Sorenson, James LeVoy. *Finding the Better Way.* Salt Lake City: Deseret Book Co., 1992

Sullivan, Dan. Proceedings of the 68th Million Dollar Round Table Annual Meeting, June 1995: General Session. (Million Dollar Round Table, 1995)

Szent-Gyorgyi, Albert. 1893-1986

The Book of Luke. *The Holy Bible (KJV)* The Church of Jesus Christ of Latter-Day Saints. Salt Lake City, UT 1979: Luke 19:12-26

The Book of Mathew. *The Holy Bible (KJV)* The Church Of Jesus Christ of Latter-Day Saints. Salt Lake City, UT. 1979: Mathew 25: 14-30

Timothy. *The Holy Bible* (KJV) The Church of Jesus Christ of Latter-Day Saints. Salt Lake City, UT 1979: 1 Timothy 6:10

Tueller, Alden. *Practical Guide to Planned Giving.* Farmington Hills, MI: The Taft Group, November 1991.

Vanderbilt, William K. 1849-1920

Weidner, Leo. "How Congress Is Peddling IRA and 401(k) Snake Oil." *US News and World Report* 1989

Zigler, Zig. *See You At The Top.* Pelican Publishing Company, Inc. Gretna, Louisiana, June 2000

About the Author

Douglas R. Andrew has extensive experience in business management, economics, accounting, gerontology (as it relates to the economics of aging), financial and estate planning, and advanced business and tax planning. He is currently the owner and president of Paramount Financial Services, Inc., a comprehensive personal and business financial planning firm with several divisions.

As a retirement specialist, Doug shows people how to accumulate money on a tax-favored basis to achieve the highest possible net spendable retirement income. His firm, Paramount Financial, helps people to successfully manage equity to enhance its liquidity, safety, and rate of return, as well as maximize tax benefits. Paramount Financial Services, Inc. and Potomac Group West, Inc. have formed Wealth Enhancement Strategies and Creative Opportunities (WESCO), an entity created for the purpose of helping affluent individuals enhance and perpetuate their wealth. Douglas Andrew is a national advisory board member of Empowered Wealth LC, a company dedicated to optimizing not only financial assets, but also human and intellectual assets.

For more information about these concepts...

    If you would like to explore and possibly implement strategies contained in this book, but are not sure how to do so, please seek advice from a financial professional.

    If this book was given or recommended to you by a financial professional, you may choose to seek his or her advice, as well as advice from your personal tax advisor.

    If you prefer, we can refer you to a professional trained in the strategies contained in this book. This network of financial professionals is referred to as The Equity Enhancement Matrix (TEEM). If you would like to contact or be contacted by a TEEM member in your area, please contact Paramount Financial Services, Inc. toll-free at 1-888-987-5665, email us at info@pfs-inc.org, or contact us through our website at www.missedfortune.com

    If you are a financial professional and would like information on how to become a certified TEEM member, we invite you to contact us in the same manner.

*   I wish to express deep appreciation to a special friend, Jerry Davis of LifeGoals Corporation, who graciously granted me rights to use some of his proprietary concepts, illustrations, presentation styles and derivations thereof in this work. His company, LifeGoals Corporation, specializes in providing virtual office solutions for financial advisors. You are invited to visit his website at www.lifegoals.com.*

*   For help with strategic mortgage planning, please seek the advice of a mortgage professional. For a comprehensive mortgage planning analysis in harmony with the concepts contained in this book, please visit www.kendalltodd.com.*

*   The use of the InsMark® Illustration System software package was helpful in preparing many of the reports and graphics in the book, and we have arranged for readers of this book to receive a $100 System discount from InsMark. Please contact InsMark at the headquarters in San Ramon, CA, at 1-888-InsMark (467-6275). If you call, be sure to mention this book in order to receive your discount.*